Industrialization in the
Modern World

Industrialization in the Modern World

From the Industrial Revolution to the Internet

Volume 1: A–P

JOHN HINSHAW AND PETER N. STEARNS

 ABC-CLIO

Santa Barbara, California • Denver, Colorado • Oxford, England

Library of Congress Cataloging-in-Publication Data

Hinshaw, John H., 1963–
  Industrialization in the modern world : from the Industrial Revolution to the Internet /
John Hinshaw and Peter N. Stearns.
    volumes cm
  Includes bibliographical references and index.
  ISBN 978–1–61069–087–4 (hardcopy : alk. paper) — ISBN 978–1–61069–088–1
(ebook) 1. Industrialization—History. 2. Industrial revolution. 3. Industries—History.
I. Stearns, Peter N. II. Title.
  HD2321.H56   2014
  338.09—dc23   2013007798

ISBN: 978–1–61069–087–4
EISBN: 978–1–61069–088–1

18 17 16 15 14   1 2 3 4 5

This book is also available on the World Wide Web as an eBook.
Visit www.abc-clio.com for details.

ABC-CLIO, LLC
130 Cremona Drive, P.O. Box 1911
Santa Barbara, California 93116-1911

This book is printed on acid-free paper ∞

Manufactured in the United States of America

Every reasonable effort has been made to trace the owners of copyrighted materials in
this book, but in some instances this has proven impossible. The authors and publisher
will be glad to receive information leading to more complete acknowledgments in
subsequent printings of the book and in the meantime extend their apologies for any
omissions.

For Ivette and Lucas, with all my love

Contents

VOLUME 2

Acknowledgments

The Department of History and Political Science at Lebanon Valley College, and its Dick Joyce Fund, provided generous support for this project. Alyssa Sweigart, Carl Zebrowski, and Tyler Reinbold each read drafts of the manuscript and helped to make the book a better one. Ivette Guzmán-Zavala and Lucas Viti-Guzmán gave me love and support and a reason to finish the project.

Introduction: The Ongoing Revolution of Industrialization

This essay situates the Industrial Revolution into the context of world history. The industrial revolution is one of the most significant changes in the history of humanity, standing alongside other revolutions such as the discovery of fire around 1 million years ago, the acquisition of language around 60,000 years ago, and the Agricultural Revolution, which is roughly 12,000 years old. The promethean discovery of fire making enabled hominids to process food more easily, allowing their bodies to possess smaller guts and larger brains. The severe ecological crisis of roughly 60 millennia ago almost led to the extinction of humanity. Instead, our ancestors survived because a small group developed language, which enabled them to cooperate and create more complex tools and social organizations (such as religion and long-distance trade). The domestication of plants and animals made possible more efficient exploitation of nature, larger settlements, and yet more complex social organization.

What made industrialization revolutionary was that it harnessed new forms of energy, namely fossil fuels that enabled people to accelerate the creation of new tools, trades, and trading relationships. Like these other revolutions, industrialization has changed the way humans work, think, relate to each other, and think. It is much more than simply working in factories. The impact of this revolution shows no signs of stopping; indeed, the pace of change is accelerating while also becoming more global.

Karl Marx was right to see that industrialization heralded the creation of two new social classes, the bourgeois who owned industry and the working class who labored in it. Workers did work long hours and were often crowded into filthy hovels in overcrowded urban slums. These proletarians generally lived short, nasty, and brutish lives. But exploitation and poverty were hardly new in human history. Marx was also prescient to see that industrialization created the possibility of something new in history. Slowly at first, and with increasing momentum, industrialization resulted in a new phenomenon in world history: the creation of mass abundance.

Goods that had always been rare, such as iron, clothing, and even food, became increasingly cheap. This was in sharp contrast with previous technological change; the discovery of a piece of technology (for instance windmills) raised living standards temporarily, only to see humanity fall prey to the "Malthusian trap" as population outstripped resources. The rapid booms and busts of industrial societies were driven by the fact that goods became increasingly better and cheaper.

In 1900, the average life expectancy in the United States was almost 50, and a hundred years later, it was around 75 years. Of course, within industrial societies terrible inequalities remained. If white American males in 1900 could expect to live to 47, and African Americans to be around 33, that was the same life expectancy of poor Romans 2,000 years ago.

In retrospect, it is clear that Marx was wrong to believe that workers would inevitably seize the means of production and control their distribution. Yet Marx's optimism (or overoptimism) helped spark the creation of workers' parties throughout the world that sought to redistribute the wealth of industrial societies downward. Especially in Europe, labor or socialist parties encouraged the expansion of voting rights, which led to the creation of state-sponsored pensions and other social insurance schemes. The Russian Revolution sought to speed up that process of socialist transformation, but instead it created a brutal and undemocratic dictatorship that ultimately stifled the development of Russia, and every country that underwent communism. Yet the Russian Revolution arguably aided the process of reform in other countries. It is noteworthy that social welfare experiments accelerated in response to the Soviet experiment, and faltered when it became clear six decades later that that experiment had failed.

Why did communism fail? It lacked many of the social and cultural ingredients that made industrial capitalism function. It is worth recalling the insights of Adam Smith. Smith observed that self-interest drove the emerging capitalist economy. Industrial workplaces made more efficient use of labor; by subdividing tasks, pin makers dramatically increased the production of pins, thereby lowering the price. This social benefit was achieved as individuals (both workers and businessmen) pursued their own self-interests.

So, if entrepreneurialism could lead to exploitation, a fact that Smith acknowledged, it also fostered technological and organizational innovation. Industrialization created more opportunities for new and old skilled trades and professions; industrial economies required more carpenters as well as electricians, more lawyers as well as engineers. Capitalism either stimulated, or reinforced, the bourgeois values of self-discipline and self-reliance that Benjamin Franklin extolled, and numerous others repeated in mass-produced newspaper and magazine articles. Industrial capitalism created enormous opportunities for businesses to develop corrupt relationships with government, but also for other entrepreneurs in mass media to make money by exposing them. If Marx saw government as the only mechanism that could bring order and justice to industrialization, Smith saw that the self-interest of an aspiring capitalist would ultimately destroy monopolies. Moreover, the growing wealth of the professional middle classes ultimately created greater social confidence and political expectations, a fact that Marx would have appreciated (even if he bemoaned that workers lagged far behind them).

Let us look at the process of industrial capitalism in some greater detail. The railroads symbolized the industrial age in the nineteenth century. They were complex pieces of machinery that burned fossil fuel (coal) and moved enormous amounts of goods quickly across continents. Before industrialization, it cost as much to ship goods 20 miles over land as it did to ship them across the Atlantic. Railroads dramatically lowered shipping costs. Linked with telegraphs, railroads revealed the ability of industrial economies to shatter ancient limits of time and space. Railroads were the first big business, and authority could not run along ties of family or friendship. They were the first to rely upon such organization innovations as double-entry bookkeeping, providing a check on the corrupt self-interest of managers. Railroads also symbolized how successful businesses could become monopolies, as most developed enormous economic power by manipulating government policies to raise prices and to stifle critics and competitors.

Yet if competition could be delayed, or distorted, it could not be denied. New industries, such as automobiles, arose in response to the primal demands of greed and gain. Long-distance trucking, private automobiles, and airlines, burning a new kind of fuel (gasoline), wrested much of the market of shipping freight and people from railroads in the first decades of the twentieth century.

The auto industry symbolized the confluence of technological and organizational change of the twentieth century. Automakers such as Henry Ford adopted the new techniques of scientific management that enabled them to dramatically expand production on mechanized assembly lines. Over the space of 15 years, Ford managed to lower the cost of his Model T by two-thirds, and ultimately paid many of his workers twice the prevailing wage. Some business leaders saw Ford as a class traitor, while others heralded him as creating a template for a new kind of society that transcended traditional class conflict. Ford exported his cars throughout the world and opened up production plants in Germany, France, Australia, South Africa, and India. By the start of the 1920s, half of the cars in the world were made by Ford. Lenin invited Ford to produce vehicles in the Soviet Union. Equally important were Ford trucks and tractors, both of which helped mechanize food production and distribution.

Industrialization allowed people to produce, transport, and preserve food, which tended to drive its cost down. The railroads opened up new areas for food production, such as the American Midwest, helping farmers and ranchers access national rather than local markets. But until the 1920s, farmers still set aside one-quarter to one-third of all agricultural land to feed the animals that powered the plough. That changed with the Fordson tractor, a notably cheap and durable product. Powered by gasoline, the tractor allowed farmers either to plant crops in areas once devoted to grasses or to open up new areas, such as those parts of the American West that had been covered by grass whose root system was so deep and tough it could not be ploughed by draft animals.

The results were a dramatic expansion in food stuffs and a corresponding reduction in food prices. Within a few years, the opening of the American prairies turned the severe drought of the 1930s into a new phenomenon: the Dust Bowl. Dust from the western prairies even darkened the skies of Washington, DC. Thus industrialization accelerated the ancient tendency of humanity to overexploit the soil, whether from farming or grazing. The return of rains, and then of the ability of farmers after World War II to use machinery to pump water from deep aquifers, prevented the vast majority from drawing the connection that while industrial farming could increase production, it also had the power to transform the environment. In some areas, the aquifers are already running dry; in some areas, sufficient water remains for another twenty years of industrial agriculture.

Following World War II, industrial farming, aided by agronomists, fertilizers, pesticides, and bioengineered crops, dramatically increased food supplies. Industrialization continually transforms the nature of food. In 1900, an orange was considered an appropriate middle-class Christmas gift for a child. By 1950, in American snow-covered cities, oranges were no longer exotic or rare. But desertification, encouraged by industrial farming as well as traditional methods, continues apace. Dust from the Sahara now reaches the Caribbean, just as particles from the expanding Gobi darken the skies over Beijing and reach the Pacific shores of the United States.

In the world of today, hunger remains a significant problem, especially in Africa, Latin America, and Asia, but in health terms, obesity is just as large of a problem. The problem of too much food is unique to the industrial age. Fast food is not just popular but industrialized. Choose any iconic fast-food chain, and the food has been carefully manufactured, relying on fossil fuels to power the machinery that produces, transports, or transforms the product. Scientists add chemicals to make the food more appealing or possess a longer shelf life. The food is packaged via an industrial process. The ancient art of persuasion has been transformed by psychologists and pollsters, and the ads come to the potential consumer via the latest technologies in telecommunications.

Fast food has become a global phenomenon, increasingly transforming the cuisine and waistlines of the world. Coca-Cola is available throughout the world, even in remote parts of the Himalayas where it has to be carried by porters for several days. Poor South Africans routinely eat crisps (what Americans call chips) or chips (what Americans call fries) and Russians (sausages). McDonald's is an expensive, though cherished, treat. Throughout the world, a rise in living standards is accompanied by an increase in meat consumption as well as fast food. Meat and fried foods trigger the pleasure centers of the brain, a holdover from the many millennia that calorically dense food (such as fats, meats, and sugars) was rare. Only in the last few decades have luxuries like chocolates or cheeseburgers become so widely available that they pose a threat to health. Thus the Industrial Revolution helps create in abundance the foods that our ancestors craved.

To fulfill the world's rising demand for meat, more and more forests are transformed into farms to raise grains for cattle. To produce one calorie of chicken, four calories of grain and fossil fuels are required. Beef can require up to 50 calories. Cattle raised in feedlots have a significant ecological impact; the nitrogen-rich runoff from cattle dung depletes oxygen from water and helps to create "dead zones" in oceans. Antibiotics fed to animals keep diseases low but make more likely the creation of drug-resistant bacteria that could harm humans.

Industrialization creates the possibility of mass abundance but also the reality of increased pressure on the environment. Humanity's demand for food has resulted in the logging of the Amazon to create farmlands for cattle and the strip mining of the ocean floor for cod and other wild food. Oil powers all societies, but oil extraction and refining often creates severe local problems, from contaminated water to carcinogen-filled air. Two and a half centuries of burning fossil fuels is transforming the climate itself, as ever-higher levels of carbon create a greenhouse effect. Industrialization is setting in motion an environmental catastrophe arguably as great as those that followed the giant meteor that ended the reign of the dinosaurs. Industrialization created this problem, and the capacity to understand it, and also the possibility of avoiding it through the adoption of greener energy sources.

The issue of oil and the environment underscores important aspects of industrialization: the production of goods and their environmental costs are increasingly global and interconnected. If there is greater awareness that the world is fragile and limited, there is concern that global supplies and flows of energy are also limited and fragile. Industrialization and rising living standards rely on increasing energy usage. Until now, the assumption has been that the earth can absorb any and all environmental costs, despite mounting evidence that the free ride that humanity has enjoyed from nature is coming to an end. Until now, fossil fuels have been cheap. It was possible to extract 10 or 20 calories of energy from coal or oil for every calorie of energy invested. Those days are behind us. Climate change, better technology, and rising energy costs all make it possible to extract oil from the ocean floor of the Arctic. This excites some and horrifies others, but it is not a sign of the return of the era of cheap energy.

Both energy and environment have the potential to limit the Industrial Revolution, but until then, there is every sign that the pace of change is intensifying. Billions of people of the world still lack access to clean water, but a majority of the world's population possess a cell phone. Manufacturing is increasingly automated, eliminating millions of jobs in China, in the United States, and throughout the world. Work is increasingly done by computers and other machines, even in law, engineering, and medicine. Even if the work is not automated, it is increasingly possible to have it done via the Internet, making it possible for professionals to work from home or to do it cheaper from across the globe. Consequently, industrialization is transforming every aspect of life of affluent Japanese teenagers as well as residents of slums from Brazil to Indonesia. Even those who have never seen a factory floor are shaped by this unique revolution. Peasants in rural Mexico and college-educated Chinese in the super cities of the Pacific coast live in a world of industrial products, electronic entertainment, and industrial expectations.

What would Karl Marx and Adam Smith make of our industrial age? Marx would point out that the costs and benefits of industrialization are unevenly shared. In much of the world, economic inequality is increasing. Public policy is one of the most important mechanisms of lessening, or increasing, the gap between economic winners and losers. Smith might well agree, as he harbored no illusions about the ways the rich could use government to their own ends. But he would observe that self-interest remained a powerful motivator, and societies that created the right mix of support for innovation (through education, infrastructure, and policies that support innovation) raised their living standards far faster than those that tried to suppress the market. In 1950, Egypt and Sri Lanka were richer and better educated than China or Singapore, but that is no longer the case.

Marx might point to the finite nature of raw materials and how important energy is becoming to the military and diplomatic strategies of powerful companies. Smith would likely observe that as energy becomes more expensive, it becomes more profitable to extract more of it. Furthermore, self-interest would dictate that the individual or company that figured out an efficient form of green energy would become richer than Croesus or Bill Gates.

Environmental problems would vex both. In the long term, it is in everyone's self-interest to reverse pollution, but in the short run, dumping pollution into oceans, rivers, or the air is a free ride. This results in the "tragedy of the commons." Marx would likely emphasize the role of government in increasing the cost of pollution, a point Smith might well concede, although pointing out that self-interest will result in new forms of technology that few can foresee.

The Industrial Revolution is here to stay. It is transforming our world, creating both possibilities and problems that are more intense. There is no way to reverse course, short of a disaster. Even in some doomsday scenarios, the society that survived would still be an industrial one, even if living in a more degraded physical and political environment.

Chronology

1563	English Statute of Apprentices requires guild regulation over skilled labor
1600s	Proto-industrialization. Beginning of plantation system in the Caribbean and spread of racialized slavery to the Americas; adoption in Europe of American crops such as corn and potatoes
1601	English Poor Law authorizes local governments to provide relief to unemployed
1619	English iron makers begin to use coal instead of charcoal
1694	Bank of England receives charter
1702	Thomas Newcomen invents steam engine
1721	Calico Act restricts imports of cloth to England
1733	Flying shuttle invented in England by John Kay
1750s–1800	Rise of the factory system in England
1757	East India Company begins to conquer India
1769	Water frame invented by Richard Arkwright; James Watt patents his efficient steam engine
1776	Adam Smith publishes *Wealth of Nations*; Matthew Boulton invents a steam engine suitable for industry
1779	Samuel Crompton invents spinning mule
1789–91	French Revolution; manorialism abolished
1790	National Bank of the United States established
1791	Le Chapelier Law in France abolishes guilds and labor combinations
1799–1815	Napoleonic Wars
1790s	Establishment of gold standard

1793	Cotton gin invented by Eli Whitney
1795	Britain wins Cape colony (South Africa) from Dutch
1799–1800	English Combination Acts prohibit strikes and unions
1802	First English Factory Act limits work of pauper children to 12 hours a day
1805–40	Muhammed Ali begins attempt at industrialization of Egypt
1809	England suspends minimum wage
1810s	Luddite risings in England
1813–14	Repeal of English Statute of Apprentices
1815	British Corn Law raises tariffs on grains
1817–25	Construction of the Erie Canal
1818	Prussia drops internal tariffs
1819	Factory Act in England prohibits employers from hiring workers younger than 9, and children under 16 can work only 12 hours a day
1820s	Beginning of Industrial Revolution in Belgium, France, and New England; property-less white males gain the vote in the United States; Prussia advocates Zollverein or customs union for Germany
1830s	Chartism in England; first department stores open in France; abolition of slavery in English colonies; charter for the Bank of the United States allowed to lapse
1830	United States has 23 miles of railroad track; beginning of expansion of railroad system
1832	Partial enfranchisement of British males
1834	England passes harsh poor relief act
1837	Telegraph developed in England by William Cooke and Charles Wheatstone and in the United States by William Morse
1839–42	Opium Wars in China
1840s	Beginning of Industrial Revolution in Germany
1842	Springfield Armory in the United States begins to produce interchangeable parts for rifles; Chinese government forced to open ports to foreign trade
1844	Rochdale Cooperative movement begins

1846	Britain repeals Corn Laws
1848	*Communist Manifesto* published by Karl Marx
1848	Democratic revolutions attempted throughout Europe; manorialism abolished in most of central Europe
1850s	Crédit Mobilier helps to finance French railroad system; half of England lives in cities
1851	First international industrial exposition in London (Crystal Palace); major U.S. cities connected by telegraph wires
1854	Henry Bessemer invents Bessemer converter for steelmaking
1854–56	Crimean War
1855–60	Second Opium Wars in China
1861	Emancipation of the serfs in Russia; California connected to the eastern United States by telegraph wires
1861–65	Civil war in United States
1861–67	Emancipation of slaves in the United States
1862	U.S. Morrill Act provides federal land grants to universities that provide technical or agricultural training
1864–76	First Workingmen's International (collapses due to conflict between Marxists and anarchists)
1866	Transatlantic telegraph cable laid; sharecropping system begins in the U.S. South
1867	English male workers receive the vote
1868	Beginning of Meiji Era
1869	Suez canal opens; formation of Knights of Labor
1870s	Rise of white-collar labor force; Sidney Thomas and Percy Gilchrist develop process to use limestone to remove phosphorous from molten iron, which allows expansion of iron making in Germany
1871	Paris Commune; English unions legalized
1873–77	Major depression
1875	Japanese government gives Mitsubishi 11 steam ships in order to compete with Western companies

1876	N. A. Otto produces first practical internal combustion motor; Alexander Graham Bell invents telephone
1877	Railroad strike in the United States
1879	First refrigerated ship built (eases transportation of meat and other foods)
1880s	Bismarck suppresses German socialists, institutes limited welfare reforms
1860s–1890s	European powers colonize Africa in the "great scramble"; widespread adoption of open hearth in steelmaking; Populist movement (backlash against Populism disenfranchises nearly all blacks and most poor whites in southern United States)
1881	First coal-fired electrical power station established in England; hydroelectric plants set up in Niagara, New York
1884	Knights of Labor successfully strike a railroad owned by Jay Gould; membership grows to several hundred thousand
1886	Formation of the AFL
1888	Zollverein (German custom's union) complete; internal tariffs dropped; Brazil abolishes slavery; Nikola Tesla sells alternating current motor to George Westinghouse; Jay Gould smashes railroad strike by Knights of Labor; membership begins to fall
1890	Sherman Antitrust Act; United States has 150,000 miles of railroad track
1892	Homestead Lockout
1892–1904	Trans-Siberian Railroad built
1894	Confédération Générale du Travail formed in France
1895	Japan annexes Taiwan
1897	Rudolf Diesel invents efficient internal combustion engine
1898	Frontier in the United States closed; United States fights and wins war with Spain and gains several colonies
1899–1920	Second Workingmen's International (collapses because nationalism during World War I overcomes internationalist principles)
1900s	Taylorism and scientific management begin

1900	Japanese Police Regulation Law makes it a crime to strike
1901	Formation of United States Steel (U.S. Steel); boom era for corporations and cartels
1902	Restrictive Bülow Tariff instituted in Germany
1904–5	Russo-Japanese War
1905	Failed revolution in Russia; formation of Industrial Workers of the World
1906	First general strike in France, led by Confédération Générale du Travail; construction began on Panama Canal; syndicalists form Brazilian Federation of Labor
1907	Jamshed Tata begins construction of steel mills in India
1909	Price of Ford Model T is $900
1910	Japan annexes Korea
1910s–1920s	Height of workers' control movement in industrialized countries; corporations seek to stem it by using Taylorism and scientific management
1911	Britain passes the world's first state-run unemployment insurance system
1914	Ford begins production of Model Ts in his River Rouge factory; price of Model T falls to $440; completion of Panama Canal
1914–18	World War I; by war's end, German, Austro-Hungarian, Russian, and Ottoman empires have fallen
1915–20s	Great Migration in the United States
1917	Russian Revolution
1917–21	Civil war in Soviet Union
1919–20	Attempted workers' revolutions in Germany, Austria, Hungary, and Italy
1920s	Fascists take power in Italy; widespread adoption of radio; 12 percent of the British workforce is unemployed
1920s–30s	Industrialized countries abandon the gold standard
1921	Major Japanese shipyard strike, union leaders arrested
1921–28	New Economic Policy in the Soviet Union

1923	John Maynard Keynes writes *Tract on Monetary Reform*, a critique of the gold standard
1924	United States limits immigration
1925	Japan eases Police Regulation Law; Bell Laboratories established
1926	British general strike
1927	Transatlantic telephone cables laid; Ford Motor Company produces 650,000 tractors a year
1928	Collectivization of Soviet agriculture, beginning of Stalinist industrialization (first five-year plan)
1929	Wall Street crash
1930	Smoot-Hawley Tariff in the United States helps spark a trade war
1930s	Global depression
1930s	Purges in Soviet Union
1931	Japan invades China
1933	Hitler comes to power in Germany; Japan invades China
1935	Formation of Congress of Industrial Organizations (CIO); Wagner Act makes it easier to form unions in the United States
1936	Sit-down strike by auto workers in Toledo
1937	CIO wins contracts with U.S. Steel and General Motors
1939–45	Europe and the United States join World War II
1944	Bretton Woods Agreement; formation of World Bank
1945	Labour government in Britain begins nationalization of industry
1945–73	Global economic boom; suburbanization of working class in the United States; 40-hour workweek common
1947	India gains independence; beginning of decolonization in Asia and Africa; Marshall Plan begins in Europe; Taft-Hartley Act limits power of unions in the United States
1948–89	Cold War
1949	Chinese Revolution; formation of Ministry of International Trade and Industry in Japan

1950s	Rapid increase of women in the labor force in Europe and the United States
1951	First five-year plan in India
1953	First (and last) five-year plan in China
1957	Soviet Union launches Sputnik satellite
1958	Formation of European Economic Community (Common Market)
1960s	Beginning of Japanese export drive; industrialization in Pacific Rim, particularly South Korea, Singapore, Hong Kong, and Taiwan
1965	Beginning of maquiladora policy in Mexico
1968	United States lands man on the moon
1968–72	Strikes and student demonstrations throughout the world
1971	United States devalues dollar, ends convertibility of dollars into gold
1973, 1979	OPEC raises prices of oil
1974	Beginning of global depression
Mid-1970s onward	Deindustrialization closes down much of the industrial base of advanced industrial countries
1978	China begins to introduce market reforms
1984	Explosion in chemical plant in Bhopal, India
1989–91	Collapse of Soviet Union
1990s	Commercialization of the Internet begins
1994	North American Free Trade Agreement
1997–2001	Dot-com bubble
2000	United States signs permanent trading relations with China
2001	China joins the World Trade Organization
2003	United States and allies invade Iraq
2008	Price of oil reaches previous high-water mark (1979); financial bubbles collapse in Europe and the United States; era of austerity begins
2011	Toyota surpasses GM in auto sales; Eurozone on brink of collapse

ABOLITIONISM

Abolitionists advocated that slavery be restricted or abolished. During the eighteenth and nineteenth centuries, these activists in England and the United States helped to end the "peculiar institution." Many scholars argue that the success of abolitionism had more to do with the economic and political changes that the Industrial Revolution wrought on European and U.S. societies and economies than with the moral suasion of abolitionists.

In the early eighteenth century, many social groups in England benefited from and supported the lucrative trade in slaves between Africa and the Caribbean. Likewise, most British supported the use of slaves and indentured servants to produce sugar produced on Caribbean plantations. Support for slavery came not only from the planters (many of whom lived in England) but also from the merchants who outfitted slave expeditions and the workers who built the slave ships. The importance of sugar gave planters enormous political and economic power, and many invested their financial surplus in early manufacturing concerns. However, the planters' enormous political influence gradually atrophied in the early nineteenth century as the price of their sugar rose relative to sugar produced in non-English colonies. In response to the increasing costs of a sugar monopoly, merchants, workers, and the growing class of industrialists advocated laissez-faire economic policies and questioned the mercantilist trade policies favored by planters. (Cheaper imports of foodstuffs would allow industrialists to effectively raise workers' standards of living without requiring a rise in wages.) The restriction of the slave trade was not a rejection of colonialism or white supremacy so much as an expression of faith in laissez-faire economic policy. Antislavery campaigns may have influenced some workers' sense of the woes facing "free" industrial wage labor.

By the 1830s, Britain had banned the international trade in slaves, but slave societies continued in the U.S. South until 1865 and in much of the Caribbean and Brazil until the 1880s. Although English abolitionists had boycotted sugar made with slave labor in English colonies, they did not argue that manufacturers should refuse to buy cotton or other goods made with unfree labor in other parts of the world.

During the late eighteenth and early nineteenth centuries in the United States, many white abolitionists opposed slavery partly out of belief in the superiority of wage labor and partly because slavery had "polluted" the racial purity of the country. These abolitionists advocated forcing slaves and free blacks to emigrate to the

An 1866 *Harper's Weekly* illustration depicts African Americans celebrating the fourth anniversary of the abolition of slavery in the District of Columbia. (Library of Congress)

Caribbean or Africa. Gradually, black abolitionists succeeded in shifting the terms of debate, and by the 1830s, an increasing number of white abolitionists favored the immediate emancipation of slaves without expatriation. However, many black abolitionists and radical whites questioned the usefulness of nonviolent tactics, such as petitions, because Congress (at the urging of Southern planters) had passed a rule that forbade any congressional debate concerning the petitions of abolitionists. Abolitionists' agitation and the vehement reaction to it in the South nonetheless brought the question of slavery to the top of the political agenda and helped to precipitate the growing divisions that led to the American Civil War.

The most consistent advocates of abolition were, of course, black slaves and freedmen themselves. Blacks' resistance to slavery took many forms, from "passive" strategies such as feigning sickness or stealing food to the social revolution of "black Jacobins" in Haiti in the 1790s. Although slave revolts in the southern United States (such as that of Nat Turner in 1830) caused widespread panic among white Southerners, they were relatively rare, for slaves were greatly outnumbered by whites. However, many slaves escaped to freedom, and a few, notably Harriet Tubman and Frederick Douglass, became famous speakers and writers for the abolitionist cause. Although abolitionists eventually succeeded in destroying the system of slavery, they were unable to overcome the institutionalized racism that turned freed slaves into sharecroppers—toiling in conditions little better than slavery.

Slavery continued into the present, particularly in Africa and the Middle East. Desperately poor families sell children to other families. Slaves have become much cheaper than in the mid-nineteenth century and can be purchased in West Africa for less than $100. Campaigns continue to abolish slavery, drawing heavily from religious movements and Human Rights campaigns.

See also Corn Laws; Emancipation and Reconstruction (United States); Racism; Slavery

Further Reading

Blackburn, Robin. *The Overthrow of Colonial Slavery, 1776–1848*. New York: Verso, 1988.
Williams, Eric. *Capitalism and Slavery*. Chapel Hill: University of North Carolina Press, 1944.

ACCIDENTS

The Industrial Revolution unquestionably increased the rate and severity of accidents at work. Preindustrial work could cause accidents, in falls, cuts, and problems with draft animals. More commonly, certain jobs caused endemic health problems—printers and painters faced lead poisoning, some weavers got chest deformities due to activating hand looms with their upper bodies. Industrial power equipment actually reduced the risk of some deformities, but it greatly heightened accidents and work-related illnesses of other sorts. Use of chemicals increased, causing various risks of poisoning. High-speed power equipment created new opportunities for loss of fingers and limbs. Boilers could and sometimes did explode. The expansion of metallurgical furnaces could cause burning or scalding. The tremendous growth of the labor force in coal mines and the need to dig mines ever deeper accounted for a series of major disasters.

Workers worried greatly about accident dangers. In early industrialization, employers seemed to take few precautions. Child workers on textile machinery, often required to repair thread while the machine was operating, frequently lost fingers. Many observers in virtually every new industrialization—including those occurring in places like Mexico or China today—claimed that employers refused to go to the modest expense of screening off exposed machine parts. Proper timbering in coal mines might be neglected. One worker in the United States recalled that in the early twentieth century, mine owners preferred losing immigrant workers to timbering mines: "Wops are cheaper than props." Of course it was not in employers' interests to ignore safety altogether; quite apart from worker reactions, accidents could damage equipment and delay production. Nevertheless, machinery became steadily more complicated, raising the risks. Growing use of power equipment in craft work—for example, machine-powered lathes in woodworking shops and on construction sites—increased the range of accidents in the later nineteenth century.

The introduction of internal combustion engines for cranes and, soon, trucks and automobiles created further risks. Unquestionably, the rate of death by work accident rose dramatically in industrial societies during the nineteenth century.

Largely at the urging of unions, governments of industrial countries began to step up factory safety requirements and inspections from about 1870 onward. Some countries, including Germany, had a tradition of government inspection of mines that went back even earlier. Workers' concern about growing accident rates, particularly as the pace of work stepped up around 1900, prompted trade unions to press for more control, and major strikes often followed mine disasters. Better safety measures almost certainly reduced accident rates, though not necessarily worker anxiety, by 1900. Mining fatalities in Belgium fell by about 10 percent in the first decade of the twentieth century, for example. Many U.S. states, as well as several European countries, began to introduce workmen's compensation laws, which required employers to pay workers injured on the job. Dominant thinking shifted from the assumptions of the early industrial period—when employers typically blamed workers for "imprudence" as the cause of accidents—to the notion that owners were accountable for working conditions.

Engineers and scientific management contributed to safer industrial workplaces. Until the early 1920s, the steel industry in the United States required many workers to labor seven days a week at 12-hour-long "turns." The term came from the fact that every week the men would switch from days to nights, providing one day off, but every other week, the men would work a long turn of 24 hours. The system saved companies from employing a third shift but almost ensured that men working with massive machines and molten metal were continuously fatigued. Workers regularly crawled off to sleep wherever and whenever they could and were sometimes horribly killed. Engineers showed that the accidents peaked when workers ended a long turn, or when they shifted from days to nights. The adoption of an eight-hour day virtually paid for itself in fewer accidents and more productivity. Even after the industry was unionized, the system of turns continued, and workers continued to rotate every two weeks between a day turn, then to afternoons, then to nights. The consequences of such schedules, or of regular night work, increases stress and results in shortened life spans.

Not surprisingly, safety regulations remained a contentious area. In the interest of maintaining war output during World War I, the United States increased federal regulation, forming a Working Conditions Service in the Department of Labor. This regulation slackened during the 1920s, however, as union power declined and greater reliance was placed on voluntary employer efforts. New Deal legislation, in addition to providing disability payments under Social Security, again encouraged more attention to industrial hygiene.

Industrialization continued to promote more work accidents in the twentieth century, particularly in countries where the process was just beginning. Safety regulations often seemed lax, as governments worked to increase output and foreign investors looked to economize on their investments. Major disasters, such as the

1984 explosion in a U.S.-owned chemical plant in Bhopal, India (over 200 people killed, over 20,000 maimed), were simply one indication of an ongoing problem. Many developing countries require minimal safety standards. Consequently, workers' risks of accidents or exposure to chemicals vary widely. Pakistan became a leader in the industry of taking apart transport ships. Older ships are filled with asbestos and other hazards. The antiquated vessels are beached and hundreds of workers using simple tools and limited safety equipment take the ships apart. Chinese coal mines are some of the most unsafe in the world. Chinese workers protest regularly, sometimes over safety issues. Yet some protections are offered to those Chinese who take apart computers and electronics, far more than their Indian or African counterparts.

Even in advanced industrial societies, the effectiveness of regulations varied; early in the 1990s, many workers claimed that U.S. packing houses were causing increasing accidents by speeding up their cutting machines. Moreover, new equipment could pose unexpected problems; excessive computer use caused a growing incidence of carpal tunnel syndrome among office workers, for example. Finally, even as some of the most overt safety problems were brought under partial control, more insidious health problems like stress, fatigue, and loss of sleep seemed to increase in the new millennium—one source of the increasing tendency among U.S. workers to retire at an earlier age.

See also Environment; State, Role of the

Further Reading

Rosner, David, and Gerald Markowitz, eds. *Dying for Work: Workers' Health and Safety in Twentieth-Century America*. Bloomington: Indiana University Press, 1986.
Stearns, Peter N. *Lives of Labor: Work in Maturing Industrial Society*. New York: Holmes and Meier, 1975.

ADVERTISING

Because the Industrial Revolution depended on growing consumer interest and generated a massive level of goods, advertising was inevitably bound up in the process. Specific industrial inventions, initially in printing and photography, also facilitated advertising by cutting the cost of newspapers and flyers and, ultimately, adding pictorial illustrations and film as well as radio outlets.

Advertising began in the eighteenth century. The growing number of store owners in England and other countries used eye-catching displays and signs to attract customers. Early newspapers routinely carried notices of products for sale, often intermingled with regular articles to blur the distinction between commerce and objective reporting. As industrialization advanced and the need to sell goods increased, advertising changed; in the West, the 1870s formed a fairly clear dividing line. After this point, advertising was increasingly geared toward the masses as well as toward middle- and upper-class consumers. The growing mass press, like the

Wire rope from the John A. Roebling company made possible suspension bridges, such as the Brooklyn Bridge, but had numerous other commercial applications. 1879. (Library of Congress)

London Daily Mail, depended on lots of advertising, which supported its cheap purchase price; in turn, flashy headlines and a gripping style helped lure working-class readers who would, of course, also see the ads. The tone of advertising changed as well. Most early advertising was informational, stressing availability, price, and quality. By the late nineteenth century, advertising took on a more emotional cast. Silk goods, for example, were described in terms of utility and price in U.S. newspaper lists even in the 1890s, but after 1900, they began to be touted as "alluring," "bewitching"—"to feel young and carefree, buy our silk." Similar transformations occurred for other products. Automobiles, for instance, were initially advertised largely in terms of economy, good mechanics, and sometimes speed. But by the 1930s, advertising increasingly stressed cars' appearance and fashionability, to appeal to a wider market that included women.

By the early twentieth century, a substantial advertising business was beginning to develop; it came into its own in the United States by the 1920s. Modern advertisers clearly gained the capacity to create demand for goods. For instance, clever advertising, rather than product quality, boosted certain brands of cigarettes over others. Advertisers were also constrained by public beliefs, however, and they worked within the culture, advertising products in terms of existing family values, ideas about gender, and so on. Companies linked their brands to popular bands, sports teams, or in some cases, new national identities.

The technological advances of the late twentieth century helped to develop a new model of niche advertising. Advertisers could identify and target increasingly specific demographic groups. At first, companies could insert different ads into national magazines. The explosion of the Internet and then social media provided companies like Google or Facebook with staggering amounts of information about consumer preferences. Consequently, companies were then able to advertise on websites and video games, or send ads to customers' smart phones. The advent of Internet advertising contributed to the sharp decline of newspapers in the United States in the 1990s and thereafter.

See also Consumerism and Mass Consumption

Further Reading

Ewen, Elizabeth, and Stuart Ewen. *Captains of Consciousness: Mass Images and the Shaping of American Consumers*. New York: Oxford University Press, 1982.
Marchand, Roland. *Advertising the U.S. Dream: Making Way for Modernity, 1920–1940*. Berkeley: University of California Press, 1985.

AERONAUTICS

Airplanes are a product of the industrial age and the rapid expansion of scientific knowledge; they are a symbol of industrialization, and aeronautics is an industry in its own right. Aircraft production, repair, air travel, and air freight have grown into a major component of the international marketplace. Early in the new millennium, aeronautics employed more than half a million workers in the European Union, more than 1 percent of its workers, and generated almost 2 percent of the European Union's economic activity. Airlines and even airports are a symbol of national pride, and governments have historically heavily subsidized the industry.

From its origins, aircraft production required the ability to manufacture and manipulate high-quality metals, steel and aluminum, and other materials such as plastics. Therefore airplanes tended to be manufactured in countries with highly developed metalworking industries. The pace of technological change in the industry has been unrelenting; aircraft companies have had to incorporate new designs for planes, engines, and propulsion, new metals or materials, as well as electronics and computers. Consequently, aeronautics required a well-developed university system, as well as research and development in the private sector.

Government played an important role in this industry, as airplanes proved crucial in many wars, starting in World War I. Initially, planes were chiefly used for observation, providing valuable intelligence to whoever controlled the air. By the end of the war, airplanes were used to shoot and bomb troops on the ground; there was also a major fight for air supremacy.

Aircraft were quickly put to use by industrial powers in maintaining control over colonies. For instance, the British used airplanes and poison gas bombs on the Iraqi Kurds in the 1920s. The Italians benefited from aircraft in conquering Libya in the 1930s. The Japanese bombing of civilians in China (and later the Germans throughout Europe) was considered brutal but horribly effective.

Once industrial powers began fighting, quality mattered more than quantity. The British initially discounted the Japanese airplanes and pilots but quickly lost several colonies and much of their navy to the Japanese, who relied heavily on air power. In 1941, the Soviet air force was the world's largest. The Germans quickly eliminated it. The air war was particularly fierce on the western front, although some historians have suggested that German bombardment of London as well as British and American bombing raids of German cities simply increased civilian support for their own governments.

Airplanes were widely seen as a symbol of a country's industrial and military might, and throughout the Cold War, governments subsidized the aircraft industry on grounds of military necessity and national pride. In the 1950s, Soviet military aircraft were well designed, although by the 1970s, they were inferior to Western counterparts. Consequently, the Soviet Union sold few commercial aircraft but was keen to sell more. When its supersonic commercial plane crashed at a Paris air show, it was humiliated. However, the United States had secretly been flying spy planes overhead, and in reality, the "Concordsky" did not fail, as was widely believed; it simply crashed into an American plane as it made a high-altitude loop. The Soviets did not make another Concordsky.

Commercial airline travel began in the 1930s and quickly expanded. Jet travel began in 1952, making international and long-distance flight quicker and cheaper. As it eclipsed oceanic travel, places such as Cairo and Cape Town became marginalized as passengers no longer had to pass by them going to and from Europe. In the United States, the air travel industry was regulated and subsidized, and so remained financially stable and heavily unionized. Newly independent countries in Africa and Asia sponsored national airlines, many of which went bankrupt, although several (such as Singapore Air and South African Air) have remained solvent and a source of national pride. In the United States, new companies and entrepreneurs entered the industry after it was deregulated in the late 1970s, where cost rather than passenger comfort became the key to survival. The low-cost model quickly spread throughout the world.

Air freight is an important aspect of global trade. As much as one-quarter of the world's goods (measured by value) are shipped by air. Air travel allows rural areas to ship to rich cities. The products themselves are diverse, from fresh-cut flowers to illegal drugs to workers themselves. Thus aeronautics ties rural Uganda to London, and highland Peru to suburban Los Angeles. Of course, most air shipping goes between, or within, industrialized countries. Six of the world's largest air freight companies are located in East Asia, not surprising given that region's dynamic growth. Since the 1990s, aeronautics has grown rapidly in China, with major companies shifting aircraft and engine assembly and production there. Companies find China's lower wages attractive, but the Chinese government also pushes companies to shift their production there if they want to service the country's large and growing market.

Aeronautics symbolizes and helps propel the global industrial revolution's erosion of time and space. It will continue for as long as there are cheap fossil fuels.

Further Reading

Pattillo, Donald M. *A History in the Making: Eighty Turbulent Years in the American General Aviation Industry*. New York: McGraw-Hill, 1998.

AFRICA

The Industrial Revolution has tended to increase the exploitation of African resources and labor. With the partial exception of South Africa, efforts to promote industrialization directly within sub-Saharan Africa have not been met with great success. Several regions have enjoyed periods of considerable economic growth but more typically as a supplier of raw materials or labor. Thus global expansion of the industrial economy has brought some benefits to parts of Africa but has not ensured direct participation in industrialization itself. The causes for Africa's dilemma are hotly debated.

Well before European imperialism began to seize sub-Saharan Africa, the subcontinent's participation in global trade had involved exports of relatively unprocessed goods—including slaves. This imbalance increased from the late nineteenth century onward. European and some American companies gained access to the region's great mineral wealth, setting up large mining operations and relying on relatively cheap local labor. Agricultural production was partially diverted from local subsistence farming to the production of export cash crops, such as vegetable oils, coffee, and cotton. Some of these crops significantly depleted the soil, causing environmental damage at further cost to economic potential. In turn, Africans largely imported factory products from the established industrial regions. Little local manufacturing occurred.

Decolonization brought political independence to sub-Saharan Africa from the 1960s onward. The newly independent states led concerted efforts to increase their economic autonomy, often through their own or regional industrial growth. At various points, many African countries received considerable funding from foreign governments, often without appreciable impact. Donors were often ignorant of African conditions and assumed that their own models of industrial development would fit. Equipment from the Soviet Union was of notoriously poor quality. African leaders themselves sometimes believed that industrial investments would pay off very quickly and did not devote attention to local economic conditions including the ongoing importance of agriculture. In many regions, foreign exploitation of mineral resources continued. The 1960s and 1970s did see several countries attempt a policy of import substitution, seeking to protect local factories that would produce some of the manufacturing goods previously acquired as imports. But lack of skilled labor and adequate technology doomed some of these efforts to failure. Many new nations were also fairly small, which meant that markets were limited. Most governments went heavily into debt, borrowing from outside the continent, which limited economic prospects. In many instances, most notoriously in Zaire, Western aid ended up in the Swiss bank accounts of local politicians. By 2000, many countries had lower living standards and life expectancies than when they won independence.

Many African countries, periodically from the 1960s onward, were also constrained by civil wars, famines, or disease, further constraining economic growth. The 1980s saw new emphasis on private enterprise, with lower government spending, and in the 1990s, there was new discussion of export-oriented industrialization. In some countries, multinationals (from Japan and South Korea as well as the West) set up factories using local labor. The goal was minimization of labor costs through low wages and long hours, with workers sometimes locked in the factory to make sure they did not wander off and to compel overtime.

By the early twenty-first century, however, several African countries began to enjoy unprecedented growth rates, of 5 to 10 percent per year. A few countries, such as Botswana, had had already achieved such rates of growth in the 1990s. The keys here were a new round of natural resource exports, now to China and India as well as the West, and investments by the rising Asian powers in regional infrastructure. Competition for oil—in Nigeria, Sudan, and elsewhere—intensified, and the same applied to other resources. Little real economic diversification occurred, and there was little sign of outright industrialization. Large segments of the population remained in subsistence agriculture.

South Africa provided a partial exception to this picture—but only partial. By the late twentieth and early twenty-first century, the nation was clearly the most economically developed in sub-Saharan Africa overall, and it rated reasonably high on international wealth measurements. But these ratings, to some extent, concealed unusually sharp divisions within South Africa between whites and blacks. The nation developed four major urban economic centers. Mining became a key source of wealth, from the late nineteenth century onward. By the late twentieth century, a number of foreign manufacturing firms had established factories in the country. South Africa thus exported automobiles, with plants developed by European and Japanese companies. Labor costs were midrange, and the country also won mid-level rankings when it came to innovation and worker skills. Overall, the industrial sector was not large, and the country did not display the dynamism visible by the twenty-first century in several parts of Asia or Brazil. Government reforms, introduced after 2004, placed greater emphasis on private enterprise, which did lead to some growth. Large sections of the population were still involved in subsistence agriculture, and many parts of the country were extremely poor; unemployment rates were high and rising.

Overall, Africa participated actively in the global Industrial Revolution, but without much control over the process, and often at a measurable and growing disadvantage. Change mainly involved additional exploitation, though some regions periodically reaped some benefits. In the early twenty-first century, there were some hopes that new earnings were possible on the global market that might in turn translate into more balanced economic development. The fact that growth rates stayed high in several resource-exporting countries, even during the global economic downturn of 2008, inspired some new confidence. Certainly, the goal of more active industrialization was widely shared. From 1989 onward, under the auspices of the United Nations Development Organization, African nations have celebrated November 20 as "African Industrialization Day," a chance to measure any progress and to recommit to further change.

Further Reading

Hopkins, A. G. *An Economic History of West Africa*. New York: Columbia University Press, 1976.

Kayizzi-Mugerwa, Steve. *The African Economy: Policy, Institutions and the Future*. New York: Routledge, 1999.

Mshomba, Richard. *Africa in the Global Economy*. Boulder, CO: Lynne Rienner, 2000.

Rodney, Walter. *How Europe Underdeveloped Africa*. Washington, DC: Howard University Press, 1981.

Tarp, Finn, and Peter Brixen. *The South African Economy*. New York: Routledge, 1996.

AGRICULTURE

The Industrial Revolution unquestionably diminishes and transforms agriculture in terms of the relative importance of its product and the proportion of the labor force it engages. Social classes based in agriculture, notably the peasantry and the aristocracy, decline, and urban workers and businessmen rise, though the process is usually gradual. Changes in agriculture are absolutely essential for industrialization, for greater productivity in food must precede any massive growth in the urban labor force.

Significant changes in European agriculture began in the late seventeenth century, initially unconnected to industrialization proper. Led by the Dutch, many farmers and estate owners began to drain marshes, expanding the land available for farming. New farming principles were introduced, such as the use of nitrogen-fixing crops like the turnip. Many groups discussed better methods, and individual promoters, like "Turnip" Townshend in England, spread the gospel of innovation. By periodically planting turnips or peas, land could be used annually, and many areas gradually moved away from the traditional three-field system in which one-third of the land had to be left fallow every year. Some new equipment was introduced, such as the seed drill, and estate owners, particularly in England, experimented with better methods of stock breeding. In other words, some of the same innovative ideas that were affecting manufacturing entered agriculture, particularly where large estate owners were eager for new profits (as in England). Peasant farming changed more slowly, though here, too, tools improved, as the more efficient

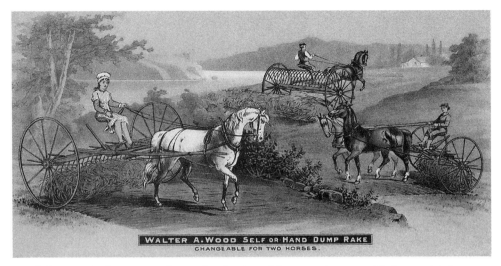

WALTER A. WOOD SELF or HAND DUMP RAKE
CHANGEABLE FOR TWO HORSES.

Until the twentieth century, the mechanization of farm equipment relied on animal power;
Walter A. Wood Self or Hand Dump Rake Advertisement, ca. 1880–1900. (Bettmann/Corbis)

scythe replaced sickles for harvesting. Most important was the increasing use of New
World crops such as the potato, which produced a greater abundance of cheap
foods, spurring population growth and releasing more starch products for sale in
urban markets. Collectively, these changes, sometimes called an "agricultural revolution," constituted the first big improvements in European farming since the
Middle Ages. They sustained both growing populations and increased urbanization.

Advances in agricultural productivity accompanied the early stages of industrialization almost everywhere. The Japanese government promoted more efficient farming in the 1870s and 1880s. Russia's emancipation of the serfs in 1861, though
complicated, did generate increased market production, and under the Soviet
government, the collectivization program strove to produce more food with fewer
workers, if only with mixed success. Governments (for example, Japan) also began
requiring tax payments in cash, which helped provide industrial capital but also
forced peasants to sell more food to meet the tax payments.

Once in motion, industrial revolutions further encourage agricultural change.
Growing urban markets help motivate increasing commercial specialization on
the farms. Science and the growing chemical industry are enlisted to produce new
fertilizers—a major development in Germany from the 1830s onward. New equipment becomes available as the principles of mechanization are applied to agriculture. Thus the harvesters and other devices introduced by the mid-nineteenth
century helped convert vast lands in North America to efficient commercial grain
farming to feed not only North American cities but also industrial centers in
Europe. By 1850, Britain had begun to reduce any effort to maintain adequate agriculture, realizing that it was more productive to concentrate on industry, including
industrial exports, while importing foods from Eastern Europe, Australia, New

Zealand, and North America. Although the British pattern was unique—no other major industrial country let agriculture slide to such an extent—world trade in foods supplemented industrialization efforts in many parts of Western Europe. Thanks to agricultural change and, sometimes, new imports, rural populations began to fall rapidly, dropping to under 50 percent of the total in England by 1850 and continuing to decline.

By the twentieth century, not only the relative size but also the absolute number of the farming population had plunged in every industrial area, thanks to the steadily increasing efficiency of industrial agriculture. The globalization of trade has accelerated the trend. In the 1990s, the North American Free Trade Agreement opened up Mexican markets to American and Canadian agricultural products, and the result was the dislocation of millions of Mexican small farmers. Many of them journeyed to the United States, where hundreds of thousands found jobs on industrialized farms, meatpacking plants, or poultry-processing factories. Similar dislocations have occurred throughout Asia, Africa, and Latin America, feeding the slums of the major cities in those regions.

The communist regimes, and their successors, provided interesting variations on the general rule of industrialization and agriculture. Soviet-style industrialization made agriculture more mechanized, but collective ownership provided few incentives for individuals to efficiently produce or distribute goods. The result was systematically stubborn food shortages. In communist Poland, almost half of food production came from a small number of privately owned farms. After the 1970s, the Chinese government encouraged entrepreneurial thinking both by collectives and by farmers. Within a generation, China not only fed its burgeoning urban population but exported food.

Concerns have been raised about the sustainability of the industrialized agricultural model. The system is heavily reliant upon fossil fuels, and one estimate holds that 16 calories of energy are required to produce, process, and transport 1 calorie of grains. Considerably more is needed for meat or dairy products. The large-scale poultry farms or beef feedlots are notoriously dirty, and are a major contributor to the contamination of groundwater. Nitrogen-rich runoff from cattle feedlots helps fuel the growth of "dead zones" in bays and gulfs. Growers rely upon widespread use of antibiotics to keep diseases in check, raising concerns that farms are helping to create drug-resistant "superbugs." Thus far, such concerns have been outweighed by the ability to dramatically increase food production.

See also Chemical Industry; Green Revolution; McCormick, Cyrus; Plantations; Potato

Further Reading

Horn, Pamela. *The Rural World, 1780–1850: Social Change in the English Countryside*. New York: Oxford, 1981.

Schlosser, Eric. *Fast Food Nation: The Dark Side of the All-American Meal*. New York: Houghton Mifflin, 2001.

Stearns, Peter N., and Herrick Chapman. *European Society in Upheaval: Social History since 1750.* 3rd ed. New York: Macmillan, 1992.

AIR-CONDITIONING

In 1922, Willis Carrier made it possible not only to cool air (through ice or mechanical fans) but to remove humidity from hot, sticky air, and thus air conditioning was born. Carrier used coils filled with highly volatile refrigerants, such as Freon, to draw heat and moisture from inside rooms and transfer it outside; as the refrigerants cooled, air was pumped back to the inside where the process began again. This technological innovation helped to speed the spread of corporate headquarters from the North to such southern cities as Houston, Dallas, and Atlanta.

Air-conditioning has accompanied the spread of multinational corporations throughout the world in the twentieth century. Initially used in movie theaters, hotels, and corporate headquarters, room and home air-conditioners were quickly adopted by the upper and middle classes. An industry in its own right, air-conditioning was increasingly installed in office buildings, public facilities, homes, and even automobiles throughout the entire world. Although they create a physical climate many find more conducive to concentrated, sustained physical or mental labor, the chemical ingredients in air-conditioning, ironically, have helped to deplete the ozone, hastening the greenhouse effect that is warming the planet.

See also Du Pont de Nemours; Environment

Further Reading

Arsenault, Raymond. "The End of the Long Hot Summer: The Air Conditioner and Southern Culture." *Journal of Southern Culture* 50, no. 4 (November 1984): 597–628.

ALGER, HORATIO. *See* Self-Help Literature

ALI, MUHAMMED (1769–1849)

Muhammed Ali Pasha al-Mas'ud ibn Agha was ruler of Egypt during the second quarter of the nineteenth century, setting up a new dynasty that survived until the revolution of 1952. He was also one of the first rulers outside the West to realize the implications of the industrialization process and to institute reforms designed to allow Egypt to develop its own industrial economy. His policies were met with mixed success, but they unquestionably introduced substantial changes into Egyptian society.

Muhammed Ali, born in Macedonia to Albanian parents, began his career in the Ottoman army. He participated in the reoccupation of Egypt after the withdrawal of French forces, around 1800, and then was able to seize power in Egypt in 1805. He hoped to promote Egypt as the regional successor to the Ottoman Empire.

The new ruler was committed to the modernization of the Egyptian economy. He used the state to manage economic affairs, particularly promoting the growth of cotton for export. Using forced labor to create the necessary workforce, he set up a number of pilot factories, particularly for military goods but also in textiles. He sent a number of Egyptians to study in Europe, to gain greater technical competence, while also establishing new schools within Egypt. On the other hand, Muhammed Ali also devoted great efforts toward military campaigns and territorial expansion, which arguably complicated his economic

Portrait of Muhammed Ali, Viceroy of Egypt, 1811. (Gianni Dagli Orti/Corbis)

goals and drew considerable and forceful European resistance. He was not successful in building an industrial economy. Instead, his main economic legacy was to tie Egypt increasingly into the production of cash crop exports, notably cotton, to generate revenues for other activities.

Further Reading

Marsot, Afaf. *Egypt in the Reign of Muhammed Ali.* New York: Cambridge University Press, 1984.

Pollard, Lisa. *Nurturing the Nation: The Family Politics of Modernizing, Colonizing, and Liberating Egypt, 1805–1923.* Berkeley: University of California Press, 2005.

Vatikiotis, P. J. *This History of Modern Egypt: From Muhammed Ali to Mubarak.* Baltimore: Johns Hopkins University Press, 1991.

ALIENATION

The concept of alienation is frequently used by social historians dealing with industrial work and the working class. The word means hostility to or estrangement from some activity or experience. Karl Marx, in *Capital*, applied the term particularly to the work processes of industrial capitalism. Because workers no longer owned producing property and because their formal training often declined, Marx argued that they were alienated from the products of their work, with no real stake or identity in the manufacturing process. His claim made good theoretical sense, though historians and social scientists have had problems coming up with practical measures of alienation that would show how and to what degree workers lost a sense of meaning.

Labor protest articulated many grievances concerning work—but can the most alienated workers even advance clear goals? Certainly some workers, at various stages of industrialization, have seemed alienated. In the early stages of the industrial experience, some workers simply left the factories, even though they had no clear options, because they could not stand the strangeness and the lack of meaning. Later, some workers—for example, the German miner Max Lotz, whose letters were published by a social scientist soon after 1900—articulated what must be judged alienation. They spoke of their work as a daily struggle, not so much because of physical toil but because the supervision was so severe, the significance so unclear, the process so nerve-racking. Lotz was a sincere socialist who hoped an ultimate socialist victory would change the framework of labor; he had no faith in stopgap reforms because he believed the problems ran too deep.

Most workers were probably not profoundly alienated, for many did make partial accommodation, such as instrumentalism, that is, reducing expectations of work in favor of higher pay. But a degree of alienation has dogged the experience of industrial work for many people, particularly assembly-line workers.

The concept of alienation has been extended in the twentieth century to include white-collar workers whose careers do not meet their expectations of middle-class success. These workers encounter alienation in midcareer and express it by working less hard and often seeking early retirement. Alienation, blue- and white-collar, may also be expressed by frequent illness. In sum, alienation is an important, if somewhat, elusive aspect of the impact of industrialization.

Further Reading

Koditschek, Theodore. *Class Formation and Urban Industrial Society: Bradford, 1750–1850.* New York: Cambridge University Press, 1990.

Shepard, Jon. *Automation and Alienation.* Cambridge, MA: MIT Press, 1971.

ALTERNATING CURRENT (AC)

Initial transmission of electricity used direct current, which flows evenly through a wire but requires a complex commutator to transmit successfully to a motor. Direct current is still used in batteries, as in automobiles, but it requires a switching arrangement—the commutator—to connect one after another to the coils on a rotating armature to act with the poles and cause the motor to rotate. This complexity inspired the search for an alternating current that would reverse flows at rapid intervals, or cycles, connecting with motors through slip rings. Alternating current, used for home appliances, simplifies both the generators and the electric motors. Moreover, it can easily be transformed to high voltages, which greatly increases efficiency over long-distance power lines. Electric transformers can step up the voltage for transmission, and then step it down for use in actual motors.

Though developed by the work of several researchers, alternating current was first utilized by Nikola Tesla (1856–1943), an electrical engineer born in Austria-Hungary. Trained in a technical school and at the University of Prague, Tesla then moved to the United States, where he invented a motor with coils arranged so that when alternating current energized them, the resulting magnetic field rotated at a predetermined speed. He patented his motor in 1888 and then sold it to George Westinghouse.

See also Electronics

Further Reading

Jonnes, Jill. *Empires of Light: Edison, Tesla, Westinghouse, and the Race to Electrify the World.* New York: Random House, 2004.

Nikola Tesla helped to create the first commercial applications of alternating current (AC) but, like many inventors, died poor. (Library of Congress)

AMALGAMATED SOCIETY OF ENGINEERS (ASE)

This great British union of skilled factory workers—the British term for machine tools workers is engineers—was formed in 1851 from a variety of strong local organizations. The union, with 11,000 initial members, was formed on craft union principles, emphasizing the valuable skills of its members and attempting to bargain carefully rather than dissipate resources in frequent strikes. Like other British "New Model" unions in the 1850s, the ASE placed a premium on respectability and self-improvement for its members, while also providing solid financial benefits such as assistance in illness and unemployment. The union also pressed for political gains and helped induce the grant of suffrage to male workers in 1867 and the legalization of unions in 1871 and 1875. Direct bargaining with employers helped to do away with nonmonetary payments and long delays between paydays. The success of this kind of union was reduced by the deep depression of the 1870s.

In later decades the union, though still strong, lost a number of bitter strikes against employers who sought to introduce piece-rate payments as a means of more fully controlling worker productivity. This more difficult context prompted the ASE to cooperate more fully with new industrial unions and to provide some of the resources and leadership for general movements such as the Trades Union Congress, though the union remained relatively moderate.

Further Reading

Haydu, Jeffrey. *Between Craft and Class: Skilled Workers and Factory Politics in the United States and Britain, 1890–1922.* Berkeley: University of California Press, 1988.

AMERICAN (U.S.) CIVIL WAR (1861–65)

The American Civil War pitted the North, the region of the United States most committed to industrial production and wage labor, against the South, the region most closely tied to plantation-style agricultural exports based on slave labor. The North had an overwhelming superiority in railroads, iron mills, and machine production; the South had some industrial facilities, but believed that Britain, the chief consumer of Southern cotton, would eventually intervene to end the war. The North's military strategy destroyed the economy of the South by blockading its exports, and Britain quickly turned India and Egypt into suppliers of cotton. The South, like many Third World countries, learned that the production of agricultural commodities rarely provides economic leverage on industrial countries. The South's defeat was ensured when the North encouraged the defection of Southern slaves, many of whom formed a crucial part of the North's army.

The economic impact of the war was enormous. Together, the North and South had expended 5 billion 1860 dollars in the struggle and sustained 700,000 deaths and several hundred thousand wounded. Many fortunes were made by those who had supplied the Northern army. In one case, J. P. Morgan bought several thousand defective rifles for $3.50 apiece and sold them to a general for $22 each. Much Southern industry, crops, livestock, and savings were destroyed. As a result of the emancipation of slaves, Southern planters lost most of their capital; the South's economic development lagged far behind the North's for many years. Although historians disagree whether the war accelerated industrialization in the North, the North definitely passed several laws during the war that stimulated national economic growth, such as the Homestead Act, banking legislation, and land grants for universities and railroads. Use of railroads and factory-produced goods made this the first "industrial" war, and it was studied as such by outside observers, including German generals.

See also Emancipation and Reconstruction (United States); Plantations

Further Reading

Andreano, Ralph. *The Economic Impact of the American Civil War.* Cambridge, MA: Schenkman, 1962.

Ransom, Roger L. *Conflict and Compromise: The Political Economy of Slavery, Emancipation, and the American Civil War.* New York: Cambridge University Press, 1989.

AMERICAN FEDERATION OF LABOR (AFL)

The American Federation of Labor (AFL) was formed in 1886 to coordinate the activities of national craft unions. After the failure of the Knights of Labor to organize industrial unions or to establish production cooperatives, the AFL advocated the view that unions should focus primarily on economic issues, using the leverage that their occupations gave them with employers. This approach favored highly skilled workers, and the mainstays of the AFL were the building trades (carpenters, plumbers, etc.). By 1904, the AFL had about 1.5 million members.

Unlike most European unions that affiliated with Social Democratic or Labor parties, the AFL's brand of pragmatism led it to downplay political issues and avoid direct affiliation with political parties. Instead, the U.S. union followed the advice of Samuel Gompers, the AFL's leader, of "rewarding your friends and punishing your enemies." In part, this was due to the fact that the American political system gave no rewards to smaller parties; moreover, there was a long history of courts striking down pro-labor legislation. Nevertheless, a large number of AFL members were indeed socialists, and a resolution in 1894 calling for the nationalization of all the means of production was only narrowly defeated. Instead, the AFL called for the eight-hour day, selective nationalization of utilities and the railroads, and other legislative reforms. Another leftist insurgency in 1903 was beaten back, and shortly thereafter, Gompers entered a short-lived alliance with some manufacturers via the National Civic Federation. By the 1940s, the AFL's policy of political neutrality was weakening, and the AFL began to acknowledge its de facto endorsement of the Democratic Party.

The AFL had a somewhat antagonistic relationship with the unskilled, black, female, and immigrant parts of the U.S. working class. During the 1910s, the AFL opposed unemployment insurance because it felt workers should simply be paid enough to take care of themselves during layoffs and feared that the benefit would make workers dependent upon the government. The AFL supported the exclusion of the Chinese from the United States, a view that most white workers shared. Although in the 1880s the AFL attempted to forbid its members from barring black workers, it had little power over its member unions; by the early 1900s, the federation allowed unions either to exclude blacks outright or to organize them into separate locals.

The AFL was largely unsuccessful in organizing workers in mass-production industries such as steel or auto, partly because of unionists' views of the unskilled but also because unions invariably confronted not only employers but also the police, state militia, or even federal troops. As the industrial sector of the economy grew throughout the twentieth century, the AFL came to represent a proportionally smaller part of the working class (although the federation's membership actually was slowly expanding). The federation proved unwilling or unable to organize industrial workers, and the AFL expelled the more radical CIO unions in 1938. Yet the labor upsurge of the 1930s also benefited the AFL, as many industries, such as paper making, preferred AFL unions to CIO ones. Some CIO unions returned to the AFL because of political reasons, and CIO attempts to organize traditional AFL strongholds (such as the building trades) failed. The two federations merged in 1955, largely on terms dictated by the AFL.

See also Industrial Workers; Knights of Labor

Further Reading

Kaufman, Stuart Brace. *Samuel Gompers and the Origins of the American Federation of Labor, 1848–1896.* Westport, CT: Greenwood, 1973.

ANARCHISM. *See* Syndicalism

APPLE

Apple was founded in 1976 and symbolizes the successes and contradictions in the fusion of computerization and industrialization. The founding of Apple is the stuff of entrepreneurial legend. Founded in a garage in Silicon Valley, the company manufactured smart, intuitively interactive computers and cultivated an avid base of customers. It battled the giants of the personal computer industry, notably IBM and Microsoft; in one ad, Apple compared its rivals to Big Brother in *1984*. The company never broke out of the niche market for personal computers. By 2000, it was on the verge of failure; by 2010, it was worth more than its nemesis, Microsoft.

These Apple products were all produced when Steve Jobs was CEO of Apple and range from the Macintosh (1984) to the iPod (2001), the iPhone (2007), and the iPad (2010). (AP/Wide World Photo)

Throughout the 2000s, Apple brought out a line of products that transformed the music and cell phone industries. In 2001, it developed the iPod, a handheld digital music player, and an online music store, iTunes, that sold individual songs for 99 cents. The combination proved wildly successful, as was its line of iPhones, which came out in the mid-2000s, and the iPad, a handheld computer tablet.

The successes stemmed from the genius of its founders, as well as the company's informal workplace culture that cultivated innovation. Steve Jobs, one of the cofounders, often walked through corporate headquarters barefoot. The company also "branded" itself through clever antiestablishment advertising that enabled it to enjoy a distinctive corporate identity and an extremely loyal customer base.

Apple's environmental legacy is messier than its informal, hipster image would allow. Computers and electronics require enormous amounts of toxic chemicals to manufacture, and many environmental groups have criticized the company for moving too slowly to reduce or eliminate them. Apple has made progress over time, though it has fallen short of the limits of what is technically (and financially) possible.

Apple fuses an extremely well-paid staff in the United States that researches, designs, and advertises its products, and a much lower-paid set of workers abroad that manufacture them. Production lines have moved from California to China, where workers are not directly employed by Apple but work for subcontractors, sometimes under harsh conditions.

Further Reading

Linzmayer, Owen W. *Apple Confidential 2.0: The Definitive History of the World's Most Colorful Company*. San Francisco: No Starch Press, 2004.

ARGENTINA

In the nineteenth century, Argentina's economy was dominated by the exports of hides, beef, and wheat from its rich pampas. Although the country made few manufactured goods, its volume of agricultural goods made it one of the 10 largest participants in the world market by 1900. By 1920, Argentina "possessed" over 20,000 miles of railroad, most of it owned by British banks, and half of its population was urbanized. Unlike most of Latin America, nearly all of Argentina relied on wages for their survival. World Wars I and II, as well as the Great Depression of the 1930s, hampered Argentina's exports and hindered its imports of manufactured goods. Argentina responded by following a policy of import substitution of manufactured products; by the 1930s, half a million Argentineans worked in industry. Industrial production soared in the 1940s and 1950s under the government of populist Juan Perón, who relied not only on the military but the trade unions for his political survival. Perón tried to diversify Argentina's economy by diverting profits from its agricultural exports into industry as well as social welfare schemes. Argentina's industrial economy slowly expanded until 1976, when it was decimated by the open-market policies of the military junta that ruled the country from 1976 to 1983.

Argentina provided a test case for the neoliberal ideas of American economists. Under the junta, the country liberalized markets and privatized state assets. The country assumed enormous debts, and sought to ensure financial stability and reassure creditors by linking its own peso to the U.S. dollar. By 1999 the system collapsed, and the economy went into a tailspin. Against the advice of the International Monetary Fund, Argentina refused a program of austerity and announced it was repudiating its foreign debt. The peso slumped in value, which made exports cheaper. A period of economic pain was short-lived and followed by several years of rapid growth. Much of the debt was eventually repaid but at a considerable discount. The Argentinean case reveals the power and limits of international financial markets to shape the policies of individual countries.

See also Neoliberalism, or Economic Liberalism; Perónism; World Systems Theory

Further Reading

Bulmer-Thomas, Victor. *The Economic History of Latin America since Independence*. Cambridge: Cambridge University Press, 2003.

Lewis, Paul H. *The Crisis of Argentinean Capitalism*. Chapel Hill: University of North Carolina Press, 1990.

ARISTOCRACY

The most significant relationship between the aristocracy and the Industrial Revolution was a negative one. Industrialization reduced the importance of the aristocracy, though often very gradually and over the long run. By promoting new ways to generate and collect wealth and encouraging a social system in which money began to replace traditional status and legal privilege as the chief criterion for success, industrialization promoted a new elite of big businessmen, who eventually dominated the traditional aristocracy. This process took many decades. Many businessmen remained impressed by aristocratic prestige and sought to imitate their traditional betters by buying landed estates, marrying their daughters to aristocratic heirs, and cooperating with the aristocracy politically (as in compromise tariff legislation). At the end of the nineteenth century, a mixed upper class of businessmen and aristocrats dominated much of Europe. The full eclipse of the aristocracy came only by the mid-twentieth century. A similar, perhaps even more durable, aristocrat-entrepreneur collaboration developed during the Meiji restoration in Japan.

Aristocrats had difficulty adapting to the principles of an industrial economy, and not only because agriculture was their primary base of power. Their class traditions argued against too much devotion to moneygrubbing and specialized training. Many aristocrats attacked industrialization by fighting for legislative protection for agriculture. Individual aristocrats played an important role in advocating labor reforms—to safeguard workers against the worst industrial hardships but also to counterbalance upstart factory owners. This latter motivation was a major source of early reform laws in Britain and, with Bismarck, in Germany. Countries without an aristocratic tradition, like the United States, were slower to moderate some of the harsh conditions of industrialization.

Individual aristocrats, finally, played a significant role in outright industrialization, even though their class as a whole might have suffered. British aristocrats, less suspicious of commerce than their counterparts on the Continent, helped set a context for the first Industrial Revolution. Several major landowners in Britain and some Prussian estate owners (the Junkers) expanded mining operations or even established factories as part of the early industrial process. Their capital and influence helped launch industrialization in many European countries and in Japan.

See also Feudalism and Manorialism

Further Reading

Spring, David. *European Landed Elites in the Nineteenth Century.* Baltimore: Johns Hopkins University Press, 1977.

ARKWRIGHT, RICHARD (1732–92)

This English inventor advanced the transition from hand spinning to power spinning in factories by inventing the water frame, patented in 1769. The water frame used rollers, revolving at different speeds, to stretch out fiber, which then was twisted into thread by flyers and bobbins operating continuously. Arkwright did not invent roller spinning, but he perfected it and made it commercially profitable. His machinery was first run by water power, but the steam engine was soon used successfully. Arkwright's thread was twisted so hard that it was mainly used for calico (cotton) wraps. Arkwright also patented improvements in accessory processes, such as carding of fiber, in 1775. He was one of the rare early industrial inventors who also succeeded in business, in contrast to most of his colleagues who saw their ideas exploited by other entrepreneurs.

See also Crompton, Samuel; Hargreaves, James; Textiles

Further Reading

Derry, Kingston, and T. I. Williams. *A Short History of Technology.* Oxford: Oxford University Press, 1961.

Mathias, Peter. *The Transformation of England.* New York: Columbia University Press, 1979.

ARMOUR, PHILIP DANFORTH (1832–1901)

Philip Armour was one of the "robber barons" of the late nineteenth century. After making a fortune providing meat to the Union army during the American Civil War, he formed Armour and Company (1870), which by the 1890s was one of the largest meatpacking companies in the United States. He helped to develop the centralized slaughtering of cows and pigs that turned butchering from a localized craft into a mass-production industry. Instead of one man killing, skinning, and

Philip Danforth Armour was an iconic "robber baron" building a fortune in the cut-meat industry. (Bettmann/ Corbis)

turning a hog's carcass into food, workers repeatedly did one stage of the work along continuously moving "disassembly lines." Armour also helped to develop modern marketing and distribution of meat by using, for example, refrigerated railroad cars to transport fresh meat to distant markets. Armour's philosophy was to "use everything from the hog but the squeal," and what could not be made into bacon or sausage was turned into lard, soap, or glue.

See also Refrigeration

Further Reading

Josephson, Matthew. *The Robber Barons: The Great American Capitalists, 1861–1901.* New York: Harcourt, Brace, 1934.

ARTIFICIAL INTELLIGENCE (AI)

Humans have long dreamed of human-made objects that could think like people. Ancient Greeks wished for chairs that would move behind their masters; Leonardo da Vinci sketched out plans for an automated knight. Novelists in the nineteenth century feared the potential of the Industrial Revolution, penning such tales as *Frankenstein*. In the twentieth century, robots were first anticipated by science fiction writers. Twentieth-century fiction and film revealed both utopian longing and deep unease that machines could replace humans in the realm of work, war, and ultimately, the act of tool making itself. Such is the power of industrialization that ancient dreams are increasingly becoming a reality.

The term "artificial intelligence," originated in 1956, has been defined as "the science and engineering of making intelligent machines." Computer scientists sought to imitate and reproduce human intelligence. If that goal has not been fully achieved, enormous gains have been made. AI resulted in new insights into how the brain functions as scientists try to replicate intelligence. Rather than a single large and general processor, the brain has numerous subsystems that interact.

AI has proven successful enough that once smart machines become commonplace, they cease to be considered AI.

AI enabled factories to utilize robots on assembly lines. By 2000, almost 2 million robots were used in factories around the world. AI enabled companies to automate telephone customer service and to flag unusual patterns in financial dealings.

By 1997, a computer was able to win the chess championship. The next frontier was language-based games; in 2011, a computer (Watson) beat out its human competitors on the television show *Jeopardy!* AI has resulted in a variety of intelligent machines, such as the programs developed in the 2000s that allowed the gaming industry to read the movement of the human body. These are not simply parlor tricks but successful efforts to mimic subsystems of human thought. For instance, Watson-style computers could provide potential solutions to medical problems. (That would make the program Dr. Watson, we presume). Computers still struggle to do what humans regard as simple tasks, for instance those that require social intelligence like reading the emotions of a stranger by their facial expressions. Other technologies, such as fully automated vehicles, already exist and should be commercially available within a generation.

As with most things computer related, the U.S. military was an early consumer. AI enabled the military to develop combat simulations, as well as robots that can help disable bombs or scout for enemies. The technology exists for automated sentries that never sleep and would always follow the rules of war.

The complex nature of reality and of human intelligence has had a way of frustrating such utopian hopes. The British government used AI to monitor thousands of cameras in urban areas to detect and prevent criminals and terrorists. The results have proven somewhat underwhelming. One comedian showed that by simply adding a moustache or a hat, a human could fool the AI programs. AI continues to make explosive progress, and there is every indication that intelligent machines will continue to spread.

Further Reading

Nilsson, Nils J. *The Quest for Artificial Intelligence*. New York: Cambridge University Press, 2009.

ARTIFICIAL SILK COMPANY (RUSSIA)

This company is an example of the role of foreign entrepreneurship in the early stages of Russian industrialization. It was founded in Myszkov in 1911 by Belgian entrepreneurs linked to a Brussels concern. The company developed an improved process for treating cellulose and producing rayon. The company did fairly well but, like many foreign firms, reported problems with Russian workers: the workers were hostile to non-Russian direction and seemed slow to pick up the necessary new skills. Strikes not only disrupted production but sometimes threatened the lives of the foreign managers and the skilled workers brought in to train local personnel.

In this context, the need to recruit Russian management emerged quickly. Foreign firms like the Artificial Silk Company were swallowed up by the state in the wake of the 1917 revolution.

See also Russia and the Soviet Union (USSR); Synthetic Fabrics

Further Reading

Stearns, Peter N. *The Industrial Revolution in World History*. 3rd ed. Boulder, CO: Westview, 2007.

ARTISANS

Artisans were one of the most important classes of workers in the industrialization process, but their role was unusually complex. All preindustrial economies had large groups of artisans, both urban and rural, responsible for all kinds of manufacturing, from textiles and food processing to traditional metallurgy.

Artisans are workers who manufacture products using relatively simple tools while relying on considerable skills. Typically, they undergo an extensive training period as apprentices. Then they serve a stint as journeymen, working in a small artisan shop alongside the owner-master, often living and dining there in conditions of considerable familiarity if not equality. Many journeymen aspire to become masters in their own right, and although the real opportunities vary, some mobility within one's lifetime is common. Many urban artisans form organizations, or guilds, that protect artisanal conditions and try to prevent undue change. Artisans and their guilds are proud of their products and seek to maintain quality.

The Industrial Revolution operated on principles different from those of the artisanal economy. Innovation replaced reliance on traditional methods; powered equipment cut into skills and artistry; mass production displaced emphasis on artistic quality; a gap between employer and worker replaced the more collaborative customs of artisans. Guild controls over technique and firm size had to be weakened before serious industrialization could take place. In the long run, industrialization reduced the size of the artisanry, while undermining its conditions of work. This was true in England after 1850 and in Japan after 1920. In Japan, artisan traditions of abundant leisure were particularly attacked during industrialization.

Individual artisans, however, were vital to the industrialization process. Many crucial inventions came from artisans eager to improve methods of production; this ingenuity was a particularly vital resource in eighteenth-century Britain, where a traditionalist guild system was less significant. Larger numbers of artisans took skilled factory jobs, where they could parlay their skills into higher earnings. This shift was essential in metallurgy and machine building, for it created an important bond between artisans and the "aristocracy of labor" in the factories and inhibited unity of action with unskilled and skilled workers. Many artisan masters expanded operations to become factory entrepreneurs, another important connection between craft experience and industrial innovation.

Artisans also sought to resist industrialization or develop new organizations to defend their position. Because of their skills and tradition, artisans were in a better position to organize than were most early factory workers. Some artisans opposed the industrial economy outright, converting to early forms of socialism or fighting in revolutions such as 1848. Other artisans formed unions to bargain for better wages and hours. Almost everywhere, artisans formed the initial trade unions, even in Russia, where artisans in newly growing cities like St. Petersburg imported goals and organizational capacity from central Europe in the 1860s. Although artisan (craft) unions often stood aloof from factory workers, seeking to bargain respectably and to rely on scarce skills, the artisanal lead helped guide larger trade union movements during the nineteenth century in Europe and North America. Artisans also provided leadership for many socialist movements and for various labor reforms and educational gains.

The number of artisans increased in most early industrial revolutions, for growing cities needed more carpenters, bakers, and jewelers. Only a few artisanal crafts, such as weaving, were substantially displaced by the new factories. Gradually, however, additional inventions, like the sewing machine or new shoe-manufacturing equipment, began to reduce the number of outright artisans. Moreover, after 1850 artisanal conditions themselves began to be affected by new equipment and a more industrial pace. Much labor strife in the later nineteenth century involved artisans (construction workers, for instance) fighting to retain some control over their jobs. On the whole, the distinction between artisans and other kinds of manufacturing workers became less important as a result of these trends, though some differentiation persisted through the twentieth century.

See also Discipline; Revolutions of 1848; Work; Working Class

Further Reading

Rock, Howard P. *Artisans of the New Republic: The Tradesmen of New York City in the Age of Jefferson*. New York: New York University Press, 1979.

Stearns, Peter N., and Herrick Chapman. *European Society in Upheaval: Social History since 1750*. 3rd ed. New York: Macmillan, 1992.

Zdatny, Steven. *The Politics of Survival: Artisans in Twentieth-Century France*. New York: Oxford University Press, 1990.

ASSEMBLY LINE

The creation of a continuous flow of production was the goal or reality in a number of late nineteenth-century industries, including oil refining, meatpacking, and steel. However, the moving assembly line was most inextricably linked to the rise of the mass-produced automobile. Like the development of the automobile itself, the development of the assembly line occurred in stages and arose from the effort of a number of different persons and companies.

In the early twentieth century, most car production was done in batches by small groups of skilled workers. Henry Ford recognized the possibilities of the assembly

Workers assemble flywheels for Ford Motor Company in 1913. (National Archives)

line, which allowed continuous production of cars by semiskilled workers. Between 1908 and 1913 Ford installed assembly lines in his factories. Although Ford recognized the value of the concept, teams of engineers worked out the details. Other auto companies quickly adopted the practice. For instance, by 1912 Buick was producing the chassis of their cars on assembly lines, though its chassis was simply pushed from one work site to another on lines of two-by-fours. Ford, however, led the industry, putting his cars on chain-driven assembly lines that were combined with scientific management techniques, and production increased dramatically. Semiskilled workers performed repetitive motions on small parts of the process as each unit moved by.

Ford's new factories were built to take full advantage of the assembly line. Instead of working in cramped quarters, new facilities allowed moving assembly lines to converge at the appropriate moment. By 1914, Ford's Highland Park factory had 14,000 workers and 15,000 machines. His new River Rouge plant was even more advanced: "In conveyers alone it was a wonderland of devices. Gracy, belt, buckle, spiral, pendulum gravity roller, overhead monorail, 'scenic railway' and 'merry-go-round,' elevating flight—the list was long both in range and in adaptation to special purpose." Ford's strategy was to radically lower the price of his product and build a "car for the great multitude." The strategy worked. Between 1909 and 1914, the price of the Model T fell from $900 to $440, and by 1923, Ford had gained 55 percent of the world market in automobiles.

The constant, brisk pace made the work difficult, and Ford had great difficulty in maintaining a workforce. At certain points, turnover in his factories was 1,000 percent a year. Because Ford had a very popular product, he was able to dramatically raise wages and institute a series of social welfare programs. Workers' adaptation to the assembly line was never complete, however, and their dissatisfaction contributed to the rise of industrial unionism in the 1930s.

The assembly line remained central to the imagery and reality of industrialization. Companies have been able to improve the speed and efficiency of the assembly process using computers and more complex tools such as robots, greatly reducing the number of workers needed.

See also Fordism

Further Reading

Flink, James J. *The Automobile Age*. Boston: MIT Press, 1998.
Meyer, Stephen. *The Five Dollar Day: Labor, Management, and Social Control in the Ford Motor Company, 1900–1921*. Albany: State University of New York Press, 1981.

AUSTRALIA

Since the nineteenth century, the Australian economy has been based in large part on exports to other industrial areas. Both agricultural products—meat and wool—and minerals were shipped, first particularly to Britain, then elsewhere; by the late twentieth century, Australia had become Japan's primary provider of all raw materials except fuel. Like Canada, Australian production was based on advanced technology, which permitted high wages and industrial living standards. Britain and (after 1950) the United States supported extensive investments. Australia also generated large industries, mainly for its own consumption. A huge steel mill was set up in 1915. By the 1950s, 28 percent of the labor force was in manufacturing. An active labor movement also developed in Australia, and the country pioneered in considerable welfare legislation.

The industrialization of East Asia has transformed Australia. The country found growing markets for its considerable mineral wealth, such as iron ore, and agricultural products, in the rapidly expanding Japanese, then Korean, and then Chinese economies. Australian exports to Asia kept its currency strong and have helped reorient its economy and even culture away from Britain and Europe. The change is dramatic and recent. Until 1973, its "White Australia" policy meant that Asian immigrants were all but excluded. In the new millennium, Chinese is taught in many public schools, an acknowledgment of its increasing integration and reliance on East Asia.

Further Reading

Macintyre, Stuart. *A Concise History of Australia*. 3rd ed. New York: Cambridge University Press, 2009.
Wilson, Charles. *Australia, 1788–1988: The Creation of a Nation*. New York: Barnes & Noble, 1987.

AUTOMATION

Automation is the mechanization of the work process and one of the classic strata-
gems by which employers can gain increases in productivity as well as enhance their
control over the work process itself. Since industrialization is by definition a replacement of human or animal power by mechanical power, the development of automation is an intrinsic, though controversial, aspect of the industrialization process.
Although automation was a constantly evolving process throughout the nineteenth
century, it definitely surged in the latter nineteenth and the early twentieth centuries
when such industries as machine building, automobiles, and shipbuilding tried to
supply a rapidly expanding market, and then again after World War II in industries
such as automobiles, electronics, and petrochemicals.

In early nineteenth-century Britain, after the putting-out system had initiated
the subdivision of the process of making cloth, industrialists began to consolidate
the workforce into factories. Using steam and water power, mill owners began to
use new machinery to help deskill the craft of certain workers, such as hand-loom
weavers or wool croppers. Some of these workers argued that the new system,
although economical in the monetary sense, upset what historians have come to call
workers' "moral economy" because it dehumanized their work and lowered their
standard of living. Some workers petitioned mill owners, threatening retribution
from "General Ludd"; in some cases, Luddite workers destroyed the machinery that
threatened their livelihood.

Whether out of a shared belief in progress or because overt machine wrecking was
futile, workers generally sought to restrict rather than oppose outright the imposition
of new machinery. Throughout the nineteenth century, skilled textile workers, some
of their crafts created by new technology, sought to limit the number of machines that
a person could operate. Whenever possible, skilled workers, such as machinists,
sought to restrict the entry of new workers, for employers often hired younger workers
to use new machines to perform tasks prohibited by the work rules.

Battling new technology and opposing the dilution of work rules was frequently a
frustrating task. Puddlers, glass blowers, and machinists were frequently successful
in slowing down the pace of automation throughout the length of the nineteenth
century, but most workers, including textile workers and cobblers, met with little
success. Even extremely highly skilled work could be automated and jobs eliminated within a short period of time. In the 1920s and 1930s, tens of thousands of
rollers of steel sheets were replaced by mechanized rolling mills as steel companies
attempted to supply the burgeoning mass market for automobiles. Displaced workers referred to the new mills as "big morgues" since they eliminated so many jobs.
Beginning in the 1910s, U.S. auto companies such as Ford and General Motors
became leaders in automation.

New technology did not always simply deskill workers: the jobs of highly skilled
machinists and open-hearth workers, for example, were both made possible by
advances in workplace technology. However, the accelerating pace of automation

in the twentieth century eroded much of the craft-like control that machinists and open-hearth workers once held over the workplace. Many of the building trades experienced a fair degree of new technology but were still considered skilled. Carpentry, a preindustrial craft, began to use mass-produced windows in the mid-nineteenth century, and by the mid-twentieth century, carpenters were using power saws and mechanical nail drivers. By contrast, the skills of plasterers were almost totally undermined by the advent of mass-produced "sheet rock" in the mid-twentieth century.

Although automation is frequently perceived as economically inevitable, governments have generally played a key role in developing automation. In the early nineteenth century, the U.S. government funded Eli Whitney's development of interchangeable parts and helped to train many of the men who would later lead the machine tool and armaments industries. Similarly, throughout the twentieth century, the U.S. military has funded defense corporations' attempts to create completely automated factories. The automation efforts of General Electric were satirized in the mid-1950s by Kurt Vonnegut in *Player Piano*. Indeed, some historians have argued that the ideal of the workerless factory captivated employers who confronted militant unions of machinists not because automation was more efficient (it often was more expensive) but because it gave the illusion of total control, free of operator error.

After World War II, the pace of automation greatly accelerated as Fordist employers sought to supply mass markets while holding down overall labor costs. At least in Europe and the United States, most unions have acquiesced to automation as long as the remaining workers shared in the productivity gains of employers. One of the classic examples is the United Mine Workers, which in the late 1940s allowed the mechanization of mining to stabilize the profitability of the industry (which was losing markets to oil) and to guarantee the remaining miners decent wages. Similarly, dockworkers' unions agreed to containerization programs, in which cargo was loaded via crane in large containers (often directly onto trains or trucks) in exchange for large wage gains. However, many workers express concern about being subordinated to the needs of machinery—a concern enhanced by the recognition that continuing technological advances may eliminate their jobs.

Since the 1960s, the increasing sophistication of computers has allowed employers to closely supervise, deskill, and automate jobs as diverse as fast-food cook, airline receptionist, social worker, and real estate agent. For instance, airline receptionists are electronically monitored to make sure they are not spending too much time with their customers and that they are meeting a quota of sales for their shift. Data-entry work is often done on computer terminals in poorer countries or regions and then transferred by satellite to companies. The accelerating pace of automation and the increase in unemployment since the 1970s have weakened the union movement throughout the world, removing an important barrier to this process.

Further Reading

Garson, Barbara. *Electronic Sweatshop: How Computers Are Transforming the Office of Tomorrow into the Factory of the Past.* New York: Simon and Schuster, 1988.

Noble, David F. *Forces of Production: A Social History of Automation.* New York: Knopf, 1984.

AUTOMOBILE

The development of the internal combustion automobile resulted from the collective accumulation of technical knowledge among European and U.S. entrepreneurs. Gasoline-powered engines triumphed over steam, electric, or diesel (which inventors had experimented with to make road vehicles) largely because gasoline engines were smaller, more reliable, and more powerful and because by the late nineteenth century gasoline had become a cheap and readily available commodity. In the late nineteenth century, European car makers such as Karl Benz produced more advanced machines (and, equally important, cars that were more commercially successful) than their U.S. counterparts. By the early twentieth century, however, U.S. car producers were closing the technical gap and were producing cars for a mass market rather than for the higher-priced European "class market."

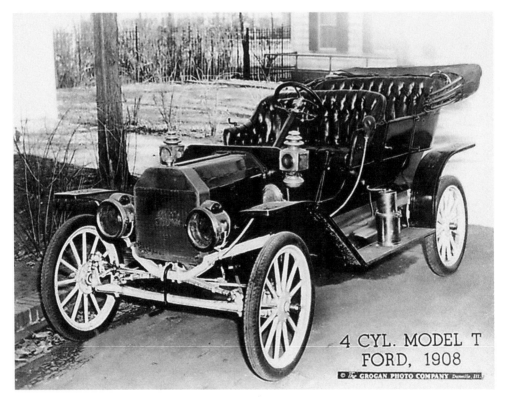

Henry Ford's Model T was the most popular car in the world in its heyday. (Library of Congress)

By the 1910s, Henry Ford's cheap and sturdy Model T had become the most common automobile in the world. Ford was able to lower the production costs of his Model T by applying the time management strategies of Frederick Winslow Taylor, which allowed Ford to use large numbers of semiskilled workers on moving assembly lines. Ford dramatically raised workers' wages, in part to compensate for the brutal pace of work and in part to retain a stable workforce. Beginning in the 1920s, General Motors, led by Alfred P. Sloan, began to market somewhat more expensive cars with a much wider range of consumer options than Ford offered. Sloan also extended credit to his customers so they could pay for their purchases over time.

The automobile has arguably transformed everyday life in industrialized countries more than any other machine in the twentieth century. The car's impact was initially most profound on rural life. Many farmers were attracted to the Model T because of its low cost and reliability. It also had a high clearance that allowed it to negotiate poor roads. Ford's cars, trucks, and tractors allowed farmers to produce more crops and to transport them to urban markets, and they facilitated socializing, thus relieving some of the isolation of rural life.

Automobiles quickly had an enormous impact on cities as well. By the 1920s, the middle class in the United States had begun to move into the cheaper land on the edges of cities, although many of them still worked in the center city. Although suburbanization was interrupted by the Great Depression, the trend greatly accelerated after World War II, as the national grid of "super" highways was developed in the 1950s. As early as the 1920s, businesses began to be able to move goods via trucks (instead of rail), which helped to decentralize the location of factories and warehouses and accelerated the movement toward suburbs. After World War II, many blue-collar workers also began to move into the cheaper land on the edges of cities—a benefit made available by mass "automobility." The federal government subsidized the suburban boom through highway construction and by giving cheap loans for suburban (but not urban) construction. As businesses and people moved to the edges of cities, the inner cities were increasingly stripped of their population, fiscal viability, and previous social functions.

Although the social and economic impact of the automobile was most extreme in the United States, many other nations attempted to manufacture cars, and even less-industrialized countries were extensively influenced by cars, trucks, and buses. Even in countries that do not produce them, trucks and buses are widespread and have greatly changed the transportation of people and commodities. Many countries, such as India, followed the model of import substitution—industrializing countries developed manufacturing capabilities that reduced dependence on imports, though they did not become major automobile exporters. Car production in developing countries such as Mexico, Brazil, Turkey, South Africa, and Eastern Europe has also greatly expanded since World War II. European countries experienced mass automobile ownership somewhat later than the United States, and their governments succeeded in ensuring that their large cities were not so adversely affected by suburbanization.

In the 50 years following the end of World War II, the most dramatic new player in car production has been Japan. Japan began to produce cars, and especially trucks, for military purposes in the 1930s, but the industry was relatively small. After World War II, the U.S. military bought numerous Japanese trucks, but only in the 1950s did car makers begin producing large numbers of automobiles. By the late 1960s, Japanese car makers, with the active support of their government, had begun to export large numbers of cars to the United States and Asia—by the 1980s Japan had become the world's largest producer of cars. Beginning in the 1970s, South Korea attempted to emulate Japan's success, although the rising technological requirements of car production, including the introduction of microcomputers in cars and on the production line and the oversaturation of European and U.S. markets, has hampered Korea's effort.

Since the 1980s, automobile production was becoming a world phenomenon, as established companies coordinated production between established and "offshore" factories. Companies both competed with each other and also formed complex alliances, sharing technology and design, as well as marketing each other's cars under familiar brand names.

In the 1970s and 1980s, the entry of lower-wage countries such as Japan and then Korea placed great pressure on European and U.S. companies; in response, U.S. companies have shifted production to maquiladora factories in Mexico or elsewhere. Yet wages are only one factor, as auto production requires large numbers of engineers, designers, and skilled technicians, and reliable transportation and electricity grids. Thus in the 1990s, Mexico and Czechoslovakia became major car producers, whereas Bangladesh and Angola did not.

Since the 1990s, China has enormously expanded its automobile production and consumption, rapidly becoming the world's largest producer and consumer of cars and trucks. The government encouraged international companies to open up production facilities in China or risk losing access to its burgeoning market. Likewise, private companies are encouraged to form partnerships with Chinese private or state-owned companies. Although much of the technology remains imported, the country has targeted electric cars as a strategic area for international prominence.

See also China; Fordism; Oil

Further Reading

Flink, James J. *The Automobile Age*. Cambridge, MA: MIT Press, 1998.

BACK OFFICE

The "back office" is a business term that refers to support staff, like Internet technology (IT), who traditionally work physically distant from the managers and workers in the corporate headquarters (the front office). Beginning in the late 1990s, back-office workers began to be outsourced to countries such as India to work on the help desk for international companies. India had a large pool of educated, English-speaking workers; those factors, along with increasingly sophisticated software, made it possible to integrate Indian support staff with workers and managers 10,000 miles away. By 2010, India realized almost $50 billion dollars' worth of back-office exports. The international outsourcing was not just in low-level workers but increasingly in technical and educated workers such as computer software programmers and researchers for banks, medical work, and lawyers. In the 2010s, India began to lose some of this work to lower-wage countries like the Philippines.

The process of outsourcing manufacturing work to lower-wage countries has a long history in the Industrial Revolution, but the ability to do so for office workers is a product of a number of trends, such as the Internet, the increasingly sophisticated university system throughout the world, and a larger and more confident class of entrepreneurs in developing countries. The process has refashioned labor and business markets, as well as the expectations of workers, professionals, and corporate leaders, in both the developing and developed world. The process should continue to accelerate in the coming years.

Further Reading

Dossani, Rafiq, and Arvind Panagariya. "Globalization and the Offshoring of Services: The Case of India." *Brookings Trade Forum: Offshoring White-Collar Work* (2005): 241–77.

BANK OF ENGLAND

European banking evolved considerably from the Middle Ages, allowing transactions in different cities by exchanging promissory notes. But a large central bank emerged only with a charter of 1694 that grouped prominent financiers in London under government backing. The new bank loaned the government over a million pounds and in return was allowed to issue paper money. Other experiments in paper money occurred at the same time, but most failed. The Bank of England alone succeeded, and for more than a century, it held a unique place in public and private finance. The existence of a strong central bank encouraged private banking activity and facilitated commercial activity throughout the nation. Local banks needed to hold only small reserves, because they could draw on accounts with the Bank of England in case of sudden demand for money; this capability facilitated not only commercial transactions but loans for investment purposes. Clearly, a strong central banking system of the sort that took shape in England during the eighteenth century was a key ingredient in early industrialization, and it was widely copied by other countries.

Further Reading

Clapham, John Harold. *The Bank of England: A History*. Cambridge: Cambridge University Press, 1966.

BANKING, INVESTMENT

Banking has played an important role in shaping the course of industrialization throughout the world. Although bankers were not extensively involved in industrialization until the 1830s, they played a crucial role thereafter by channeling savings into railroads, new banks, or governmental borrowing for infrastructure projects or wars. Many investment bankers were originally merchants, such as the Barings brothers, who were slave merchants before becoming financiers and establishing the Barings Brothers & Co. of England.

Railroads and industries required massive amounts of capital to purchase machinery or raw materials and to pay workers. Andrew Carnegie remarked: "It is astonishing the amount of working capital you must have in a great concern, it is far more than the cost of the works." After 1880, investment bankers in both England and the United States began to take an active interest in running the industries that they had financed. J. P. Morgan and other bankers justified their increasing control by arguing that they were able to supply money only as long as they maintained the trust of other investors. As a result, bankers tended to discourage their corporations from risk taking or innovation, although they were instrumental in shifting operations from the original entrepreneur or his family to more bureaucratic forms of organization. Operating in the "regulatory vacuum" of the laissez-faire state, bankers often encouraged the formation of monopolies or cartels to limit risk and maximize profit.

Since the 1930s, however, the U.S. government has sought to limit the control of individual banks over industry by prohibiting banks from owning stock in industrial companies, which they were allowed to do in Europe or Japan. Critics of this regulation argue that it has discouraged U.S. banks from lending to industry, which often earns a lower return than real estate, and thus has contributed to deindustrialization and an oversupply of commercial real estate.

See also Banking System; Finance Capital; Gold Standard; Mellon, Andrew; Money; Westinghouse, George

Further Reading

Carosso, Vincent P. *Investment Banking in America*. Cambridge, MA: Harvard University Press, 1970.
Davis, Lance Edwin. "The Capital Markets and Industrial Concentration: The U.S. and U.K., a Comparative Study," *Economic History Review* 19 (1966): 255–72.

BANKING SYSTEM

The banking system is composed of the various institutions that help to facilitate or regulate the circulation of money and capital. It includes private or public banks and government agencies like the U.S. Federal Reserve. Before the Industrial Revolution, individuals or firms acquired loans from private banks, but in the eighteenth century, national banks were established in England, the United States, and other countries to stimulate industries and economic growth. National banks also facilitated national and international commerce, permitting deposits and exchanges associated with growing change. Supplying individuals and firms with sufficient capital to keep the economy expanding (without triggering inflation or depression) has proved to be an extraordinarily difficult task.

Many bankers were leery of industrial firms until the 1830s, when they began to play an increasingly important role in developing manufacturing. In the 1850s, the French bank Crédit Mobilier facilitated the growth of railroad networks and other industries by pooling the capital of thousands of individuals. However, there were

Federal Reserve members pose with bankers and governors in 1914. (Library of Congress)

few effective regulations on banks or investments to prevent unscrupulous individuals like Jay Gould (or even established banks like Crédit Mobilier) from cheating investors by "watering" stock or otherwise manipulating their finances.

By the late nineteenth century, bankers were not only loaning money to firms but increasingly helping to open up new industries. For instance, the Mellon family helped to develop the aluminum industry in the United States, and the French Rothschild family initiated and then controlled the Russian oil industry prior to the 1917 Russian Revolution. By the late nineteenth century, many European and Japanese banks had developed close relationships with industrial concerns and often acquired enough stock to exercise monopolistic or oligarchic control. In Japan, these zaibatsus were termed "monopolies of capital."

Although the government was always an important part of the banking system, the philosophy of laissez-faire limited governmental activity until the twentieth century. For instance, the charter for the National Bank of the United States (established in 1790) was allowed to lapse in the 1830s. Without a national bank, the federal government had few tools to intervene in depressions or financial panics—or even to regulate the circulation of currency. Economies generally entered a crisis after financial speculations or manipulations caused investors to sell their currency in favor of gold, causing a short-term capital shortage. Federal control over the currency was briefly reestablished in the 1860s and 1870s and then abandoned once again until the establishment of the Federal Reserve in 1913. The "Fed" attempted to ensure that the currency was elastic enough (and strong enough) to facilitate economic growth.

In the 1920s and 1930s, the role of government underwent a significant transformation. With great reluctance, most countries abandoned the gold standard in favor of paper currencies. However, the inability of most countries to regulate their economies and currencies disrupted the international system of trade—some governments arbitrarily devalued their currencies to encourage exports—and these factors greatly contributed to the Great Depression and World War II. During the 1930s in the United States, laissez-faire principles gave way to a more interventionist role for government. Faced with a crisis in the banking system, the New Deal government increased its power to regulate the fiscal solvency of banks and the stock market. In 1933, the United States adopted the Glass-Steagall Act, which had prohibited privately owned banks from also making investments. The law also created the Federal Deposit Insurance Corporation, which guaranteed the savings of individuals for banks that followed federal guidelines.

In the 1940s, most of the world's governments agreed to greater control over international trade, and the U.S. dollar (backed by gold reserves) became the accepted standard against which other currencies were measured. This period of international banking and economic stability began to break down in the late 1960s as changes in the international economy outpaced the institutional controls placed on it; in 1971, the United States devalued its dollar and no longer converted its currency into gold. In the 1970s and 1980s, banks followed their corporate clients and became increasingly international. National governments have found it more and more difficult to control the exchange rate of their currencies—largely because of the significant amounts of money held by international investors and banks.

Since the 1980s, the banking system has become less regulated. Large banks have grown much larger. A key example of deregulation occurred in 1999 when the Glass-Steagall Act in the United States was amended to allow commercial banks to make direct investments. Banks dived into investments with reckless abandon, making increasingly exotic financial instruments such as bonds based on risky or subprime mortgages. Trillions of dollars' worth of such bonds were issued and rated as ultrasafe, even though, in retrospect, they were anything but. Bankers created more complex financial instruments, such as collateralized debt obligations, which sliced up returns from assets (such as mortgage-backed securities) based on risk. Bankers throughout the world, especially in Europe and the United States, encouraged investors to buy these instruments. In theory, these instruments and investments limited risk, but instead they amplified it throughout the global financial system. The result was the global financial crisis of 2007–8, which resulted in the worst economic downturn since the Great Depression.

See also Banking, Investment; Bretton Woods Agreement; Finance Capital; Keynesianism; Morgan, John Pierpont; New Deal

Further Reading

Brett, E. A. *International Money and Capitalist Crisis: The Anatomy of Global Disintegration.* Boulder, CO: Westview, 1983.
James, John A. *Money and Capital Markets in Postbellum America.* Princeton, NJ: Princeton University Press, 1978.
Kindleberger, Charles P. *A Financial History of Western Europe.* London: Allen and Unwin, 1984.

BEHAVIORAL ECONOMICS

Most economists use the model of a rational, self-interested person to understand or predict economic behavior. By contrast, behavioral economics incorporates the findings of scientific research of psychologists into its studies. People can be rational, but more often it is their emotions that drive their behaviors.

Psychologists find that people are acutely aware of their social status and invest heavily in making sure they improve their standing with others, or at least do not lose ground. This drives much economic behavior as individuals make choices influenced by what others around them are doing. For instance, everyone can understand that unpaid overtime is not in his or her self-interest; most people would be happier having extra time to spend with family, friends, or on their hobbies. But ambitious individuals may calculate they can get promoted by working 4 extra hours a week. But as others respond, everyone may end up working 20 or 30 hours more with little or no advantage conferred. This situation describes many managers at Asian and U.S. companies.

High status confers a number of benefits, notably longer life, greater choice in choosing mates, and increased likelihood that children and grandchildren survive. Some economists have argued that the Industrial Revolution was actually an *industrious* revolution as individuals in early modern Britain who deferred gratification, saved, and invested gradually increased their numbers so that their behaviors defined the cultural and legal norms.

How humans respond to low status is also important. Men in the poorest districts of Chicago will likely live a full 20 years less than their more affluent counterparts a few miles away. Even controlling for race, lifestyle, smoking, etc., makes little difference; those with higher status live longer, healthier lives. Those with low status experience it as physically and emotionally painful and are more prone to attempt to gain status through physical aggression.

Further Reading

Clark, Gregory. *A Farewell to Alms: A Brief Economic History of the World.* Princeton, NJ: Princeton University Press, 2007.
Frank, Robert H. *Falling Behind: How Rising Inequality Hurts the Middle Class.* Berkeley: University of California Press, 2007.

BELGIUM

Belgium was the second country to industrialize (Britain was first). Belgium had been a major center of urban commerce and domestic manufacturing, particularly in textiles, since the Middle Ages. The area also had extremely rich coal resources, the basis for a rapidly growing mining industry. Just across the English Channel from Britain, Belgium was an obvious target for expansion efforts by British entrepreneurs, like the influential Cockerill family. Mechanization began in Belgian textiles in the 1820s, though, as in many areas where complex hand weaving prevailed, factories gained ground only slowly. By 1846, less than half of all textile workers were in large factories. Metal crafts also survived well, even as modern metallurgical operations developed. The massive expansion of coal mines, however, quickly added to the factory labor force. Railways developed rapidly, initially under private ownership; the state began taking control after 1870. A substantial machine-building and armaments industry arose, supplying other parts of Europe, including France, as well as Belgium itself. Belgian industrial leadership played an active role in spreading the Industrial Revolution, notably to Russia, and Belgium also became a major colonial power with the acquisition of the Congo in the 1880s.

The revolution of 1830 that established Belgian independence set up a regime dominated by middle-class interests; Belgium was slow to grant the working class the vote or to introduce some of the common late nineteenth-century labor reforms, and a substantial socialist movement arose by 1900 in this context.

Further Reading

Mokyr, Joel. *Industrialization in the Low Countries*. New Haven, CT: Yale University Press, 1978.

BELL, ALEXANDER GRAHAM (1847–1922)

Alexander Graham Bell invented the telephone in 1876. Bell was interested in human speech and, like his father and grandfather before him, taught deaf students. In the mid-1870s, Bell worked on a multiplexing system that would allow overburdened telegraph systems to simultaneously send more than one signal. Competing against other inventors, Bell developed the telephone system. Bell reproduced the variations in human speech via variations in electricity, transmitted it, and then translated the electrical signals into sound. Numerous technical hurdles had to be overcome before the system was commercially viable, but Bell extended the communications revolution, which facilitated the development of large corporate bureaucracies. Most major inventions after Bell were developed by systems of university-trained engineers and scientists; he was one of the last of the breed of lone brilliant inventors. Bell's company remains in existence, still commercially viable and a leader in communication technology

See also Bell Laboratories; Inventions; Technology

Further Reading

Bruce, Robert V. *Alexander Graham Bell and the Conquest of Solitude*. Ithaca, NY: Cornell University Press, 1990.

Replica of Bell's magnetic transmitter and receiver, 1876. (Library of Congress)

BELL LABORATORIES

As industrialization has accelerated, the scale of economic activity has increased and technology has grown more complex. Bell Labs represents the shift of invention from lone inventors, like its namesake, Alexander Graham Bell, to systems or institutions that are sponsored by corporations or even consortiums of companies in conjunction with the government. Bell Laboratories was set up by American Telephone and Telegraph in 1925. It is an enormous conglomeration of university-trained engineers and scientists whose mission is to carry out primary and applied research for the telephone system. Many important scientific advances have come out of Bell Labs, including lasers, the transistor, microwave radio relay, and solar-powered battery cells.

See also Inventions; National Aeronautics and Space Administration (NASA); Technology

Further Reading

Reich, Leonard S. *The Making of American Industrial Research: Science and Business at GE and Bell, 1876–1926.* New York: Cambridge University Press, 1985.

BESSEMER, HENRY (1813–1898)

Henry Bessemer was an Englishman who in 1856 "invented" and, more importantly, helped to perfect a process for transforming iron into steel. (An American, William Kelly, had independently invented the same process in 1856.) The Bessemer converter (so called because it converted iron to steel) blew air through molten pig iron, which removed its carbon, making it more malleable. The heat generated by the interaction of oxygen and carbon also increased the temperature of the molten iron, allowing steelmakers to avoid using additional fuel. Robert Mushet introduced a crucial chemical intervention when he discovered that manganese added to molten steel removed excess oxygen and sulfur, thus allowing the steel to be more uniform in quality. Although it had been possible to make steel before the Bessemer process, the new process was cheaper and allowed the metal to be made in larger quantities, and steel began to replace iron. By the 1870s, the process was widely used in the United States, allowing industrialists to use cheaper labor and circumvent puddlers.

See also Open Hearth

Further Reading

Krause, Paul. *The Battle for Homestead, 1880–1892: Politics, Culture, and Steel.* Pittsburgh, PA: University of Pittsburgh Press, 1992.

BIOTECHNOLOGY

Biotechnology has an ancient lineage. The United Nations defines it as "any technological application that uses biological systems, living organisms, or derivatives thereof, to make or modify products or processes for specific use." Consequently,

Ears of genetically modified corn, produced by Monsanto; genetically modified corn is widespread in North America but largely banned from Europe. (Monsanto U.K.)

biotechnology would include the plants and animals domesticated since the Neolithic Revolution, as well as such processes as the making of cheese, bread, and beer.

The modern view of biotechnology is that it is the scientific manipulation of biological organisms to solve a medical or industrial problem; generally, biotechnology is done by corporations to make a profit. Examples of biotechnology are genetically modified crops, manufacturing a drug that responds to a specific kind of DNA, and altering, cloning, or creating bacteria for a specific purpose. Consequently, biotechnology exemplifies how industrialization has harnessed the scientific breakthroughs of the late twentieth century.

The industrial saga of biotechnology begins with the brewing of beer. Since the late nineteenth century, brewers had researched better and cheaper ways to achieve fermentation. During World War I, Germans relied on industrially developed yeast for the majority of feed for cattle. The British manipulated starch to manufacture acetone, a critical ingredient for explosives. Biotechnology continued to be applied to the industrial production of food, as well as medicines such as penicillin. Scientists opened up many novel avenues, but not all of them proved successful, such as the effort in the early 1970s to solve world hunger by processing protein from petroleum. In that instance, consumers balked at such foods, and by 1974, the price of oil quintupled. This is not the first time that the benefits, or hazards, of biotechnology were oversold to the public.

Since the late twentieth century, biotechnology has enormously expanded as a result of the advances of science. This expansion has generated the expectation that, by the early twenty-first century, biotechnology will add several trillion dollars to world markets. Real and potential industrial biotech applications are in agriculture, drug design and manufacture, disease detection and diagnosis, as well as bioremediation, such as bacteria that break down industrial pollution. The development of recombinant DNA techniques makes possible a historically unprecedented level of control over the genetic composition of organisms. Also referred to colloquially as "genetic engineering," recombinant DNA technology has sparked impassioned public debate regarding its possible (and ultimately unpredictable) consequences; but it also has precipitated many encouraging industrial and medical breakthroughs, the first of which was the commercial production of synthetic human insulin in 1982. It is hoped, for instance, that similar advances in agricultural genetics could eventually eliminate world poverty. Another area with enormous potential is the engineering of bacteria to break down algae and emit ethanol or other alternative forms of liquid fuels.

Almost as important as the technology were changes in U.S. law. In 1980, U.S. courts ruled that an individual or company could hold a patent on living organisms, including specific genes, crops, or bacteria. Since that time, the U.S. government and companies have pressed to open markets for goods; European countries have largely resisted out of concern for public safety. Companies modified grains such as corn to outgrow weeds or to resist insect predation, thereby limiting the need for herbicides and insecticides. New strains can drift into other farmers' fields; companies have forced those farmers to pay for the crops they did not plant. There is concern that such drift will corrupt the genes of key crops developed over thousands of years, with unintended consequences. The vast majority of genetically modified crops are soybeans, corn, cotton, and canola grown in Argentina, Canada, Brazil, India, and the United States.

Since the completion of the human genome project in 2000, genetic cloning and manipulation has received an influx of funding, although practical applications have lagged behind both fears and expectations. The problem of understanding how tens of thousands genes interact with each other is no mean task.

Further Reading

Bud, Robert. *The Uses of Life: A History of Biotechnology*. New York: Cambridge University Press, 1993.
Smith, John E. *Biotechnology*. 5th ed. New York: Cambridge University Press, 2009.

BLACK WORKERS

Since the rise of racialized slavery in the Americas in the sixteenth century, the labor of black workers has been an important (if unacknowledged) part of global industrialization. Slave labor created many of the raw materials (notably cotton) for Europe's factories and many of the foodstuffs (sugar, for example) for its increasingly urbanized population. The capital surplus from the slave trade and plantation production helped to underwrite industrialization in Europe and the United States. Even when slaves were freed, black workers suffered the burden of racism, for most industrialists and workers barred blacks from factory employment. Nonetheless, black workers were a crucial part of the working class in the United States, Latin America, and Africa.

Africans brought with them many important skills that helped build the emerging slave societies in North and Latin America. Many of the blacksmiths on Brazil's slave plantations had gained their expertise in Africa. West Africans from the "Grain Coast" were skilled agriculturists, and Africans' skill with rice growing was absolutely central to the development of that crop in the Americas. After the development of plantation crops (sugar, cotton, and rice), most slaves were used in labor gangs, although by the mid-nineteenth century in the southern United States, slaves were used as coal miners and as factory workers in textile mills or iron foundries.

After their emancipation, most black workers were economically marginalized as sharecroppers, and many jobs or economic sectors were closed to them. In the United States, most factory owners asserted that blacks were too inherently lazy to adapt to industrial production, and most trade unions prohibited blacks from membership. Andrew Carnegie recruited most of his unskilled laborers from eastern and southern Europe, although he did hire a small number of skilled black furnace men from Virginia—a signal to his white workers not to take their privileges for granted. During the period of the Great Migration, when European immigrants became unavailable (due to World War I and changes in immigration laws), industrialists discovered the virtues of black workers. With the rise of social history since 1970, historians have begun to describe the impact of the black working class on the black community and the rest of the working class. Black industrial workers formed the basis for markets for black entrepreneurs and political or union movements. Because blacks were still blocked from many white-collar jobs, deindustrialization in the 1970s and 1980s hit the black working class particularly hard.

Black workers were an important source of labor throughout the world. In Africa, colonial governments displaced black peasants from the land (generally through taxation) to create a local working class to work on plantations, in mines, or in emerging cities. Though not industrial workers per se, black labor produced many of the raw materials (rubber, copper, tea, and coffee) necessary for industrial production (or consumption) in the "cosmopolitan" center. After World War II, many formerly colonized black workers migrated to Europe or North America, where most of them worked in low-paid positions in the service economy. In South Africa, the black working class played a crucial role in that country's exploitation of its mineral resources and, more recently, in the transition to a democratic government.

See also Dual Labor Markets; Emancipation and Reconstruction (United States); Underclass

Further Reading

Harris, William Hamilton. *The Harder We Run: Black Workers since the Civil War*. New York: Oxford University Press, 1982.

Trotter, Joe William. *Coal, Class, and Color: Blacks in Southern West Virginia, 1915–32.* Urbana: University of Illinois Press, 1990.

BOBBIN BOYS. *See* Child Labor

BŌREN (ALL-JAPAN COTTON-SPINNERS TRADE ASSOCIATION)

This Japanese association, formed in the 1880s and operating over the subsequent 50 years, demonstrated the high level of cooperation among Japanese manufacturers. Private enterprise dominated the industrialization of Japanese textiles, but it did not preclude extensive exchange of information. Bōren helped coordinate policies with the government. It also issued trade publications to promote technological modernization and even arranged to loan engineers from one company to another to facilitate technical advance. Bōren went even further than most Japanese collaborative arrangements, arranging reduced rates on raw cotton with Japanese shippers and setting production quotas for each member to limit competition. Entry to Bōren was easy, but almost all producers had to belong. The cartel's successful management helps account for Japan's rapidity in replacing imports of British cottons and in beginning to export by the 1920s.

See also Cartels

Further Reading

Patrick, Hugh, ed. *Japanese Industrialization and Its Social Consequences.* Berkeley: University of California Press, 1976.

BORING ENGINES

These engines are vital components in making precision metal products. Boring machines powered by horse-drawn windlasses had been developed between the fifteenth and seventeenth centuries in Europe to bore cannon from bronze or cast iron. Cannon were suspended over a drill and held against it by their own weight as the drill was turned by the horses. These engines were used to make cylinders for the Newcomen steam engines, but they were very imprecise because the diameter of the cylinders was so large. John Wilkinson (1728–1808) developed greater accuracy, and further improvements were introduced in the 1790s. Drill heads were now carried on heavy rods running completely through the cylinder; the power was still supplied by horses turning a shaft. Accurate boring machines, to which new sources of power were later applied, were a vital component of the early machine tools industry, making the equipment essential for steam engines and for textile operations.

See also Machine Building; Wilkinson, John

Further Reading

Dickinson, Henry Winran. *A Short History of the Steam Engine*. New York: Cambridge University Press, 2011.

BOULTON, MATTHEW (1728–1809)

Boulton was a pioneer in building the steam engine. When James Watt had exhausted his financial resources in experimental work on a usable engine, Boulton came to his aid with the mechanical and financial resources of his factory near Birmingham, England. The first successful engine was built in 1776. Boulton, no technical genius, was one of the English businessmen profoundly influenced by the eighteenth-century Enlightenment ideas of progress and material improvement. He played a significant role in forming groups to promote technical advances, arguing that such developments would promote general well-being.

Further Reading

Dickinson, Henry Winran. *A Short History of the Steam Engine*. New York: Cambridge University Press, 2011.

BOURSES DU TRAVAIL

The Bourses du Travail was a movement of French workers in the 1880s and 1890s to build federations of local and regional unions. In the wake of the Paris Commune of 1871, the French government banned unions, but by 1884, it legalized them again.

French workers confront police after a meeting at the Bourse du Travail, in 1947. (© Bettmann/Corbis)

The government subsidized bourses that were supposed to operate as employment agencies, but they were quickly taken over by syndicalists who sought to use strikes and unions to bring about a revolutionary society—preferably a stateless one (anarchism). The bourses helped to strengthen the syndicalist tradition in France, and by 1902, the local and regional bourses had merged with the national organization of the Confédération Générale du Travail.

Further Reading

Geary, Dick, ed. *Labour and Socialist Movements in Europe before 1914*. Oxford: Berg, 1989.
Stearns, Peter N. *Revolutionary Syndicalism and French Labor: A Cause without Rebels*. New Brunswick, NJ: Rutgers University Press, 1971.

BOYCOTT

A boycott is a ban on conducting business with an individual or employer. Captain C. C. Boycott (1832–1897), an agent for a landlord in Ireland, was the first to be boycotted after his tenants refused to have any dealings with him (even social interactions) because they felt he was a rude, arrogant symbol of British colonial rule and exploitation. The boycott was brought to the United States by Irish immigrants and adopted by trade unionists seeking to punish an employer. A boycott was potentially more effective than a strike because any unionist could participate, not just employees of the offending industrialist. In 1894, for example, the employees of George Pullman struck, and unionized railroad workers enforced a boycott against Pullman by refusing to connect sleeper cars (which Pullman owned and operated) to trains. The boycott spread to any railroad that attempted to operate using Pullman cars. With the aid of the federal government, Pullman and the railroad companies won that battle, but boycotts remained a formidable weapon in labor's arsenal. So formidable did the practice prove that in the 1890s a group of employers established the American Anti-Boycott Association, which prosecuted the United Hatters of North America for a consumer product boycott under the Sherman Antitrust Act. Their action resulted in liens being placed on several workers' homes to pay for damages. Secondary boycotts, aimed against employers other than one's own, continued to be practiced by unionized transportation workers (dockworkers, railroads, truckers, and airlines) until banned by the Taft Hartley Act in 1947.

Trade unions still enforce consumer product boycotts, particularly if a company has locked out its employees or is breaking a strike by using permanent replacement workers (scabs). Since the 1960s, unions in the United States have attempted to use these consumer boycotts to isolate and punish particular companies through "corporate campaigns." They have succeeded in forcing employers to rehire fired employees or to open factories that have been closed. However, corporate campaigns are time consuming and the outcome far from certain. For instance, in the mid-1980s, unionists at a Hormel meatpacking plant in Austin, Minnesota, were engaged in a particularly brutal strike and urged other unionists not to buy Hormel products. The strikers then attempted to isolate Hormel from its traditional source of capital by encouraging members of the community to withdraw their savings from a particular bank until the strike was settled. Although this form of boycott can be embarrassing (or even costly) to employers, it is generally less effective than secondary boycotts: despite their thorough efforts, the Hormel strikers lost their campaign.

Boycotts have also played a role on the international scene. Indian boycotts of British goods were part of the independence movement in the early twentieth century. The boycotts also encouraged the growth of Indian industry.

See also Industrial Unions

Further Reading

Tomlins, Christopher L., and Andrew J. King, eds. *Labor Law in America: Historical and Critical Essays.* Baltimore: Johns Hopkins University Press, 1992.

BRAZIL

Brazil won its independence from Portugal in 1822 and was ruled by an emperor until 1889. Although by 1871 the children of slaves were declared freed, slavery itself was not abolished in Brazil until 1888. Until well after World War II, Brazil's economy remained dominated by its colonial exports: coffee, cotton, and sugar. There was a small industrial working class in cities such as São Paulo, which had large numbers of women in its textile mills because industrialists sought to restrict black workers from industry.

During and after World War II, authoritarian governments took an increasingly interventionist role, seeking to promote industry by building infrastructure projects such as highways and hydroelectric dams. The military also intervened to prevent social reforms in the style of Argentina's Juan Perón. Active government sponsorship developed in reaction to Brazil's vulnerability during the Great Depression of the 1930s. During World War II, the government helped to construct a major steel mill and later organized a highly competitive computer industry. Brazil borrowed heavily from abroad to finance the development of steel mills, trucks, mining, and other heavy industry.

Development was rapid: in 1957, the country did not make any automobiles; by the 1980s, it exported large numbers of cars, as well as military equipment and computers. Development was also uneven. Brazil has entrenched poverty; millions live in urban shanty towns. The deep rural poverty drove landless laborers from the northeastern areas to the Amazon to cut down the forest.

Like many developing countries, Brazil suffered mightily from the oil shocks of the 1970s. Imported oil became more expensive, leading to inflation as well as a stagnant economy. In the late 1970s, Brazil had to obtain loans from the International Monetary Fund, the terms of which resulted in a long period of hardship for most workers. Investment and wages in the public sector fell, although workers who worked in export sectors, such as cars, but also oranges, sugar, and other products, did better. In the 1980s and 1990s, inflation remained a serious problem.

Yet Brazil made significant gains. The industrial sector continued to grow, accounting for about one-third of the economy. The country has long had enormous agricultural wealth, but for centuries, Brazil exported raw materials. Since the 1980s, Brazil's large and diverse industrial sector allowed it to transform sugar into ethanol for its automobile industry. Brazil's industrial base is allowing it not only to import technology, such as for its vast oil drilling platforms off its shores, but to improve upon it as well. The domestic oil industry expanded rapidly, and by the 2000s, Brazil was exporting oil.

Yet high levels of income inequality remained, as did racial discrimination. Brazil has one of the most uneven distributions of income of any industrializing country; only South Africa, with its long history of legalized discrimination, comes close. The political system encouraged corruption by the politicians and their allies and cynicism among the citizenry.

Brazilian politics was reshaped by its industrialization. In 1980, trade unionists and Catholics influenced by liberation theology and left-wing activists critical of the Soviet Union formed the Workers' Party (PT). The PT looked to Poland's Solidarity as an example of political independence from the state that had controlled unions since the 1960s. In the 1980s and 1990s, the PT won control of major cities and a few provinces. The party garnered a reputation for anticapitalist rhetoric, and highly creative and environmentally friendly policies. By 2002, it won the presidency and many seats in Parliament, and had become a more traditional Social Democratic Party. The PT's reforms helped to make society less unequal and politics less corrupt. Brazil is an increasingly wealthy society whose influence is just beginning to be felt in Latin America and the world.

Further Reading

Skidmore, Thomas E. *Brazil: Five Centuries of Change*. New York: Oxford University Press, 2010.

Wolfe, Joel. *Working Women, Working Men: São Paulo and the Rise of Brazil's Industrial Working Class, 1900–1955*. Durham, NC: Duke University Press, 1993.

BREAD RIOTS

These riots were one of the most common forms of preindustrial urban protest (there were also rural grain riots). Bad harvests caused rising food prices; these price hikes not only hit urban workers directly but also reduced the market for manufactured goods, thus causing unemployment. Workers often rioted against bakers for unfair prices, asking also that the state intervene to provide affordable food. Women and men alike were active in bread riots. As industrialization progressed, food supplies became more adequate. Protest shifted increasingly to the workplace and to politics. Bread riots declined and with them the involvement of women in lower-class protest.

Bread riots did however occasionally recur in industrial societies, as in France around 1912. In developing countries, bread riots remained a tradition. Many postcolonial regimes subsidized grain (for instance, Sri Lanka) or bread (Egypt). When the Egyptian government eliminated the subsidy in 1977, at the urging of the International Monetary Fund, bread riots grew in intensity until the government reversed itself.

After 2007, food prices rapidly increased due to factors ranging from bad weather to the increased use of farmland to grow crops for biofuels or other export crops. For the billions of people who live on less than two dollars a day, there is little ability to afford

Confederate bread riots were widespread; this one is depicted in *Frank Leslie's Illustrated Newspaper* on May 23, 1863. (Library of Congress)

higher food prices. Riots and protests spread throughout the world, and some governments refused to export grains. Riots over food contributed to the unrest leading to the "Arab Spring" of 2011. Because it is likely that climate change will cause crop failures in the near future, it is likely that bread riots will remain a feature of world history.

See also Moral Economy; Strikes

Further Reading

Bush, Ray. "Food Riots: Poverty, Power and Protest." *Journal of Agrarian Change* 10, no. 1 (2010): 119–29.

BRETTON WOODS AGREEMENT

After the 1930s, the international system of banking and trade was in crisis. The failing British Empire did not have the economic clout to maintain the gold standard. Many nations devalued their currencies and imposed protectionist tariffs hoping to increase exports and decrease imports. Instead, the result was a severe truncation of international commerce. The Great Depression contributed to the rise of fascism and then World War II. In 1944, over 40 countries met at Bretton Woods, New

Hampshire, at the United Nations Monetary and Financial Conference to determine the institutional framework for international trade, banking, and economic development for the post–World War II era.

The problems confronting the diplomats and bankers at Bretton Woods were as much political as economic. Would the new institutions that regulated world trade encourage low tariffs and open markets, as favored by the economically and financially stronger nations such as the United States? Or would new institutions provide financial assistance to weaker governments that needed aid in rebuilding their economies to compete in the global marketplace?

The Bretton Woods agreement established goals of more liberalized global trade with lower tariffs while providing some assistance to economically weaker, debtor nations. The International Monetary Fund (IMF) was created to stabilize national currencies and to encourage the expansion and liberalization of world trade. The IMF established the U.S. dollar as the de facto currency of world trade by pegging the exchange rates of other currencies to the dollar. The Bretton Woods conference also founded the International Bank for Reconstruction and Development (the World Bank) to help rebuild the economies of countries devastated by war. The World Bank would also become an important conduit of credit for countries seeking to industrialize.

Bretton Woods did result in greatly expanded world trade. However, the IMF and the World Bank did not play the role of relatively autonomous institutions capable of counterbalancing the economic and political power of the stronger nations. These banking institutions emerged as enforcers of laissez-faire principles or neoliberalism on debtor nations, particularly those in Latin America and sub-Saharan Africa. Although key provisions of Bretton Woods have disappeared, and the agreements relating to fixed currency exchanges were abandoned in 1971 as a result of a greatly deteriorating U.S. economy and currency, Bretton Woods's institutions and compromises continue to greatly influence the course of world trade and economic development.

See also Banking System; Development Theory; Great Depression (1930s); Neoliberalism, or Economic Liberalism

Further Reading

Brett, E. A. *International Money and Capitalist Crisis: The Anatomy of Global Disintegration.* Boulder, CO: Westview, 1983.

Cline, William R. *International Monetary Reform and the Developing Countries.* Washington, DC: Brookings Institution Press, 1976.

BREWING AND DISTILLING

Making beer from fermented grain involved techniques going back to ancient Mesopotamia. In the late nineteenth century, industrialization had an impact on brewing by facilitating the construction of larger vats that could increase output and by giving big brewing companies increasing advantages over small, local operations. Improved transportation and bottling also favored bigger operations in brewing. In some countries, large commercial breweries were among the first new enterprises intruding on largely traditional economies, in the nineteenth century. The great Guinness brewery was one of the first modern factories in Ireland, developing rapidly from 1855 onward after a more modest start. The Cervecería Cauahtemoc of Mexico, which was named after the last Aztec ruler but set up in the 1880s by a businessman of German descent, José Schneider, became so successful that it had to set up a bottle factory as well. Breweries also played a role in late nineteenth-century Japanese industrialization.

Industrial procedures had a bigger impact on the distilling of alcoholic drinks (distilling involves separating alcoholic liquors from fermented materials). Early in the 1800s, several inventors—J. B. Cellier-Blumenthal and L. C. Deroux in France, Aeneas Coffey in Britain—introduced continuous stills for recovery. In 1850, new distilling towers were devised that increased output. These developments expanded the production of alcoholic drinks and also tended to increase their potency. Supply factors played a role in the increased drinking that accompanied the Industrial Revolution.

In the postwar world, developing countries became avid consumers of bottled beverages, especially alcoholic ones. Consequently, alcohol and beverage companies became industrialized, even in countries with few factories. In apartheid South Africa, laws prevented blacks from buying liquor, but they could buy a potent form of "traditional" beer from South African Brewery (SAB) Company sold through government shops. Illegal "shebeens" sold home-brewed beer and liquor. After the end of apartheid, and the international sanctions against it, SAB expanded throughout sub-Saharan Africa, buying up local companies. That success allowed SAB to expand into Europe and the United States, becoming a major force in the ongoing contest for the beer-drinking public.

Further Reading

Forbes, R. J. *A Short History of the Art of Distillation*. Leiden, Netherlands: E. J. Brill, 1970.

BRIC (BRAZIL, RUSSIA, INDIA, CHINA)

This abbreviation refers to Brazil, Russia, India and China. Coined by economist Jim O'Neill in 2001, the collection draws attention to the shift in global economic power away from the long-standing industrial leaders (mainly the United States, Western Europe, and Japan), with the increasing industrialization and global economic presence of the several large countries at a "newly advanced" stage of economic development. At times, other countries may also be included in this grouping, notably South Africa. (Mexico and South Korea, to some extent comparable to the BRIC group, are regarded as somewhat more fully developed.) India, China, and Brazil, particularly, have all been displaying very rapid economic growth in recent years, and all survived the 2008–10 global recession with unusual strength. Many forecasts hold that the BRICs by 2050 may eclipse the current richest economies of the world, combined. Collectively, the BRIC nations cover a quarter of the world's land area and contain more than 40 percent of the world's population. In 2009, BRIC countries held their first formal summit, pushing for greater mutual economic collaboration.

Obviously, forecasts of the BRIC future are not without critics, who argue that one or more of the group may well fail to live up to current forecasts. The Russian population, for example, is shrinking, and the populations of China and Brazil will soon stagnate. Environmental issues loom large in China. Or other unforeseen mishaps might occur.

Further Reading

O'Neill, Jim. "BRICs Could Point the Way Out of the Economic Mire." *The Financial Times*. Last modified September 23, 2008. http://www.ft.com/intl/cms/s/0/0dcb6f1c-8906 -11dd-a179-0000779fd18c.html#axzz1v2D6i34F.

Wilson, Dominic, and Roopa Purushothaman. "Dreaming with the BRICs: The Path to 2050." Goldman Sachs, Global Economics Paper No. 99. *CEO Confidential* 2003/12 (October 1, 2003). http://www.goldmansachs.com/ceoconfidential/CEO-2003-12.pdf.

BRITAIN

The British Industrial Revolution has drawn more attention than any other because the process was first chronologically, and long set a standard for the rest of the world. What caused British primacy? The nation shared many features with other Western societies, but it had dropped serfdom and a strict guild system by the late Middle Ages, giving it a flexible labor force and encouraging the kind of artisan-inventor responsible for the amazing array of British innovations during the eighteenth century. Britain was an especially successful maritime and colonial power, and its export markets motivated industrialization. The British government, though mercantilist until the late eighteenth century, was small and flexible, in contrast to the more heavy-handed French state. Britain's aristocracy tolerated commerce, even allowing aristocratic younger sons to go into business outright without losing status; again, this contrasted with the more conservative Continent. British culture, Protestant at base, may have encouraged a special entrepreneurial spirit that was eager to use business success to prove God's favor. Distinctive resource patterns— good location of coal and iron, good river ways, but also an exhaustion of forests that encouraged use of coal to replace charcoal in metallurgy—favored British development.

Britain's early success spurred high earnings, which meant additional capital for further expansion. Britain—"the workshop of the world"—maintained a world industrial lead well past 1850. British confidence allowed repeal (1841) of regulations that had tried to limit exports of new technology and skilled workers (the regulations had not worked well anyway). British industrial expansion even began to

Paper for bank notes is made in a British mill in 1854. (The Illustrated London News Picture Library)

push out agriculture, and the British decided to import foods in exchange for the industrial exports in which they excelled. Early industrialization had costs, however: compared to the United States and many other parts of Europe, British labor suffered particularly bad urban conditions, unusual exploitation of child labor, and other problems as manufacturers sought to economize. Those factors helped propel numerous middle- and working-class British and Irish to emigrate to the United States, Canada, or other parts of the British Empire.

The next issue of particular interest in British industrialization, after causation and initial success, involves Britain's relative industrial decline from the late nineteenth century onward. Eclipsed by the faster growth of the United States and Germany, Britain began to lag badly in the twentieth century, despite continued innovations such as the development of a television industry in the 1930s. After World War II, particularly, Britain became a decidedly lesser industrial power, still in the top rank but only barely. Why did Britain fade? British cultural values may have been more appropriate for the entrepreneurial phase of industrialization, when individual ingenuity was at a premium, but they were less suited for corporate organization and structured research. British education lagged in technical areas. Resources were less appropriate for late nineteenth-century metallurgical techniques than for earlier processes, given the chemical composition of British iron ore. Labor gains, thanks to powerful unions, may have cut British flexibility. Exhaustion after colonial and the world wars played a role as well. The precise combination and concentration of reasons for the decline are debated, as is the relevance of the British example to other still-great but nervous industrial leaders like the United States.

See also Causes of the Industrial Revolution; Standard of Living

Further Reading

Deane, Phyllis. *The First Industrial Revolution.* Cambridge: Cambridge University Press, 1969.
Musson, A. E. *Growth of British Industry.* New York: Oxford University Press, 1979.
Wiener, Martin. *English Culture and the Decline of the Industrial Spirit, 1850–1980.* Cambridge: Cambridge University Press, 1981.

BUBBLES

Bubbles occur when above-market rates are paid for some good or asset for a sustained period of time. A classic bubble occurred in the early seventeenth century when the newly rich Dutch began paying ever-higher prices for tulips. At the height of tulip mania, in 1637, single tulip bulbs were purchased for a price that was 10 times the annual wage of a skilled craftsman. Obviously, such a state of affairs was unsustainable, and tulip mania ended with a crash.

The development of stocks, bonds, and markets has resulted in several bubbles. There were speculative bubbles in railroad stock in the 1840s, in all stocks in the 1920s, and in technology stocks in the 1990s. Gold and silver prices experienced a rapid run-up in prices in the 1970s and then a correction; some believe there was a gold bubble after 2008. Sometimes bubbles are located in one country; for instance, Australian mining shares had a bubble in 1970, and Japan had a massive bubble in stocks and real estate in the 1980s. The housing bubble that popped in 2007 was particularly severe in the United States, Ireland, and Spain. As of 2011, there is discussion that a housing and stock bubble has developed in China.

Most economists tend to see individuals as self-interested actors who make decisions on the basis of a rational weighing of costs and benefits, with the caveat that each person can have different desires (or "utility"). That view explains why someone buys a Chevrolet as opposed to a Ford or might pay extra to have a red car.

Bubbles operate because of the emotions that occur within groups. A rule of thumb in the price of stocks is that they tend to trade at 15 times their earnings. A stock that produces a dollar in dividends a year typically trades for up to 15 dollars. Less than that and the stock is undervalued; more than that and it is overvalued. During the depths of the great depression, stocks were so undervalued (and cash so rare) that the total value of many companies was less than the cash value of companies' buildings and cash on hand.

By the logic of price over earnings (the P/E ratio), past performance is the best predictor of success. But what if one stock is Dell and the other is Apple in the late 1990s? Both are valued similarly. But in the next 10 years, Dell's stock price did not rise while Apple's increased 3,000 percent. Which would you rather own? This helps explain why at the height of the tech bubble that burst in March 2001, companies that never paid a dividend (or even showed a profit) were valued at tens or even hundreds of billions of dollars. Millions of buyers wanted to own the next big thing.

Such uncertainties about the future of the stock market (or any market) help make bubbles happen. Each bubble has its own dynamic, but in every instance, people convince themselves that "this time it's different." In other words, buyers convince themselves (often with help from brokers and the media) that the asset you are paying a premium for is Apple in 1996, not tulips in 1637, or Priceline in February 2001. What people around you are doing influences individual decision making. People look at each other (or the smart fellow who bought tulips in 1633, or Priceline in 1999) and try to emulate them. After all, the person who makes a killing on the stock market can buy a better house, in a better school district. People also overestimate their own ability to assess information. After all, many people, including this author, did not buy Apple stock in 1996.

Experimental economists suggest that in the laboratory, bubbles form more often than a view of people as rational actors would suggest. In those scenarios, many traders understand that there is a bubble, but they overestimate their ability to engage in timing. Overconfidence of individuals to sell at the precisely right time is a major factor in bubbles.

Understanding that most people are irrational and/or overconfident, or else are seeking to exploit those that are, puts additional weight on the role of those actors or regulators who are supposedly rational and/or looking out for the integrity of the system. In the U.S. housing crisis, banks made numerous "subprime" or less-than-safe loans because they knew they would not hold them. Instead, the loans were bundled and sold off to investors who (ironically) wanted a safe, steady stream of income. Rating agencies rated the bundles as ultrasafe, chiefly because they were paid by the banks that were selling the loans. Individuals at rating agencies that gave what came to become labeled "toxic assets" a less than stellar rating were disciplined because they were losing the firms' business. Government regulators did not do anything about this either because they believed that markets were invariably rational and self-correcting and/or because they did not understand these complex new instruments.

There is evidence that effective regulation can keep financial bubbles from emerging. The Glass-Steagall Act of 1933 prevented U.S. banks that accepted deposits from investing in stocks. Investment banks could invest in stocks, but they were not protected by the various agencies that protected banks and banking consumers (like the Federal Deposit Insurance Corporation). In 1999, those provisions of Glass-Steagall were rescinded. In 1999, 5 percent of bank loans were subprime; in 2006, 30 percent of loans were. The housing bubble did not occur in Texas in the 2000s, not because Texans were particularly smart, but because their banks were regulated more closely (because of an earlier banking crisis that affected the region in the 1980s).

Further Reading

Reinhart, Carmen M., and Kenneth Rogoff. *This Time Is Different: Eight Centuries of Financial Folly*. Princeton, NJ: Princeton University Press, 2009.

BÜLOW TARIFF (1902)

Passed in 1902, this German tariff established high rates on manufactured but also agricultural goods. It represented a deal between heavy industrialists, who wanted to protect finished products but ideally preferred low food prices, and big landowners, particularly the East Prussian Junkers, who sought to protect all foodstuffs, most particularly grain. This tariff was the famous "marriage between rye and iron," as a combined upper class agreed to compromise at the expense of lower prices for working-class consumers. The tariff was also a response to the rising tariff rates in France and the United States. The government hoped to use the new tariff, named for the chancellor, to bargain with other nations, and in fact, the highest industrial rates were not actually imposed. Nevertheless, the tariff fed the growing sense of national exclusiveness and economic competition before World War I.

See also Protectionism

Further Reading

Gerschenkron, Alexander. *Bread and Democracy in Germany*. Berkeley: University of California Press, 1943.

BUREAUCRACY

Bureaucracy refers to a hierarchy of administrative officials. Bureaucracies are known for set rules of operation and careful record keeping, defined responsibilities, and expert knowledge. The earliest major bureaucratic tradition arose in China, where officials received explicit training and specialized functions. Administering complex empires created a need for bureaucracies, such as in ancient Egypt and Rome. European bureaucracies began to emerge in the Middle Ages. Until the Industrial Revolution, bureaucracies grew up primarily in relation to the state and the military, though the Catholic Church also maintained an important bureaucracy. Training and specialization increased notably in the seventeenth century; grades of military officers and division of functions—combat, supply, and so on—were particularly impressive innovations.

The efficiency of European bureaucracies contributed to some of the functions governments performed in promoting industrialization. Ministries of commerce sponsored technical expositions; artillery officers provided one spur to further training in engineering. Industrialization, in turn, demanded new bureaucratic functions, such as the administration of school systems, welfare operations, and factory inspectorates. Bureaucracies began to expand rapidly in the later nineteenth century as these government activities grew. European bureaucracies by this point were providing models for administration in other societies. Many colonies were forced to adopt their "mother" country's bureaucracies, but Japan (which had never been colonized) selected those that it thought were state-of-the-art. Civil service principles, supporting hiring and promotion by merit rather than birth or influence, were adopted in most European countries and the United States in the 1870s, while specialized training opportunities in fields like economics and public health increased as well. Japan's bureaucracy is widely credited with guiding that country through industrialization beginning in the 1860s, although it later steered the country toward a disastrous war with the United States.

Bureaucratic principles had spread to the private sector by the 1870s, with the growth of large corporations with extensive management operations and specializations according to production, research, procurement, sales, advertising, and so on. In the development of management hierarchies, with detailed promotion procedures and expert functions and training, big business rivaled the state in bureaucratization as industrial societies matured.

The rise of large businesses in the late nineteenth century created vast internal labor markets for various professionals from accountants to lawyers. Professionals gained access to greater security but gave up autonomy. The shift created a certain degree of anxiety and stress. Americans worried about the growth of conformity. The Japanese "company men" gained lifetime employment but sacrificed enormous amounts of time with their family. Ironically enough, when the systems of lifetime corporate employment began to come apart in the 1980s, new stresses and anxieties were created as well.

See also Managers

Further Reading

Chandler, Alfred D., Jr. *Managerial Hierarchies*. Cambridge, MA: Harvard University Press, 1980.
Torstendahl, Rolf. *Bureaucratization in Northwestern Europe, 1880–1985*. London: Routledge, 1991.

BUSINESS CYCLES

During the Industrial Revolution, years of relative prosperity alternated with slumps. During downturns, levels of employment and wages fell, causing immense hardship. In the early Industrial Revolution, workers starved. Workers pawned furniture, reduced diets, and sometimes returned to the countryside. When prosperity returned, employment went up and wages usually followed, though sometimes after a lag. The year after a slump ended was particularly ripe for strikes or riots; this phenomenon was an important element in the revolutions of 1848, which followed the crisis of 1846–47. Workers needed to wait for better times to afford the risks of protest and to express the grievances that had built up during a slump. Moreover, they grew impatient for more rapid improvements when the cycle finally turned upward. The frequent oscillations caused by business cycles discouraged workers, reducing

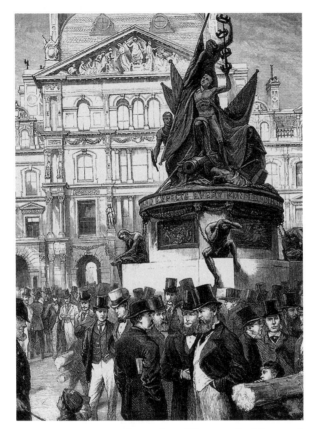

Businessmen were calm and confident at the Liverpool Stock Exchange in 1877. (The Illustrated London News Picture Library)

their sense that any coherent planning made sense or that they had control over their fate.

Before 1850, slumps were usually caused by bad harvests; prosperity returned when harvests improved. During bad harvests food prices rose, reducing demand for manufactured goods; unemployment could hit one-third of the urban labor force. After 1850, better transportation and agricultural improvements eliminated major food crises in Western Europe (though not yet in Russia). A brief slump in 1857 prefigured the more common sort of industrial recession. These modern recessions occurred when production pushed past available sales, for productive capacity had overexpanded in economies where low wages often limited consumer demand. Investments became overextended. Bankruptcies caused investment banks to fail, particularly ones that had offered speculative loans. Bank failures frightened potential investors, so purchases of capital goods (mainly from heavy industry) declined. Depressions in the United States were termed "panics" for this reason. This decline led to lower consumption in other industries, and the familiar downward spiral of declining wages and unemployment began. Recovery occurred only when prices fell and interest rates dropped enough to encourage new purchases and new investment. Business orders gradually went up and employment began to recover. Modern business cycles are international in scope. Many slumps have been triggered by bank failures in the United States, and the effects then spread to Europe. Industrial slumps bring lower prices and hit workers less heavily than agricultural failures once did, but they tend to last for several years, causing great insecurity.

The first major recession of this sort was the prolonged crisis of the mid-1870s, which gripped most of the industrial nations. Another recession occurred in the 1890s, and a few shorter ones after 1900 and again after World War I; the Great

Depression that began in 1929, a massive global crisis, extended this series of business cycles.

Business slumps had a positive economic function in one important sense. They drove out the less efficient producers—business failures went up rapidly—while employers introduced new methods and more advanced technology to permit them to cut prices and stimulate sales. The result was a more productive economy when the next phase of the business cycle kicked in. Slumps also promoted new business forms, like the trusts and cartels that responded to the 1870s depression by attempting to avoid "overcompetition."

After the Great Depression, Western countries became more confident that they could manage business cycles. Government-run social welfare programs took much of the bite out of downturns, and countercyclical spending increased the speed of recovery. Regulation of the financial system also reduced panics. Confidence in Keynesian economics was shaken by the stagflation of the 1970s and resulted in more market-based approaches in much of the English-speaking world. Western Europe continued along its Social Democratic path. The deregulation of the financial sector in the 1980s and 1990s helped unleash other financial panics, such as the one that refashioned the Japanese economy in the late 1980s. The result in Japan was a "lost decade" of sluggish economic growth and growing unemployment. Other regional financial panics resulted, such as the one in East Asian economies in the late 1990s. Ultimately, a worldwide downturn began in 2007. Debates over whether to use government to stimulate the economy or to impose austerity measures shaped political debates for the next several years.

See also Cartels; Inflation and Deflation; Keynesianism; Trusts

Further Reading

Josephson, Matthew. *The Robber Barons: The Great American Capitalists, 1861–1901.* New York: Harcourt, Brace, 1934.

Krugman, Paul. *The Return of Depression Economics and the Crisis of 2008.* New York: Norton, 2009.

C

CALICO ACT (1721)

This English law of 1721 was designed to protect English woolen and silk manufacturing against the importation of cotton cloth made in India. It forbade the sale of calico and levied stiff fines against anyone wearing calico material. The Calico Act is an example of the mercantilist interest in using taxes and tariffs to protect national industry. It had a severe impact on traditional cotton manufacturing in India by reducing the available export market. As Indian imports declined, a new English cotton industry took hold, for cotton clothing had become popular. English cottons, in turn, provided the setting for much of the mechanization associated with the early Industrial Revolution.

See also Deindustrialization; Protectionism

Further Reading

Smith, Woodruff. *Consumption and the Making of Respectability, 1600–1800.* New York: Routledge, 2002.

CANADA

Canadian industrialization relied heavily on foreign investments and railway development. Major railway building began in the 1870s. Canadian agriculture, wood pulp, and mineral production grew rapidly, and the nation became a major exporter to Western Europe and the United States. Canada has the world's largest holdings of nickel and asbestos, and modern mining equipment allowed the nation to expand output amid a rising standard of living. Extensive immigration around 1900 (2.7 million between the years 1903 and 1914) provided needed labor. After World War I, U.S. investment increased, and U.S. firms located manufacturing subsidiaries in Canada; Canadian automobile production, for example, was one such subsidiary. Canada's industrial economy was unusually heavily tied to other countries and to exports. By the 1950s, Canada exported a full third of its total output and imported a third of its manufactured goods. Because of its dependence on import-export trade, Canada suffered greatly from international setbacks like the 1930s depression, but it boomed when war needs or prosperity elsewhere stimulated international demand.

Throughout the twentieth century, Canada became increasingly interdependent with the United States. In 1965, Canada signed the "Auto Pact" with the United States, which essentially created a free-trade zone for that industry. American companies could sell cars in Canada, and vice versa; employment boomed in southern Ontario. Canada has a free-market system, like the United States, although with some significant differences. Canada became an increasingly attractive location for manufacturing because of its government-administered health insurance, called Medicare. The system is paid for by taxes and is cheaper than the company-based plans in the United States. Canadian labor law, while based on the American Wagner Act, has proven over time to provide unions more protections. After the 1980s, the steel industry fared far better than its American counterpart, in part because of health care but also because the tax system encouraged more investment.

Since the 1990s, Canada's economy has proven healthier than its American counterpart. The government has generally run surpluses, and its balance of trade is generally positive, thanks to a booming energy sector as well as traditional exports from mining, logging, and agriculture. The Canadian dollar, long weaker than its American counterpart, has grown stronger; government debt is relatively low for a developed country. Canada is one of the few countries that may be a relative "winner" from global climate change, as agriculture should be more viable, and it will be able to access more petroleum from under the Arctic sea.

Further Reading

Marr, William L., and Donald G. Paterson. *Canada: An Economic History*. Toronto: Macmillan of Canada, 1980.

Norrie, Kenneth, Douglas Owram, and J. C. Herbert Emery. *A History of the Canadian Economy*. 3rd ed. Scarborough, Ontario: Nelson, 2002.

CANADIAN PACIFIC RAILWAY

Railroad building began extensively in Canada in the 1870s. The Canadian Pacific was completed in 1905, linking the country from the Atlantic to the Pacific and connecting the rich western prairie provinces to the international economy. Immigration from Europe to western Canada greatly increased, as did both wheat and mineral output for world trade. The rail line, built mainly with British capital, greatly advanced the Canadian economy, including the significant industrial development in Ontario.

See also Railroads

Further Reading

Taylor, Graham D., and Peter Baskerville. *A Concise History of Business in Canada*. Toronto: Oxford University Press, 1994.

CANALS

The early Industrial Revolution created huge new transportation needs, both to ship finished products and, especially, to move raw materials, such as ores, grains, and construction items. Roads were inefficient and costly for heavy goods, and internal

Canals lowered the costs of transporting raw materials and finished goods; this picture is of Sheffield, England, in 1879. (The Illustrated London News Picture Library)

rivers were not always well located or sufficiently deep and wide for transporting goods. An enthusiasm for canals developed in the context of dealing with industrial requirements and encouraging industrial development. Canals also allowed governments, the sponsors of most projects, to take a major role in spurring economic growth. Canal systems spread widely in later eighteenth-century Britain and then, in the early nineteenth century, in Western Europe and the United States. The Erie Canal, linking the Hudson River with the Great Lakes, was a striking project, one example of how canal networks flourished throughout the new industrial world. The Erie Canal connected a vast area that could ship its agricultural goods to market and simultaneously import manufactured products from New York City.

Construction of canals depended on massive crews of unskilled laborers aided by draft animals but otherwise using manual equipment. Irish immigrants provided much of the labor for canals in the United States. Available cheap labor was vital, and working conditions were harsh and arbitrary.

The importance of canals began to decline with the railroad, which provided faster hauling and more flexible routes. Barge operators frequently tried to delay railway projects, without ultimate success. Canals nonetheless continued to serve industrial needs, and in France, among other places, active canal building continued alongside railway development into the 1880s. A few massive oceangoing canal systems, such as the Panama Canal and the St. Lawrence Seaway, were completed in the twentieth century.

See also Panama Canal; State, Role of the

Further Reading

Way, Peter. *Common Labour: Workers and the Digging of North American Canals, 1780–1860*. Cambridge: Cambridge University Press, 1993.

CANNING

Canning was a result of the Napoleonic Wars (1799–1815), as the French leader sought alternatives to the high death rate of soldiers from spoiled food and poor nutrition. He set up a Society for the Encouragement of New Inventions, with a prize for a method of preserving food. Pursuing the prize, a candy maker, Nicolas Appert, discovered that air caused food to spoil. In 10 years of experiments, he found that cooked foods, sealed in tightly corked bottles and cooked again, would remain edible for a long time. He won his prize in 1810. But glass bottles often broke, and an English method that used metal containers or canisters (soon, simply cans) was more fruitful. Canning spread widely, but it was Louis Pasteur's discovery of bacteria's role in food spoilage, in the 1850s and 1860s, that first explained why the method worked. This discovery led to more effective procedures for sterilizing closed containers.

Further inventions, like the threaded Mason jar (1858) and the rubber sealing ring (1902), advanced the process. Canned goods still remained subject to spoilage, which is why the H. J. Heinz Company bottled its ketchup and other goods, so that consumers could see for themselves that the food was fresh and contained no contaminants. Canning served as the basis for a growing food-processing industry, more reliable food supplies, and new forms of retailing featuring more elaborate grocery stores.

Further Reading

Toussaint-Samat, Maguelonne. *A History of Food*. 2nd ed. Chichester, UK: Wiley-Blackwell, 2009.

CAPITALISM

Capitalism is a system of production in which capital in a variety of forms (money, credit, machinery, and goods) is owned by a relatively small class of capitalists who employ a class of wage laborers to produce the goods, with the owners then expropriating the profits. As a term for economic system, capitalism only came into usage in the mid-nineteenth century; however, historians agree that by the fifteenth century, capitalism had begun to emerge in Europe.

The reason for the evolution of capitalism in Europe is a point of great controversy. Some scholars believe that capitalism first emerged from a crisis in feudalism or manorialism that resulted in capitalistic forms of agriculture in England and, to some extent, in France and Germany. Other scholars hold that new systems of global trade encouraged the spread of capitalism. In either case, capitalism preceded the Industrial Revolution, and the changes that capitalism wrought upon European, and especially English society, enabled the development of industrialization there.

Between the fifteenth and eighteenth centuries, even English society was not yet fully dominated by capitalistic values, for many poor and rich people had not internalized the values of the market. At this stage of capitalism, merchants, big farmers, and planters were the chief capitalists. "Commercial capitalism" helped to lay the groundwork for the Industrial Revolution by rewarding entrepreneurialism, transforming the role and political form of the state, and building up the necessary financial surplus that would later be invested in industry. By instituting harsher labor systems and more market-oriented patterns of trade, commercial capitalism also began to transform a number of societies throughout the world system—a process that would accelerate in the next two centuries.

Between the late eighteenth and late nineteenth centuries, capitalism and the Industrial Revolution fundamentally remade European society and, indeed, much of the world. Although capitalism had begun to create an industrial working class, the number of factory workers was relatively small—even by the mid-nineteenth century. However, the process of industrialization quickly began to transform work habits, patterns of trade, and the daily lives of people throughout the world.

This stage of capitalism was relatively competitive, and many inventors and entrepreneurs became rich. Later in the nineteenth century, large corporations and cartels began to monopolize manufacturing to maximize their profits. During this phase, the industrial corporations began systematically to exploit the scientific process for new products and processes. Mass-production techniques produced more goods than ever before, but, according to the logic of production for profit, the result was increasingly desperate competition among industrialized countries over markets, resulting in a scramble for colonies and captive markets. The rapid expansion of new goods and technologies contrasted with the growing international instability that led to the disaster of World War I.

To maximize production for the war, the states of industrialized countries began to take a much stronger role to regulate domestic production (and to a limited extent, international trade). During World War I, and particularly during the Great Depression of the 1930s, the laissez-faire ideology of the competitive era of industrial capitalism was abandoned in favor of various forms of corporatism throughout the industrialized world. Britain laid the foundations for its welfare state, and in the United States, the New Deal initiated a tentative form of Keynesianism. Italy, Germany, and Eastern Europe experimented with fascism, and the Soviet Union developed an economy in which the state assumed all control over the market. However, the capitalist competition among industrialized countries for markets continued and contributed to World War II.

After World War II, the industrialized nations developed much stronger institutions to regulate international trade and finance. From the 1940s until the early

1970s, an unprecedented period of economic expansion occurred that spread capitalist institutions throughout the world and dramatically improved the standards of living of many workers in industrialized countries. Many observers spoke of mixed systems, in which private capital and capitalist competition continued to motivate business but state regulation and welfare systems moderated the process. After the late 1970s, laissez-faire capitalism gained ground in China and Latin America—reducing the role of the state. Some scholars argue that since the 1970s capitalism has entered a new "postindustrial" phase in which industrial production has become far more globalized than ever before. As a result, the position of workers and many local communities has become more destabilized—threatening to undo many of the gains of modernization.

Free-market capitalism enjoyed a period of ascendency in the decades following the fall of the Soviet Union. Few politicians or media commentators questioned that markets were efficient in allocating goods and services, and many argued that social questions were best left to them as well. That logic arguably led to the financial crisis that started in 2007 and has led to widespread public criticism. It is unlikely, however, that capitalism itself will be challenged, as it was in the late nineteenth century, although the rules governing it may be rewritten. Indeed, one example is that welfare systems are being expanded throughout East Asia.

See also Bretton Woods Agreement; Finance Capital; Fordism; Imperialism; Merchant Capital; Moral Economy; Plantations; Research and Development (R&D); Science; "Second" Industrial Revolution; Slavery; Stalinism; World Systems Theory

Further Reading

Klein, Naomi. *The Shock Doctrine: The Rise of Disaster Capitalism*. New York: Henry Holt, 2007.

Tucker, Robert C. *The Marx-Engels Reader*. New York: Norton, 1978.

Wolf, Eric. *Europe and the People without History*. Berkeley: University of California Press, 1982.

CARNEGIE, ANDREW (1835–1919)

Andrew Carnegie exemplified the ruthless industrial entrepreneur of the late nineteenth century, though his rags-to-riches mobility was unusual. A poor immigrant from Scotland, Carnegie rose rapidly within the Pennsylvania Railroad but left in 1865 and eventually formed his own steel-making company. Much of Carnegie's genius lay in his reorganization of the workplace. Previously, iron and steel were produced in a variety of stages by different firms in scattered locations. Carnegie centralized and reorganized production for maximum speed and efficiency; he quickly became the low-cost producer of steel rails, with a guaranteed market in his former employer, the Pennsylvania Railroad. Carnegie bought additional mills and turned them into low-cost, state-of-the-art production facilities. He also vertically integrated his company, setting up operations in all stages of production, from coal mining to finished steel products. One such venture included a merger with Henry Clay Frick, who controlled vast supplies of cooking fuel, the energy needed to make steel.

Carnegie incorporated a number of innovations that helped make him enormously successful. His accounting methods were unusually meticulous. He required managers to maintain careful records and rewarded those who met targets with bonuses, not in cash, but in company stock. Carnegie's stock plan encouraged managers to root out waste and decrease costs. His company was the lowest-cost producer of iron rails, a fact that he used to pressure other companies.

Andrew Carnegie rose from poverty to enormous wealth in the postbellum United States. (Library of Congress)

During depressions, Carnegie slashed prices, forcing other producers out of business; as the market recovered, he raised prices. In some instances, he bought out more technologically advanced companies, paying them a fraction of the price they had paid for new equipment. Moreover, Carnegie paid them with his own company's stock. Carnegie sought to retain his cost advantage by breaking the power of skilled craftsmen, such as the iron puddlers who were essential to the production process. After a series of confrontations with the union in the 1880s, Carnegie threatened skilled workers at his Homestead Works with a pay cut. The workers refused to accept the cut, and Carnegie locked them out. Pinkerton guards who had been sent to escort strikebreakers were driven out of town by strikers. Eventually, the facility was reopened on a nonunion basis by the Pennsylvania militia.

Carnegie sold his company in 1901 to J. P. Morgan's United States Steel Company. Reportedly, railroad companies were worried that Carnegie would get into the transportation business and undermine the monopoly companies there. Part of the deal was that Carnegie could not buy a new company. One of the richest men in the world, Carnegie devoted his subsequent years to philanthropy. Carnegie also served as a spokesman for the virtues of capitalist competition, espousing Social Darwinist ideals.

See also Homestead Lockout (1892)

Further Reading

Wall, Joseph Frazier. *Andrew Carnegie*. Pittsburgh, PA: University of Pittsburgh Press, 1970.

CARTELS

Cartels were voluntary agreements between large corporations to exercise monopolistic control over the market. In the late nineteenth century, national cartels began to form in Western Europe that established sales prices, allocated market share among companies, cooperated to block the entry of foreign corporations or cartels into domestic markets, limited production, and sometimes pooled patents or shared technologies. In contrast to the United States, where the formation of monopolies caused widespread alarm (but formed anyway), European governments did not seek to ban cartels but sought to protect the public from flagrant abuses. By the 1930s, Germany, Japan, Italy, and much of Scandinavia and Eastern Europe, as well as South Africa, not only enforced cartels' agreements but had begun to encourage the formation of domestic cartels. Critics of the New Deal charged that the U.S. government had adopted a similar policy.

The chemical industry led the way in the formation of cartels. Cartels had proved crucial to the development of the German chemical industry because collective agreements between companies helped to raise prices, thereby subsidizing the research and development of new products. By the 1880s, German chemical companies were hiring university-trained chemists (many had been unable to find academic jobs) and later establishing corporate research and development laboratories. The German cartel maintained its lead over foreign producers by taking out patents abroad—in the early twentieth century, German firms held over 40 percent of U.S. patents relating to the chemical industry and were several times larger than their British, French, or U.S. counterparts. The German cartel's hold over patents blocked foreign chemical companies from beginning production of many different product lines. During World War I, the U.S. government effectively subsidized its own chemical industry by distributing patents to its own domestic corporations. In the case of telephone and radio corporations, technologies and patents overlapped and a patent pool was established to facilitate a division of markets; subsequently, some companies concentrated on telephones, others on radios.

German cartels took the lead in establishing international cartels. In 1925, I. G. Farben, which accounted for half of all German production, was formed, and soon the German-led dye cartel accounted for almost two-thirds of the international market. Although powerful, the German-led cartel's impact was affected by governmental policies in different countries. In cases where the governments failed to protect small firms, the international cartel bought out or closed down chemical producers; in larger countries where governments were strongly protectionist, local firms were invited to join the cartel. In general, separate agreements were made with U.S. and Japanese firms or cartels. International cartels were often able to use their technological superiority and profitability to force domestic manufacturers into sharing markets. Cartels proved an important factor (or barrier) for countries seeking to build domestic industries with a significant scientific or high-technology base.

See also Capitalism; Finance Capital; Monopoly

Further Reading

Amatori, Franco, and Geoffrey Jones. *Business History around the World*. New York: Cambridge University Press, 2003.

Kudo, Akira, and Terushi Hara. *International Cartels in Business History*. Tokyo: University of Tokyo Press, 1992.

CAUSES OF THE INDUSTRIAL REVOLUTION

The analysis of historical causation involves identifying what combination of preexisting conditions and new elements brought about significant change. The Industrial Revolution was a massive change launched by an unusual mix of factors. Basic conditions for industrialization in Western Europe included changes in culture emanating from the scientific revolution and the rationalist movement of the eighteenth century known as the Enlightenment. These movements improved scientific knowledge, and some specific scientific advances, as in the study of gases, directly fed initial inventions like the steam engine. More generally, the Enlightenment promoted beliefs in material progress and in the value of hard work and innovation, forming the outlook of many pioneering entrepreneurs.

The second basic condition for industrialization rested in Western Europe's dominant role in the world economy. Since the sixteenth century, England, Holland, and France had dominated world trade. This position brought huge profits, some of which could be converted into capital for further investment. Greater prosperity also encouraged new consumer interests that became quite evident by the eighteenth century, as large numbers of people sought new clothing and other items, providing a clear internal market for manufactured goods. Their dominance of world trade also encouraged Europeans to concentrate increasingly on manufacturing, for manufactured products commanded better prices when they could be exchanged for raw materials or foods in places like Eastern Europe or the Americas. Europe's manufacturing gains brought gradual technical improvements in metallurgy and textiles, and by 1700, Europe had the most advanced technology in the world in virtually every manufacturing branch. Finally, increased manufacturing created a workforce increasingly familiar with a market economy and ever more skillful. From skilled workers came many of the inventions crucial to industrialization. To an extent, the Industrial Revolution simply continued these trends in a dramatically new format.

Specific factors triggered the Industrial Revolution. Under mercantilism, governments became more interested in promoting national industry. Some measures were heavy-handed and counterproductive, like the French government's attempts to regulate craft methods; but other moves, like British tariff protection for the new cotton industry, helped spur change. Britain faced the depletion of its forests, which encouraged businessmen to experiment with coal, rather than wood-derived charcoal, for smelting metals. The most important specific trigger for industrialization was the huge population growth that erupted in the eighteenth century. The populations of England and Prussia increased by 100 percent between 1730 and 1800; France gained 50 percent. Supported by new food supplies from the Americas— for instance, the potato—and a lull in epidemic disease, population growth forced many people to seek jobs off the land, making formation of a new labor force easier. Middle-class families produced growing numbers of surviving children, which spurred them to seek innovation simply to sustain their growing families.

Every Industrial Revolution outside Britain was also caused by knowledge of the power and wealth industrialization could create. Britain's success in the Napoleonic Wars convinced many European governments that they had to imitate simply for military reasons. Businessmen in Europe and the United States saw the prosperity of leading British manufacturers and again vowed to imitate. Later Russian and Japanese industrializations were prompted by firsthand knowledge of the military power generated by Western industrialization. By providing motivation and example, the imitation factor could supplement other causation—for example, many later industrializers did not have huge capital or a favorable position in world trade, but they could copy strides made elsewhere in textiles and heavy industry.

Other factors need to be considered in explaining industrialization. Resources are obviously crucial. Most industrial revolutions took place in societies with access to coal and iron, though Japan proves that a poor resource position can be overcome. Education may also play a role. Most European industrializations began before the existence of a mass school system, but a large minority of the population was already literate. In later industrializations, education may be essential to provide a sufficiently skilled labor force along with the basis for necessary technicians. Of course, many developing countries expanded the levels of education in their societies but failed to spark or sustain industrialization.

See also Demographic Transition; Entrepreneurial Spirit; State, Role of the

Further Reading

Hartwell, R. M., ed. *The Causes of the Industrial Revolution in England.* London: Methuen, 1967.
Stearns, Peter N. *The Industrial Revolution in World History.* 3rd ed. Boulder, CO: Westview, 2007.

CELL PHONES

Cell phones are one of the most significant inventions of the postindustrial age. In the space of 50 years, this form of communication technology has gone from the stuff of science fiction to the realm of necessity. Mobile telephony has transformed daily life as much as electricity or running water.

Cellular phones developed out of the radio telephones, which were developed for the military and widely used in World War II. Car-based phones were commercially available as early as 1946; they remained bulky and expensive, although progressively less so. Handheld cell phones were a popular feature of the late-1960s science-fiction television show *Star Trek*. The "communicator" was compact and slim; it allowed person-to-person communication over long distance without the use of copper lines for the transmission of sound.

In reality, the first handheld sets were developed in the early 1970s and weighed several pounds. They remained a luxury item until the early 1980s. The Japanese developed the first nationwide cellular network, followed quickly by the Nordic countries. By the early 1980s, the United States, the United Kingdom, Canada, and Mexico were developing their networks. The world quickly followed and never looked back. Because they were initially expensive, mobile phones became a status symbol, and in poorer countries, a totem of modernity.

Cell phones quickly changed from luxury to necessity for the world; here a Buddhist monk talks on his phone in Tibet. (Angelo Cavalli/zefa/Corbis)

By the mid-1990s, cells morphed into "smart phones," adding calculators, texting, cameras, music, and Internet connection. Increasingly, the cell became a mobile entertainment device and portable computer, a heavy user of software, and an increasingly large market for movies and games. Phones have become a form of interactive credit card; people can pay bills or deposit checks with their phones. Smart phones have proved enormously popular; by 2010, more than one-quarter of all phones sold were smart phones.

Whereas computers and Internet connection are highly correlated to the income of the individual or the wealth of the society—the so-called digital divide—the picture is somewhat different for cell phone usage. Cell phones are a form of conspicuous consumption, but by 2010, there were almost as many cell phones throughout the world as people. Richer countries have more phones per person. The United States has almost one phone per person while Vietnam has one phone for every three people. Yet even in rural Africa, many people have access to cell phones, often charged from car batteries.

The advantages of cell phones make them an important aspect of life for poor villagers. In countries without widespread traditional telephone coverage, routine trips to gather information or fill out forms can take all day. Cell phones help farmers and the poor waste less time. Another aspect that facilitated the spread of cell phones is that the infrastructure for them (communication towers) is cheaper to develop than a traditional copper-wire system. Cell phones became popular because they are convenient and a symbol of modernity; consequently, they have spread from Wall Street to the suburbs, from the malls of Cairo to the slums of Mumbai and Rio de Janeiro.

The dramatic spread of cell phones has spawned a host of new social trends. Numerous parents have seen their children (or spouses) disappear into the games, texts, YouTube, and music contained in their own individualized worlds. Cell phones and the Internet have helped to weaken traditional print media like newspapers and magazines, especially so in the United States. Increasingly, people get news or gossip via short text messages, "tweets," or social networks like Facebook.

The addictive quality of cells and smart phones is a cause of concern or "moral panics." There is increasing evidence that texting and driving are a very poor mix; while a cell phone can multitask, the human brain cannot. As with other new forms of media, such as novels when they were introduced centuries ago, cell phones symbolize the alienation of individuals from one another.

Yet cell phones have played a role in the democratic revolutions of the new millennium. Some repressive regimes in the Arab world shut down the Internet, but not Twitter, which some have argued aided the process of developing mass demonstrations in Egypt. Antigovernment activists in Libya and Syria used cell phones to upload videos and photographs to foreign newspapers and human rights groups. When the United States and NATO intervened in Libya, they shut down the government's communications, including cell phones.

Cell phones also represent the globalization of international production. The design, software engineering, and research for cell phones is chiefly done in the Organization for Economic Cooperation and Development countries, with production increasingly done in East Asia, especially China.

Further Reading

Hansen, Jarice. *24/7: How Cell Phones and the Internet Change the Way We Live, Work, and Play*. Westport, CT: Praeger, 2007.

Klemens, Guy. *The Cell Phone: The History and Technology of the Gadget that Changed the World*. Jefferson, NC: McFarland, 2010.

CENTRAL UNION OF GERMAN INDUSTRIALISTS

This group was formed in 1876 during the severe depression of the mid-decade. It grouped leading industrialists, particularly from heavy industry, in an early display of their growing political muscle. The union clamored for tariff protection as the only way to save German industry. Bismarck, Germany's effective ruler, was eager to conciliate this bloc, and he did raise rates in his 1879 tariff, which was one step toward the growing protectionist climate of the later nineteenth century.

See also Protectionism

Further Reading

Whitfield, Bob. *Germany, 1848–1914.* Oxford: Heinemann Educational, 2000.

CHARITY

The tradition of giving money and goods to the poor goes far back in human history. Religious traditions such as Islam and Christianity have long supported charity. Charity connects with industrialization in several ways. First, extensive charity may sometimes have delayed more systematic attempts to deal with working-class poverty. This argument has been made for Russia, where Orthodox commitment to personal charity was extensive and may have impeded more systematic reforms. Second, in Western industrialization many business people and liberal economists argued against charity, claiming that it simply made workers idle and perhaps encouraged more childbirth, thus making conditions ultimately worse. Instead of charity, workers should be encouraged to help themselves, gain education, and save. Arguments of this sort motivated the Poor Law reform in England. Third, the criticism notwithstanding, charity during the Industrial Revolution was extensive. Often, middle-class women sponsored charities while their husbands concentrated on business. Some business families sought status and respectability by highlighting their charitable endeavors. Reports on the poverty of urban areas and fear of popular disorder motivated ongoing charity. Thus charity remained a vital resource even as conflicting attitudes and other reform measures took shape.

See also Social Insurance; Underclass

Further Reading

Barry, Jonathan, and Colin Jones. *Medicine and Charity before the Welfare State.* London: Routledge, 1991.

Jordan, W. K. *Philanthropy in England, 1480–1660.* New York: Russell Sage Foundation, 1959.

CHARTISM

Chartism was a mass movement for democratic rights that flourished throughout England, Wales, and Scotland from 1838 to 1848. While calling on older ideas of the rights of free Englishmen, the Chartist movement was also a major stage in the evolution of protest in an industrial society. Factory workers, particularly in northern England, participated strongly in the Chartist movement, and artisans attempted to use the movement to compensate for their increasingly precarious position in an industrial economy.

Chartism protested the exclusion of the working classes from the extension of the vote in the 1832 Reform Act and also the harsher requirements for poor relief enacted in 1834. The movement took its name from the People's Charter, drawn up by the cabinetmaker William Lovett and published in 1838 by the London Working Men's Association. Chartists demanded universal male adult suffrage and the opening of Parliament to working-class representatives. Women took a subordinate role in the movement, signaling their decline in working-class protest activities. Chartists also urged government-sponsored education and other measures that could facilitate working-class social mobility. The Chartists presented massive petitions to Parliament at several points that were also backed by large gatherings and some riots; factory workers tended to be more prone to violence than artisans. In 1848, the failure of the final petition effectively ended the movement, but Chartism nevertheless advanced the political consciousness of the working class. At the same time, the Chartist period and the movement's collapse highlighted ongoing tensions between skilled artisans—those, for example, who dominated the London Working Men's Association—and factory operatives. The artisans put more faith in the political system and in respectable, if vigorous, petitioning. They were suspicious of the newer, less skilled segments of the working class. After the Chartist movement, many artisans turned to separate, largely peaceful craft unionism; a full working-class movement did not resume in Britain for some decades, even as industrialization continued to advance.

Further Reading

Chase, Martin. *Chartism: A New History*. Manchester, UK: Manchester University Press, 2007.

CHEMICAL INDUSTRY

Until the Industrial Revolution, chemical production, mostly fairly local, focused on dyes and paints. Only explosives were made on a somewhat larger scale, usually in government-owned or -licensed plants. The rise of a modern chemical industry began with new scientific discoveries in the 1820s. New products were isolated (benzene in 1825) or analyzed (coal tar in 1849). The first aniline dye was synthesized by accident in 1856, and other artificial dyes followed. An organic-chemicals industry was poised to take off, and growing demand for fabrics created an obvious new market. New explosives were also invented, beginning with nitrocellulose in 1846; TNT was later developed by the Swedish inventor Alfred Nobel. Work on organic fertilizers advanced in Germany from the 1830s onward. Plastics were introduced, and paper made from wood pulp spread widely from the 1840s onward. The use of chemicals in making metals and other products expanded, though a bit later; this movement included the Hall-Héroult electrolytic process for deriving aluminum from bauxite (1886), which made the mass production of aluminum possible for the first time. Meanwhile, growing uses were found for compounds like sulfuric acid. Finally, demand for soaps exploded after 1860, as bathing became more common. British production of alkalis for soaps tripled between 1852 and 1878.

Amid this explosion, new procedures were introduced to make chemicals with less labor, including larger vats, revolving furnaces, and mechanical roasters. Companies subsidized extensive research to find new ways to make soaps. The Belgian chemist Ernest Solvay (1836–1922) introduced a new process to make soda, using towers to mix carbon dioxide with ammoniacal brine, recovering the ammonia in a still; the Solvay process gained ground rapidly in making alkali, though Britain lagged, as it did in advanced chemicals generally, after

Prior to the Industrial Revolution, most people made their own soap, which was harsh. (Vintage Literature Reproductions)

1870. Led by Germany and the United States (which innovated less but copied rapidly), chemical output soared, doubling or tripling in each decade by the late nineteenth century. German sulfuric acid production, for example, more than tripled between 1900 and 1913. The growth of the largely semiskilled labor force was also considerable, though unionization came slowly in this new industry. In Germany and most other companies, a few big firms cornered an increasing percentage of chemical production, with a diverse array of products from fertilizers to medical compounds. The military and environmental implications of the rapidly growing industrial sector were also important.

See also Cartels; Du Pont de Nemours; Environment; Science

Further Reading

The Unbound Prometheus: Technical Change and Industrial Development in Western Europe. Cambridge: Cambridge University Press, 1969.

CHILD LABOR

Use of child labor in factories and mines prompted concern quite early in the Industrial Revolution. Though children had always worked, their employment in more dangerous settings, outside the home and sometimes apart from other family members, obviously posed new problems. At the same time, middle-class ideas about children increasingly emphasized better care and more education—another source of reform ideas. Meanwhile, however, workers frequently depended on children's earnings to supplement adult wages, and employers (though middle class) eagerly sought child labor because it was cheap and docile and trained children for factory life. Employers also had a fierce sense of private property and resented any outside intrusion into their management of their firms.

The long-range impact of industrialization, however, was to reduce child labor. Most industrial societies moved fairly quickly toward a separation of work and childhood and later to a considerable separation of work and early adolescence, defining these stages as necessary for education.

Use of child labor in the early Industrial Revolution followed from the fact that children from the age of about five had always been used to work. Both employers and worker families found child labor fairly normal. Children received low wages. They could be used on jobs where agility and small size were at a premium. Bobbin boys, for example, tied thread when it broke on looms in the cotton industry while the looms were running, suffering frequent accidents in the process. In early industrial Britain, children were also used to haul coal from the mines or to pick slate from coal before it was shipped to market. British need for cheap child labor drove many cotton factory owners in Lancashire to recruit gangs of children from urban poorhouses. The children were housed in miserable dormitories and often beaten, working alternate day and night shifts. British exploitation of children seems to have been particularly severe, because of the need for low wages and docile labor in this first industrialization process. But child labor emerged in factories, particularly in the textile industry, in France, Belgium, the United States, and elsewhere.

Although child labor, even for the very young, was not novel, factory conditions were. Many children worked under the direction of strangers, rather than family members. More frequent accidents and the driving pace of work also posed problems. Middle-class reformers were soon appalled at child-labor practices, particularly because middle-class standards were changing to emphasize growing affection, care, and education for children. Many working-class families depended on children's income, but workers too began to worry about the treatment of children, particularly as factories became more impersonal. There was a growing realization that children were not being trained well, as apprenticeship standards declined. Many child workers were doomed to a life as unskilled factory hands. This situation prompted growing appeals for education to replace work, at least for children under 12.

Child labor reform began early and overcame the resistance of many employers who relied on the labor of children. Britain enacted restrictions on the employment of pauper children placed in factories in 1802, and in 1819 Parliament passed a child labor law applicable to all children working in textile mills. The Factory Act of 1819 made 9 the minimum age for employment and prohibited a workday of more than 12 hours for children under age 16. A new law in 1833 cut the workday to 9 hours for textile workers under age 13 (there were then about 56,000 such workers) and introduced factory inspection for the first time. British laws were revised and extended several times during the nineteenth century, most notably in 1878 when the minimum age for employment was raised to 10, and hours for children under 14 were limited to 6. The Factory Act of 1833 also required some schooling for factory children.

British laws helped stimulate legislation elsewhere, so that most industrializing countries began to act on child labor earlier in their industrial revolutions than the British had. Prussia passed a law in 1839. Several industrial states in the United States passed measures and also began to require primary education, though national laws withstood constitutional challenge only in 1940. France passed its first law in 1841, after extensive debate in which many employers claimed that child labor was benign and in which liberal principles were widely invoked to claim that fathers' rights to determine their children's activities and owners' rights to do what they wished in their factories must take priority.

Most early laws were badly enforced. They applied only to larger factories, leaving small shops free to use children as they wished. France began to develop a system of paid inspectors free from employer intimidation only in the 1870s. Also in the 1870s, most industrial countries had begun to require primary education, and although this requirement was sometimes evaded, it did cut the use of younger children considerably. By this time, too (earlier in England, beginning in the 1830s), many workers turned against child labor because their children were now being bossed by strangers and because children's low wages could hold down those of adults.

By 1900, a period of schooling was virtually universal in the Western industrial countries and also in Japan, which installed a mass education system even before industrialization was fully under way. As childhood became separated from work, families began recalculating the expense of having children, a major factor in the falling birthrates associated with the demographic transition. In most industrial societies, factory work for young adolescents began to be regulated as well, as the age of first employment crept up past 12. In the twentieth century, limits on labor were extended to teenagers in many industrial countries. By the 1920s, child labor was becoming rarer in industrial Europe and North America, and school attendance became virtually universal. As late as 1940, however, only 10 percent of the U.S. population had a high school diploma. Japan, by installing compulsory primary education even before full industrialization, also limited the use of children. Population pressures still existed, however, generating families with many mouths to feed, and the need to seek earnings encouraged continued reliance on child labor in most nonindustrial countries well into the later twentieth century.

Child labor continued to loom large in most less industrial countries. UNICEF estimates that as many as 250 million children continue to work in industries as diverse as agriculture, textiles and carpet making, toy making, and prostitution. Child labor remains widespread in much of Asia, Africa, and Latin America. The weakening of the state in sub-Saharan Africa since the 1970s means that many children cannot afford school fees. India, for example, passed laws against children in factories, but extensive use of children continued in other branches of the economy, particularly because there was no compulsory education. In the town of Sivakasi, for example, 45,000 children under the age of 15 worked in the local match industry by the 1980s. Coercion plays a role; Chinese children in the 2000s were kidnapped and forced to make bricks in the city of Shanxi. Organizations seek to limit the use of children in making clothes and toys sold in Western countries, though the obstacles range from the desperate poverty to the decentralized nature of outsourcing production that diffuses corporate responsibility.

See also Liberalism; State, Role of the

Further Reading

Heywood, Colin. *Childhood in Nineteenth-Century France*. Cambridge: Cambridge University Press, 1988.

Humphries, Jane. *Childhood and Child Labour in the British Industrial Revolution*. New York: Cambridge University Press, 2010.

International Labour Organization. *Stopping Forced Labour*. Geneva, Switzerland: International Labour Office, 2001.

Nardinelli, Clark. *Child Labor and the Industrial Revolution*. Bloomington: Indiana University Press, 1990.

Trattner, Walter. *Crusade for the Children: A History of the National Child Labor Committee and Child Labor Reform in America*. Chicago: Quadrangle, 1970.

Weissbach, Lee. *Child Labor Reform in Nineteenth Century France*. Baton Rouge: Louisiana State University Press, 1989.

CHINA

China's history of industrialization has been influenced by political factors such as the terms of trade, the basis of state power, and revolution, as well as by new technology. The Chinese government in the early nineteenth century attempted to resist incorporation into world trade but was too weak to prevail. In the Opium Wars (1839–42 and 1858–60), Britain and France forced the Chinese government not only to allow the sale of opium throughout the country but to make a series of humiliating trade concessions. Other European powers, the United States, and especially the Japanese also won trade concessions, such as allowing foreign-owned banks to issue their own currency. The foreign domination of China prevented the Chinese government from erecting protective tariffs for local industry, although by World War I, some industry had developed around Shanghai and Manchuria.

The Japanese government's annexation of Manchuria in 1931 and the subsequent war for the conquest of all of China discouraged further industrialization.

The Chinese Communist Party (CCP) came to power in 1949 after a long and bloody war with the Japanese and nationalist forces. The CCP, led by Mao Zedong, had relied on the peasantry (not the urban working class as in Russia). Mao charted a uniquely Chinese path to socialism. Heavy industry was initially encouraged, in part to follow the Soviet model of industrialization and to ensure that China would no longer be dominated by foreign powers, but later, light industry and agriculture were emphasized. Agriculture was collectivized, but slowly; still, food production lagged. After the economically disastrous Great Leap Forward in the late 1950s, industry was tied to the needs of the countryside, producing fertilizer, agricultural machinery, and material for irrigation systems. From the early 1950s until the early 1980s, steel production increased by a factor of 30 and electrical production by a factor of 50. China was developing the infrastructure for industrialization, but the right combination of policies had yet to emerge to raise living standards.

After Mao's death in 1976, the CCP under Deng Xiaoping opted for a less ideological and more pragmatic course of action. As Deng often remarked, "It doesn't matter whether the cat is white or black as long as it catches mice." Investment and trade with foreign companies were encouraged and agriculture was decollectivized. Peasants could not own land, but they could buy and sell lengthy leases, and they were eligible for compensation for their productive investments. Socialism continued to shape China's economy; for instance, part of the profits from semiprivatized communes in the countryside was allocated to their villages' social spending, such as pensions. However, the government attempted to break the "iron rice bowl" of permanent employment in state firms. State-run firms provided social welfare functions and typically had far more employees than necessary for effective production. Throughout most of the 1980s, industry grew at a 10 percent annual rate (one of the world's highest), and China became a leading producer of steel, machine tools, and textiles.

Throughout the 1990s, China attracted enormous amounts of direct foreign investment. China had several advantages, such as a large and low-paid workforce. The authoritarian government made sure that land for factories was acquired regardless of property rights. Workers' wages were kept in line by the government and communist unions. Also, there were few or no environmental restrictions. The theme was to industrialize and become wealthier, and then to deal with issues such as water or air pollution.

China posed major benefits for foreign companies, who could manufacture parts or goods for a fraction of the price in Japan, the United States, or Europe. Yet the Chinese regime caused headaches for foreign companies. The Chinese government turned a blind eye to pirated goods, and often seemed to encourage the process. (The irony that American companies in the nineteenth century had stolen technology from more-advanced British companies went unnoticed.) The Chinese placed numerous barriers against foreign companies exporting goods to China. Tariffs, both formal and informal, helped ensure that China exported far more than it imported.

Throughout the 1990s, however, China had to annually apply for a permit to trade with the United States. The annual review process was an occasion for companies to complain about unfair trading practices, and for unions and human rights groups to excoriate the regime. In 2000, President William Clinton convinced the United States Congress to grant China the right to trade with it on a permanent basis. The idea was that China would lower its tariffs and that the United States, and other countries, would gain access to the Chinese market. The reality was different. Once it became clear to companies that the United States would not block Chinese goods, foreign investment boomed and Chinese exports surged.

Other forces were at work. The Wal-Mart corporation developed the unique ability to pressure companies to lower their prices. Even companies that did not want to produce in China were effectively pushed in that direction because otherwise they would lose access to the world's largest retailer.

The pace of industrialization in China was blindingly fast. It was as if a hundred years of development were being crammed into a decade. Changes were rapid and profound. The communist regime had for decades restricted individuals from moving to the cities. The rapid expansion of exports caused the coastal regions, especially the cities, to grow. Communist officials turned a blind eye to the tens of millions of impoverished rural residents who migrated to the cities for jobs. Migrants found jobs, but benefits such as education were still restricted.

In many ways, the patterns of industrialization proved familiar. Workers lived in tightly regulated dormitories and complained about the fast pace of assembly-line work, the harsh rules of the workplace, and pollution from assembling electronics, shoes, or computers. Yet in many ways, this was a decidedly different style of industrialization. Thousands of workers toiled in electronic factories, "farming" for goods that had only an online market (such as *World of Warcraft*). Gamers in rich countries would buy goods or characters that had been farmed and then sold online. The industry was larger than the GDP of nonindustrialized countries such as Nepal. Ironically, the favorite nonwork activity of online farmers was playing online games.

Income inequality grew, which led to increased cynicism about the government that still maintained it was a communist country. Yet most Chinese recognized that life was getting better, and focused on getting ahead or becoming wealthy. Tens of millions moved into the middle class; by 2011, around 1 million had become millionaires. Coastal cities such as Shanghai became as wealthy as industrialized countries such as Italy. Rural areas remained far poorer, with living standards closer to Pakistan than to Europe. Yet no longer did Chinese peasants face starvation, as had been the case as recently as the 1960s. The rising living standards of the Chinese mean that more are eating meat or dairy products, creating a vast market for farmers throughout the world. Migrants could use cell phones and the Internet to keep in touch with parents and children back home. When they returned to the countryside for holidays, or during rare slumps, they could decide whether to travel by traditional trains or their high-speed counterparts.

The Chinese have been extremely successful in manufacturing goods. For instance, China manufactures most Apple computers and products. China has been able to encourage companies to produce not just parts but entire products or product lines in the country. The American dream of exporting cars to China proved impossible, but American cars produced in China are seen as high-quality status symbols. The Chinese government seeks for China to become a country that produces innovative products. In the 2010s, China identified several industries as strategic, such as solar power, electric cars, and high-speed trains. As of 2012, the country has succeeded in producing much of the world's solar photovoltaic cells.

Problems remain. The rapid pace of industrialization has meant that Chinese companies often produce low-quality products. One Chinese company exported gypsum board to the United States that contained low-level radioactive waste. Once put into American homes, the boards caused electrical systems to malfunction and had to be removed from homes at enormous cost. In the 2000s, China became notorious for selling tainted or poisoned food products. The "Made in China" label is ubiquitous but often seen as low in cost and low in quality.

The rise of China has remade economies throughout the world. Some countries, such as Australia, have grown rich exporting minerals and food products to China. Thousands of Chinese students study at universities from New Zealand to Canada, becoming a growth market for those institutions. In the 2000s, Chinese companies have become a major presence throughout Africa. Chinese companies built or rebuilt railroads, mines, oil fields, and pipelines. The practice angered some Africans, because they often imported Chinese construction workers, but pleased others who saw China as developing much-needed markets for their products.

Asian countries, such as Korea and Hong Kong, which could once count on being low-priced competitors to Europe and the United States, have had to rethink their strategies. Manufacturing jobs have often moved to China, but Korean and Japanese companies have been able to help develop the Chinese infrastructure. Nowhere is the balancing act more delicate than Taiwan, which China maintains is a breakaway province. Throughout the Cold War, Taiwan could count on a military alliance with the United States, but the rise of China has created a more distant relationship with its former patron. Taiwan has opened up certain kinds of trade, such as tourism, though it has been controlled by the Chinese government.

The rise of China as an economic power has military implications. A modern China has resulted in a more modern military, a fact that is not lost on its neighbors. Chinese industrialization has helped propel oil prices higher, meaning that territorial disputes are as much over deep-water sources of oil as fishing rights. The Chinese military has apparently been engaged in cyber warfare, such as stealing military and industrial technologies.

Ironies abound. The Chinese maintain an avid focus on the stock market and status symbols such as cell phones and cars. Yet China has thousands of illegal strikes and workers' demonstrations, angry at being ill-treated or not paid. Peasants often protest losing their land or government corruption. When protests become too widespread, the national government often punishes local or provincial leaders.

Further Reading

Fallows, James M. *Postcards from Tomorrow Square: Reports from China*. New York: Vintage, 2009.

MacFarquhat, Roderick, and John K. Fairbank, eds. *Cambridge History of China*. Vol. 15. New York: Cambridge University Press, 1991.

Riskin, Carl. *China's Political Economy: The Quest for Development since 1949*. Oxford: Oxford University Press, 1987.

CHINA MOBILE COMMUNICATIONS

Before the 1930s, China was overwhelmingly rural and struggled to develop an industrial infrastructure. Until 1949, it was engaged in a brutal war with the Japanese, and between the nationalists and the communists, which left the country in shambles. The communists emerged as the victors, and industrialization proceeded in line with Stalinist policy. The government made steady progress in developing a wire-based telecommunications network; by the 1960s, all cities and major market towns had telephone and telegraph connection. In the 1970s, the government prioritized, developing a radio and wireless network. By the mid-1980s, the country had imported more foreign technology, and access to telephony was rapidly expanding, if limited in rural areas. After 1990, the country developed a fiber-optic network. In 1993, there were 3.5 million cell phone users; a decade later, that number had increased a hundredfold.

China Mobile is the world's largest telecommunications company, with over 600 million subscribers. It services about 70 percent of the Chinese market, although it has begun to expand internationally by buying other companies. China Mobile began as a fully state-owned company, although 30 percent was sold to private investors. It is listed on the New York and Hong Kong stock exchanges.

The company reveals the successes and tensions of the Chinese path to industrialization. Compared to its Maoist era, twenty-first-century China has made enormous progress in expanding access to telecommunications. Even so, there is enormous potential for further growth as Chinese cell phone usage is only at the average for developing countries. As the country's wealth rises, more affluent cell consumers will likely demand more smart phones, etc. The government also carefully monitors and controls political expression over the Internet and cell phones. Indeed, the Chinese model of government control is a model that some authoritarian regimes have imported.

Further Reading

Lu, Jia, and Ian Weber. "State, Power and Mobile Communication: A Case Study of China." *New Media and Society* (December 2007): 925–44.

CHINESE COMMUNIST PARTY

The Chinese Communist Party has reshaped the dynamics of the global economy. In 1949, China became the world's largest communist county. After 1978, communists engineered a turn toward capitalism. By 2011, China has become the second-largest industrial economy in the world, with extremely rapid growth rates. Not unlike the Japanese a century before, the Chinese had studied how to hold onto political power while modernizing the economic basis of the country.

Formed in 1921, the Communist Party came to power in 1949 after a long war with its Nationalist opponents, as well as the military forces of Imperial Japan. In China, the peasantry, not the urban working class, provided the critical support for the revolution. In 1949, starvation was a real threat, and famine stalked China for many years afterward.

When the party prevailed in 1949, China seemed an unlikely candidate for industrialization. The country was overwhelmingly rural and devastated by almost 20 years of war and civil war. For several decades before the communists came to power, China had made fitful progress in responding to the challenge of industrial powers such as Britain or Japan. Until the late 1980s, the Communist Party pursued various communist approaches to industrialization. It broke with the Soviet model in 1961, but from 1966 to 1976, the country and party were wracked with intense ideological conflict. During the Cultural Revolution, millions were reeducated in

Chinese poster from 1968 encouraging the people to "Respectfully wish Chairman Mao eternal life." (Stefan Landsberger)

rural camps after being accused of being landlords or spies for the capitalist powers. Hundreds of thousands, perhaps many more, died from starvation or execution.

There were always factions in the party, not surprising in a country as large and diverse as China. Mao Zedong led efforts to revolutionize the Chinese economy and society, such as the Great Leap Forward and the Cultural Revolution, but they ended up in disaster. In the former case, millions died as a result of poor decisions; in the latter, millions were "reeducated" amid economic chaos. After 1978, a more pragmatic bloc came to dominate the country, led by Deng Xiaoping. As he famously put it, "It doesn't matter whether the cat is white or black as long as it catches mice." The object of the party was to raise living standards; if Maoism had failed, then perhaps "socialism with Chinese characteristics" would succeed. And most would agree it did.

Various reforms were implemented that reintroduced market forces and private property into the economy; these can be compared to Lenin's New Economic Policy of the 1920s. China's centuries-long tradition of entrepreneurialism reasserted itself. The party clarified its control over the macro economy, relying on trained technocrats to create the incentives to create economic growth. Peasants were allowed to own small plots, sell their surpluses, and retain their profits. The threat of mass starvation receded, and a few began to amass wealth. Local governments were encouraged to develop light industries that exported goods and to keep the profits. The result was that economic output increased and living standards rose. By the early 1990s, the experiment had resulted in dramatic economic expansion, even if rural poverty remained widespread. Thousands of foreign-owned factories were encouraged to set up shop in China.

The party allowed individuals to enrich themselves; by the 2000s, China had a rapidly growing class of millionaires and billionaires. Rural poverty continued to be a problem, but a rapidly growing middle class emerged, especially in coastal cities. The party continued to direct the overall economy, protecting key companies or sectors. The party retained its political rule, jailing dissidents who push too hard over environmental, land-claim, or labor rights issues.

The party succeeded by allowing individuals to get rich. Free speech or democracy would not follow. The Internet and press are closely monitored, and criticisms of the regime for environmental problems, suppression of workers, or ethnic tensions have landed many in jail. Ironically, protests and riots are endemic, with as many as 20,000 a year. Unlike in the Soviet Union, which fell apart, the communists in China retained power. There are numerous problems in China, from land being seized with little or no compensation, to political corruption and cronyism. Yet the party is also credited with being able to direct the country away from decades of near-famine toward a rapidly growing economy that is raising living standards. As in many authoritarian regimes, nationalist anger is directed against enemies of the nation (the United States or Japan), and protests of this kind are allowed, and sometimes encouraged.

Some observers note that the communists have perfected the strategies of suppressing organized protests or movements. Many of those elements have been adopted by other authoritarian governments seeking to hold onto power regardless of the cost, such as Zimbabwe's Robert Mugabe. However, Mugabe destroyed his country's economy since the 1990s; by contrast, the Chinese Communist Party greatly expanded their country's productive capacity. The party's transformation of the economy, and its ability to retain control, is essential to the successes and problems of China in the twenty-first century.

Further Reading

Chow, Gregory C. *China's Economic Transformation*. Oxford: Blackwell, 2002.
Joseph, William A., ed. *Politics in China: An Introduction*. New York: Oxford University Press, 2010.

CHUNG, JO YUNG. *See* Hyundai

CIO. *See* Congress of Industrial Organizations

CLASSICAL ECONOMICS

Following the example of Adam Smith, a number of British economists from the early to mid-nineteenth century worked out a system of economic laws that, they argued, described optimal economic behavior and policy. These laws are the foundation of classical economics. Some of the economists have been dubbed the "Manchester School," as the chief theorists worked out of this city. The term "liberal economist" is sometimes also used, though not all liberals agreed fully with classical economics. Although the principal economists were British—T. R. Malthus, David Ricardo, Nassau Senior, and John Stuart Mill—others, including J. B. Say in France, shared similar views.

The classical economists argued that free competition was the desired economic state. They spoke of profits as the reward for risk and saving in a competitive economy. Entrepreneurs would move to operations where profits were promising, and the resultant competition would drive profits down; this was an example of classical "laws" designed to prove how free competition would ultimately work to the general good. Many classical economists argued that wages could not improve much above subsistence, for every increase in wages would draw new workers (or cause workers to increase their birthrate), thus driving the level down again. This view was called the "iron law of wages" and helped label economics "the dismal science." Classical economics also tried to describe rent income and often criticized it as unproductive since it could less fully be brought into the competitive system.

Classical economics helped justify the policies of laissez faire, including a good bit of indifference to working-class poverty, as well as attacks on tariffs and other restrictions of trade. Proponents of pure classical economists dwindled somewhat after the 1860s—John Stuart Mill even changed his views to allow for more state-sponsored social reform—but classical assumptions have remained an important ingredient in economic theory in the West even to the present day.

See also Keynesianism; Liberalism

Further Reading

Heilbroner, Robert L. *The Worldly Philosophers: The Lives, Times, and Ideas of the Great Economic Thinkers.* New York: Simon and Schuster, 1986.

CLOTHING

The manufacture of clothing traditionally occurred at home, except that the upper classes employed skilled artisanal tailors. The Industrial Revolution vastly increased the production of thread and cloth, requiring new systems for assembling of clothes. Simultaneously, demand for clothing rose during the eighteenth century. The result was a rapid expansion of hand work. The invention of the sewing machine, in the middle of the nineteenth century, increased the output of workers in the industry and diluted traditional skills, though a great deal of manual manipulation was still required. The result, however, was not a factory system but a growth of sweatshops that employed primarily women workers. Some sewing was also done by women working from their homes or tenements. Sweatshops expanded rapidly in cities like New York, Paris, and London in the late nineteenth century. Skills were limited on the new machines, and women workers were abundant. Immigrant workers were often used, as in the New York garment district. The result was long hours and low pay in an industry that, although mechanized to a degree, continued to have high labor costs in relation to the total product. To add to the difficulty, many sweatshops were badly lit and ventilated. Several European governments, and also U.S. states like Massachusetts, introduced some regulation of nonfactory industries around 1900, precisely because of sweatshop conditions in the clothing trade. Unionization also developed, and the International Ladies Garment Workers in the United States became a significant force in the twentieth century. At the same time, the continued search for low-cost labor drove much clothing manufacture to less industrial areas, like parts of the Pacific Rim. Some manufacturing still remains in New York and Paris because of the demand for the work to be delivered quickly.

See also Light Industry; Women Industrial Workers

Further Reading

Perrot, Philippe. *Fashioning the Bourgeoisie: A History of Clothing in the Nineteenth Century.* Princeton, NJ: Princeton University Press, 1994.

Stansell, Christine. *City of Women: Sex and Class in New York, 1789–1860.* Urbana: University of Illinois Press, 1982.

COAL. *See* Coal Miners

COAL MINERS

Coal miners were essential players in the industrialization process. Britain's rise as an industrial power was clearly linked to its huge supplies of coal as fuel for iron making, steel mills, locomotives, and steam power in general. Coal was often located in proximity to iron ore fields, and thus coal mining was closely associated with the iron and steel industry. The rapid expansion of mining, without major new technologies, required a great increase in the labor force. The hazards of coal mining led miners to form unions relatively early, and mine workers' unions were a strategic part of the union movement in Britain, Germany, and the United States. Coal was increasingly important throughout the nineteenth century, but oil began to displace it as a fuel for ships, homes, and factories. By the late 1940s, the use of coal was clearly declining; in the United States, many miners lost their jobs to automation. Coal miners have been unable to reassert their once formidable political and economic power, symbolized by the defeat of a major strike at the hands of a conservative government in Britain in the mid-1980s.

See also Congress of Industrial Organizations (CIO)

Further Reading

Berger, Stefan, Andy Croll, and Norman Laporte, eds. Towards a Comparative History of Coalfield Societies. Aldershot, UK: Ashgate, 2005.

Feldman, Gerald D., and Klaus Tenfelde, eds. *Workers, Owners, and Politics in Coal Mining: An International Comparison of Industrial Relations.* Oxford: Berg, 1990.

Men and draft animals bringing coal out of an English colliery in 1869. (Hulton Archive/Stringer)

COCKERILL, WILLIAM (1759–1832)

The Cockerill family played a vital role in the spread of the Industrial Revolution beyond Britain. William Cockerill brought modern textile machinery to France in the 1790s; Napoleon made him a citizen in 1810. Cockerill operations spread to Belgium, where a machine-building plant in Liège employed 2,000 workers by 1812. Cockerill boasted of his ability to import new technology from England just days after it was introduced. By the 1830s, the Cockerill operation included the largest integrated metallurgical and machine factory in the world, and it had expanded into mining, shipbuilding, and railroad development. Cockerill realized the quick profits to be made from using British inventions in regions where older methods still predominated; there were risks but less competition. Although Cockerill's role in Belgium was particularly great, his family also spread factories into Germany. By the later nineteenth century, the parent Belgian company set up establishments in Russia.

See also Causes of the Industrial Revolution

Further Reading

Henderson, William Otto. *The Industrial Revolution in Europe, 1815–1914.* Chicago: Quadrangle Books, 1968.

COLD WAR

Because of its length (over 40 years) and intensity, the Cold War between the capitalist and the communist world had a large impact on world industrialization between 1948 and 1989. Massive investment in military research resulted from the rivalry between the United States, the Soviet Union, and their respective allies. Many technologies such as nuclear power, satellite communications, computers, and the Internet were developed first for military use and later applied to the civilian world. The development of enormous standing armies, navies, and air forces also created markets for new kinds of products or in novel parts of the world. The United States and Soviet Union never fought directly, but there were a number of proxy wars in Korea, Vietnam, Afghanistan, and numerous other places.

The impact of the Cold War on the Soviet Union and Eastern Europe was enormous. The Soviet Union, which had struggled to industrialize in the 1920s and 1930s, was first devastated by its war with Nazi Germany and then locked in an economic struggle with the United States, the wealthiest, most advanced industrial power in the world. Stalin and his successors favored the development of steel mills and other forms of heavy industry over civilian industries. The military received preferential treatment in labor and materials, which further hampered production for civilian uses (such as housing). The military did have short-term utility and was used to control Eastern Europe and to protect revolutionary governments in China, Vietnam, and Cuba. In the 1950s, Soviet military equipment was comparable to the American counterparts. For instance, the AK-47 was a cheap, reliable, and powerful automatic rifle. By the late 1970s, however, an escalating arms race with the United States consumed an increasing portion of the Soviet Union's resources and was a contributing factor to the eventual collapse of its economy. In 1979, the Soviet Union intervened in Afghanistan, and the United States armed the opposition. Soviet forces spent a decade trying to control the country, only to meet with frustration. The Afghan war helped bankrupt the Soviet Union.

This 1951 poster from the United States appeals to parental instincts in order to build support for the Cold War. (Swim Ink/Corbis)

The military-industrial complex was proportionally smaller in the United States, directly involving about 20 percent rather than nearly 40 percent of the economy by the 1980s, but it nonetheless had a profound effect on that country's industrial development. The relocation and expansion of military industries to the southern and western portions of the United States was crucial in the spectacular growth of cities such as Los Angeles, San Diego, San Antonio, and Seattle. Industries such as aircraft, electronics, and computers became highly dependent upon military support for research and development and then on the government to buy their finished products. A large proportion of the nation's scientists and engineers worked on military-related projects, and the expansion of the university system after World War II was based in part on the need to mobilize a skilled and educated workforce in the global struggle. New academic fields, such as computer science, emerged from the military, and established fields, notably physics and electrical engineering, became quite dependent upon military financing. The Internet was one spinoff of military research.

The Cold War greatly influenced the shape of industrial development in Europe and Asia. In the early phases of the Cold War, the United States greatly desired to stimulate the reindustrialization of West Germany and Japan, but it took steps to prevent either country from remilitarizing. As a consequence, both countries were largely freed from the financial burden of defending their own borders, a decision that by the 1980s the United States had reason to regret. In fact, some economists view the foreign military expenditures of the United States as an informal way to balance its trade surpluses from 1948 to 1968—and as a contributing factor in its subsequent trade deficits.

The Cold War was a major factor in the rise of Japan, South Korea, and Taiwan as industrial powers. Because these were all "front-line" states (bordering communist countries), the United States helped to underwrite their early efforts at industrialization, offering technical assistance, grants, and eventually access to markets. For instance, the Japanese car industry was given a boost during the Korean War when the United States bought its military trucks. As late as 1960, 10 percent of the Japanese economy derived from the military spending of the United States.

Although the Cold War technically ended in 1989 with the collapse of the Soviet system, the military continues to play a large role in the United States and Europe. As politicians have discovered, the "peace dividend" that many taxpayers looked forward to in the early 1990s went unrealized as many cities and industries mobilized to save what had become essential to their survival. Some analysts observe that the opportunity costs of continuing to subsidize military industries over civilian ones is a major factor in the decline of manufacturing of the United States.

See also Internet; Military-Industrial Complex; State, Role of the

Further Reading

Leffler, Melvyn P., and Odd Arne Westad, eds. *The Cambridge History of the Cold War*. New York: Cambridge University Press, 2009.

Markusen, Ann R., and Joel Yudken. *Dismantling the Cold War Economy*. New York: Basic Books, 1992.

COLONIZATION. *See* Imperialism

COMBINATION ACTS

In 1799 and 1800, inspired by fear of revolutionary agitation spreading from France, Britain passed acts forbidding combinations (what today are called unions) among workers—effectively making unions and strikes illegal. During the next two decades, the difficult early period of British industrialization, the acts were frequently invoked to justify arrest of working-class protest leaders. They were one factor (similar to laws in most other early industrializing societies) in keeping agitation down. Liberals often supported the acts, arguing that workers should negotiate freely but individually, for any group activity distorted free-market competition. As Britain passed through its most repressive phase, opinion shifted, as various leaders (including many liberals) saw that workers needed new rights to balance the power of employers. The Combination Acts were repealed in 1824, though various legal restrictions affected trade unions.

Further Reading

Hudson, Pat. *The Industrial Revolution*. New York: Bloomsbury, 1992.

COMMUNISM

Communism is the belief that economic production should be socially (or communally) controlled, directed, and owned. Although industrialization caused social upheaval for workers, many observers recognized that the new economic order could not only meet people's material needs but eventually liberate humanity from the scourge of poverty. Although each regional or national movement has its own influences, traditions, and history, the Paris Commune (1871) and the 1917 Russian Revolution are crucial moments in the history of world communism.

The Paris Commune was a complex and contradictory event, and many Communards were influenced by Karl Marx as well as by the anarchism of Mikhail Bakunin and Pierre-Joseph Proudhon. By operating factories, arming workers (to defend the city from the advancing Prussian army), and establishing free schools, Communards were attempting, and in many ways succeeding, to establish the first worker-run society. The implications of the Commune inflamed the passions of revolutionaries and reactionaries alike. Lenin would later term it a "festival of the oppressed," and many socialists and anarchists looked to the event as a precursor of a society struggling to be born. The upper and middle classes were also

Street demonstrators in Petrograd shot by the provisional government in July 1917. (Associated Press)

obsessed with the Commune, though for obviously different reasons, and they generally tolerated the French government's brutal suppression of Communards: twice as many people were killed as died in the French Revolution (1789–93).

Many communists believed that self-regulating communities of producers would form the basis of a new society and the communal ideal would play an important role in the Russian Revolution. The Bolsheviks came to power in 1917 in large part by promising to allow workers and peasants to run the factories and farms. However, whether by necessity (to defeat counterrevolutionaries) or by design, power quickly became concentrated in the Bolshevik, or Communist, Party. In 1921, revolutionary sailors near St. Petersburg (Krondstadt) rebelled against the Bolsheviks' suppression of the self-governing councils (soviets) of workers and soldiers. Many socialists and anarchists viewed the suppression of this commune as the final betrayal of the revolution. Subsequently, "large C" Communism became identified with Stalinist tactics, although "small c" noncommunist leftists tried to differentiate the ideal of communism from the flawed but "actually existing" socialism to be found in the Soviet Union. Communist revolutions throughout Europe after World War I failed; instead the Red Army proved the most efficient means of exporting Stalinism.

At the end of World War II, the Soviet Union occupied part of Germany, and all of Poland, Romania, Bulgaria, Czechoslovakia, and the Baltic states. Chinese communists won their civil war. By the late 1950s, the Soviet Union's method of economic development and intolerance of dissent had alienated even Mao Zedong, who advocated a different variation of Stalinism for China. Communism still attracted adherents, notably in Cuba and Vietnam. The Cubans sought to export revolution throughout the 1960s and 1970s, helping to push the Soviet Union to expand its support for various African societies. None benefited from the experiment.

Under Stalin's heirs, Soviet society had developed an informal social contract that many workers joked was "we pretend to work, you pretend to pay us." By the 1980s the Soviet Union had entered into an economic and political crisis from which it failed to recover, and Chinese leaders had begun to embrace capitalism more fully.

After 1989, communism was in full retreat worldwide. The Soviet Union lost control over Eastern Europe; soon enough, nationalist rebellions broke apart the Soviet Union. Communist parties in democratic countries struggled to remain viable; most found it prudent to rename themselves, dropping "communist" entirely. By the 2000s, communism was restricted to China, North Korea, Vietnam, and Cuba. In China, communists monopolized state power but abandoned most of the Soviet-style economics.

See also Great Leap Forward; Internationals; Stalinism; Syndicalism

Further Reading

Avrich, Paul. *Anarchist Portraits*. Princeton, NJ: Princeton University Press, 1988.

Claudin, Fernando. *The Communist Movement: From Comintern to Cominform*. New York: Monthly Review, 1975.

Eley, Geoff. *Forging Democracy: The History of the Left in Europe, 1850–2000*. New York: Oxford University Press, 2002.

Haupt, Georges. *Aspects of International Socialism, 1871–1914: Essays*. New York: Columbia University Press, 1986.

COMPANY UNION

The term "company union" is most commonly used to describe a union sponsored by a particular company to avoid negotiations with an independent union. Many Western firms intimidated or cajoled their workers into company unions around 1900, sometimes offering paternalistic benefits to its members. The effort won some success but did not deflect the growth of independent unions in Europe and the United States. Sometimes company unions developed into independent unions.

The related "enterprise" unions represent the workers at a particular firm. Enterprise unions generally exercise less leverage with companies than independent labor organizations. Enterprise unions are common in Japan and in the 1950s triumphed over left-wing industrial unions that made political and economic demands. While enterprise unions are not company unions, they did receive help from employers in defeating left-wing unions. Japanese enterprise unions typically maintained that they must help improve their company's productivity, whereas industrial unions saw their role as extending benefits to the entire working class rather than to one set of workers. Although enterprise unions do cooperate with each other in "spring offensives" to win better wages and working conditions, the temptation and pressures to strike an independent deal with one's own employer generally undermine unions' solidarity. Korean enterprise unions are extremely militant and then encourage workers to work hard to make up for production lost during strikes.

Further Reading

Brody, David. *Labor Embattled: History, Power, Rights*. Urbana: University of Illinois Press, 2005.

Rose, James D. *Duquesne and the Rise of Steel Unionism*. Urbana: University of Illinois Press, 2001.

COMPRADOR

In 1842, China was forced by European countries to open several of its ports (e.g., Hong Kong) as conduits for international trade. Compradors were Chinese middlemen (the term is Portuguese in origin) who put their knowledge of China's languages, culture, laws, and economy to use for Western companies—and often amassed their own fortunes. The term "comprador" has generally been used to describe a class of merchants or ruling class that relies on extensive foreign support to maintain its position.

In nineteenth-century China, merchants had lower status than artisans, farmers, or scholar-bureaucrats (the most prestigious social group). However, compradors' knowledge of Western languages, business practices, and technology made them invaluable to the Chinese government and to Chinese merchants. Compradors often headed Chinese industrial firms, such as the first steamship line, which was formed in 1873. Unlike traditional merchants, compradors generally did not seek to become scholars but preferred to stay in business.

Compradors were able to use networks of Chinese traders to help European merchants expand their trade throughout East Asia. By the early twentieth century, the comprador system began to decline as both Chinese and foreign merchants gained greater knowledge of each other's languages and markets; compradors disappeared entirely in the 1940s.

Further Reading

Bandarage, Asoka. *Colonialism in Sri Lanka: The Political Economy of the Kandyan Highlands, 1833–1886.* Berlin: Mouton, 1983.

Hao, Yen-p'ing. *The Commercial Revolution in Nineteenth Century China: The Rise of the Sino-Western Mercantile Capitalism.* Berkeley: University of California Press, 1986.

COMPUTERIZATION

Thinking machines have an ancient lineage. But modern computers owe much to the machine-tool industry. By the late nineteenth century, Hollerith machines mechanically sorted cards, which enabled national governments to amass and analyze vast amounts of data. The U.S. Census used Hollerith technology to compile social statistics for its decennial censuses. In the 1930s and 1940s, the Nazis relied on Hollerith machines to establish lists of who was Jewish or Aryan under their racial laws. The U.S. Social Security system used Hollerith machines to compute the benefits for millions of citizens. During World War II, both the Allies and the Axis used this technology to help organize complex logistical tasks, such as coordinating the shipment of goods and armies by rail.

After the war, computers began to refashion factory production; that process has accelerated over time. In the late 1940s, the U.S. government encouraged military contractors to use computers to help mechanize the machine tool industry. This process was described by novelist Kurt Vonnegut in the 1952 book *Player Piano.* Vonnegut had worked at General Electric and witnessed how workers' motions in tooling complex parts were copied by a machine and then played back, like a player piano. However, during the 1950s, most computerization was restricted to large companies using computers to process pay and benefits for its workers.

In the 1960s and 1970s, companies used computers to monitor the flow of materials in industrial processes. Computers enabled steel makers to accurately monitor and record the heat of a furnace as well as its ingredients. In time, computers made it cheaper to make smaller batches of specialty metal. By the 1990s, even in many developing countries such as South Africa, furnace workers no longer needed physical prowess so much as computer literacy. Computers enabled new facilities to eliminate production workers, relying on a handful of workers to oversee the machinery and to do repairs.

The growing processing capacity of computers, and their decreasing size and cost, accelerated the process of factory automation throughout most industries. For instance, in wine-bottling plants, computer-run machinery put wine into bottles, attached labels, and loaded crates onto pallets, and then stacked them onto the loading docks. In the 2000s, more factory jobs in the United States

Illustration of Herman Hollerith's electric sorting and tabulating machine, ca. 1895. (Library of Congress)

were lost to computerization and automation than to China. At the same time, automation was the leading cause of Chinese job loss as well.

Computers originally remade and automated the work of machinists, but in time, it has been applied to bank tellers and secretaries, as well as engineers, doctors, lawyers, and (ironically) computer scientists. Factories and offices have been emptied of workers, freeing them up for new forms of work, although some fear they will instead face a world without work.

Further Reading

Noble, David F. *America by Design: Science, Technology and the Rise of Corporate Capitalism*. New York: Knopf, 1977.

Zuboff, Shoshana. *In the Age of the Smart Machine: The Future of Work and Power*. New York: Basic Books, 1988.

COMPUTERS

Since the seventeenth century, mathematicians have recognized the desirability of a machine that could automatically process information. In the mid-seventeenth century, Blaise Pascal developed "thinking machines." In the 1830s, Charles Babbage and his female programmer, Augusta Ada, used punch cards in their "difference engine." Punch cards were later used in the partial automation of the U.S. Census in the 1890s. During World War II, the U.S. military turned to universities and corporate research laboratories, such as Bell Labs, to make important advances in both mechanical and electronic computers, such as automatic machines capable of rapid, complex calculations. Until the late 1950s, computers were expensive, used only by large governmental and corporate bureaucracies. Beginning in the 1960s, however, the size and cost of computers decreased, largely through the use of microchips; computers' speed increased; and their use expanded throughout society. Computers have helped to automate many different kinds of jobs and, combined with advances in communications technology, have made it easier for companies to decentralize production and distribution.

See also Computerization; University

Further Reading

Ceruzzi, Paul E. *A History of Modern Computing*. Cambridge, MA: MIT Press, 2003.

Cortada, James W. *Before the Computer: IBM, NCR, Burroughs, and Remington Rand and the Industry They Created, 1865–1956*. Princeton, NJ: Princeton University Press, 1993.

CONFÉDÉRATION GÉNÉRALE DU TRAVAIL (CGT)

Founded in 1894, this French national federation of unions long attempted to bypass the socialist political movement and its various disputing factions. Strongly influenced by the bourses du travail movement—local, largely artisanal labor exchanges—the CGT reflected France's strong craft traditions and revolutionary heritage. The movement did embrace industrial federations as well and combined frequently strident rhetoric with practical efforts to promote union growth. A general strike for an eight-hour day in 1906 brought government repression, and the federation became more moderate. After World War I, it was caught in splits between socialists and communists but remained the largest national union organization.

See also Internationals; Syndicalism

Further Reading

Moss, Bernard. *Origins of the French Labor Movement*. Berkeley: University of California Press, 1976.

CONGRESS OF INDUSTRIAL ORGANIZATIONS (CIO)

The Congress of Industrial Organizations was the largest federation of industrial unions in the United States. It was formed in 1935 as the Committee for Industrial Organization by a number of unionists within the American Federation of Labor who wished to organize unskilled workers in mass production industries. (The CIO changed its name to the Congress of Industrial Organizations in 1938.) After a brief period in the 1920s of "welfare capitalism," in which corporations sponsored new benefit programs, industrialists had responded to the Great Depression in the 1930s by slashing the wages and benefits of their workers. In sharp contrast to previously antiunion administrations, President Franklin Roosevelt signaled his tentative support for unions when he helped to pass legislation that aided unions, such as the National Industrial Recovery Act in 1933 and the Wagner Act in 1935. In the desperate conditions of the Depression, workers followed radical leaders who organized mass strikes of truck drivers in Minneapolis and dockworkers in San Francisco. Clearly, many unskilled workers, considered "unorganizable" by the AFL, were ready for unionization. At this juncture, it was the AFL that was not ready to change; it expelled the CIO in 1936.

The CIO used new tactics to organize mass-production industries. In 1936, autoworkers in Toledo seized upon a new tactic: the sit-down strike. Because of the continuous nature of production within automobile plants, even a small number of workers who shut down one part

A Congress of Industrial Organizations (CIO) strike in New York City, ca. 1938. (Franklin D. Roosevelt Presidential Library)

of the production process idled hundreds or even thousands of other workers. Workers learned that employers were far less likely to resort to violence inside their plants, because valuable machinery could be damaged. Thus sit-down strikes forced employers to negotiate with workers, which increased workers' sense of their power: employers had previously refused to even meet with unions. To organize workers throughout the industry, however, CIO organizers had to distribute leaflets to workers on the streets, leaving themselves vulnerable to attack. Before the industry was organized, unionists and company guards battled on many city streets around the entrances to factories. The turmoil of the auto industry probably convinced U.S. Steel in 1937 to recognize the CIO union, simply to avoid that kind of upheaval in its mill towns.

In a clear break with the AFL, the CIO organized both white and black workers. To this end, the CIO hired many communists as organizers, who were staunch antiracists. The head of the CIO, John L. Lewis of the United Mine Workers, was an anticommunist but rationalized his use of communists by observing: "Who gets the bird, the hunter or the dog?" By the 1940s, Lewis fired most of them from unions he controlled, such as steel and coal, although many communists remained in CIO unions in auto, meatpacking, electrical, and elsewhere. In the late 1940s, the CIO expelled the communist-dominated unions, leaving the labor movement divided and weak. In the postwar years, the CIO continued to expand its membership but slowly grew more conservative, and in 1955 it merged with the AFL. Though less radical than their predecessors, CIO unions proved instrumental in extending social welfare benefits such as raising the minimum wage, increasing the federal government support for education, and providing care for the aged. Former CIO unions, such as the Auto Workers, were also instrumental in promoting the passage of civil rights laws in the 1960s.

Further Reading

Bernstein, Irving. *Turbulent Years: A History of the American Worker*. Boston: Houghton Mifflin, 1970.
Lichtenstein, Nelson. *Labor's War at Home: The CIO in World War II*. Philadelphia: Temple University Press, 1982.

CONSTRUCTION INDUSTRY

Throughout the nineteenth century, most home construction was done by small-scale employers using highly skilled workers. Most contractors were former workers themselves. The growth of cities from the early nineteenth century onward necessitated a rapid growth in the construction industry. This growth, plus well-defined skills for carpenters, masons, and others, encouraged the spread of craft unionism throughout the industry. Although most employees retained their skills, there was some innovation in housing construction. Beginning in the 1830s, working-class homes in the United States were made with "balloon" frames of inexpensive wood studs held together with machine-made nails (instead of complex joints); by the 1870s, precut wooden studs were widely available. By 1900, new equipment, including mechanized saws and preformed concrete, was altering work patterns. In the 1940s, homes for the lower middle class were mass produced throughout suburban "Levittowns." Levitt relied not only on what mechanization was available (power saws, bulldozers) but on a simple, repetitive design in which the work was subdivided, allowing gangs of workers to increase their productivity. Large-scale construction projects, such as skyscrapers, dams, or airports, have been dominated by large companies because they require vast amounts of technical expertise and capital—as well as political connections to obtain the contracts.

See also Infrastructure; Kaiser, Henry

Further Reading

Christie, Robert A. *Empire in Wood: A History of the Carpenter's Union*. Ithaca, NY: Cornell University Press, 2011.

CONSUMERISM AND MASS CONSUMPTION

Consumerism is the term used to describe "a culture of consumption," which analyzes not only the influence of mass consumption on economic development but also the cultural and social dimensions of what Marxists call "commodity fetishism," a preoccupation with turning human qualities—like beauty—as well as goods into consumption items. Since the mid-nineteenth century, mass consumption of manufactured goods and services has become more important to developed industrial societies.

Some of the most exciting recent work on consumerism has uncovered the origins and rapid gains of the phenomenon in the eighteenth century, particularly in Britain but also to an extent in Western Europe and North America. Large numbers of people acquired a new passion for imported goods like sugar, tea, and coffee. New home furnishings and table settings became more sought after. The eagerness for stylish clothing led to a rise in secondhand shops and in clothing thefts. Store owners began to set up more attractive displays and to advertise. Fads—always a facet of consumerism—supported abandoning old clothing styles in favor of the latest fashion. Early consumerism responded to new opportunities based on Europe's favorable position in world trade. Cheaper clothing allowed ordinary people to mimic and subtly challenge the lifestyles of the upper classes. This phenomenon was observed by Adam Smith. Above all, consumerism helped set the market for greater output, thus motivating new industry and production methods. Although the pressures of early industrialization reduced the interest of poor urban workers (or work-oriented manufacturers) in consumerism, the pattern was launched; the next round of consumerism, later in the nineteenth century, clearly built upon earlier trends.

While a large portion of manufactured goods (railroads, iron and steel, machine tools, and chemicals) produced by industrial corporations in the mid-nineteenth century were directed toward factories or infrastructure projects, an increasing number of goods, such as sewing machines and processed foods, began to be mass marketed to middle-class consumers. Furthermore, by the late nineteenth century, more middle-class people worked as clerical workers or professionals than as farmers and small businessmen, and consequently, their cultural values began to change. The dominant virtues of hard physical work, savings, and self-reliance began to be replaced by new mores that valued leisure and the goods and services available for purchase in the market.

The transformation in middle-class lifestyle (and, equally important, the changed expectations of what daily life should be) was painful and resulted in heightened levels of anxiety. While ministers and the new professions of doctors and psychologists attempted to put the collective mind of the middle class at ease, advertisers began to suggest that consumption of goods could also alleviate troubles. By the late nineteenth and early twentieth centuries, advertisers began to shift from offering technical information about their products to suggesting that their products could fulfill their customers' emotional needs and desires. Interestingly, to invoke a higher modern authority, by the 1910s and 1920s many advertisers relied on white-coated "doctors" and "scientists" who promoted their products by promising they would cure real or imagined problems.

Because members of the working class had less money to spend (or saved what little they had to get them through bouts of unemployment), workers were slower to join the culture of consumption. However, many poor families could go to the movies or amusement parks, buy processed foods and cigarettes, or purchase a radio. The lack of workers' purchasing power was seen by some industrialists in the early twentieth century, such as Henry Ford, as a problem. Because industrial workers in mass-production industries (such as automobiles or electrical equipment) produced more and more goods, some employers felt they could pay their workers higher wages (which also prevented the unionization of their factories). Nonetheless, it was uncommon before 1920 for working-class families to purchase "consumer durables" such as radios, washing machines, refrigerators, or automobiles. That quickly changed. In the 1920s, companies began to extend consumers' credit to purchase items, encouraging greater consumption and production of goods. During the Great Depression, many workers lost the radios, cars, and furniture they had bought in more prosperous times.

Many of the Keynesian policies after World War II were directed at expanding the purchasing power of workers and the middle class in developed countries such as North America, Western Europe, and Japan. Consumerism was an important feature that offset the crisis of "under consumption" and prevented the global industrial system from slipping back into depression after 1945. The ability of workers to participate in consumerism (albeit interrupted by the Great Depression in the 1930s) was seen by many workers and most middle-class observers as proof of the genius of the capitalist economic and political system. In 1959, Vice President Richard Nixon told Nikita Khrushchev in the famous "kitchen debate" that the United States was more of a "workers' state" than the Soviet Union because "44 million families own 56 million cars, 50 million television sets, 143 million radios ... and 31 million own their homes."

By offering workers the opportunity to improve their standard of living, particularly after World War II in the West, consumerism has long been assumed to have depoliticized workers. Rank-and-file communists recall that during the 1950s it was hard to interest workers in socialism when workers had "never had it so good." Even in Japan, which lagged in consumerism because of low wages and devotion to savings, consumer interests increased by the 1950s, a process encouraged by large department stores and advertising. Before the 1980s, many observers argued that Eastern European and Soviet workers chafed under their regimes because they were denied consumer products such as cars. Some scholars have observed that even in the United States the influence of consumerism on politics has more often been assumed than proven; they point to examples of boycotts led by unions or civil rights groups. Current studies of consumerism explore how different groups establish personal meanings by acquiring goods and how consumerist values spread to other areas, as in the "selling" of political candidates.

Beginning in the 1990s, social scientists began to pay more attention to the ways that consumption is linked to social status. The increasing purchasing power of the wealthy, due to more favorable tax policies, globalization, and other factors, enabled them to spend more money on larger homes, luxury cars, and status symbols such as expensive clothes and watches. The result was to increase the cost of "respectability" for the near-rich and the increasingly hard-pressed middle class. The size of homes grew larger than incomes, a fact made possible by consumer debt. This phenomenon fueled the housing bubble in the United States, Spain, and other countries and contributed substantially to the financial crisis beginning in 2007.

Further Reading

Brewer, John, and Roy Porter, eds. *Consumption and the World of Goods*. London: Routledge, 1993.

Cohen, Lizabeth. *Making a New Deal: Industrial Workers in Chicago, 1919–1939*. New York: Cambridge University Press, 1990.

Fox, Richard Wightman, and T. J. Jackson Lears, eds. *The Culture of Consumption: Critical Essays in American History, 1880–1980*. New York: Pantheon, 1983.

Frank, Robert H. *Falling Behind: How Rising Inequality Hurts the Middle Class*. Berkeley: University of California Press, 2007.

CONTAINERIZATION

Shipping has always been an important cost for manufacturers. Late in the twentieth century, international shippers arrived at a standard-size metal container. Once loaded onto the box, goods could be transported by rail, truck, or ship. The weight of the metal increased the fuel costs, but that was more than made up for by the lowered labor costs in loading and offloading containers. In the twenty-first century, an iconic image of globalization is that of cargo ships, some almost 400 meters long, with hundreds of boxes packed on their decks.

Early in the Industrial Revolution, it was often cheaper to ship goods across the Atlantic than to move them 50 miles over land. Part of the reason was that ships had to be unloaded by gangs of men, and then horse-drawn wagons had to be prepared by men as well. A few mines or manufacturers packed goods into wooden boxes or barrels to make it easier to load onto barges or ships. In the early 1900s, railroads in the United Kingdom used metal or wooden rectangular boxes for shipping, but the practice did not spread to other countries. Beginning in the late 1920s, some U.S. railroads carried trucks on railroad cars, and one shipping company loaded railroad cars onto ships bound for Cuba.

The American military helped develop containerization because it had to ship enormous quantities of goods. During the Korean War, the military shipped steel boxes (CONEX, or Container Express) that cut shipping times in half and also reduced theft at ports. There were huge advantages to loading a box once and then shipping it by truck, rail, or ship (intermodal) across the country or around the world. By the mid-1950s, ships were being built just to handle intermodal boxes. There was a lengthy process of arriving at standard sizes and labeling practices that finally culminated in the early 1970s.

New types of cranes were needed on docks to handle the containers and the new ships; they dramatically reduced the need for workers. As ships grew larger, ports had to invest in new cranes, handling facilities, and computers, or lose most of their business.

Containerization increased the speed, and lowered the costs, of international shipping. Along with improved electronics, computerization, and the Internet, containerization helped accelerate the process of shifting factories to lower-wage countries. In the early twenty-first century, over one-quarter of all shipping originated in China; 8 of the 10 busiest ports in the world are in East Asia.

There are environmental costs to increased shipping. Ships transport maritime species from one port to another. New species of fish can drive out commercially viable stocks; fast-growing mussels can clog the intake pipes for factories. Dealing with invasive species is an expensive proposition. It is unclear how many goods wash overboard from container ships. In one case, rubber ducks shipped from China were swept overboard in the North Pacific and washed up on shores as far away as Alaska and North Carolina.

Further Reading

Levinson, Marc. *The Box: How the Shipping Container Made the World Smaller and the World Economy Bigger*. Princeton, NJ: Princeton University Press, 2006.

COOPERATIVES

Early industrialization was launched on a firmly capitalist basis, with major firms regarded as the private property of the owner. Not surprisingly, many people who objected to industrialization, at least as currently organized, began to think of alternatives to this arrangement. Ideas of cooperative organization were part of almost all utopian socialist schemes, such as those of Robert Owen in Britain and Charles Fourier and Pierre Proudhon in France. Utopians argued that private property allowed some people to profit from the labor of others—hence Proudhon's dramatic phrase "property is theft." A cooperative alternative, or cooperative, in which ownership would be shared by those involved, would distribute rewards equitably and would allow all participants to make decisions about how work was to be organized. Utopian communities in Europe and the United States always used cooperative principles.

The first large-scale cooperative effort originated with the British Rochdale Equitable Pioneers in 1844. The founders, 28 weavers in a town near Manchester, focused on buying groceries, selling them at standard market prices (to avoid annoying other shopkeepers), but then distributing profits to members of the cooperative, in proportion to purchases, at the end of the year. Members also voted

A bird's-eye view of one of the model communities at New Harmony, Indiana, in 1825. (Library of Congress)

on all policy issues, and a small part of the profits was reserved for mutual education efforts. The cooperative flourished, numbering 8,000 branches by the 1870s; by the 1860s, the movement branched out into wholesaling and began to manufacture some of the commodities sold. Well before this point, cooperative stores modeled on the Rochdale example began to spread to other countries. In Germany, a large cooperative movement sprang up in the 1850s, organized by Franz Schulze-Delitzsch and emphasizing banks and credit societies as well as cooperative stores. Consumer cooperatives never displaced other forms of retailing, though they caused concern to private store owners, but they definitely added a new option for consumers.

The cooperative movement also spread strongly among peasants in Western Europe and farmers in the United Sates from the 1860s onward. Cooperatives could help small agricultural producers acquire seeds, fertilizers, and equipment at lower cost through buying in bulk; they could provide credit; and they could help market and process produce. Cooperatives helped Danish peasants obtain the capital needed to convert to more market dairy farming, and cooperatives in many countries helped sell dairy products at favorable prices. The movement allowed rural producers to bargain more effectively with large wholesalers, shippers, and equipment manufacturers.

Cooperatives were sometimes attempted in factory production, but they rarely succeeded. Because factories seemed to need a management hierarchy, cooperative insistence on lots of participation and joint decision making could prove inefficient. Other cooperatives, trying to be efficient, disappointed their worker-members by failing to change working conditions appreciably.

A variation on the cooperative model is the employee stock ownership plan (ESOP). ESOPs are owned in part or in total by the workers at the company. ESOPs encourage higher productivity because workers see the company as their own. Workers at ESOPs have about three times the levels of savings of workers at traditional corporations. About half of *Forbes* magazine's annual list of "best companies to work for" are ESOPs. ESOPS are vastly more difficult for other companies to take over, and consequently, they can invest in new machinery with greater confidence. There are ESOPs in a variety of countries, such as the Mondragon cooperatives in Spain. About 8 percent of corporate equity is ESOPs, with more than 10 million workers covered by a plan.

Further Reading

Williams, Richard C. *The Cooperative Movement: Globalization from Below.* Aldershot, UK: Ashgate, 2007.

CORN LAWS

Britain began levying tariffs on grain imports to protect its farmers, as early as the sixteenth century; more modern regulations, called Corn Laws for the generic British term for grain, began in 1660. Rates rose and fell as a result of eighteenth-century legislation. Grain growing increased during the Napoleonic Wars, but when peace returned, farmers (including aristocratic estate owners) faced falling prices. A new Corn Law in 1815 established higher tariffs (though in fact prices continued to fall).

For years thereafter, manufacturing interests battled to reduce grain tariffs; their interest was in cheap food, whether imported or not, so that workers might be given lower wages. The issue was also ideological—liberal theory argued for free trade as the best way to stimulate production and maximize prosperity; and it was symbolic—the growing industrial middle class battled the aristocracy for political power. Several partial reductions did not end the dispute. An Anti-Corn Law League emerged in 1836, headed by the liberal Richard Cobden and backed by many factory owners. The league benefited from the larger middle-class vote that was allowed in the Reform Bill of 1832. After much agitation, the Corn Law was repealed in 1846, establishing Britain as a leader in free trade.

See also Agriculture; Enclosure Movement; Protectionism

Further Reading

Hudson, Pat. *The Industrial Revolution.* New York: Bloomsbury, 1992.

CORPORATIONS

Corporations are companies that can accumulate investment funds from many individual investors. They emerged only after industrialization was well under way. The need to amass extensive capital to form and expand large industrial firms emerged quickly with the Industrial Revolution. The initial response in Western countries

A political cartoon from 1873 shows Uncle Sam scolding corporate miscreants for stealing the cake; the cartoon refers to the Crédit Mobilier scandal, which purportedly raised moneys for the construction of the transcontinental railroad. (North Wind Picture Archives)

was to apply the joint stock form, which was already well established in overseas commerce. Joint stock operations allowed several wealthy investors to pool their capital to set up such enterprises as new metallurgical factories or railroads. But the conventional joint stock operation had one obvious constraint: any investor could be held liable for the debts of an entire firm, should it go bankrupt or be sued. This constraint limited the number of joint-stock companies and confined most investors to the ranks of the very wealthy, who could know the industrial operation intimately as well as gain some assurance about the solidity of their coinvestors.

One way out of this constraint on pooling capital was through government involvement via government-backed bonds. This method was used for many railroads (in the United States, large land grants to railroads had somewhat the same effect, making investment less risky) and also for big industrial investment banks like the Crédit Mobilier, formed by the French government in 1852 to promote business financing.

The common solution after 1850 was to pass legislation permitting joint stock companies, or corporations, to form with limited liability—that is, the investor was liable only for the amount of his or her investment. Many countries hesitated to embrace this innovation, worried that it would encourage irresponsible corporate behavior; but the lure of amassing more capital from more diverse investors, including relatively small ones, was too great to resist. Limited liability laws passed in most European countries. France, for example, passed a law in 1863 and further liberalized it four years later. The corporate form spread very rapidly thereafter; it was used in most branches of industry, particularly in heavy industry. Mergers were often arranged in the corporate form, for example, the United States Steel Corporation, which carried on the firms of Andrew Carnegie and many mine owners. Joint stock financing was widely used in investment banking, helping banks assume a growing role in setting up and rearranging industrial operations, particularly toward mergers and vertical and horizontal integrations. Hundreds of corporations formed each decade after 1870 in the major industrial countries, allowing massive industrial expansion and greatly increasing the size of the average firm. Thus corporations promoted further industrial growth and innovation and also served as the financial basis for the age of big business—an age that still describes most capitalist countries.

Nations seeking to industrialize usually imitated this feature of Western business law. Russia gained its first joint stock bank in 1864. During the reform era of the 1860s and 1870s, limited liability law was extended, and the number of corporations rose rapidly.

The rise of the limited liability corporation also promoted the growth of business investment on the part of the middle as well as the upper class. It served as the basis for the rapid growth of stock markets, where limited liability shares could be bought and sold. In the twentieth century, it became an increasingly international phenomenon, as investment in foreign as well as domestic corporations surged—an obvious way to direct capital from wealthy countries to settings where capital was in short supply but industrial opportunity growing. Also in the twentieth century—quite visibly by the 1920s and again after World War II—the corporate form could support nonproductive investment behavior, as stocks were bought and sold not because of industrial potential but as means of manipulating stock prices and earning windfall investment profits.

See also Joint Stock Companies; Mergers

Further Reading

Chandler, Alfred D., Jr. *The Visible Hand: The Managerial Revolution in American Business.* Cambridge, MA: Belknap Press, 1977.

CORPORATISM

This economic policy was designed to organize an industrial economy in a way that offered an alternative to capitalism and socialism. It harks back somewhat to preindustrial traditions in which artisans or merchants organized into guilds or corporations to assure quality of production, harmony within the group over any divisive competitive advantage, and good relations among various segments of the labor force. Corporatism of the twentieth-century variety was touted as a means of checking the exploitation possible under capitalism while also reducing class conflict.

Corporatism was widely discussed in many countries, by certain British socialists as well as by conservative leaders in Europe and Latin America. Fascist leaders, however, actually came closest to implementing corporatism as a policy. Mussolini's Italy moved first. During the 1920s, the Italian government abolished strikes and required government approval of all worker associations. Corporatist rhetoric urged collaboration between employers and workers. The government regulated work by adopting an annual vacation with pay and some improvements in social insurance (Labor Charter, 1927). Employer and worker associations were required to cooperate with government agencies. The idea was that each major industry would form an overarching corporation to further labor-management cooperation, topped by a National Council of Corporations. In fact, most of the corporations were little more than paper constructions, though fascist leaders tried to use some councils to coordinate economic policies. Private enterprise still prevailed, along with fairly rapid industrial growth, and the main result of the corporate economy was to undermine independent trade unions. A similar pattern took shape in Nazi Germany.

Corporatist policies also spread to Francoist Spain and to parts of Latin America. In Brazil between 1930 and 1945, under the regime of Getulio Vargas, corporatist rhetoric flourished, and the government intervened regularly in labor disputes in the interest of preventing strikes. Here, too, industrial growth occurred, but labor was held down.

See also Perónism

Further Reading

Malloy, James M. *Authoritarianism and Corporatism in Latin America*. Pittsburgh, PA: University of Pittsburgh Press, 1977.

COTTON

Cotton, one of the principal fibers to be utilized in mechanized textile production, had been grown and used in manufacture in India but was a new product in Europe in the eighteenth century. Increasing British production (resulting partly from bans on Indian imports) thus fed a new consumer interest, one of the first cases of the connection between industrial production and changing taste. American Cotton had longer threads and worked well with machines because it did not break easily. Cotton clothing was lighter and cooler than wool, and became quite popular. Carding, spinning, and weaving devices were applied from the mid-eighteenth century onward, and because there was little traditional production and so little stake in preindustrial procedures, machines gained ground very rapidly. The utility of cotton was boosted by the invention of the cotton gin, which separated the seed from the fiber of the cotton plant. Cotton became cheaper and more prevalent.

Cotton cloth could be dyed and printed in many colors and designs. This, plus its low cost, attracted popular taste, changing clothing habits very quickly. Cotton was also easily laundered, which improved hygiene. Conversion to cotton clothing was a significant improvement in the standard of living of the lower class and in the variety and fashionability of apparel widely evident by the 1820s and 1830s. The rapidly expanding production of cotton, a major industrial export, called for increasing supply. Not only the southern United States and India but also Egypt and, later, parts of Africa turned to cotton growing for commercial export. Some of these regions benefited from export earnings, but others (such as Mozambique under Portuguese rule) relied on poorly paid labor. Some land was put to cotton production at the expense of basic foodstuffs, worsening economic conditions for the local peasantry, as in parts of sub-Saharan Africa such as Mozambique in the first half of the twentieth century. In short, cotton reflected a variety of features, both advantageous and disadvantageous, of industrialization as a global process.

Further Reading

Riello, Giorgio, and Prasannan Parthasarathi, eds. *The Spinning World: A Global History of Cotton Textiles, 1200–1850.* New York: Oxford University Press, 2009.

COTTON GIN

The cotton gin was invented by Eli Whitney in 1793 to separate cotton fiber from the seed. Before the existence of this machine, a person had to spend a full day handpicking the seeds from a pound of fiber. With cotton fabric gaining popularity,

The cotton gin revitalized the U.S. cotton industry. (Library of Congress)

and machines increasing the output of thread, the need for a better method of initial processing was pressing. The gin feeds harvested cotton through a row of rapidly revolving saws, the teeth of which pull the cotton from the seeds; ribs between the saws prevent the seeds from passing through. The cotton gin not only supported the industrialization of cotton production, it also increased the importance of slavery in the southern United States, where cotton cultivation spread to new areas such as Alabama and Mississippi.

Further Reading

Lakwete, Angela. *Inventing the Cotton Gin: Machine and Myth in Antebellum America.* Baltimore: Johns Hopkins University Press, 2005.

CRANES

Loading cranes, based on cranks (winches) and pulleys, are an ancient device long used by merchants and ship owners. With industrialization, especially by the late nineteenth century, new materials and machines could be applied to cranes, making them bigger, more mobile, and capable of carrying much heavier loads. Metal cranes, using metal cables instead of rope and powered by internal combustion engines, spread in metallurgical plants and on docks and construction sites. Cranes could also be placed on rails, for lateral mobility, or on truck beds. Many unskilled workers, previously employed for crude hauling, were displaced by the new kinds of cranes, though the increasing volume of goods to be moved or loaded preserved some employment. Mechanical cranes and derricks allowed construction of new structures like the skyscraper, introduced in the United States soon after 1900, for which materials had to be lifted to great heights. Mechanical cranes, a logical, fairly simple technical outgrowth of industrialization, thus transformed a number of aspects of labor, transportation, and urban life. Throughout the twentieth century, cranes became larger, for instance, to move shipping containers.

See also Containerization; Dockers

Further Reading

Cipolla, Carlo M. *Before the Industrial Revolution: European Society and Economy, 1000–1700.* New York: Norton, 1993.

CROMPTON, SAMUEL (1753–1827)

The inventor of the spinning mule (1779) was one of a long line of eighteenth-century English inventors who established the technological basis for the industrialization of textiles. The mule, like the spinning jenny, contained a movable carriage with spindles, but rollers were used automatically to feed the fibers to the spindles; when the yarn was partly spun, the feed rollers stopped and the spinning was completed at high tension. This made possible the spinning of finer cotton threads for muslins (in contrast to Arkwright's cruder water frame). Thread could be spun not only far faster but also much finer than by the human hand. It was estimated that by 1812 one-half to two-thirds of the English cotton industry depended on mule-spun thread. Both processes, the frame and the mules, are still used in modern textiles. Crompton had to sell his patent for next to nothing because of poverty.

See also Lawrence, Abbott; Textiles

Further Reading

Hills, Richard L. *Power in the Industrial Revolution.* Manchester, UK: Manchester University Press, 1970.

CRYSTAL PALACE EXHIBITION (1851)

Sponsored by Britain in 1851, this great international exhibition, held in an iron and glass pavilion itself a mark of industrialization, celebrated the British industrial lead. Huge crowds of people from all social classes pressed to see the latest industrial wonders in a display designed to convince that industrialization meant progress. Foreign observers were stimulated to greater efforts at imitation, seeing the triumph of British machines, though individual displays, like Krupp's in metallurgy, surprised the British hosts by their sophistication. Many industrial exhibitions followed in the nineteenth and twentieth centuries as a means of competitive display; they spread industrial knowledge, and they certainly showed the increasingly international scope of economic change.

View of the south side of the Crystal Palace in London during the 1851 Great Exhibition of the Works of Industry of All Nations. (Library of Congress)

Further Reading

Hobhouse, Hermione. *The Crystal Palace and the Great Exhibition: Art, Science, and Productive Industry*. New York: Continuum, 2002.

CUNARD STEAMSHIP COMPANY

This British company, founded by Samuel Cunard (1787–1865) in 1840, was the first great transatlantic steamship line. Steamship development had concentrated in the United States, where it was vital on river ways. But British coastal steamships began to increase after 1827. Seagoing steamships were not developed until 1838, when four steam vessels crossed the Atlantic. The results pleased the owners, though tremendous amounts of coal had to be used. On the basis of these results, the Cunard Company launched its service with a fleet of four ships, which had to use about 40 percent of their carrying capacity for coal. Until the 1860s, the Cunard operation focused on shipments of mail. But then improved engine construction, using higher pressures, reduced the coal needs, and the steamship began to come into its own for passenger as well as transport use. Cunard himself introduced iron steamers (1855) and screws instead of paddle wheels (1862). The Cunard line remained a major player in Atlantic and other oceanic operations into the later twentieth century.

See also Steamboat

Further Reading

Butler, Daniel Allen. *The Age of Cunard: A Transatlantic History 1839–2003*. Annapolis, MD: Lighthouse, 2003.

D

DAEWOO

Daewoo is a South Korean "chaebol" or holding company. Its strategy in the world market has been to compete fiercely at the bottom rungs of a number of different markets rather than concentrating on a single product. This strategy was remarkably successful. In the early 1970s, for instance, Daewoo produced no ships, but by the mid-1980s, it had become the second-largest shipbuilder in South Korea, which had become the world's premier shipbuilding nation. Daewoo's rise depended not only on the assistance of the Korean government but also on the collective technical, financial, and organizational assets of the different companies within the chaebol.

Further Reading

Graham, Edward Montgomery. *Reforming Korea's Industrial Conglomerates*. Washington, DC: Institute for International Economics, 2003.

DECOLONIZATION

Decolonization is the process by which former colonies rid themselves of direct political and economic control from metropolitan countries. World War II greatly weakened the industrialized European countries with colonies in Asia and Africa (England, France, Holland, and Belgium) and destroyed outright the empires of Italy and Japan. By the mid-1960s, most of the Asian and African nationalist movements had won their independence from colonial powers through either wars (Algeria, Kenya) or mass movements (India, Ghana). However, more difficult than winning political freedom was the struggle for economic independence.

As a matter of policy, most metropolitan countries had shaped their colonies into suppliers of cheap raw materials. Decolonized countries often attempted to industrialize and thereby gain more control over their economic lives and to increase the standards of living of their populations. However, the legacy of colonialization was difficult to overcome. The colonies inherited physical infrastructure such as railroads and roads that had been developed to move raw materials efficiently from the interior to the coast. Moreover, the social infrastructure such as education and social services was generally quite underdeveloped. The former Belgian Congo provides an extreme example: upon independence it had less than 20 college graduates. After decolonization, the state played an important role in the industrialization process (or attempt) because former colonies lacked a vigorous class of capitalists and in part because many nationalist leaders were influenced by socialist theories of

Louis Mountbatten was the last viceroy of India and oversaw (some say engineered) the partition of India and Pakistan in 1947. (Library of Congress)

development. After 1947, the Indian state expanded the educational system, nationalized certain industries, and offered financial incentives for others. In South Korea, the state encouraged the formation of large business conglomerates very similar to the zaibatsus of their former colonizers, the Japanese.

Many of these new nations have experienced severe political instability such as ethnic wars, border conflicts, and political repression. This has been compounded by economic turmoil. By the 1980s, the economies of many countries in sub-Saharan Africa were in outright decline. The historical experience of Latin America in the nineteenth century, which also underwent a process of decolonization, suggests that it often takes decades to develop the institutions necessary for a stable nation-state. Even a stable nation-state, however, is no guarantor of successful industrialization, as the case of Argentina makes clear. The difficulty of Latin American countries to industrialize has led many scholars to analyze the neocolonial policies of industrialized countries, which discourage industrialization by refusing to open their markets to industrial goods or by dumping manufactured goods in local markets and thus undercutting fledgling industrial firms.

In the late 1980s, a third wave of decolonization occurred as countries in Eastern Europe and the former Soviet Union gained their political independence. Much of

Eastern Europe was industrialized, but most countries have found it difficult to make the transition from a centralized economy to the capitalist marketplace. A few countries, such as Yugoslavia and some of the countries in the Caucus mountains, experienced wars that devastated them. In most cases, political independence was swiftly followed by rapid deindustrialization. East Germany was absorbed into a wealthy West Germany, but for many, the process has been painful. A few countries, such as Hungary, Poland, and the Czech Republic, have prospered following their decolonization. Proximity to Western Europe helps; Slovakia, for instance, has developed into a major automobile producer. Many of the countries that were once part of the former Soviet Union appear headed for a prolonged period of political autocracy with limited prospects for economic development.

See also Finance Capital; Maquiladoras; World Bank; World Systems Theory

Further Reading

Grimal, Henri. *Decolonization: The British, French and Belgian Empires, 1919–1963*. Boulder, CO: Westview, 1978.
Smith, Tony, ed. *The End of the European Empires: Decolonization after World War II*. Lexington, MA: Heath, 1975.

DEFLATION. *See* Inflation and Deflation

DEINDUSTRIALIZATION

Deindustrialization is the dismantling or destruction of manufacturing or industry. Over the last 200 years, the dynamic nature of capitalism has generally involved the spectacular rise and fall of specific industries in regions or countries. The history of deindustrialization suggests that market forces, new technology, governmental policies, and industrialists' decisions and investment patterns are possible causes of deindustrialization.

The rise of the British textile industry in the late eighteenth century destroyed the hand-loom trade in Great Britain and textile producers in India. Although the replacement of mechanized looms for hand-powered ones was inevitable in economic terms, the fate of Indian textiles was sealed by the mercantilist policies of the British imperial government, which actively sought to create a reserve market for British products. The government maintained policies that largely kept India as a captive market for British textile mills; deindustrialization here meant the displacement of hundreds of thousands of workers. Throughout the nineteenth century, the technological supremacy of British industry meant that if national governments could not protect local manufacturers through tariffs, as in the case of France and the United States, the cheaper British imports rapidly displaced local producers. Thus, throughout much of Latin America, many women lost their textile manufacturing jobs in the 1830s and 1840s. As industrialization proceeded throughout the world, even well-established industries could fall. By 1919, jute-weaving mills in

Scotland (at least the ones that produced twine and coarse bagging for raw cotton) were successfully displaced by mills in Calcutta, which had cheaper labor and were located closer to raw materials. In some cases, Scottish mills were dismantled and moved to India.

Even within national boundaries, established crafts or industries can be deindustrialized by new technology, market forces, or corporate policies. In the 1850s, the petroleum industry replaced whale oil with its own products as a source of light and eventually robbed coal of much of its market for heating homes and powering industry. Advances in mechanized rolling of sheet metal in the 1920s, a response to the rising demands of the automobile industry, displaced many hand-rolling mills in the Pittsburgh region. Large coal regions in Europe and the United States began to experience deindustrialization in the 1920s, which resulted in a massive loss of jobs. Deindustrialization can also result from corporate policies to avoid unions or move to be closer to cheaper labor. After a bitter textile strike in the 1920s, for instance, many New England-based companies shifted their mills to the nonunion South.

After World War II, corporations' ties to specific countries weakened as multinational corporations took advantage of the global lowering of tariffs that resulted from the Bretton Woods Agreement. The experience of coordinating production and distribution of goods throughout the world further weakened the ties between corporations and their "home" country. From the 1970s onward, many U.S. firms shifted their factories to northern Mexico after the U.S. and Mexican governments had reduced tariffs and other trade barriers. As a result of the efforts of the World Bank/IMF, many countries throughout the world have reduced their barriers to foreign investment by limiting taxation and easing restrictions on the export of profits. Not surprisingly, there has been enormous growth in free-trade zones in places as diverse as the Caribbean, Chile, and the Philippines. In this scenario, companies shift production plants from one country to another in search of the most favorable business climate. Sheer international growth has produced new levels of production in important industries such as steel and textiles, resulting in deindustrialization in parts of the United States, Europe, and Japan. Since the 1970s in the United States, deindustrialization has dramatically reduced the size of the manufacturing labor force. In the 2000s, one-third of the manufacturing workforce disappeared.

Perhaps the most dramatic case of deindustrialization occurred in the 20 years following the breakup of the Soviet Union. Industrial production has fallen by more than 50 percent, partly in response to the shutdown of inefficient facilities. Even relatively modern factories—in Poland, for example—lost their former markets in the Soviet Union and suffered until they gained access to new markets. Western Europe, coping with its own problems of deindustrialization and unemployment, initially refused to allow Eastern European producers access to their markets.

Another factor resulting from the collapse of the Soviet state is sheer larceny. The proceeds from the sale of valuable machines, raw materials, or products such as petroleum have often simply been stolen by unscrupulous managers. Moscow has become the largest consumer of German luxury automobiles even as many former industrial workers are desperately seeking day-labor jobs throughout Western Europe.

The systematic loss of industry not only results in direct unemployment and massive disruption in many working-class families but also causes a negative ripple effect as service sector workers are displaced. In the United States during the 1970s and 1980s, small tool-and-die shops that relied on contracts with automobile companies also went out of business. Perhaps the most pernicious effect of deindustrialization is that it reduces tax revenues and weakens the ability of government to respond to economic and social crisis. In the early 1980s, some local governments in U.S. "rust belt" towns unscrewed the lightbulbs in streetlights because they simply could not afford to pay their electric bills. Numerous corporations have used the threat of relocation to lower their tax bill or to request easing of environmental or safety regulations.

Different countries have responded variously to the problems of deindustrialization. In the case of the United States, the federal government under both Democratic and Republican regimes has refused to intervene to directly subsidize heavy industry. Aid to hard-hit areas has been minimal; many steel-mill towns in Pennsylvania and Ohio that were deindustrialized in the 1970s and 1980s are still largely devastated. Japanese steel towns benefited from their companies' paternalism, for the companies have subsidized new industries. Because of their strong trade unions and Social Democratic traditions, Western European governments generally expanded unemployment benefits, added jobs in government industries, or increased their emphasis on education. French unions have forced their government simply to increase state subsidies to the steel industry there. In the late 1970s, Margaret Thatcher, in England, pioneered the path of radical reduction of government services to workers.

Globalization has created new levels of competition, resulting in the closing of older or less efficient factories. Advocates of reduced tariffs argue that it costs the country more to protect a job in shoe making or textiles than it saves the country as a whole in cheaper prices. Some labor economists argue that the result is not "free trade." Workers in manufacturing face competition from abroad, but numerous protections are placed in agreements for drug companies, or for professionals. Numerous laws and policies prevent the immigration of qualified doctors, lawyers, and dentists from poorer countries to richer ones.

Deindustrialization is a major problem for many formerly industrialized countries. The ability of government to counteract the loss of jobs is limited. Another factor is the growing power of corporations to relocate plants from one region or country to another. In the United States, hundreds of billions of dollars have been spent by local and state governments since the 1970s to attract new jobs. While this makes perfect sense for a locality, the effect on the number of jobs within the nation has been limited. Throughout the world, some countries (notably Hong Kong) or regions, such as the Docklands in the East of London, have benefited from free-trade zones. But overall, factories are far more mobile than workers.

See also Dual Labor Markets; World Systems Theory

Further Reading

Bluestone, Barry, and Bennett Harrison. *The Deindustrialization of America: Plant Closings, Community Abandonment, and the Dismantling of Basic Industry.* New York: Basic Books, 1982.

DEMOGRAPHIC TRANSITION

This term describes the process by which a society's population system changes from the traditional one of high death and birthrates to one with much lower birth- and death rates. Usually death rates drop first, then, as people realize the problems associated with the resultant population increase, the birthrates begin to decline as well, gradually restoring greater population stability. The new system, however, is much different from the old, for the percentage of children in society goes down (the lower birthrates) and that of older people rises (due to effect of declining mortality rates and higher life expectancy).

This demographic transition first occurred in Western Europe and the United States and was closely associated with industrialization. Rising population in the eighteenth and early nineteenth centuries resulted from declining death rates, thanks to better food supplies and some new sanitation measures. Increasingly, industrial economies helped people realize that a new level of birth control was essential. Middle-class people usually led the way, seeking fewer children so that they could be sure to have the capital necessary to educate the children they did have and to provide them with a start in business or the professions (or for women, marriage) at an appropriate middle-class level. They sought to upgrade human capital while cutting human numbers. Industrialization increased the requirements for education and capital and thus motivated more rigorous birth control. Working-class conversion to new levels of birth control occurred a bit later—1870 is the standard date for Western Europe. Workers found that children could not work until they entered their teens and that they also needed some education; their own low wages prompted concern for birth control simply as a matter of family survival, particularly given recurrent economic slumps like the one that hit Europe in the mid-1870s. By 1900, the average family size was dropping rapidly. Ironically, fewer children per family also promoted better care for children, so Europe and the United States also experienced a massive reduction of infant mortality between 1880 and 1920, motivating still greater levels of birth control.

Birth control during the demographic transition in the Western world was first accomplished primarily by sexual abstinence or coitus interruptus. Artificial methods were used but were suspect for moral reasons and were not fully reliable in any event. Gradually, however, greater reliance on factory-produced items like condoms and diaphragms (called pessaries in the nineteenth century) increased, which reduced the sexual tension occasioned by the demographic transition.

Other societies that industrialized went through a roughly similar demographic transition as the relationship between fewer children and family and national prosperity was recognized. Birthrates declined in the Soviet Union from the 1920s. Japan's demographic transition, backed by the government and involving considerable use of abortion, occurred after World War II. East Asia followed the pattern set by Japan. By the 2000s, the average family size had fallen from five or six to two and a half. By the 1980s, Russian and Japanese fertility declined so much that the overall population is expected to fall in the coming decades. Germany would also have experienced a population decline, but immigrants raised the overall numbers. By 2000, most European countries were on the road to smaller populations with an average number of children of less than one and a half per adult woman. Another important factor is that as the status of women rises, they tend to have fewer children, a fact made easier by access to birth control.

After 1978, China enforced a one-child policy, discouraging larger families and encouraging abortions. The approach was heavy handed; families that were larger paid a variety of penalties and fees. It is estimated that over the first 30 years of this policy, 400 million fewer children were born. The policy is extremely controversial; infanticide rates for girls are higher than for boys, but the policy appears widely popular within China.

Many nonindustrial or partially industrialized societies have experienced unprecedented population growth in the twentieth century. Many experts argue that (as the death rate has fallen due to better medical technology and food supplies) these countries must introduce a demographic transition simply to be able to industrialize fully; otherwise, the increasing population will drain too many resources. In keeping with these beliefs, China, India, and most other countries have tried with varying success to introduce greater population control in the later twentieth century. In some cases, poor women have been sterilized, an approach that has been abandoned as immoral and counterproductive. Some societies with expanding industrial sectors have experienced a demographic transition even though the legacy of fast growth will continue to spur population expansion for some decades; these societies include Brazil (1950s), Mexico (1960s), and probably China (1980s). The exact patterns of demographic control necessary or desirable for industrialization are matters of dispute. In the 2010s, China's deep wells of cheap labor have begun to run dry, and some factory work is shifting to poorer countries such as Vietnam. Japan has a smaller population, but the workers that remain are vastly more productive and should be able to support the larger number of retirees.

The general pattern is that the less industrialized the continent, the more children per family. Latin America, while unevenly industrialized, follows the general pattern as East Asia. The Middle East and North Africa have larger families, about three and a half children per woman, but far lower than in the 1950s. The real outlier has been Africa, whose average family size has only partially decreased to about five and a half children per woman. By 2050, Africa's population should double. Overall, however, the growth of the world's population has begun to slow.

See also Child Labor; Green Revolution; Population Growth; Retirement

Further Reading

Caldwell, John. *Theory of Fertility Decline*. London: Academic, 1983.

Coale, Ansley, and Susan Watkins, eds. *The Decline of Fertility in Europe*. Princeton, NJ: Princeton University Press, 1986.

DEMOGRAPHY. *See* Population Growth

DENG XIAOPING (1904–97)

Deng Xiaoping is best known as the communist leader who moved China toward a market economy during the 1970s. Deng never officially held top office in China or in the Communist Party but was China's principal leader from 1978 to 1992.

Of peasant origin, Deng studied in France during the 1920s, where he converted to Marxism. He participated in the communist movement in China and then, after 1949, held a variety of provincial positions. Long interested in economy policy,

Chinese vice premier Deng Xiaoping and President Jimmy Carter smile as they faced photographers in the Oval Office of the White House in 1979. (AP/Wide World Photo)

his views clashed with those of Mao Zedong, and he was twice removed from office. But during the maneuvering following Mao's death, he managed to gain power.

Like Marxists generally, Deng believed in the importance and, under a proper social system, the benefits of industrialization. He was deeply troubled by the economic stagnation heightened by key policies under Mao, notably the Cultural Revolution. In power, he became the chief architect of the idea of a socialist market economy, in which greater economic openness and competition would be combined with communist political control. Under his leadership, China opened to foreign investment, global trade, and considerable private enterprise. In turn, his policies helped convert China into one of the world's most rapidly growing economies, based above all on the rapid expansion of industrial manufacturing.

Further Reading

Marti, Michael. *China and the Legacy of Deng Xiaoping*. Washington, DC: Brassey's, 2002.

Shambaugh, David. *Deng Xiaoping: Portrait of a Chinese Statesman*. New York: Oxford University Press, 1995.

Yang, Benjamin, and Bingzhang Yang. *Deng: A Political Biography*. New York: East Gate, 1998.

DEPARTMENT STORES

Department stores, which offered a large variety of items for mass consumption, were a clear product of industrialization. They served the need to find new ways to display and sell increasing quantities of manufactured goods. They thus followed the growth of urban shops in the eighteenth century. The stores carried all sorts of products, from kitchenware to clothes, and geared themselves to wide sales rather than to neighborhood shopping. Department stores were also industrial in their organization: the labor force (salespeople) was specialized, largely unskilled, supervised, and trained to be efficient. Discipline imposed on sales clerks, though distinctive in emphasizing the need to be polite and mimic middle-class dress and manners, was as severe as in the factories. Goods were arrayed precisely, in machinelike fashion. Unlike many traditional shops, department stores did not allow bargaining over price, and limited chatting and socializing.

The first department store, an expansion of a clothing shop, opened in Paris in the 1830s. The idea quickly spread. After the 1850s, most Western cities offered several major department stores. Great stores opened in the United States, like Macy's in New York and Marshall Fields in Chicago. Their owners resembled industrialists in seeking to innovate in quest of profit. Department stores were launched outside the West, though most often by Western businessmen. Most of the stores in St. Petersburg and Moscow, around 1850, were foreign owned, the first started by a French businessman. The rise of department stores (called depato) in Japan in the twentieth century, some of them unprecedentedly large, was an integral part of the nation's industrial growth; by the mid-twentieth century, these stores featured huge arrays of standardized industrial goods including cameras, audio equipment, and other delights of high-tech consumerism.

The spread of department stores provoked massive debate in the late nineteenth century and beyond. Many observers criticized the stores for luring women into excessive consumption and moral decline. Others worried about the impact on the lower classes. Although most department stores' shoppers were middle- or upper-class, the stores did seek mass sales, and many poor urban people at least wandered through, developing what one historian has called "dream worlds" of material luxury. New kinds of theft developed amid the opportunities department stores offered; in both Europe and the United States, kleptomania, a new disease, emerged in the 1870s. Its victims were mainly women, often from wealthy families, who stole out of compulsion. Some Russian intellectuals also attacked department stores for their foreignness: "With the colossal houses ... the former good nature, the conviviality ... [of shopping] is disappearing. The tenor of life is becoming disciplined, is being chained to the pace of the machine."

In the United States, urban department stores declined in the postwar period. Department stores relied on streetcar lines to bring customers to their doors. Department stores quickly moved to the suburbs. Cities, like Pittsburgh, had more than a dozen department stores in 1945; by 1990, all but one had closed or relocated. Department stores flourish in the suburbs, but Internet shopping and rising economic inequality, which decreases the purchasing power of the middle and working classes, threatens them.

See also Consumerism and Mass Consumption

Further Reading

Miller, Michael. *The Bon Marché: Bourgeois Culture and the Department Store, 1869–1920.* Princeton, NJ: Princeton University Press, 1981.

Pasdermaijan, Hrant. *The Department Store: Its Origins, Evolution, and Economics.* London: Routledge, 1954.

Williams, Rosalind. *Dream Worlds: Mass Consumption in Late Nineteenth-Century France.* Berkeley: University of California Press, 1982.

DEPENDENCY. *See* World Systems Theory

DEVELOPING COUNTRIES

The idea of a "developing country" is an effort to distinguish, in the world economy, between nations that have completed an industrial revolution and those that are still in the process, or have yet to change much at all. The term is a contested one, for several reasons. One, of course, is any implications that developing countries are inferior to developed ones, or that there is a standard, possibly Western, model of economic development to which all should aspire.

The idea of a "developing" category may also express some confusion about whether the primary measurement is industrial development, or rather more general relative poverty. A few societies, after all, particularly in the oil-rich Middle East, have relatively modest levels of factory industry but are quite wealthy. Most commonly, "developing" applies to cases where industrial levels lag behind those of the West or Japan but also where measurements of material well-being (life expectancy, per capita income, educational levels) lag as well.

The greatest problem with the "developing" term is the lack of clear standards that distinguish between a developing stage and achievement of industrialized status. Some now use the term "newly industrialized" for certain economies that are still measurably different from the established industrial cases (the West including Australia, Canada, New Zealand, Japan, and usually South Africa and Israel) but are equally industrial. China, however, despite its rapid industrial and economic growth over the past two decades, still usually refers to itself as "developing" ("the world's largest developing economy"). Another point of confusion involves the fact that countries in the former Soviet Union, including Russia, are usually not labeled either developed or developing. Economists and global institutions continue to debate the most useful criteria to deploy in explaining different economic categories among the world's major regions.

Probably the clearest emerging distinction is the growing use of the term "less economically developed country" (LEDC) for the poorest nations that cannot at this point be regarded as developing.

Further Reading

Bozyk, Pawel. *Globalization and the Transformation of Foreign Economic Policy*. Aldershot, UK: Ashgate, 2006.

United Nations Statistics Division. "Composition of Macro Geographical (Continental) Regions, Geographical Sub-Regions, and Selected Economic and Other Groupings." October 2008. http://unstats.un.org/unsd/methods/m49/m49regin.htm.

Waugh, David. *Geography, An Integrated Approach*. 3rd ed. Walton-on-Thames, UK: Nelson, 2000.

DEVELOPMENT THEORY

Development theory arose in the late 1940s, elaborated by economists and other social scientists in the United States and in international economic organizations like the World Bank. The theory attempted to identify the changes that could move impoverished, largely agricultural, "Third World" economies into the industrial age. Sweeping changes were seen as necessary, but the primary attention of development theory was directed at increasing levels of science and education, introducing new technology, and accumulating capital, on the assumption that these ingredients, similar to those available in the Western industrial countries, would cause governments, labor forces, and entrepreneurs to adjust appropriately. Specific government forms, or prior traditions of work, did not matter much in this scenario. Development theorists paid some attention to agricultural productivity, though they were sometimes accused of neglecting the agricultural majority in favor of showcase industrial projects. With time, they devoted increasing attention to demography, as rapid population increase threatened to prevent significant industrial gains, no matter the inputs of foreign advisors, technicians, or investment capital.

Development theory sought to sum up what was understood about the causes of successful industrialization, though many historians have argued that the summary oversimplified and downplayed human and cultural factors. The theory was spurred by sincere, if somewhat patronizing, concern about massive world poverty, as colonial regions achieved political independence without corresponding economic gains, and by a desire to improve economic levels to bar the spread of communism in the context of the intensifying Cold War.

Development theory formed the basis of serious policy. In 1949, the International Bank for Reconstruction and Development (World Bank) sent a mission to Colombia that called for sweeping reforms in the name of industrial development. Science, technology, planning, and the guidance of international organizations constituted the launching pads. Special attention was paid, in this and other cases in Latin America, Africa, and Asia, to the problem of capital formation. During the 1970s, development theory had to adjust to the stubborn fact that industrialization had not gained ground as rapidly around the world as initial planning had anticipated. New attention went to agriculture with the "Green revolution," which is one result of technology applied to farming in the tropics.

Development theory has been criticized for more than over optimism and vagueness about sources of new capital. It has been seen, like modernization theory, as an unexamined Western judgment on very different world societies. It has been attacked for putting industrial advance ahead of any real attention to poverty, which often has remained untouched by apparent change at the industrial level. The strong planning emphasis has also been questioned, particularly as free-market theories gained ground in the 1980s.

Naive expressions of development theory have declined. Nevertheless, many of the goals and some of the premises of development theory persist in efforts to stimulate industrial growth by cutting rates of population increase, expanding education, or enhancing investment.

See also Causes of the Industrial Revolution; Modernization Theory

Further Reading

Escobar, Arturo. *Encountering Development: The Making and Unmaking of the Third World.* Princeton, NJ: Princeton University Press, l995.
Nurkse, Ragnald. *Problems of Capital Formation in Underdeveloped Countries.* Oxford: Oxford University Press, 1953.

DIESEL, RUDOLF (1858–1913)

A German mechanical engineer, Diesel developed an internal combustion engine in 1897 that used oil as a fuel. It was more efficient than gasoline engines and simpler in design, making it especially appropriate for large equipment such as steamships and locomotives. Diesel was an example of the later-industrial kind of inventor, because he was formally trained (in Munich). He based his work on other engineers' designs and on the theory of heat engines. He set up a factory to make his engines. In 1913, he mysteriously disappeared from a German ship bound for London.

Diesel engines work on compression ignition, rather than spark plugs. Air, compressed by a piston in each cylinder, ignites the fuel. Diesel oils are cheaper than refined gasoline, and their energy is easily converted to rods that can turn crankshafts, providing rotary power for heavy engines.

Further Reading

Oakes, Elizabeth H. *A to Z of STS Scientists.* New York: Infobase, 2002.

German inventor Rudolf Diesel. (Library of Congress)

DISCIPLINE

New forms of discipline were essential for the work processes of early industrialization for three reasons. First, workers operated in relatively large groups. Even though most early factories were small, the owner could not keep his eye on the whole crew, which was composed of strangers unaccustomed to working with each other. Second, powered machinery required unprecedented speed and co-ordination. If one member of a team operating a machine strayed, the whole machine might have to be shut down, resulting in a great loss of production. Third, factory owners generally shared a rigorous work ethic (for others, and often for themselves as well) that held that good, disciplined work was life's highest goal and the clearest demonstration of good character. Since many workers brought from their rural or artisanal pasts had different work values that emphasized a slower pace with more interruptions, new forms of discipline seemed essential to whip them into shape.

The goals of factory discipline were diligence and regularity. Workers had to arrive on time. They could not dirty the material they were working on. They could not sing, chat, or wander around. They had to obey orders and display loyalty, and, of course, they could not steal materials. Several mechanisms were used to enforce this unfamiliar discipline. Shop rules stipulated the major regulations and were prominently posted. Fines were administered. A worker who arrived late to work was locked out of the factory for a half-day, receiving no pay and owing an additional half-day's pay as penalty. Watchmen frequently controlled exits and even searched workers suspected of stealing material. Increasingly, foremen were employed to make sure that workers toed the line. They replaced more informal methods of supervision, such as hiring a skilled worker and making him responsible for the behavior of his assistants.

Eventually, the rigor of discipline tended to increase. Workers were told not to try to fix a machine but to leave it to a specialist. The advent of efficiency experts—industrial engineers—in the 1890s signaled an effort to regulate workers' motions ever more strictly, to avoid loss of time. Factory workers were to be made as machinelike as possible. New electrical devices like time clocks systematically checked arrivals and departures.

Although the most rigorous work discipline applied to the factories, new systems spread to other branches of work. Sales personnel and clerks were required to adhere to dress codes and were taught politeness and other forms of emotional control to please their bosses and customers. This trend gained momentum in the twentieth century. Some scholars argue that the subtle regulations, particularly over emotional expression, enforced on white-collar workers have now become particularly severe, distorting emotional life even off the job. Airline flight attendants carefully taught to smile no matter what the provocation from a passenger—a major component of company training—are a recent example of workers disciplined to make their public personalities fit the job.

At no stage in the industrialization process did workers accept all the new discipline with docility. Individual efforts to evade rules were legion, and thefts from the workplace expressed defiance as well as desire for material gain. Mocking the supervisors was a favored past time—when it could be enjoyed safely. Specific conflicts with foremen were the source of many small but bitter strikes. Larger efforts, in strikes and the union movement, to modify employers' rights unilaterally to determine discipline were a major stimulus to the labor movement from the late nineteenth century onward. On the whole, however, workers increasingly accepted many aspects of industrial discipline, one of the major changes in the human experience of work brought by industrialization.

See also Scientific Management

Further Reading

Joyce, Patrick. *Work, Society, and Politics: The Culture of the Factory.* New Brunswick, NJ: Rutgers University Press, 1980.

Pollard, Sidney. *The Genesis of Modern Management*. Cambridge, MA: Harvard University Press, 1965.

Stearns, Peter N. *Paths to Authority*. Urbana: University of Illinois Press, 1978.

Voss, Kim. *The Making of American Exceptionalism*. Ithaca, NY: Cornell University Press, 1993.

DISTILLING. *See* Brewing and Distilling

DIVISION OF LABOR

The process of subdividing the role of each worker in the manufacturing process has been a central feature of industrialization since its origin in late eighteenth-century England. In one of the classic examples of the advantages of the division of labor, Adam Smith observed in the 1770s that an artisan working alone could produce only a handful of pins; whereas, once the labor process has been subdivided, a few dozen workers repeating different tasks in a pin factory can produce thousands. The division of labor has continued because each industrialist or employer has an interest in producing goods more cheaply to gain a greater market share or simply to remain competitive.

In contrast to artisans who produced an entire product from beginning to end, factory owners separated workers into skilled, semiskilled, and unskilled laborers. In the late eighteenth century, for example, the New England shoe industry relied on the "putting out" system, in which rural artisans produced entire shoes in their workshops. In the early nineteenth century, merchants centralized production of shoes in factories; some workers became foremen or skilled workers (such as those who made the patterns that other workers followed), but most employees became factory "hands" who repeated one or two steps in the production process. Shoe factories relied on steam-powered machinery, but the "deskilling" of workers was also a significant factor in allowing shoemakers to raise production of shoes and lower prices. Many of the deskilled workers were women. Given sexual division of labor, women's jobs were always categorized as low-skill, even when (as in garment making) their jobs actually required a number of skills.

Even as industrialization destroyed many workers' preexisting skills, it also created entirely new skill requirements, as exemplified in the work of puddlers or machinists. By the late nineteenth century, however, most machinists did not create whole machines but were employed in large workshops completing one stage of machine making. Many young workers were still enrolled in apprentice systems around 1900, but only a small proportion of them (less than 25%) learned all the different features of the craft. Battles between an increasingly craft-conscious machinists' union and employers set the ground for the counteroffensive led by Frederick Winslow Taylor and the scientific management movement. During the Cold War, military contractors relied on machinists to build aircraft and ships, but both employers and the military eagerly attempted to use automation to create workerless factories.

Because of the increasingly hierarchical division of labor in manufacturing, the number of people engaged in supervisory tasks rose rapidly in late nineteenth-century corporations. These people included both foremen and managers, as well as white-collar employees who staffed the new bureaucracies as accountants, engineers, and low-level clerical workers. These occupations could also become deskilled when new technology was implemented or when new opportunities opened up for men and the old jobs were staffed with women. Secretarial work, for example, once a slot for educated, responsible men, was increasingly divided into filing, receptionist, and typing tasks as women took over the field and new equipment downgraded skills like handwriting.

There is also an international dimension to the division of labor. The pressure on industrialists to shift production to regions or countries where wages are lower has existed since the beginning of the industrialization process. The English textile industry displaced Indian manufacturing (which was often of higher quality) in the eighteenth century, but by the mid-nineteenth century, Indian manufacturers began to displace English mills from low-quality markets such as bagging. However, low wages are only one aspect of industrialists' costs, and the extreme division of labor and the more capital-intensive nature of many industries in developed countries allowed them to capture high-end markets or to dominate mass markets by using high-volume production.

Since the early 1970s, however, the ongoing industrial investment in developing countries has accompanied increasing unemployment in developed countries. For instance, automobile companies have increased investment and production in relatively poor countries such as Brazil and Mexico. Many scholars have argued that the international division of labor has resulted in the shift of low-skill, low-wage industrial jobs to industrializing countries while highly skilled, high-tech, high-wage jobs remain in the advanced industrialized countries. Because multinational corporations are headquartered in industrialized countries, this tendency persisted until the late 1980s, when middle-class jobs began to lose ground. For instance, U.S. corporations are subcontracting the designing of cars to Japanese companies; South Korea has emerged as a site for engineering; and Bangalore, India, has become a site for writing computer software.

See also Assembly Line; Deindustrialization; Fordism; Maquiladoras; Pink-Collar Workers; Postindustrial Economies; Protoindustrialization

Further Reading

Braverman, Harry. *Labor and Monopoly Capital: The Degradation of Work in the Twentieth Century*. New York: Monthly Review, 1974.

Montgomery, David. *Workers' Control in America: Studies in the History of Work, Technology, and Labor Struggles*. New York: Cambridge University Press, 1979.

DOCKERS

Dock work was a traditional, largely unskilled operation. Many dockworkers—dockers—in ports like Hamburg, Germany, alternated dock work with agricultural labor, though a more skilled core of ship loaders provided a stable element. Some European ports had traditional organizations of dockers that helped regulate work habits and distribute jobs. Demands for dockers grew with industrialization, as ocean commerce expanded, but supply grew even more quickly than demand, thanks to population increase. By the late nineteenth century, irregular employment was widespread. New technology, especially loading cranes, altered the nature of dock work. Around 1900, employers (themselves organized increasingly in large shipping companies) tried to speed the pace of work, using foremen for closer supervision; the tonnage handled per worker rose, even aside from new technology.

In this increasingly industrial atmosphere, a number of big dock strikes erupted: the great 1889 movement in Britain, the 1896 strike in Hamburg, and the 1899 and 1904 protests in Marseilles. The strikes, though usually defeated, helped unionize dockers and other unskilled workers, providing a new and often radical membership for the union movement as a whole for the next several decades. Dockworkers, still distinctive in many ways, became part of mass unionism and the industrial working class.

Further Reading

Davies, Sam. *Dock Workers: International Explorations in Comparative Labour History, 1790–1970.* Aldershot, UK: Ashgate, 2000.

DOMESTIC MANUFACTURING

This traditional, but capitalist, system of production developed in Europe starting in the Middle Ages. Also called the putting-out system, domestic manufacturing involves work in the home, usually by several family members cooperating in various tasks. Many domestic manufacturers also engage in agriculture, though some are full-time. Equipment is simple, usually purchased by the family—a spinning wheel or a hand loom. Domestic workers receive material from an urban merchant, who usually sends out agents to provide the material and give instructions on what product is desired. The workers complete the manufacturing, and the agent then returns to get the thread, cloth, or small metal goods, paying workers by the piece. Workers occasionally go directly to cities to negotiate their own purchases and sales. Occasionally, also, merchants provide the tools.

Domestic manufacturing requires little capital; merchants only have to invest in the raw material. It requires few adjustments by workers, who can pursue a traditional rural family life. Some domestic manufacturing also occurs within cities. This is why the system spread so rapidly when demand for manufactured goods went up in the eighteenth century, drawing hundreds of thousands of new workers into the process. The system does not encourage high productivity, however, unless workers are very needy. And there is little supervision of quality. Thus some merchants in domestic manufacturing saw the desirability of shifting to a factory system when it became possible.

In the long run, domestic producers could not compete with factories and equipment. But domestic manufacturing regions survived in Western Europe throughout the nineteenth century, and it has been argued that this tenacity often made it easier to set up factories in new areas, rather than trying to get traditional workers to change jobs and locations. By accepting lower pay, by getting other family members (particularly women and children) to work harder, and by concentrating on either high-quality or very cheap products, domestic weavers could eke out a living for decades, as they did, for example, in parts of France or Ireland.

Domestic manufacturing was not exclusively a European system. It spread in the United States right before industrialization began. It spread also in Turkey, for the production of rugs for Western markets, and in other areas. Domestic manufacturing could actually grow in response to new demand even after industrialization began.

See also Proto-industrialization

Further Reading

Liu, Tessie. *The Weaver's Knot: The Contradictions of Class Struggle and Family Solidarity in Western France*. Ithaca, NY: Cornell University Press, 1994.

DONGFENG MOTORS

Dongfeng is the second-largest carmaker in China. It was founded in 1969 as a government-owned company, or the "Second Automobile Works," originally making heavy trucks. There was a strong military rationale for creating the company; it was located in the interior of the country, to keep it safe in case of invasion.

The firm began to operate as something like a private company in the 1980s, although it remains under government ownership. This ambiguity causes friction. Government ownership helps the company to enter into partnerships with foreign companies such as Nissan and Honda. Dongfeng has more collaborative relationships with foreign automakers than any other Chinese carmaker. Because the Chinese government sees electric cars as a growth industry, Dongfeng is entering into that field.

In the late 1990s, the company lost money. In the 2000s, the company's sales quadrupled. The company was made public in 2007, but the government retained 70 percent ownership. While the Chinese market is growing rapidly, the company faces stiff competition. Public ownership has proven essential for this company, and it has benefited from it. But state ownership tends not to benefit most companies; the task of making a quality car that consumers want at an affordable price often goes against what governments want or need companies to do.

In this file photo taken in 2010, a model stands next to the all-electric I-Car, a concept car debuted by state-owned automaker Dongfeng Motor Corporation at the Beijing Auto China 2010 show in Beijing. (AP Photo/Ng Han Guan, File)

Further Reading

Zhang, Wenxian, and Ilan Alon, eds. *A Guide to the Top 100 Companies in China.* Singapore: World Scientific, 2010.

DRINKING

Drinking habits were greatly transformed by industrialization. Before the Industrial Revolution, many British peasants or farm laborers began the day with a mug of beer, and drinking throughout the working day was common (for instance, sailors received a daily ration of rum). In fact, in the United States until the 1820s, it was considered impossible to build a house without liquor on the job site. However, drinking in the preindustrial workplace was closely supervised by the master artisan or owner who determined the timing and amount of drink.

Factory owners desired a sober workforce and fired or fined workers who drank on the job. Although many craft workers continued to hold to older traditions, industrialists generally succeeded in changing attitudes toward drinking and work. Indeed, during the nineteenth century, there was a rise in coffee and tea consumption among the urban working classes throughout Europe and North America. Still, industrialists, the middle classes, and some labor leaders were troubled by the fact that many workers spent much of their leisure time in saloons. A saloon offered more than simply a place to drink—it was a site for workers to socialize, find jobs, read the paper (often in immigrant workers' native languages), and enjoy a nickel lunch. After the repeal of Prohibition, drinking patterns changed. Saloons were replaced by taverns, which were more accepting of women, although most taverns catered to specific audiences that were often segregated by race and class.

The relationship between alienated industrial labor and drinking remained. As Ben Hamper, a working-class writer, put it: "Go to any General Motors plant in Flint. Turn your back to the building gaze directly across the roadway. I guarantee you'll be peering at a tavern, perhaps several of them. . . . Find a factory, you'll find a bar." Alcohol helped dull the pain of rigidly segmented work. In the late twentieth century, the use of illegal drugs (such as marijuana) or prescription drugs (notably OxyContin) skyrocketed. In the United States, many workers began using methamphetamine to handle multiple jobs or work on the night shift. Meth and OxyContin (often prescribed for chronic back pain) became major scourges among the white and rural working class. Employers turned to testing workers for drug and alcohol use, suggesting that many workers continued to self-medicate.

See also Alienation; Temperance

Further Reading

Rosenzweig, Roy. *Eight Hours for What We Will: Workers and Leisure in an Industrializing City, 1870–1920*. Cambridge: Cambridge University Press, 1983.

DU PONT DE NEMOURS

This famous Delaware family established a great chemical company, one of the leading business dynasties in the United States. The first Du Pont in the United States was a French-born economist who fled the revolution. His son, a student of the French chemist Lavoisier, set up a plant near Wilmington, Delaware, to provide gunpowder to the U.S. army in 1802. This enterprise was the basis for the Dupont Company. Subsequent descendants served in the U.S. military and government. Thomas Du Pont (1863–1930) made a fortune in coal and iron. Under his presidency (1902–15), the Dupont Company consolidated. The company had branched out from gunpowder to high explosives in the 1880s. It became interested in cellulose products in the 1890s, producing plastics and paints. Under Thomas Du Pont, the product list expanded to several hundred items. In imitation of German chemical companies, a formal research division was established, one of the first in the United States. Dupont took the lead in developing nylon, and after World War II, the company became active in nuclear power and developed Teflon and new fibers such as Orlon and Dacron.

See also Research and Development (R&D); Synthetic Fabrics

Further Reading

Hounshell, David A., and John K. Smith. *Science and Corporate Strategy: Du Pont R&D, 1902–1980*. New York: Cambridge University Press, 1988.

DUAL LABOR MARKETS

Almost all observers would agree that some jobs, such as for large automotive companies, generally pay well and lead to better jobs, while other jobs, such as french-fry cook at a fast-food restaurant, are poorly paid dead ends. Dual labor market theory seeks to explain this situation by showing how jobs are divided into primary and secondary labor markets. Primary job markets consist of jobs that pay decent wages and benefits, offer year-round, full-time employment, and, just as important, provide on-the-job training or opportunities for advancement. The secondary labor market consists of unstable jobs that pay poorly with little or no opportunity for upward mobility. All jobs in the secondary labor market are entry level; a subsequent job in the secondary labor market is likely to have the same pay, no matter how much time was spent on the first one.

The preindustrial job markets for workers were highly stratified, for the gap in skill and living standard between artisans and the unskilled was quite extreme. When they could, artisans and skilled workers restricted the entry of new workers into their labor markets to keep wages high. The barriers to entering these labor markets could be legal, but they were more often a combination of social and technical factors. In the nineteenth century, an aspiring artisan or skilled worker generally had to learn his trade from a knowledgeable older man. In the case of puddlers, sons frequently learned how to manipulate molten iron from their fathers. Sometimes, a father would have to retire before his son could become a full-fledged practitioner, which could lead to a certain degree of friction within families. Recruiting new workers from family or friendship networks, however, facilitated the solidarity that ensured the survival of craft unions. It also had the effect of barring women, racial, and ethnic minorities from skilled jobs.

Industrialization undermined or eliminated the skill of many trades, and some historians have argued that this effect created a great deal of homogeneity among workers. Employers' increasing reliance on mechanization and the minute division of labor did effectively de-skill many trades, greatly decreasing the time it took to learn to make shoes or weave cloth. However, much evidence suggests that, even in factories, skilled workers maintained relatively privileged positions. (Their high pay and partial autonomy in the workplace led them to be called "labor aristocrats" in the nineteenth century.) Even after shoemaking and textile factories had emerged, many former artisans became skilled workers or foremen, overseeing the work of unskilled workers, who were sometimes women or recent immigrants. The turnover rate was frequently highest for unskilled workers who occupied jobs in the secondary labor market, while skilled workers were much more likely to stay at their jobs.

In the 1900s, large corporations began to develop internal labor markets in an attempt to convince unskilled workers not to change employers. Employees were offered opportunities to improve their pay when they switched jobs within the corporation. Although the difference in skill was often negligible between jobs, many workers welcomed the chance to earn more money and perhaps one day to become a skilled worker. Employers generally continued to encourage divisions between skilled, unskilled, and semiskilled workers to discourage the formation of unions. In the U.S. steel industry during the early twentieth century, most of the laborers in the steel mills were Catholic immigrants from eastern and southern Europe. Through internal labor markets, many immigrants had become semiskilled workers, although employers carefully extended numerous privileges to its skilled workforce, most of whom were native-born Protestants. Skilled workers refused to identify with immigrants, contemptuously referring to them as "hunkies" and "dagos." In 1919, unskilled workers in steel sought to build an industrial union movement open to all workers, but skilled workers crossed the picket lines of the immigrants and helped to break the strike.

There has been a strong correlation between race, gender, or ethnicity and position in industrial job markets. At the turn of the century, in the northeastern industrial cities of the United States, the daughters of skilled workers frequently became clerical workers, saleswomen, or telephone switchboard operators. Employers generally reserved these jobs for "American" women, and the daughters of eastern and southern European immigrants had to settle for factory jobs. Although black women were certainly bona fide Americans, they occupied the bottom of the female job market. Employers generally refused to hire black women for either factory or clerical work, and most were relegated to jobs as domestics or clothes washers.

Although unionization of heavy industry raised the standards of living of many black workers (and to some degree of women), the disparity between working-class labor markets increased after World War II. Particularly as manufacturers abandoned inner cities, a process well under way by the 1950s, black workers and recent immigrants from Latin America and the Caribbean were forced to take low-wage jobs in the service sector. By the 1970s, deindustrialization was eliminating the sources of livelihood for many blue-collar workers; black workers were especially hard-hit because they were largely barred from suburban and white-collar job markets. Even when manufacturing jobs have returned, unions have been too weak to force employers to pay high wages; in Los Angeles and New York, many immigrant workers are employed in low-wage "sweatshops" in the garment, woodworking, and electronics industries.

Labor market patterns in Western Europe have followed roughly the same chronology as in the United States. Advancing industrialization reduced skill disparities and separate labor markets in the late nineteenth and early twentieth centuries. But advancing technology after World War II, along with labor shortages in a rapidly growing economy, prompted many native-born workers to move into skilled ranks or out of the blue-collar labor force altogether. Immigrants from other parts of the world filled the unskilled jobs, particularly in service industries like restaurants or transportation. These workers lacked the training to compete for the better-paying positions and were often targets of racial discrimination. Low pay and frequent unemployment characterized this labor sector.

Racial factors often created somewhat separate labor markets, even apart from skill requirements. Employers and workers sometimes sought to exclude or restrict new immigrants from their labor markets altogether. In Australia, white workers successfully agitated for legislation to exclude Asian workers; in California, white unionists barred Asians from all but the most menial jobs. Under the apartheid regime, black workers from the South African countryside had to apply for work permits to work in urban centers or even in the gold mines. Polish immigrants to the coal mines of northern France were often deported when unemployment threatened French workers. In response, Polish immigrants formed their own unions to advocate their interests. France and Germany allowed "guest workers" to work for a short period before being sent back to Algeria, Turkey, or Poland. Over time, these guests have become integrated into German society.

Because of the stronger laws and policies protecting Western European workers, fewer immigrants have obtained jobs in countries like France. The result is that many immigrants are shut off from primary labor markets, and in many instances, their children are shut off from all labor markets. The result is to increase social tension, which occasionally spills over into social unrest.

See also Underclass; Work

Further Reading

Gordon, David M., Richard Edwards, and Michael Reich. *Segmented Work, Divided Workers: The Historical Transformation of Labor in the United States*. New York: Cambridge University Press, 1982.

Harrison, Bennett, and Barry Bluestone. *The Great U-Turn: Corporate Restructuring and the Polarizing of America*. New York: Basic Books, 1988.

E

EAST CENTRAL EUROPE

This region, whose definitions fluctuate but that include contemporary countries running from the Baltic States and Poland, to the Balkans, has had a varied experience of industrialization since the nineteenth century. Much of the region was primarily agricultural, and as Western Europe industrialized, the region exported raw materials and grains in return for manufactured goods. To many observers at the time, and since, the region constituted something of a case study of "economic backwardness."

By the later nineteenth century, however, significant pockets of heavy industry developed based primarily on holdings of coal and iron ore, particularly in Poland (then part of Russia) and Bohemia (then part of the Habsburg Empire and now the Czech Republic and Slovakia).

The region was disrupted by World War I and then the creation of a number of small, independent states, often fiercely nationalistic and bent on protecting the local economy through high tariffs. Little industrial advance occurred. Hitler and Nazi Germany thought of the region as a source of raw materials and foods to Germany, which in fact was largely the case even before the German conquests prior to and during World War II.

After the war, the region fell directly or indirectly into Soviet hands. The Soviets removed some industrial assets and benefited from regional resources such as Romanian oil. But ultimately, some support for industrial development emerged, particularly in established centers such as Poland and Czechoslovakia, where, among other things, a thriving armaments industry helped supply weapons to various countries during the Cold War. Five-year plans in countries like Hungary and Romania, following the Soviet model, included efforts to further industrial growth, sometimes at considerable cost to the local environment.

After the end of the Cold War, most countries in the region ultimately joined the European Union, and worked to convert to a market economy. The transition was complex but surprisingly successful in a number of cases, advancing industrial growth. Amid continued national variety, the region by the early twenty-first century was substantially industrial, but at lower levels, and with lower standards of living than regions that had undergone a full industrial revolution.

Further Reading

Berend, Ivan T., and G. Ranki. *The European Periphery and Industrialization 1780–1914.* Cambridge: Cambridge University Press, 1982.

Janos, Andrew. *The Politics of Backwardness in Hungary, 1825–1945*. Princeton, NJ: Princeton University Press, 1982.

Komlos, John, ed. *Economic Development in the Habsburg Monarchy and the Successor States.* New York: Columbia University Press, 1990.

EDISON, THOMAS A. (1847–1931)

The "wizard of Menlo Park" was a prolific inventor and industrialist. Edison developed several products that transformed the twentieth century: incandescent lights and electrical streetlight systems, the phonograph, and the motion picture camera. Edison was more of a tinkerer than a scientist; he distrusted theoretically minded academics, but he did develop one of the first industrial laboratories to bring together scientific minds in his "invention factory." Edison pursued applied research—he wanted his inventions to be commercially viable—and he or his associates patented over a thousand different products or processes. Although Edison believed direct current would provide the basis for electrical systems, he was bested by George Westinghouse and Nikola Tesla, who advocated alternating current. Edison helped form one of the world's largest manufacturing conglomerates: General Electric.

See also Research and Development (R&D); Research Laboratories

Further Reading

Millard, Andre J. *Edison and the Business of Innovation*. Baltimore: Johns Hopkins University Press, 1990.

EDUCATION AND LITERACY

Education has been associated with industrialization in many ways. Regions that have industrialized have usually had relatively high educational levels already. Western Europe had expanded literacy to a growing minority from the sixteenth century onward, and the United States had the most literate population in the world by the late eighteenth century. Japan's preindustrial literacy rate was quite high, and the nation improved it by imposing a universal primary school requirement in the 1870s.

Literacy and numeracy are important to an industrial labor force by providing workers who can do simple calculations and read instructions and shop rules. Advancing consumerism also depended on people who could read advertisements and product labels. Historians have cautioned, however, against positing too close a link between basic education and industrialization. Uneducated workers often did just as well, in terms of productivity, wages, and mobility, as workers with some schooling; this was true among immigrants to Canada, for example. Even some factory owners have been uneducated, even illiterate. How much education is needed to launch an industrial revolution is thus not entirely clear.

A school in Norfolk, England, during the late nineteenth century. (Library of Congress)

Despite this complexity, there is no question that in all cases to date, education continued to expand after the Industrial Revolution began. Although extensive use of child labor sometimes inhibited schooling, the issue was addressed in child labor laws. Primary education spread because of belief in the economic utility of basic education and because child labor became less useful: children had to be given something else to do and some other controls. Many paternalist employers set up schools for their workers' children. By the 1870s, most Western countries required primary education. Schools taught not only literacy and arithmetic skills but discipline, including time discipline, which helped to form habits useful in factories. Schools often tried to teach loyalty to the nation and the existing economic system, with some effect (particularly in societies like Japan, where nationalistic education in the 1920s built on older Confucian loyalty). By the 1890s, literacy rates had risen as high as 95 percent of all adults in most industrial countries. By then, also, most families, even in the peasantry, had accepted the necessity of education for later work life. Interestingly, education for women made particularly good sense by 1900, for it prepared them for clerical jobs.

Technical education was absolutely vital to advancing industrialization, for a certain number of people simply had to have access to specialized technical knowledge. In very early stages of industrialization, training could be provided on the job. By the mid-nineteenth century, however, schools and night courses increasingly took over part of the task of providing technical knowledge of chemistry, accounting, design, and other skill areas essential to industrial technicians and low-level engineers. Big companies, like Le Creusot in France or Tata in India, set up technical high schools for the most talented graduates of their primary programs and recruited their top skilled workers and foremen from this group. Technical courses spread in most industrial cities, widely attended by artisans. Germany set up technical high schools; U.S. high schools offered technical tracks. Britain, which lagged in providing a technical education system, clearly suffered from the lack of well-trained technicians and managers by the late nineteenth century. Japan and, after 1917, the Soviet Union used effective technical education to improve the quality of its industrial labor force.

Most countries trying to industrialize in the late nineteenth and early twentieth centuries worked on expanding both primary and technical education, though the strain on resources sometimes limited results. Specific patterns varied. India featured superb technical training for a minority but introduced mass education less rapidly. Latin America moved forward in mass education, with 75 percent literacy by the 1990s, while technical facilities, though expanding, gained more slowly. The cause-effect-cause relationships of industrialization and education remain complex.

See also Child Labor; University

Further Reading

Graff, Harvey. *The Legacies of Literacy*. Bloomington: Indiana University Press, 1987.
Kaestle, Carl, et al. *Literacy in the United States*. New Haven, CT: Yale University Press, 1991.

EDWARDS, PERSIS (1816–96)

Persis Edwards found a job in the then-new textile factories of New Hampshire in 1839. She had grown up on a farm, expected her mill work to be a sojourn of only a few years. She was like most of the new factory hands, intending to save her wages to send back to her family in the countryside or to accumulate as a nest egg for her marriage. Indeed, at one point she wanted to come home but accepted uncomplainingly her mother's decision that the family still needed her wages. Edwards seems fairly representative of this unusual first generation of American factory women, save that her letters have been preserved.

In 1839, she wrote a cousin that she liked her job "very well—enjoy myself much better than I expected." But she also felt confined by factory conditions—"could wish to have my liberty a bit more." Some of Edwards's colleagues were a bit bleaker in their assessments, noting their low status and claiming to be "sick" of factory conditions. Fairly well paid and housed in good barracks, most New England factory women stuck it out until they had saved what they wanted; conditions did not begin to deteriorate until the 1840s, when new immigrant workers and increasing employer efforts to lower wages reduced workers' satisfaction. Persis Edwards did finally return home, and she later married.

See also Textiles; Women Industrial Workers

Further Reading

Dublin, Thomas, ed. *Farm to Factory: Women's Letters, 1830–1860*. New York: Columbia University Press, 1981.

ELECTRICITY

The applications of electricity provided new flexibility to the Industrial Revolution, particularly from the later nineteenth century onward. Electrical energy could be transmitted over long distances, allowing power use well away from the original energy source. It could be applied to large motors or very small ones, permitting power equipment in small factories, nonfactory sites, and homes. Thus industrial technology spread to many artisans, housewives, and others using small electrical motors, such as farmers. Applications of electrical energy also created a massive new industry, providing electrical appliances and equipment for a variety of uses. Finally, electrical power could be used not only for motion but also for light and heat.

Industrial uses of electricity depended on prior scientific discoveries: Volta's chemical battery in 1800; Oersted's discovery of electromagnetism; the statement of the law of the electric circuit in 1826; and work by several scientists including Faraday on electromagnetic induction in 1831. Subsequent significant inventions included the electromagnetic generator, in 1866–67; the ring dynamo, producing the first commercially practical direct current, in 1870; and later development of high-voltage alternating current. Advances in the manufacture of cables and insulation and in generator construction were also vital.

Early uses of electricity, like the telegraph, required little power and could be run on batteries, but electrical motors and lighting depended on larger power stations. The first station in Europe was set up at Godalming, in England, by the Siemens brothers in 1881. Coal- and water-powered stations soon sprang up throughout the industrial world. Early stations were small, but it was soon discovered that big stations, close to the power source, were more efficient, even with some power loss in transmission. Additional discoveries quickly reduced the transmission loss, particularly through the use of alternating current. Power stations generating 225 kilowatts over 200 kilometers at 30,000 volts were introduced in Germany in 1891, and advances were rapid thereafter.

Power stations of this sort could run a variety of large motors, city lighting and tram systems, and home outlets. Electricity was applied to trains, with a Siemens model in 1879; to city lighting, in several U.S. cities in 1882; to metallurgy and chemistry in the 1880s (electrical manufacture of sodium, aluminum, and other products); and also to the mechanical kneading of bread, the sewing of clothes, and other shop and sweatshop production branches. Huge electrical equipment companies arose in Germany and the United States; two firms, AEG and Siemens, dominated the German market. Rates of power production multiplied. New industrializers adopted electricity quickly. In Japan, however, use of electricity began slowly, though the Tokyo Electric Light Company formed in 1882. Japanese power-generating capacity rose over sevenfold between 1905 and 1920, then tripled again before 1930. Japanese conversion to electricity was the most rapid in the world by this point, and Soviet expansion of electrical networks was not far behind. Here were clear cases in which latecomer industrializers, with less established commitment to older methods like steam engines, could forge ahead rapidly.

In the late twentieth century, electrical appliances have become more efficient. Yet consumption of power continues to rise, as the number of electrical devices are multiplying, notably personal computers and handheld electronics, but also electric cars. Thus new sources of electricity are a necessity for industrial and industrializing countries. In the 2000s, China was building two power plants a day, expanding its electricity generation by more than 10 percent per year. In theory, wind or solar power could supply the world with electricity. In practice, however, sustainable energy seems likely to supplement rather than supplant fossil fuels.

See also Electronics; Hydroelectric Power; Westinghouse, George

Further Reading

Hughes, Thomas Parke. *Networks of Power: Electrification in Western Society, 1880–1930.* Baltimore: Johns Hopkins University Press, 1993.

ELECTRONIC WASTE OR E-WASTE

Electronics and computers are sometimes extolled as a technology that is "green," vastly different than the smokestack industries of the second Industrial Revolution. Disposing of outdated electronics involves a combination of cutting-edge technology and labor practices from the early nineteenth century.

Electronic waste is a side effect of the explosive growth of personal computers, laptops, portables, and handheld electronics. Gordon Moore, one of the founders of Intel, observed that processing power doubles every two years. "Moore's Law" means that the life span of cell phones and other electronic devices is just a few years as new software and faster chips make them obsolete. In the mid-2000s, China threw away more than 2 million tons of electronic waste; the United States threw away half as much.

Most electronics make their way into landfills; as they break down, they leach heavy metals. Indeed, e-waste is the largest source of heavy metals in U.S. groundwater. Only 20 percent of e-waste is recycled, and only a fraction of recycling is done in an environmentally responsible way. Typically, if consumers recycle their

Electronic waste, a large pile of unwanted computer monitors. (Shutterstock)

outdated electronics, it is shipped to a poor country, such as Ghana or China where the recycling takes place.

Computers and cell phones can either be disassembled for their component parts or smelted down to extract the amounts of valuable metals, such as gold or copper. In those instances, ancient technologies are employed to do the smelting, notably wood fires under heavy iron pots. As the plastic burns off, the clouds of smoke provoke a variety of symptoms, from severe headaches to asthma to blood poisoning. Child labor is often used because children are cheap, almost disposable workers, who are much less likely to complain than adults.

The most valuable material in the e-waste is not gold but information. After criminals learned that they can find out personal information about credit card or banking accounts, the price of functional computers shot up, vastly more than valuable metals they contained. E-waste is one reason why so much computer spam and so many Internet scams begin in West Africa.

Disassembly involves removing various components such as chips and batteries to be reused. Here, too, the technology involved is low-tech; nonetheless, it results in a significant part of the flow of metal into Chinese industry (40% of copper in China comes from recycling). The industry has its defenders, such as blogger Adam Minter, who points out that skilled recyclers in China can earn more than an engineer. Chinese recyclers are paid several times more in China than in India, and Indian workers work without the minimal protections (face masks, etc.) that are common in China.

There has been a history of richer nations encouraging poorer countries to accept storing toxic waste, or recycling industrial products that contain large amounts of toxic materials. For instance, ships typically contain large amounts of asbestos and other known hazards to health. The disassembly of ships was taken on by countries like Pakistan, who have a large and desperate working class. When workers become sick, there is no compensation. For that reason, the United Nations developed the Basel Convention on the Control of Transboundary Movements of Hazardous Wastes and Their Disposal in 1992. The vast majority of the world's countries formally protect workers, though in practice the convention is not upheld. (The United States never ratified the convention.)

Further Reading

Carroll, Chris. "High-Tech Trash." *National Geographic*, January, 2008. http://ngm
    .nationalgeographic.com/2008/01/high-tech-trash/carroll-text.html.
Minter, Adam. "Reprise: Wasted 7/7, from the Motor Breakers to the Sample Room."
    Shanghai Scrap (blog), March 7, 2011 (6:32 a.m.). http://shanghaiscrap.com/?p=6448.
Minter, Adam. "The Motor Breakers of China." *The Atlantic*, February 27, 2011. http://www
    .theatlantic.com/international/archive/2011/02/the-motor-breakers-of-china/71759/.
Puckett, Jim. Interview with Terry Gross. "After Dump, What Happens to Electronic
    Waste?" *Fresh Air*. NPR, December 21, 2010.
Royte, Elizabeth. *Garbage Land: On the Secret Trail of Trash*. New York: Little, Brown,
    2005.

ELECTRONICS

Electronics is a branch of the science of electricity that deals with the flow of electrons, or current, passing through vacuum tubes, transistors, or other devices instead of merely running along a wire. Vacuum tubes, the first electronic device, removed air molecules that interfered with electron flow, amplifying currents and producing signals by oscillation. The simplest tube, the diode, changes electromagnetic waves sent out by radio broadcasting stations into signals that can be heard. Electronics generally uses tubes to control small electrical signals, capable of bringing not only sounds (radio) but also pictures (television). The first practical use of electronics came in the 1890s with the X-ray, which was produced by electronic tubes. This was followed by electronic tubes in radio, spawning a massive consumer goods industry by the 1920s, as well as a significant shift in home recreation patterns. By the 1950s, electronics had become the fifth-largest manufacturing industry in the United States, employing over a million and a half workers. In the coming decades, much of that work would shift overseas or be automated.

The electronics manufacturing giant of the postwar era was Japan. American military technological prowess shocked many Japanese. The war left the country extremely poor but with widespread experience with factory employment, and a high level of education and technological knowledge. Japanese production of radios boomed after the war; by 1955, they were being exported in large numbers. Japan benefited from access to American technology; the case of Sony's adoption of the transistor is a famous case in point.

Japan also benefited from its long history of government aid to industry. The Ministry of Industry and Technology helped the electronics industry by helping to establish common standards for the industry. Its efforts to shape the industry were not flawless, and often it was frustrated by small companies who grabbed the lead on larger, more well-connected firms.

Electronics manufacture, featuring fairly simple wiring boards, could also easily be taken up by new industrializers, like Taiwan, giving them a competitive export product early in the industrialization process. The pace of technological change was rapid, not only proving an obstacle to industrializing countries but also providing them with a major opportunity for growth.

South Korea provides a case of a country that began by assembling components for foreign companies and then moved into developing its own technologies. Like Japan, Korea was devastated by World War II, and especially by the Korean War (1950–53). Korea also benefited from occupation by the United States, which stimulated demand and provided access to the American market and technology. By the mid-1970s, South Korea sought to emulate Japan's success. Like Japan, the Korean government made electronics a national priority. Korean workers were largely literate and paid roughly 5 percent of their American counterparts. Korean wages were a fifth of Japanese workers, making the country a logical place for Japanese companies to locate factories. Korea's government supported industrial research and sought to stimulate domestic demand for products, but more importantly, oriented producers toward exports. By the 1980s, Korean firms were producing their own goods such as cassette radios for export; by the 2000s, electronics accounted for 20 percent of industrial production.

The electronics industry has shown enormous growth since World War II. Electronic advances moved from radios to computers, microwaves, and smart phones, products widely used both by industry and by consumers. Consumers throughout the world have revealed tremendous appetites for electronic products. The pace of change is enormous, with many countries designing, producing, and advertising electronic goods. The industry has its critics, those who suggest that humans are poorly prepared for a wired world because, while it stimulates us, it ultimately makes people less happy. The industry has been better at producing creative products than dealing with the toxicity for workers and communities that is a byproduct of electronics production.

See also Apple; Electricity; Electronic Waste or E-waste; Sony

Further Reading

Cyhn, Jin W. *Technology Transfer and International Production: The Development of the Electronics Industry in Korea.* Cheltenham, UK: Edward Elgar, 2002.

Nakayama, Waturu, William Boulton, and Michael Pecht. *The Japanese Electronics Industry.* Boca Raton, FL: Chapman and Hall, 1999.

Smith, Ted, and David A. Sonnefield, and David N. Pellow, eds. *Challenging the Chip: Labor Rights and Environmental Justice in the Global Electronics Industry*. Philadelphia: Temple University Press, 2006.

EMANCIPATION AND RECONSTRUCTION (UNITED STATES)

The emancipation of several million slaves was a major turning point in the economic and social history of the United States and was one of the most significant results of the American Civil War. Because the war destroyed slavery, furthered the growth of industry in the North, and strengthened the ability of the federal government to promote industrialization (by reducing the political power of planters), many historians have labeled the Civil War the "second American revolution." Once the war was over, however, there remained the enormous task of reconstructing Southern society. Freedmen (ex-slaves) were free, but free to do what? Who would control the land, the government, and the direction Southern society would take? Reconstruction is the period between 1863 and 1877 in which many different groups (freed slaves, former slave masters, Northern politicians) resolved these questions.

President Abraham Lincoln had sought to win the war with the South without abolishing slavery, but he was gradually convinced by abolitionists and by the difficulties of winning the war that attracting slaves to the North would deprive the South of its labor supply and supply the Union army with much-needed troops. Although the date of Lincoln's Emancipation Proclamation (January 1, 1863) is popularly believed to be "the" date of emancipation, historians argue that emancipation is best viewed as a process rather than as an event. For one thing, Lincoln's proclamation applied only to those parts of the South outside of the military control of the United States; within the several slave states loyal to the Union, emancipation of slaves was problematic, for slave owners loyal to the United States tried to retain their "property." In the Confederacy, the effective end of slavery was tied to the advances of the Union army. However, word of the remarkable document quickly spread throughout the South and resulted in what W. E. B. Du Bois termed a "general strike" that mortally wounded the slave regime. Numerous slaves found their way to the Union lines, and these "contrabands" proved to be capable and effective soldiers.

Presidential Reconstruction (1863–66) allowed the vast majority of former confederates to easily reenter political life. Radical Reconstruction (named after the Republican congressional faction) imposed far harsher restrictions on the political rights of former confederates who had made it clear they would refuse freedmen any significant political, social, or economic rights. During Radical Reconstruction, blacks participated in Republican state governments in the South that attempted to broaden educational opportunities and protect the rights of laborers. However, ex-slaves' demands for land redistribution went unanswered, and most freedmen ended up as sharecroppers. The political aspects of Reconstruction were bitterly contested in the South, and white Democrats used a combination of terror and appeals to white supremacy against white and black Republicans. By the mid-1870s, Northern Republicans were tiring of the South's constant political turmoil. In 1877, to help resolve a bitterly contested presidential election, the last of the federal troops were withdrawn from the South, leaving black voters at the mercy of white Democrats. Within 20 years, most Southern blacks had been disenfranchised. Many historians have argued that the failure of the South to continue the political and social reforms of Reconstruction and the continued reliance on cotton production (and other raw materials) hampered industrialization of the region. The demise of Reconstruction also ended the experiment of federal intervention to solve social problems for another 60 years.

See also Black Workers; U.S. South

Further Reading

Foner, Eric. *Reconstruction: America's Unfinished Revolution, 1863–1877.* New York: Harper and Row, 1988.

Litwack, Leon. *Been in the Storm So Long: The Aftermath of Slavery.* New York: Knopf, 1979.

EMANCIPATION OF THE SERFS (RUSSIA) (1861)

Czar Alexander II emancipated the serfs, or Russian peasants tied to estates owned by nobles or the government, in 1861 in an attempt to modernize Russia, which had been humiliated in the recent Crimean War by industrialized countries; the czar

Famine-stricken former serfs head to St. Petersburg, Russia, during the late 1800s. (Library of Congress)

was also seeking to avoid peasant unrest. After emancipation, serfs were no longer owned by their landowner and could buy property, marry, and use the courts. Access to the land remained a crucial question—as it did with freed slaves in the post–Civil War South in the United States, where emancipation had been settled on terms decidedly favorable to landowners. The Russian government eventually loaned money to former serfs to buy parcels of inferior land at inflated prices. The situation drove many peasants further into poverty, and as a result of the revolution of 1905, the government canceled these debts. Peasants' dissatisfaction with the issue of land ownership was a major cause of the 1917 Russian Revolution. Nevertheless, emancipation did promote a more mobile labor force and provided some fuel for early Russian industrialization.

See also Feudalism and Manorialism; Serfs

Further Reading

Zaionchkovsky, Petr Andreevich. *The Abolition of Serfdom in Russia.* Gulf Breeze, FL: Academic International, 1978.

ENCLOSURE MOVEMENT

The English enclosure movement occurred between the sixteenth and early nineteenth centuries as entrepreneurial farmers gained control over what had previously been "common lands." By requiring owners to fence their lands, an expensive process, enclosure forced many small owners to sell to large estates. During the period of manorialism, the legal status of land was different from its status under capitalism. Land was not unencumbered private property: it often came with certain rights and obligations—peasants could owe dues (payable in cash, agricultural goods, or labor) to their manorial lords and the church. Peasants could also claim "traditional" rights to gather fuel, graze their cattle, and hunt on what was technically private property but had come to be viewed as common lands. In the sixteenth century, market-oriented farmers realized they could increase profits by fencing in or enclosing their land, expelling their tenants (or keeping them from "poaching"), and growing cash crops—often raising sheep or growing grain. The enclosure movement helped to create the entrepreneurial ethos and legal system necessary to allow the emergence of capitalism throughout the economy—which in turn facilitated the rise of the Industrial Revolution. Although estates employed laborers, they did not provide work for the growing rural population. Hence, the enclosure also created a class of landless workers who gradually became employed in proto-industrial manufacturing. Karl Marx saw this process as "primitive accumulation."

Many societies that became tied to the world system of trade also experienced somewhat similar enclosure movements. In Meiji-era Japan, peasants were denied access to common lands, and the government forced them to pay their taxes in cash, not grain. In nineteenth-century Sri Lanka (then Ceylon), the British colonial government sold what it considered "waste" lands to English planters who began to raise tea, rubber, and coffee on these mountain plantations. Although Kandyan Sinhalese peasants had used these lands to supplement their incomes, they did not generate products for the market (and thereby were unable to pay the taxes in cash) as the planters did. Throughout the world, market-oriented farms or plantation systems were created through similar enclosure movements that caused the decline of peasant producers. Government was crucial in this process of enclosure, for it changed both the legal status of land and the tax requirements.

Although enclosure movements allowed the spread of market-oriented production, the social effects seldom replicated the results in England (creation of capitalism, entrepreneurs, and landless free-wage workers). Occurring at roughly the same time as in Western Europe, enclosures in Eastern Europe also caused a growth of market-oriented production but caused a tightening of manorial relations—peasants retained some rights to land but had far less freedom of movement than Western European workers. The harsh serfdom in Russia and Eastern Europe later inhibited industrialization. The spread of the plantation system throughout colonial Asia and Africa in the nineteenth century created economic relationships and social classes that would complicate industrialization efforts in the twentieth century.

See also Decolonization

Further Reading

Bandarage, Asoka. *Colonialism in Sri Lanka: The Political Economy of the Kandyan Highlands, 1833–1886.* Berlin: Mouton, 1983.

Neeson, J. M. *Commoners, Common Right, and Social Change in England, 1700–1820.* Cambridge: Cambridge University Press, 1993.

ENERGY

Perhaps the most revolutionary part of the Industrial Revolution was harnessing new types of fuel for human activity. Thus the quest for new forms of energy continues an ancient pattern. Agricultural societies harness and consume two or three times more energy (such as charcoal to make iron) than traditional hunting and gathering societies. Industrial societies consumed several times more energy than agricultural societies. Modern societies consume several times more energy than their late-nineteenth century counterparts.

Fossil fuels allowed humans to dramatically increase production of once-rare goods, such as steel. Machines powered by coal enabled prices for steel, clothing, and shoes to fall. Industrialization allowed greater specialization of trades. By the early nineteenth century, farm families no longer spun wool, ground their own corn or wheat, or made their own shoes. By the mid-twentieth century, many farmers did not even grow a vegetable garden.

Coal was gradually displaced. Beginning in the late nineteenth century, industrial societies began to use petroleum, although coal remained more important for several decades. Hydropower provided some electricity, and in the mid-twentieth

This 1926 photo shows peasants viewing the electrification of the Moscow district—proof that the Soviet experiment was making life easier. (Bettmann/Corbis)

century, nuclear power also expanded the energy repertoire. There is enormous potential in green, or alternative, sources of energy, such as wind, solar, geothermal, or liquid fuels produced by bacteria. At present, the world is still highly dependent on petroleum; coal is still important for electricity production, especially in China, developing countries, and the United States. Petroleum remains critical for transportation, heating, and electricity generation.

For more than a century, petroleum was cheap. For every unit of energy spent on energy drilling, refining, and transporting oil, people received 10 to 20 units of energy back. That changed in the 1970s when OPEC quadrupled the price of oil in 1973; another price shock occurred in 1979 following the Iranian revolution. Higher prices spurred more production, and by the mid-1980s, prices returned to historically-low levels. That situation changed around 2003. There is considerable evidence that energy prices will remain at high levels, although high prices should result in new sources becoming available and/or greater conservation taking place. Importers, such as the United States, produce enormous amounts of natural gas via "fracking." Japan hopes to extract frozen methane that lies under the ocean floor. Twice as much energy exists in methane deposits as in all other conventional fuels.

In some countries, that process is well under way. Following the 1973 spike in prices, European countries began to conserve energy. Taxes kept oil prices high, and that slowed the growth of car sales. Europeans also encouraged people to use trains and buses, and in cities, to walk or use bicycles. Denmark ultimately eliminated its petroleum imports, in part by emphasizing alternative fuels and in part by increasing oil production in the North Sea. There is considerable research that the United States could reduce its energy usage by one-third through measures such as conservation, new fibers to transport electricity, etc.

In general, there is a strong relationship between energy-intensive societies and wealthier ones. For instance, Egypt uses less energy per capita than the United States, and it is less productive and less wealthy. Western Europe is a relatively modest user of energy but remains highly productive. There are exceptions to the rule: Russia and Saudi Arabia are energy inefficient and poor largely because it takes energy, and increasing amounts, to produce petroleum. Societies such as China and Brazil need to consume energy to raise standards of living, and as they do, they consume more energy. In 2009, China bought more cars than the United States, and its rate of car ownership is around 2 percent of the United States.

Further Reading

Stearns, Peter N. *The Industrial Revolution in World History*. 3rd ed. Boulder, CO: Westview, 2007.

ENGINEERING

Engineering is essentially a modern profession devoted to organizing materials and power for human use. Prior to the eighteenth century, design of tools, roads, and mines was a function of artisans, who often operated by trial and error. There was no formal training and little by way of theoretical principles. Growing technical knowledge in Europe and a rising demand for a more organized approach to nature stimulated the emergence of specialized training and a growing body of manuals and textbooks aimed at teaching design. France and other countries began to set up schools of mining engineering and what is now called civil engineering—the design of roads and bridges—in the late eighteenth century. Artillery services in the military also demanded engineering training. Several prestigious technical schools were set up under the French Revolution and Napoleon that turned out mechanical and chemical engineers as well. The term "civil engineering" entered the English language about 1750, introduced by John Smeaton, an English engineer. The first formal engineering training in the United States was offered at the military academy, West Point, in 1802. Rensselaer Polytechnic Institute, in Troy, New York, taught engineering from its foundation in 1824 and offered the first engineering degrees in the nation in 1835.

Engineering became increasingly vital to the Industrial Revolution, educating people not only to plan infrastructure but also to design and adapt equipment, testing materials, and so on. Trained engineers played a growing role in invention, particularly from about 1850 onward, as amateur inventors gave way to organized programs of technical development. By the late nineteenth century, engineers also began to design work systems, plotting efficient routines with their time-and-motion studies. This development led to an increasing association of engineers with management, as well as a new level of intensification of work. Engineers in the United States spearheaded this development, which was capped by the work flow systems devised by Frederick Taylor soon after 1900. New industrializers, like Japan, rapidly developed a training system for engineers. By the late twentieth century, Russian and Japanese production of engineers exceeded that of the West.

The emergence of engineering as a formal profession was complicated. Engineers, particularly in industry, long preserved a trace of manual, artisanal labor; the distinction between skilled workers, capable of installing machinery, and formal engineers was not always clear-cut. Even the development of formal training at technical schools did not eliminate the ambiguity. Technical schools operated at various levels, turning out technicians as well as genuine engineers. It was hard to get engineers to agree that they belonged to the same group, and rival associations often formed. By the late nineteenth century, however, the professionalization of engineering was clearly under way in most industrial countries. Associations were formed, licenses were established, and standards of training were raised, with increasing amounts of pure science supplementing the applied work. Engineering training also involved the inculcation of a rigorous work ethic. French technical schools in the late nineteenth century, for example, imposed strict schedules on students that were designed to serve as a model for work life.

See also Technocracy; University

Further Reading

Layton, Edwin, Jr. *Revolt of the Engineers: Social Responsibility and the American Engineering Profession.* Baltimore: Johns Hopkins University Press, 1986.

Noble, David F. *America by Design: Science, Technology and the Rise of Corporate Capitalism.* New York: Knopf, 1977.

ENGLAND. *See* Britain

ENTERPRISE UNION. *See* Company Union

ENTREPRENEURIAL SPIRIT

The role of businessmen in the Industrial Revolution is obvious. Particularly in early industrializations, like those of Britain or the United States, where the government role was relatively modest, ambitious, risk-taking entrepreneurs—businessmen who undertake new ventures—played a crucial role in introducing new equipment, factories, and organizational innovations such as corporations. Many of these industrialists seemed to possess distinctive values and energy—an entrepreneurial spirit—that historians have sought to describe and explain as part of understanding what industrialization was all about. Some historians, following the lead of the great sociologist Max Weber, author of *The Protestant Ethic and the Spirit of Capitalism*, have attributed a kind of religious zeal to industrialists, particularly those of Protestant origin, as they sought to demonstrate God's favor by pressing for ever greater industrial success. Other cultural values, including the general Enlightenment faith in progress and hard work and later social Darwinist beliefs in struggle and competition, both caused and reflected the entrepreneurial spirit of nineteenth-century industrialists.

The beliefs of industrialists varied, of course. A few were ardent reformers, like Robert Owen, eager to expand but

Robert Dale Owen was a successful British industrialist and reformer who came to the United States and helped found the utopian community of New Harmony, Indiana, in 1825. (Perry-Castaneda Library)

also anxious to produce better conditions for their workers. Many early industrialists, not surprisingly, sought business success only to ape the lifestyle of aristocrats or established merchants. In every European industrialization, a number of factory owners pulled out of industry when they had made some money, buying land and imitating the gentry, or encouraged their sons to enter respectable professions instead of business. At the same time, most industrialists shared with the wider middle class a set of beliefs about the importance of respectability, hard work, education, the weakness but moral virtue of women, and so on. They were quick to criticize workers for excessive drinking or sexuality, and in their shop rules sought to discipline labor according to middle-class standards.

Many leading industrialists, however, went beyond middle-class conventions; they did seem to display a distinctive spirit. These people might introduce new equipment in a given region not once but many times. They schooled their sons to succeed them, establishing family industrial dynasties like the Krupps or the Wendels. France, for example, had many industrialists who pioneered in setting up cotton factories, then branched out into machine building, and soon spearheaded regional railway development as well. Lesser industrialists often recognized, and sometimes criticized, the drive of these leading entrepreneur leaders. In the north of France, for example, the parents of industrialist Motte Bossut ran a small textile operation; they thought in terms of a family business, keeping an eye on all branches of production and sales themselves. Their son, however, wanted to imitate British success; he thought big and set up one of the first big spinning and weaving factories in the area. His parents lent him some money but refused to set foot in his giant factory because they felt its scale and risk were immoral.

Industrialist leaders had immense self-confidence. They worried about failure but usually felt that God was on their side. "The rich are in effect destined by Providence to be the leaders of work," as one French business paper put it. They took pride in their boldness: "You have everyone against you, and you find no resources other than your own courage." They loved hard work, often refusing to take vacations and feeling extremely uncomfortable when illness kept them from the job. They saw themselves as authors of their own fortune but also, in providing jobs, the source of general prosperity as well—"the soul of the whole industrial development of a country." They pushed for steady growth, confident in the power of their own will to overcome obstacles: "We had then only one goal, only one thought: always to expand."

Religion spurred this spirit. So did new political principles, like those of the French and American revolutions, which seemed to open new opportunities for men of talent and allowed businessmen to claim that they had replaced aristocrats and other traditional leaders as the source of dynamism in their societies. Accidents of personality undoubtedly help explain why some entrepreneurs had this driving spirit and why others were content with more modest success or shunned risk altogether.

Entrepreneurial spirit cannot be measured; its role in industrialization is impossible to quantify. But it was relevant. It also helps explain some of the conflict that industrialization engenders. The same spirit that prompted industrialists to grow also made them peremptory with their workers and intolerant of demands to share power. It was hard to get most of these entrepreneurs, so confident of their own worth, to think in terms of bargaining. It was easy for them to consider workers a breed apart, almost a different species, and therefore malleable according to the interests of the firm. Several historians have noted the particularly severe discipline imposed by U.S. industrialists in the later nineteenth century. They attacked unions and sought new ways to regulate work in the interests of efficiency, in a context in which many workers were also immigrants and so viewed as foreign as well as socially inferior. Entrepreneurial spirit helps explain why a singularly undemocratic work organization prevailed in one of the oldest Western democracies.

See also Causes of the Industrial Revolution; Entrepreneurs, Origins of; Liberalism; Religion

Further Reading

Casson, Mark. *The Entrepreneur: An Economic Theory*. 2nd ed. Northampton, MA: Edward Elgar, 2003.

Pollard, Sidney. *The Genesis of Modern Management.* Cambridge, MA: Harvard University Press, 1965.

Stearns, Peter N. *Paths to Authority: The Middle Class and the Industrial Labor Force in France.* Urbana: University of Illinois Press, 1978.

ENTREPRENEURS, ORIGINS OF

New kinds of businessmen played a vital role in the Industrial Revolution everywhere. Their role was particularly obvious in early industrializations, as in Britain, where the government was not particularly active. But entrepreneurs loom large in early Russian industrialization, in Japan (particularly in textiles), and more recently in places like South Korea and China. Because early industrial entrepreneurs were by definition willing to take considerable risks, investing in untested new machinery and organizing new kinds of business operations (over 50% of all businesses failed in the early industrial period), historians have long been interested in explaining where they came from and why some societies seem to produce more of them than others. By the late nineteenth century, the most successful industrial entrepreneurs were becoming part of a new upper class in industrial societies, influencing politics and military activity as well as business; again, the question of origins becomes significant.

Individual industrialists came from all sorts of backgrounds. Different industries obviously had different kinds of access; textiles, with relatively low capital requirements, recruited a wider variety of people than did heavy industry. Some aristocrats became entrepreneurs. A few, often very visible, industrialists came from working-class backgrounds, beginning as factory hands and working their way up through sheer talent and energy. Many cultures liked to celebrate these rags-to-riches stories. This kind of mobility was very rare, however, far rarer than historical myths like to acknowledge. By 1848, for example, only one industrial entrepreneur in Alsace came from a worker background. At the other end, most entrepreneurs were not from established merchant or aristocratic families, which tended to look on these new forms of business as dirty and chancy.

Most entrepreneurs came from families in the middle ranks of society, eager to move up or at least find new ways to defend family position in a changing environment. Some industrialists were former artisans who expanded their operations. Some simply gradually converted shop production into a small factory operation. Many had initially participated in a domestic manufacturing system as foremen; over several generations, the family acquired a bit of capital and set up a small factory. Commercial farmers were another source of industrialists, particularly in the United States and Japan. Most industrialists, in other words, came from families with some commercial or manufacturing experience.

Some entrepreneurs also came from minority religious groups, eager to seize new opportunities for business success to establish themselves in the status hierarchy, precisely because standard educational and political opportunities were closed to them. A disproportionate number of early English businessmen were Dissenters (minority Protestants in an Anglican society). Old Believers in Russia and Protestants in France provided important sources of entrepreneurship. An important theory— the Weber thesis, devised by sociologist Max Weber—argues further that Protestantism provided a culture of self-denial and a need to demonstrate success as a sign of God's favor that was ideal for capitalism. In fact, the religious origins of industrialists, including many Catholics in places like Belgium and northern France, are too diverse to sustain the Weber thesis fully, but some elements may be applicable.

See also Entrepreneurial Spirit; Middle Class; Ruling Class

Further Reading

Crouzet, François. *The First Industrialists: The Problem of Origins.* New York: Cambridge University Press, 1985.
Jaher, Frederic. *The Urban Establishment.* Urbana: University of Illinois Press, 1982.
Rubinstein, W. D. *Men of Property: The Very Wealthy in Britain since the Industrial Revolution.* New Brunswick, NJ: Rutgers University Press, 1981.

ENVIRONMENT

From its early stages, the Industrial Revolution has damaged the natural environment, though the industrialization process can also remedy some of the damage it creates. Early industrialization in Western Europe and the United States created

Slash-and-burn agriculture is as old as the Neolithic Revolution, but chain saws and trucks ensure that vast areas are burned every year—a contributor to global warming. (Media Clips/Fotosearch)

massive, smoke-belching factories, whose unsightly intrusion was often noted and deplored. Early railroads cut through farmland, often injuring livestock. Clearer environmental impact came from expanding uses of water power. Dams to facilitate water power created lakes covering former farmland and often disrupting more modest uses of power like mill wheels. Diversion of water for power use affected other users of rivers. A number of environmental court cases focused on these issues. Growing cities also polluted, thanks in part to unprocessed handling of human and animal wastes; this was a major environmental problem, for river and water quality began to decline.

By the mid-nineteenth century, environmental problems had widened. The expansion of metallurgy and the development of the chemical industry added to the amount of industrial wastes and by-products, most of which were dumped into waterways. At the same time, concentration of heavy industry radically worsened air quality because of the intensity of smoke. Slag heaps intruded on farmland, creating eyesores. In this context, countermeasures began to develop. Sewage treatment was advocated, along with underground sewers to reduce urban health hazards. By the 1880s, spurred by several epidemics, regulations about dumping wastes into waterways began to be actively discussed. A strong environmental movement developed in the United States, combining public health officials with wider elements of the middle class, some of whom were hostile to all-out industrialization. Regulations were opposed by most factory owners, and many workers placed the security of their jobs over environmental niceties. Aside from sewage treatment, effective regulation developed only slowly. Nevertheless, from the early twentieth century, the quality of waterways in the Western world began to improve. Other measures set aside park lands, like the national parks in the United States, to limit industrial exploitation of nature. Not only regulation, but also new technologies—use of petroleum instead of coal, for example—facilitated some environmental gains. Even smoke abatement occurred. Pittsburgh, a metallurgical center often so blackened by smoke in the 1920s that streetlights had to be turned on at noon, reduced smoke pollution notably by the 1950s by requiring home owners to use oil and gas for cooking and heating instead of coal.

Water and local smoke problems were tackled with some effect, but air pollution as a whole tended to worsen in the twentieth century; as the geographical range of emissions widened, the internal combustion engine created dangerous exhausts, and the chemical composition of air pollution became more complex. Adoption of tall smokestacks aided smoke abatement locally but spread pollution to other areas. Thus midwestern smoke harmed forests in Canada through acid rain, while emissions from the Ruhr killed trees and lakes in Scandinavia. There was general agreement that air pollution had replaced water pollution as the leading industrial environmental issue. Beginning in the 1960s, environmental concerns became increasingly important in Western society; "Green" parties developed considerable strength in Germany and Holland. Consciousness of these issues spread internationally until the United Nations Conference on the Human Environment, held in

Stockholm in 1972, brought representatives from over 100 countries together to discuss the global environmental. The declaration produced at the event provided further impetus to an international environmental movement, stating that "to defend and improve the human environment for present and future generations has become the imperative goal of mankind." In 1997, the Kyoto Protocol, part of the United Nations Convention on Climate Change, was adopted as a measure to combat global warming. The protocol, which came into effect in 2005, and as of 2011 included 191 countries, seeks to limit emission of greenhouse gases by committing member countries to a schedule of specific national reduction targets.

However, despite the apparent urgency indicated by such initiatives, the debate about trade-offs between environmental damage and economic growth continues. Since the early 1970s, claims in the United States that legislation such as the Clean Air Act and the Clean Water Act would depress industry by imposing overwhelming operating costs have become a constant refrain in policy debates. The "cap-and-trade" system was implemented as one way to balance environmental and economic concerns by creating tradable emissions permits that individual firms could buy or sell according to their particular needs while keeping overall emissions at a fixed level. Many preferred this method of emissions regulation because it allowed users more flexibility in controlling emissions than earlier, more rigid "command and control" regulations. At the same time, it brought environmental controls under the purportedly more efficient sway of market forces, an inherent virtue for many friends of industry.

As the emergence of a strong international environmental movement over the last several decades indicates, the Industrial Revolution also had an important impact on environments in other parts of the world from the late nineteenth century onward. In tropical countries, rubber plantations expanded over forests. In Australia, Argentina, and the American Great Plains, commercial agriculture, or sheep and cattle ranching, transformed prairies. The spread of mining and quarrying also damaged environments in Asia, Africa, and Latin America. Massive deforestation occurred in the nineteenth century, both near industrial centers and around mining and grazing operations outside the West. Brazil cut down tropical forests to make way for coffee plantations, to export products to the industrial, caffeine-hungry West. Brazil's later exploitation of its massive rain forest for agriculture and cattle farming, after the mid-twentieth century, has had a deep impact on the chemical balance of the atmosphere there and throughout the world.

Industrial revolutions outside the West have typically been at least as heedless of environmental consequences as the West has been, and have added to the overall global effect. Indeed, sometimes the pressure to compete with the West has encouraged even more recklessness. Western firms established in other parts of the world often exploited lax regulation to economize on environmental procedures; this was a major issue with U.S. firms with branches on the Mexican border, where chemical runoffs coursed freely over the ground and into waterways. Japanese pollution increased notably during the twentieth century until several serious cases of pollution-induced illness, and the sheer intensity of air pollution, forced more active regulation and the development of a substantial environmental industry by the 1970s.

The Soviet Union and its satellites were particularly careless as their industry expanded after World War II amid Cold War competition. Chemical wastes burned out large stretches of land and many waterways. By the 1980s, it was estimated that at least a quarter of Russian territory had been seriously damaged by pollution, and the health of many Russians was adversely affected as well, contributing to a rising mortality rate. Projected clean-up costs were mind-boggling, and some sites simply had to be abandoned. China's industrial push after 1978 frankly put growth ahead of environmental quality. Water and air pollution increased; the Chinese referred to airborne emissions in the cities as the "Yellow Dragon," and the nation became one of the leading industrial contributors (after the United States) to the emissions that seem to cause global warming. Countries like China often charge that established industrial powers, with enough wealth to cope with some of their own environmental problems, are trying to impose unduly rigorous standards on the rest of the world.

Environmental history is just beginning to open up as a field of inquiry. We will learn more about industrialization's impact on the environment and people's reactions to it, especially before recent times, in the future. Of course, not all modern environmental issues are directly a result of industrialization itself; sheer population and urban growth also play a role, even in nonindustrial areas. Thus, where many call for tighter industrial regulations to combat environmental degradation, some experts suggest that economic resources spent in this way could be better utilized fighting world hunger and other more immediate social problems.

See also Minimata Disease; Population Growth

Further Reading

Brimblecombe, Peter. *The Big Smoke: A History of Air Pollution in London*. London: Methuen, 1987.

"Global Issues: Environment." United Nations. http://www.un.org/en/globalissues/environment/ (accessed May 30, 2012).

Hays, Samuel. *Conservation and the Gospel of Efficiency*. Cambridge, MA: Harvard University Press, 1959.

Hays, Samuel. *Beauty, Health, and Permanence: Environmental Politics in the United States*. New York: Cambridge University Press, 1987.

Lomborg, Bjorn. *Cool It: The Skeptical Environmentalist's Guide to Global Warming*. New York: Knopf, 2007.

Merchant, Carolyn. *American Environmental History: An Introduction*. New York: Columbia University Press, 2007.

Steinberg, Theodore. *Nature Incorporated: Industrialization and the Waters of New England*. Cambridge: Cambridge University Press, 1951.

Tucker, R. P., and J. F. Richards, eds. *Global Deforestation and the Nineteenth-Century World Economy*. Durham, NC: Duke University Press, 1983.

ERIE CANAL

Prior to canals, rural areas that were not near rivers or the seacoast were at a severe economic disadvantage due to the extremely high cost of shipping goods by horse or oxcart over dirt roads. The Erie Canal was built between 1817 and 1825 and connected Buffalo with Albany, a distance of 363 miles; goods were then shipped down the Hudson River to New York City and from there to international markets. This infrastructure project was paid for by New York State and was a stunning success—transportation rates from western New York to New York City fell by 90 percent. The Erie Canal made it economically feasible for farmers to export their grain and other products to Europe; river towns in upstate New York, such as Rochester, boomed. Many other states, notably Pennsylvania, also financed the construction of canals to facilitate trade with their hinterlands. By the 1840s, railroads, which did not have to close in the winter, began to replace canals as a means of connecting markets. Canals remained more important in parts of Europe and Asia. Oceangoing traffic was also facilitated by the Suez and Panama canals, among many others.

Further Reading

Taylor, George Rogers. *The Transportation Revolution, 1815–1860*. Armonk, NY: M.E. Sharpe, 1977.

ETHNICITY

Ethnicity is an identity based on national heritage and is thus akin to nationalism, although it is generally subsumed under another national identity (e.g., Italian Americans are Americans first and Italian second). Much of the work done by historians of ethnicity has examined how ethnic communities and identities were shaped by the processes of immigration and industrialization, particularly in the United States.

Immigrants to industrial cities of the late nineteenth-century United States encountered a situation ideally suited to the creation of ethnic identities. Industrialists hired and placed workers on the basis of their supposed "national character." Slovaks were considered strong and docile, and this stereotype and the process of chain migration (whereby established immigrants helped their family and friends acquire similar jobs) resulted in most Slovak immigrants working in the coal mines and steel mills of Pennsylvania. (Their Czech counterparts spread much more widely throughout the United States.) From the late nineteenth century through the first decades of the twentieth century, relatively stable employment allowed immigrants to buy homes near their workplace and to establish a network of churches, newspapers, ethnic clubs, and self-help societies that reinforced ethnicity.

Most of the established urban ethnic neighborhoods dwindled or disappeared after World War II with the decentralization of housing and employment.

Immigrants arriving from Asia, the Caribbean, and Latin America after World War II encountered volatile job markets that afforded fewer opportunities for long-term employment or upward mobility. As a result, their ethnic neighborhoods have not been as stable as earlier ones.

Like national identities, ethnic identities are not "natural" but have to be created. Before the 1930s, for example, "Italian" migrants to the United States often identified more strongly with their specific village or region of origin than with Italy. Once in the United States, however, Italians were assumed by others to have a common language, cuisine, and culture. The ethnic identity of Italians was shaped by mass-media stereotypes, Italian nationalists, and the Italian government, which was itself in the process of creating an Italian national identity in an effort to unite a deeply divided country. Italian ethnicity in the United States began to acquire cohesion in the 1920s, although disputes between fascist and communist Italian Americans deeply divided the community.

The relationship between ethnicity and racial identity is complex and problematic. Although, at least in the United States, there are many similarities between ethnicity and race, many scholars are beginning to investigate the ways in which some migrants (such as Italians) become "white" and others (such as Mexicans or Puerto Ricans) become "black" or "brown."

See also Postindustrial Economies; Racism

Further Reading

Bodnar, John. *The Transplanted: A History of Immigrants in Urban America*. Bloomington: Indiana University Press, 1985.

Takaki, Ronald. *Strangers from a Different Shore: A History of Asian Americans*. New York: Penguin, 1989.

EUROPEAN UNION (EU)

The European Union is an economic and political grouping of 27 member states, which evolved from other coordinating bodies set up in the aftermath of World War II. The idea of greater European unity responded primarily to the conflicts that had generated two major European wars. By focusing particularly on economic coordination, European leaders believed that national rivalry could be supplanted, but that in the process economic growth and stability would be encouraged as well—as against the narrow and counterproductive national responses that had greeted the Depression of the 1930s. Core members of the coordinating effort were also advanced industrial countries, so the European bodies automatically became major players in global economic discussions and in the further development of industrialization itself.

The first postwar European body to emerge, linking France, Germany, Italy, Belgium, the Netherlands, and Luxembourg, was the Coal and Steel Community, focused on coordinating the redevelopment of heavy industry and designed to link resurgent Germany firmly to a larger European interest. This was followed by the European Economic Community, which was replaced by the European Union in 1993. The Community, and now the Union, gradually developed a single market, by undoing national tariffs, while also facilitating the movement of labor across borders; trade policies were coordinated, and the European body also provided development subsidies to less-developed regions within the community. A single monetary zone, using the euro as currency, united some members from 1999 onward.

The EU was hailed as a "United States of Europe," an antidote to the long history of warfare and economic rivalry on the continent. The EU was also seen as a counterweight to the North American Free Trade Agreement (NAFTA), which bound together Canada, Mexico, and the United States. In some ways, the EU went further than NAFTA: citizens of the EU could cross borders and work anywhere they could find a job.

Poorer members of the EU had been skeptical of creating a free-trade zone; they believed it would benefit global companies in Germany or France. In contrast to NAFTA, the EU spent considerable money in poorer countries to improve physical infrastructure (roads, airports, etc.) and to help raise living standards. In the early 1990s, countries like Spain and Ireland enjoyed a boom that resulted from EU spending. As average income approached average EU levels, those countries started paying money toward raising living standards in new member states, such as Poland and Slovakia. Richer countries, such as Germany, gained access to a larger market for their goods. In the 2000s, the value of the euro rose far beyond the U.S. dollar and was beginning to be seen as a credible alternative to that hegemonic currency.

Most former communist countries clamored to join the EU. For Poland, the Czech Republic, or Romania, EU membership was a way to not only raise living standards but join Western Europe. Numerous Poles, for instance, found work throughout the continent, even in Ireland, which had traditionally been a labor exporter. Countries had to prove that their financial house was in order (even if it was not), that the rule of law covered the economy, and that basic human rights were respected. Many former Warsaw pact members also joined NATO, the military alliance. The rapid extension of the EU stopped at the Bosporus, however. Turkey applied for membership, and while it seemed to have met all the criteria, it was rejected. Turkey turned its attentions to the Islamic world.

The European Community benefited from rapid economic growth of most member states. Economists debate how much the new levels of coordination promoted growth, or whether growth occurred somewhat independently and fostered growing acceptance of the coordinating body. Certainly, industrial expansion and coordination proved mutually supportive.

The European Union has not been without controversy. Even amid the original members, economic disputes, including the amount of assistance to provide farmers, surfaced periodically. Later expansion added many less industrialized states, prompting concern about other issues such as financial stability or the out-migration of workers. The Union was also periodically accused of overregulation from its headquarters in Brussels, in its attempts to protect product quality or in its environmental measures. And the Union always walked a fine line between its own coordinating powers and the national independence of member states. The economic crisis that opened in 2008 revealed new fissures, even within the euro currency zone, as stable economies headed by Germany were called upon to loan money to countries like Greece that had gone deeply into debt.

There were some basic problems with the EU that were not immediately apparent to all. EU members were to have their government's debts under 3 percent of their gross domestic product. Virtually all the countries used accounting tricks to cover up the fact that they did not, in fact, meet that standard. At first it did not matter, although that fact has come back to haunt the EU in the wake of the financial crisis that began in 2008. If a member country defaulted on their public debt, as Greece first threatened to do (and then Ireland, and then Portugal, and perhaps Spain and Italy), what would that do to the value of the euro?

If countries had their own currency, they could default on their debts, which would severely devalue their national currency. But that would make it easier for those countries to export goods or attract tourists and import fewer goods. Argentina in the 1990s and Iceland in the 2000s followed the strategy of currency devaluation with relatively mild negative consequences. But with a strong euro, the only choice was to make painful cuts to public services, which drove the local economy deeper into recession. That made the government less able to repay their loans, and they would restart the process again. There was no central bank, akin to the U.S. Federal Reserve, that could help stimulate the overall economy.

The European Union has constituted a powerful economic bloc, with great influence in global trade. By 2010, it had half a billion inhabitants and generated about 28 percent of the total world economy, with 161 of the world's top 500 corporations. The EU is the culmination of a long-standing dream to create a united, prosperous, and peaceful Europe. Whether this is the mechanism to make that dream a reality is not clear.

Further Reading

Dina, Desmond. *Origins and Evolution of the European Union*. New York: Oxford University Press, 2006.

McCormick, John. *The European Union: Politics and Policies*. Boulder, CO: Westview, 2007.

Pinder, John, and Simon Usherwood. *The European Union: A Very Short Introduction*. New York: Oxford University Press, 2008.

Yesilada, Birol, and David Wood. *The Emerging European Union*. 5th ed. Boston: Longman, 2010.

EXPLOITATION

The concept of exploitation owes much to the theories of Karl Marx. Marx did not believe that exploitation was created by oppressive working conditions per se; he argued that through a variety of means capitalists were able to "appropriate the

Lewis Hine's photographs of exploited children, taken on assignment for the National Child Labor Committee, in the early 1900s. (Library of Congress)

unpaid labor" of workers. In part, they achieved this end by imposing new forms of work discipline, by lengthening the workday, or by instituting new technology (which Marx believed was also derived from workers' labor). Higher production resulted, but wages did not rise. Marx wrote that the "appropriation of unpaid labor is the basis of the capitalist mode of production . . . even if the capitalist buys the labor power of his laborer at its full value as a commodity on the market, he yet extracts more value from it than he paid for," and this surplus becomes the basis for the increasing wealth of industrialists. Workers' belief in exploitation, whether Marxist or not, motivated many labor struggles, particularly between the 1870s and the 1950s.

See also Capitalism; Marx, Karl; Surplus Value

Further Reading

Marx, Karl. *Capital: A Critical Analysis of Capitalist Production.* London: Penguin, 1976.

EXPORTS

Exports are the sale of goods or services from one country or region to another. Countries can rely on high levels of exports without industrialization. For instance, throughout the nineteenth century, actual or de facto colonies (such as India, Argentina, or the U.S. South) were dependent upon exporting raw materials or agricultural products to purchase manufactured goods. However, exports are a vital means by which industrializing countries finance the purchase of machinery, technical assistance, or necessary raw materials. Exports do not need to be finished products: in the 1930s, the Soviet Union exported food products to help pay for its industrialization effort, while Argentina in the 1940s relied on its exports of meat and hides to help offset the initial cost of industrialization. Exporting goods is vital to certain latecomer industrializers, such as South Korea, whose internal markets cannot absorb their production.

See also Import Substitution; World Systems Theory

Further Reading

Moykr, Joel. *The Economics of the Industrial Revolution.* Lanham, MD: Rowman & Littlefield, 1985.

F

FACTORIES IN THE FIELD (McWILLIAMS)

The book *Factories in the Field* was written by Carey McWilliams to describe the history of migrant farm workers who toiled on California's enormous commercial farms—what McWilliams termed California's first factories. Unlike farmers in the rest of the country, these rural proletarians would never become independent landowners because the vast majority of available farmland was controlled by a handful of corporations and families (who received subsidized water to irrigate their land). The phrase "factories in the field" has been applied to other large-scale commercial farming operations, such as eighteenth-century Caribbean sugar plantations that relied on slave labor. Although planters relied on slaves and not free workers for their labor supply, these enterprises were "modern" because planters viewed land and labor simply as inputs that could produce wealth.

See also Slavery; World Systems Theory

Further Reading

McWilliams, Carey. *Factories in the Field: The Story of Migratory Farm Labor in California.* Boston: Little, Brown, 1939.

Wolf, Eric. *Europe and the People without History.* Berkeley: University of California Press, 1982.

FACTORY ACTS

Factory acts were early laws regulating working conditions. Soon after 1800, the British government gradually began to introduce new laws about work, after having removed older restrictions as part of the growing adoption of laissez-faire policies. Knowledge of deplorable factory conditions became widespread, however, forcing a new, if still rather limited, approach. Various parliamentary inquiries produced ample evidence of abuse of children in unsafe conditions. The first Factory Act (1802) provided twice-yearly washings for the dormitories of pauper apprentices and forbade more than 12 hours of work. It was not enforced. An 1819 law banned children under 9 from cotton factories, and limited children between 9 and 16 to 12 hours a day. Still, the law was not enforced. The law of 1833 again forbade use of children under 9 in textile mills, set a 9-hour day for older children, and provided for paid inspectors and some enforcement. The 1842 law regulated women's work in the mines; an 1844 law reduced children's hours of work. The 1847 Ten Hours Act applied to women and children. Men were excluded out of deference to laissez-faire, since they presumably could bargain for themselves. Other regulations dealt with fencing in dangerous machinery, educating child workers, and sanitation.

See also Child Labor

Further Reading

Cooke-Taylor, Richard Whately. *The Factory System and the Factory Acts.* London: Methuen, 1894.

FASCISM

Fascism is a totalitarian ideology and movement that opposes communism while still granting the state a large role in organizing society and the economy. In the 1920s and 1930s, fascists came to power in industrializing societies that were in economic crisis, where living standards were low or declining, and where traditions of political democracy were weak—Italy, Germany, Japan, Spain, and Eastern Europe.

In the early 1920s, the first fascist state arose in Italy, led by Benito Mussolini. Although Italy was a "victor" of World War I, the war had caused numerous deaths, economic chaos, and political destabilization. In 1919, communists sought to emulate the 1917 Russian Revolution. They launched a series of strikes and attempted to establish political control through councils (soviets) of workers. Though the strikes failed, they provoked widespread fear among the wealthy. Mussolini, a former socialist, borrowed much of the rhetoric of the left while receiving financial backing from wealthy landowners and industrialists. He used this money to pay street thugs and put them into uniform. Once in power, Mussolini arrested leftists and greatly expanded the state's role in the economy, underwriting the formation of large cartels. The fascist state was unable to raise standards of living or stimulate the Italian economy. Largely to compensate for these failures, Mussolini launched a series of ill-fated imperialist adventures in Libya, Ethiopia, and Albania.

Adolf Hitler at a Nazi Party rally in Nuremberg, Germany, ca. 1928. (National Archives)

Fascists (called National Socialists, or Nazis) seized power via the ballot box in Germany in 1933. World War I had devastated the German economy, and the resulting severe inflation ruined many white-collar workers and other members of the middle classes. German fascism, too, was financed by industrialists who feared that workers would turn from Social Democratic parties to communism. Industrialized countries with well-established parliamentary systems tolerated fascist regimes because they seemed preferable to communism. Once in power, Nazis relied upon repression of leftists and other opponents as well as propaganda through the mass media of radio and film to legitimize their rule. Germany quickly launched a military buildup (a kind of military Keynesianism) that stimulated the industrial economy and concentrated production in cartels. Employment increased, though wages were low. Tolerance of big business and profiteering created economic inefficiency. Nazi Germany's attempt to conquer other countries arose from its need for raw materials and markets that had already been seized by advanced industrialized countries, as well as from its theories of racial superiority.

World War II destroyed the fascist regimes in Germany, Italy, Eastern Europe, and Japan—but it did not destroy fascism itself. Francisco Franco, Spain's fascist leader, came to power with the backing of Mussolini and Hitler and survived until the mid-1970s. Quasi-fascist regimes have come to power in Latin America, and fascist movements have gained strength since the 1970s as living standards for many workers and white-collar workers have declined. In countries as diverse as Italy, France, Spain, the United States, and India, fascists (or those influenced by fascism) have offered racist explanations for their countries' economic (and allegedly moral) decline.

See also Imperialism; Japan; Racism

Further Reading

Kershaw, Ian. *The Nazi Dictatorship: Problem and Perspectives in Interpretation.* New York: Arnold, 1989.

Laqueur, Walter, ed. *Fascism, A Reader's Guide: Analysis, Interpretations, Bibliography.* Berkeley: University of California Press, 1976.

FEMINISM

Feminism, the movement that works to promote women's rights, has two relationships to the Industrial Revolution. First, although industrialization did not cause Western feminism, it certainly influenced it; second, feminism in recent decades has greatly affected interpretations of the Industrial Revolution.

Western feminism resulted from new ideas associated with Protestantism and the Enlightenment, and changes in family structure and limits on women's work developed well before the Industrial Revolution. In fact, many industrial societies, like Japan, have never developed feminism similar to that of the West in range or intensity. Nevertheless, industrialization encouraged feminism by reducing women's economic roles and creating new grievances, while simultaneously promoting an ideology of purity. Middle-class beliefs in the nineteenth century in Western Europe, Canada, Australia, and the United States emphasized women's freedom from commerce and their greater virtue. Many feminists urged new political and economic rights for women on the basis of their presumed virtue; since women were purer, they should have at least equal rights. This element was especially strong in late nineteenth-century feminism. After achieving the vote, and particularly after World War II, feminist concerns shifted more directly to the economic front. Betty Friedan's influential *Feminine Mystique* (1963) argued against women's confinement to the home and helped justify and motivate new work roles. Since industrial society continued to emphasize work as the basis of worth, women demanded their share, particularly as birthrates dropped and educational levels rose (two other results of industrial society).

Contemporary feminist theory has altered the study of the Industrial Revolution in several ways. It has emphasized gender as a factor in industrialization. The male-centeredness not only of manufacturers but of most male workers, now a commonplace in historical research, is a valuable contribution of the feminist emphasis. The omission of women from most labor movements and the assumptions even of many apparently sympathetic socialist leaders that women's real place was in the home have been more fully grasped, thanks to feminist research. Feminists also encouraged historians to expand their analysis from women in factories to women in society more generally. As a result, historians paid greater attention to processes such as the industrialization of household work, which lightened the labor of traditionally male work (such as grinding grains) in the nineteenth century. The mechanization of water systems or cleaning tools came much later. Feminism has prompted reinterpretation of several standard landmarks in industrial history. Movements to limit women's hours of work, like the British law of 1847, were once seen as belated triumphs of humanitarianism, as reformers finally realized how difficult factory life was for women. Now these same measures are judged to be products of male assumptions about women's frailty and as efforts to limit women's economic competitiveness. Historians of industrialization continue to try to understand the complex relationships of gender to work.

See also Women Industrial Workers

Further Reading

Rendell, Jane. *The Origins of Modern Feminism*. New York: Schocken Books, 1984.
Scott, Joan W. *Gender and the Politics of History*. New York: Columbia University Press, 1988.

FEUDALISM AND MANORIALISM

Feudalism was the dominant legal, political, and economic system in Europe between the eleventh and seventeenth centuries. In legal terms, feudalism was a series of reciprocal obligations between vassal and lord, in which both had obligations to each other. A vassal held land under a lord, in exchange for which the vassal had to provide his lord fees or services (often military ones). Feudalism was a decentralized system of political authority based on the amount of military force, particularly cavalry that elites could lead into battle. In both Europe and Japan, feudalism was associated with frequent warfare. Economically, feudalism was based on manorialism, in which nominally landowning lords exacted fees, taxes, or labor from their tenants. Feudalism ended in Western Europe in the seventeenth century and in Japan in the nineteenth century.

Manorialism was a system of agricultural management in which both serfs and landlords had ownership rights. Under manorialism, most people were peasants or tenants on large estates. Population tended to increase beyond the productivity of the land, resulting in famines or plagues. Due to a limited market for goods (mostly luxury goods, such as weapons and textiles), cities were small. Elites could increase their wealth by attempting to extract more financial surplus from their serfs (which peasants resisted) or by expanding their holdings through warfare or colonization. The constant warfare of the period encouraged the formation of stronger states that could resist outside powers or conquer more lands.

By the fourteenth and fifteenth centuries in Western Europe, the increased wealth of elites led to more commerce and manufacturing, which adversely affected peasant production (the main source of wealth) by straining food production. In response, elites attempted to increase peasants' dues and taxes. The resulting class conflict fundamentally reshaped the manorial system. Peasants in parts of Germany and France gained clear title to the land, although elites obtained wealth through the state. English elites maintained title to their land and gained higher rents, though they were forced to give their tenants greater day-to-day freedom. Once freed from pre-market reciprocal obligations of the manorial system, many producers in Western Europe were able to reorient themselves to the rising tide of international commerce. The emerging capitalist system of agriculture and commerce helped to promote the entrepreneurial ethos and to provide the surplus food and population necessary for the Industrial Revolution.

Manorial systems also developed in Eastern Europe, Japan, Latin America, and elsewhere. The conditions of serfs were worst when landlords tried to increase agricultural exports to industrial areas in the eighteenth and nineteenth centuries. Manorial labor proved to be too inflexibly tied to the land for industrialization, which is the reason the system was progressively abolished.

See also Agriculture; Emancipation of the Serfs (Russia); Serfs

Further Reading

Ashton, T. H., ed. *The Brenner Debate: Agrarian Class Structure and Economic Development in Preindustrial Europe*. Cambridge: Cambridge University Press, 1990.

Sweezy, Paul M. *The Transition from Feudalism to Capitalism*. London: Verso, 1978.

FINANCE CAPITAL

Finance capital is a concept developed by Marxists around the beginning of the twentieth century to explain the increasing power that banks exercised over industry in capitalist societies. By the late nineteenth century, industrial corporations came to rely on bankers to supply them with capital, either through loans (as in Germany, Japan, and to some extent the United States) or through selling and controlling stocks (as in England and the United States). Marxist economists believed that finance capitalists constituted one segment of the capitalist class that exerted a specific political and economic force. Finance capital was believed to be economically and territorially aggressive, resulting in various forms of imperialism including World War I. By encouraging patterns of international industrialization that favored keeping some regions as cheap producers of raw materials, finance capital helped to prevent regions such as Latin America from acquiring enough capital for industrial development.

See also Mellon, Andrew; Morgan, John Pierpont, Sr.; Neocolonialism; Zaibatsus

Further Reading

Hilferding, Rudolf. *Finance Capital: A Study of the Latest Phase of Capitalist Development.* London: Routledge, 1981.
Johnson, Simon, and James Kwak. *13 Bankers: The Wall Street Takeover and the Next Financial Meltdown.* New York: Pantheon, 2010.

FIVE-YEAR PLANS

Five-year plans were developed in the Soviet Union in the late 1920s to implement Stalin's economic goals of industrialization and collectivization. The Soviet economy was still recovering from the economic devastation of World War I, the revolution, and the years of civil war that followed 1917, but the first five-year plan in 1928 nonetheless set ambitious targets in heavy industry and agriculture. Unlike the preceding period (the New Economic Policy), where entrepreneurs were tolerated and even encouraged, the first five-year plan made economic decision making the province of the state. Central economic planners attempted to anticipate and coordinate the nation's existing or planned production facilities toward a single goal.

The five-year plan effectively marked the beginning of the Stalinist period of economic development and attempted a bold departure from the dominant logic of capitalism, which advocated (if it did not always follow) laissez-faire principles. Western governments predicted disaster, though in fact their own economies soon succumbed to the worldwide crisis of the Great Depression. Stalin's gambit stimulated an enormous economic boom, a point that communists throughout the world (with strong encouragement from Moscow) were happy to point out. The state poured massive amounts of capital into schemes that established blast furnaces, rolling mills, and various factories throughout the country. One visitor to the Soviet Union in the 1930s remarked that "I have seen the future and it works," an observation that appealed to many unemployed workers.

The five-year plans, which instituted centralized planning, production quotas, and the replacement of markets with a command economy, also created problems for the Soviet Union. Stalin had redirected resources from agriculture to industry, and from consumption to capital investments. Moreover, industrial firms were not free to reject poor-quality goods but continued to circulate them throughout the economy; machinery made with defective steel had to be made bulkier to compensate. Left-wing critics termed the system a "planless plan" because even central planners abandoned parts of the plan to exceed quotas in one sector or factory—thereby creating shortages elsewhere. Despite its limitations, many capitalist countries, including India, South Korea, and Japan, have adopted informal five-year plans as a means of galvanizing their economies. In these countries, the government helps to establish national production goals and allocates its resources, tax burdens, and incentives accordingly.

Woman welds beams at the site of a tractor factory in Belarus, May 9, 1947, part of Stalin's Five-Year Plan. (Bettmann/Corbis)

See also Stakhanovites; Stalinism; State, Role of the

Further Reading

Nove, Alec. *An Economic History of the USSR, 1917–1991*. Harmondsworth, UK: Penguin, 1992.
Preobrazhenskii, Evgenii Akekseevich. *The Crisis of Soviet Industrialization: Selected Essays*. White Plains, NY: M.E. Sharpe, 1979.

FLYING SHUTTLE

This device, invented by the Englishman John Kay in 1733, was intended to increase output in domestic manufacturing. Previously, two weavers were needed to operate a loom, one to move thread vertically and the other to guide it horizontally. The flying shuttle operated in a grooved runway on each side of the loom, propelled by a handle or treadle; it carried the horizontal thread, or weft, automatically.

Thus one worker, instead of two, could operate even a broad loom, and the whole process was speeded by the more rapid movement of the shuttle. Later improvements allowed different shuttles carrying various colors for making patterns. The shuttle responded to the increasing demand for cloth, but it increased demand in turn, necessitating greater production of thread—a key incentive for subsequent innovations in spinning. This was part of the accelerating pattern of technological change. The flying shuttle could be combined later with powered equipment in mechanical looms.

See also Crompton, Samuel; Hargreaves, James; Jacquard, Joseph; Textiles

Further Reading

Hills, Richard L. *Power in the Industrial Revolution*. Manchester, UK: Manchester University Press, 1970.

FORD, HENRY (1863–1947)

Henry Ford was the "inventor" of the moving assembly line. He created an industrial empire by mass manufacturing automobiles. Ford began making cars in the 1890s and established the Ford Motor Company in 1903. Production of the Model T

Henry Ford and his first car, which had bicycle tires. (Library of Congress)

began in 1908, and by 1913, Ford had utilized the assembly line technique to radically increase the number of cars he produced; prices also dropped steadily, and by the early 1920s, the Model T was the most popular car in the world. The River Rouge factory became the world's largest industrial facility, employing 60,000 workers, making its own steel and forging parts, and assembling the finished product. In 1914, Ford shocked the world by announcing a policy of paying five dollars a day for unskilled labor, an extremely high wage. Workers had to live up to Ford's rural Protestant standards of morality and adapt to the monotonous and brutal work regime. The pace of work was so grueling that Ford workers frequently fell asleep on Detroit's streetcars, and "Ford widows" were a staple of workers' humor. Ford's empire began to fray in the 1920s when General Motors began to attract customers by offering a wide selection of styles and models.

See also Fordism; Sloan, Alfred P.

Further Reading

Meyer, Stephen. *The Five Dollar Day: Labor, Management, and Social Control in the Ford Motor Company, 1900–1921*. Albany: State University of New York Press, 1981.

FORD MOTOR COMPANY

Henry Ford founded Ford Motor Company in 1903. The company enjoyed a rapid rise through the success of its Model T. The company exported Model T's and was building them all around the world. By 1919, half of all cars sold in the United States were made by Ford. In the 1920s, however, General Motors and its head, Alfred P. Sloan, replaced Ford as the industry leader. On principle, Ford would not sell on credit; GM would. All Model T's were black; GM offered a wide variety of cars for every purse and purpose.

In the 1930s, Ford almost went under, but unlike most car companies, it did not. Ford brought out the Model A, a relatively cheap car with a powerful V-8 engine. The car helped Ford hang on. In the 1920s, Ford built tractors in the Soviet Union. He seemed to sympathize with Adolf Hitler; in 1938, he received the highest medal the Nazi regime could give to a foreigner. Like all U.S. manufacturing firms, Ford was rescued by the flood of orders during World War II.

Ford remained family-run, although it was a publicly traded company. Henry Ford passed control to his son shortly after World War II; by the end of the 1950s, Ford had brought out a number of popular cars. For a period, it surpassed Chevrolet as the biggest producer of cars. During the 1960s, the company, along with GM, seemed to build cars that fell apart relatively quickly; critics charged it was "planned obsolesce." In the early 1970s, Ford was forced to give way to the wave of Japanese imports. By 1979, Ford bought a stake in Mazda, in part to have access to high-quality, energy-efficient engines.

The company struggled to build quality small cars in the United States, but managed to do so in most of the 25 other countries it made cars. Beginning in the 1980s, and continuing through the 2000s, Ford made most of its profits in the United States from the sales of trucks and SUVs. The F-150 pickup was the single most popular vehicle for many years running. By the end of the 1980s, Ford bought British Jaguar, a sign of its newfound profitability. It would sell the company to Tata Motors, an Indian company, in 2008.

Further Reading

Banham, Russ. *The Ford Century: Ford Motor Company and the Innovations That Shaped the World.* New York: Artisan, 2002.

Feldman, Richard, and Michael Betzold, eds. *End of the Line: Autoworkers and the American Dream.* Urbana: University of Illinois Press, 1990.

FORDISM

Fordism, an approach developed by Henry Ford and adopted and modified by many other industrialists, strictly controlled the production process to maximize output, sales, and profitability. In the early 1900s, automobiles were a luxury item, produced in small batches by groups of highly skilled workers. Ford believed that an enormous potential market existed in the United States for a cheap, durable automobile. He sought to meet that demand by mass producing the Model T on continuously moving assembly lines manned by large numbers of semiskilled workers. Time-and-motion specialists analyzed the variety of tasks performed by craftsmen to meticulously subdivide their skills into actions that could be performed by numerous unskilled laborers. If they could conform to the regime of the assembly line as well as to the strict standards of Ford's Sociological Department, which frowned upon drinking, political radicalism, and other bad habits, workers were promised generous wages. Ford's strategy was an enormous success. In the early 1910s, the Model T became the most popular car in the world, purchased by professionals, farmers, and even prosperous workers. The company's increased sales, and hence profits, enabled it to continue the welfare programs for its workforce.

Ford's labor innovations provoked other industrialists to label him a radical. Leftists sharply criticized Ford for his paternalist attitude toward his workforce and called the pace of his assembly line inhuman. However, industrialists who adopted Ford's mass production ultimately undermined the first phase of Fordism. By the late 1920s, General Motors, led by Alfred P. Sloan, captured much of Ford's market share by extending credit to consumers and offering them a wide variety of models at a time when the Model T had to be paid for in cash and was available only in basic black. Sloan's strategy undermined both Ford's profits and his paternalism. Although Ford was able to regain much of his market share with the Model A, his self-interested benevolence toward his workers disappeared. The social workers once employed by Ford to investigate workers' living habits were replaced by armed goons who intimidated workers and sought to keep the workplace free of unions.

Between the 1910s and the 1970s, many American corporations applied Ford's approach in a modified form both to their workforces and to the market. The essentials of the system remained the use of assembly-line techniques and primarily semi-skilled labor, who were rewarded for repetitious work with relatively good pay. Although Fordist companies bitterly fought unions in the 1930s, Fordism eventually managed to survive the unionization of the industrial work force. A major turning point came in the lengthy strike of 1946. The United Auto Workers argued that GM should "open its books" to reveal that it could provide workers a substantial raise without raising the price of its cars. In the end, workers got their raise only after the union acquiesced to GM's price hike. Throughout the postwar period, GM and other Fordist employers retained strict control over the marketing of their products and continued to insist on "management's right to manage" the workplace. The union won a privatized welfare system for its members, with substantial health and pension benefits, but these gains came at the expense of workers who worked for companies in more competitive sectors of the economy through rising car prices. Although Fordist companies continued to automate the workplace, which eliminated jobs and degraded the work environment, their workers' standard of living continued to rise as mass consumption became an accepted fact of life.

Elements of Fordism had become dominant in most advanced industrialized countries, but the system began to unravel in the 1970s. Companies in the United States began to lose their monopoly position in the market when competition from abroad undercut their prices. High wages were only one factor in the demise of Fordism; more importantly, management had become accustomed to passing along their poor investment decisions to consumers. Global industrialization undermined the ability of Fordist firms to force others to subsidize their social contract. Fordist employers eventually abandoned their unofficial social contract with their workforces by laying off workers and cutting wages and benefits. Fordism was so entrenched, however, that it is still in the process of being unmade in some parts of the economy.

Post-Fordist corporate strategy seeks to adapt to a far more competitive international market by adopting "flexible production," using a variety of plants and firms throughout the world to manufacture products rather than centralizing production in the home country. As a social system, post-Fordism is still being implemented, and its consequences will be global. It will clearly foster the spread of industrialization throughout the world and has already contributed to the stagnation or decline in living standards among many workers in advanced industrialized countries.

See also Long Waves of Capitalism

Further Reading

Gramsci, Antonio. *Selections from the Prison Notebooks*. New York: International Press, 1971.

Lichtenstein, Nelson, and Stephen Meyer, eds. *On the Line: Essays in the History of Auto Work*. Urbana: University of Illinois Press, 1989.

FOREIGN TRADE

Foreign trade has been a crucial aspect of all countries' efforts to industrialize. Mercantilist theories had been discredited by the nineteenth century, but most countries sought to promote exports to promote employment and to protect their currencies. Throughout most of the nineteenth century, when English manufacturing was the most advanced in the world, England advocated free trade, arguing that countries should pursue industries in which they held a "comparative advantage." However, most industrializing countries (such as the United States, Germany, and Japan) sought varying degrees of protectionism for domestic industries—as did English manufacturers in the twentieth century when their industries became increasingly uncompetitive.

The difficulties that industrialized countries faced in regulating trade among themselves led to the colonization of Africa and Asia in a search for markets. Another attempt to regulate international trade was the creation of cartels that allocated market share between countries. In the 1920s and 1930s, the informal institutions that could have countered "trade wars," such as the gold standard, broke down, and increasingly protectionist measures, such as the Smoot-Hawley Tariff

While foreign trade contributes to a healthy economy, it must be balanced against domestic needs. The Congressional Steel Caucus supports the domestic steel industry, and its workforce. In 2002, President George W. Bush passed tough foreign steel tariffs due to the Caucus's efforts. (U.S. House of Representatives/Office of Pete Visclosky)

in the United States, resulted in a sharp curtailment of global trade. While the Soviet Union and fascist regimes in Germany and Italy attempted to create a measure of "autarky," or independence from foreign trade, all regimes relied on technology or raw materials from abroad, which had to be paid for by exports.

After World War II, the United States (now the world's largest creditor and exporter) created new institutions to regulate foreign trade. Free trade would be the goal of international agreements, although that trend was balanced by institutions such as the World Bank that provided loans to weaker economies. Between the 1950s and the 1990s, these institutions helped to increase the size of international trade by over 10 times; in the 1950s, imports and exports accounted for 10 percent of the U.S. economy, and in the 1980s, that figure had grown to 25 percent. Although the United States ran a significant trade surplus until the early 1960s, it was balanced by the Marshall Plan and by assuming the responsibility for the defense of Germany and Japan. Direct military spending in Asia and Europe was another way the United States countered its trade surpluses. By the 1960s, high levels of military spending contributed to the erosion of the balance of trade for the United States. By the 1970s, Germany and especially Japan emerged as the world's strongest export economies. Unrestrained trade remains the goal of international agencies (such as GATT), although regional free-trade zones such as the European Union and NAFTA may signal a turn to regional trade "cartels."

See also Bretton Woods Agreement; Division of Labor; Imperialism; Import Substitution; Smith, Adam

Further Reading

Itoh, Makoto. *The World Economic Crisis and Japanese Capitalism*. New York: St. Martin's Press, 1990.

FOREMEN

Early in the Industrial Revolution, factory owners realized that they could not supervise all their workers directly. They employed intermediaries, called foremen, to oversee and often also to hire and fire. (These agents were sometimes called overseers, as in New England textiles.) Foremen had also worked in the old putting-out system, bringing orders to workers in the countryside and picking up products; so the idea of a subordinate director of labor was not new. In factories, foremen often acquired considerable personal power. The quality of work life often depended on the foreman's personality, for although most foremen began their lives as workers themselves, many became harsh and arbitrary. Many small strikes occurred over brutal treatment by foremen, and physical blows and sexual intimidation of women were not uncommon. By the early twentieth century, the power of foremen was diluted; employers no longer trusted them to run the work process at maximum efficiency. Engineers now studied factory arrangements and set basic work rules, which foremen were supposed to carry out. By the 1920s, beginning in the United States, foremen were also expected to quench potential labor protest, becoming grievance experts who knew how to control their own emotions in the interests of calming workers down. The position remained an important one, and foremen still formed an important bridge between labor and management, but the heyday of the foreman was over.

See also Engineering

Further Reading

van den Eeckhout, Patricia. *Supervision and Authority in Industry: Western European Experiences, 1830–1939.* New York: Berghahn Books, 2009.

FRANCE

French industrialization began in the 1820s with the establishment of several large metallurgical firms, the expansion of coal mining, and the rapid spread of factory production in textiles. This stage involved active imitation of Britain and imports of British equipment (generally illegal, by British law), as well as employment of British workers when skilled French operatives were lacking. Heavy industry concentrated in the north, in Lorraine, and in a few scattered factory towns like Le Creusot; the most modern textile center emerged under the auspices of Protestant manufacturers in Alsace. Industrial growth accelerated with concerted government

Otto von Bismarck's German Army crosses the Loire River to confront the French during the Franco-Prussian War. (North Wind Picture Archives)

backing during the Second Empire (1852–70), when the main railroad network was completed, and government-sponsored banks stimulated industrial capital. France was hurt by the loss of Alsace and much of Lorraine in the Franco-Prussian War (1871), but industry grew in 1900 and again in the 1920s. The Great Depression hit France late but fairly hard. Very rapid industrial growth characterized the post–World War II period, when France became one of Europe's industrial leaders.

France's lack of extensive coal holdings (the nation had to import coal from England) in combination with possibly undue government protection and relatively slow population growth held industrialization back in the nineteenth century, though growth rates approximated those of Britain. France emphasized light industry and luxury goods production (furniture and silk), pressing craftsmen into more rapid, uniform manufacturing operations. This characteristic accounted for a large artisanal voice in French trade unionism. Silk workers in Lyons, for example, pressed to work faster and with less artistry, recalled earlier rhetoric from the Revolution of 1789 in arguing for new political rights to provide greater voice and status. From the 1880s until 1914, French unionism included more radical goals and heavier emphasis on producer control than was common to union movements in other countries. By 1900, France also employed more women workers than Britain or Germany, though the rate of urban growth still lagged slightly. Historians used to charge France with a lack of dynamic entrepreneurial spirit, but their claims have faded as France's rapid productivity gain has been better understood. It is nevertheless true that French industry, particularly during the nineteenth century, was overshadowed by the more impressive growth of Germany.

See also Confédération Générale du Travail (CGT); Germany; Syndicalism

Further Reading

Cameron, Rondo. *France and the Economic Development of Europe, 1800–1914*. Princeton, NJ: Princeton University Press, 1961.

FRANCHISE

The history of the franchise, or voting rights, is more a part of political development than of industrialization, but there is an important connection between franchise and industrialization. As industrial working classes became better organized, they typically pressed for voting rights, believing that if they had a voice in government they could win important legislation to improve their lot. Chartism in England was an early expression of this impulse in the 1830s and 1840s. German workers sought political rights in their early socialist movements. Where voting rights were slow to come to the urban working class, as in Belgium, Austria, and Italy, important agitation, including general strikes, ensued between 1900 and 1914. The desire for franchise was a vital ingredient in the revolutionary agitation among Russian workers in 1905 and 1917, as well. Where voting rights came early, however, they could provide workers enough voice in the political process to actually limit the development of political radicalism.

For example, free male workers gained the vote in the 1820s in most U.S. states, before industrialization had really begun. As a result, the labor movements they formed did not reflect a sense of exclusion from the political process. This aspect of the U.S. labor movement has often been used to explain why socialism gained far less ground in the United States than in Europe or even Japan.

Most commonly, voting rights were granted to male workers after several decades of industrial developments—1867 in Britain, the 1860s in Germany. When the vote came, governments fairly quickly began to develop programs that would appeal to the working class, to prevent the growth and radicalism of socialism. The German leader Otto von Bismarck's social legislation of the 1880s exemplifies this reaction, though it actually failed to blunt the socialist movement. From the late nineteenth century, use of the vote helped European and U.S. workers, socialist or not, to gain new laws regulating conditions of work and developing welfare programs. A similar pattern developed in Japan in the 1920s, when the government began to encourage more protective policies in the major companies, including greater employment security, as well as heightened nationalism, as means of improving relations with new working-class voters. The history of workers' parties expanding rights for workers tended to open the way for other groups to gain rights, such as women, ethnic minorities, and eventually, for sexual minorities.

See also State, Role of the

Further Reading

Eley, Geoff. *Forging Democracy: The History of the Left in Europe, 1850–2000*. New York: Oxford University Press, 2002.

FREE ECONOMIC SOCIETY

This organization, based in St. Petersburg in 1765, was one of several in Russia that preached technical improvements similar to those being introduced in British farming. The society maintained contact between Russian leaders and the economic practices of the West. Only a few estate owners actually introduced new measures, however. For the most part, greater grain output for export was achieved by requiring more labor from the serfs.

Further Reading

Blackwell, William L. *The Beginnings of Russian Industrialization, 1800–1860*. Princeton, NJ: Princeton University Press, 1968.

FREE TRADE. *See* Protectionism

FRENCH REVOLUTION (1789–93)

The French Revolution has generally been interpreted by Marxists as one of the great "bourgeois" revolutions—a political corollary or preparation for the industrial

On July 14, 1789, a peasant uprising culminated in the storming of the Bastille, the armory-prison that had become a symbol of the tyranny of the ancien régime. (John Clark Ridpath, *Ridpath's History of the World*, 1901)

revolution. Many historians have revised the view that the French Revolution was based primarily on a class conflict between a rising capitalist bourgeoisie and a feudalistic aristocracy, noting, for instance, that most revolutionaries were themselves aristocrats (albeit ones that criticized royalist practice and ideology). However, France's revolution did transform the political and legal framework of the French state and spurred the development of a capitalist and industrial society.

The French Revolution arose out of the enormous social and fiscal crises of the feudalistic and manorial "ancien régime," or "old order." The constant warfare of the French king had bankrupted the state, and its escalating demands for taxation led aristocrats to call a parliament to limit the king's expenditures. The aspirations of other social classes for political representation and economic relief, however, resulted in a far more radical and democratic regime than that envisioned by the king's aristocratic critics. A fierce struggle ensued between political factions from different social classes over how to democratize society and reform the ancien régime. Artisans' guilds were abolished, which allowed workers more flexibility in adjusting to the new forms of production and technology that were emerging. Internal tariffs on commerce were dropped. Peasants managed to eradicate their manorial payments, although the dissolution of the manorial system allowed the introduction of more efficient forms of agricultural production—which ultimately harmed the peasantry.

The French popular struggle to reform the old order led to a counterattack by conservative monarchies that plunged Europe into a long series of wars, concluded only when Napoleon Bonaparte (the usurper of the revolution) was defeated in 1815 by allies led by a smaller but far more industrialized Britain. Although artisans, peasants, and the urban poor had ceased to control political power relatively early in the revolutionary process, the principles of political democracy and new economic legislation spread far beyond France's borders. The French Revolution established new legal codes to regulate trade, property, and labor that aided the spread of the Industrial Revolution throughout Europe.

See also Le Chapelier Law; Revolutions of 1848

Further Reading

Goodwin, Albert, ed. *The American and French Revolutions*. Cambridge: Cambridge University Press, 1965.

Hunt, Jocelyn. *The French Revolution*. New York: Routledge, 1998.

Lefebvre, Georges. *The French Revolution*. New York: Columbia University Press, 1964.

FRONTIER SETTLEMENT

The development of white settler colonies throughout the Americas, Africa, and Australia beginning in the sixteenth century helped to spread the industrial system throughout the world. These settler societies frequently expanded the amount of farmland in production for the global marketplace by further colonizing the country. Frontier settlement offered European societies an outlet for excess population, expanded the amount of raw materials available for the urbanizing population, and provided important markets for manufacturers.

The social cost to the indigenous peoples was profound. Throughout the Americas, most indigenous inhabitants died from disease, although war and outright theft of land also occurred when Europeans expanded into already settled areas or grew impatient with the sometimes slow rate of the Indians' decline. In parts of Latin America, where the precontact population had been large, and in Africa, indigenous people became a significant source of labor for farms and later industries, although whites reserved the best jobs for "civilized" workers.

In most cases, white settler societies exported agricultural products and minerals to centers in Europe. Throughout the nineteenth century in Australia, Argentina, and New Zealand, exports enabled the upper classes in the white populations to enjoy relatively high standards of living. Strong personal, cultural, and financial ties to Europe facilitated the transfer of technology and capital necessary for industrial production and efficient agriculture and mining. By the mid-twentieth century, settler countries that had not successfully industrialized, notably Argentina and New Zealand, began to suffer economically, both because the prices of raw materials declined and because European countries ended their preferential trading relationships.

See also Dual Labor Markets; Primitive Accumulation; Racism; South Africa; United States

Further Reading

Denoun, Donald. *Settler Capitalism: The Dynamics of Dependent Development in the Southern Hemisphere*. New York: Oxford University Press, 1983.

FULTON, ROBERT (1769–1815)

Robert Fulton is best known for designing the first commercially successful steamboat, the *Clermont*. Born in rural Pennsylvania, Fulton showed a talent for design at an early age, making skyrockets for a town celebration and household utensils for his mother. Apprenticed to a jeweler, he went to Europe to become an artist. He traveled widely in Europe, studying science and mathematics. Fascinated by technology, he designed various canal boats and locks, plus a dredging machine for cutting canal channels.

In 1797, he began to work on a submarine, creating several prototypes but failing to gain full backing either from Napoleon or from the British. In 1802, a U.S. ambassador urged him to concentrate on the steamboat. His first effort, launched on the Seine River, sank because its engine was too heavy, but a second model worked. Fulton ordered a new engine from England and returned to the United States, building the *Clermont* in 1807. It became a regular passenger vessel on the Hudson. Part of the boat's success owed to Fulton's concern with passenger comfort. Fulton built a small fleet for use on various rivers, and he continued work on military warships and underwater guns.

Further Reading

Judson, C. I. *Boat Builder: The Story of Robert Fulton*. New York: Scribner, 1940.

G

GENERAL COMMISSION OF FREE TRADE UNIONS (GERMANY)

The major German labor federation was formed in 1890 under the auspices of the Social Democratic Party. The "free" union movement was distinct from important though smaller Protestant, Catholic, and Polish organizations. The German federation formed at roughly the same time as major national union federations in other countries, when working-class leaders felt the need for greater coordination and more political influence in the face of the growing power of employer federations and giant corporations. The German federation was distinctive in its close and sometimes subordinate relationship to the Socialist Party; French unions stayed more separate from politics, and in Britain unions were actually more powerful than the Labour Party itself. The German federation did press socialists for greater pragmatism, for members wanted to see concrete gains, and it deviated somewhat from socialism in the attempt to recruit union members. Initially composed primarily of craft unions, the federation grew to encompass the growing industrial movement. Although local movements often insisted on great autonomy, the influence of the federation grew fairly steadily; in 1896, it was even able to expel a printers' union for bargaining too closely with employers. The federation was disbanded by Hitler and then revived after World War II.

See also Internationals

Further Reading

Eley, Geoff, *Forging Democracy: The History of the Left in Europe, 1850–2000*. New York: Oxford University Press, 2002.

GENERAL ELECTRIC (GE)

General Electric was formed in 1892, in part with power plants owned by Thomas Edison. In its early years, the company was a classic trust and owned or controlled numerous power plants and utilities. GE was also a major manufacturer, making machinery for power plants, lightbulbs, lamps, and electrical appliances such as radios, washing machines, and air conditioners. The company also made complex machines such as turbines, locomotives, and components for military contractors. GE made the first U.S. jet engine, in 1942. By 1930, the company was making plastics; in the 1950s, computers. By this point in time, it operated around the world.

Thomas Edison was relatively uneducated compared to today's standard, but proved to be one of the most prolific and revolutionary inventors in American history. (Library of Congress)

In the 1950s, GE looked like a traditional manufacturing company, albeit one that was moving into the computer age. It was a tough negotiator with unions. The company shifted production out of large unionized plants to smaller ones in rural areas where unions never got a foothold.

In 1981, Jack Welch became CEO. He is reputed to have reviewed each arm of the company and sold off the 10 percent that was least profitable. Under his direction, GE diversified and spun off numerous divisions, such as computers and aerospace. In 1986, it bought NBC. Finance (GE Capital) became an increasingly important part of its profits. In the 1990s and the early 2000s, GE seemed unstoppable and was the first company to make $10 billion a year in profit. After Welch left, GE fortunes and stock prices sagged; like many financial companies, GE had overstated profits and understated liabilities.

It is rare for a company to last 100 years. GE was an original member of the Dow Jones, and remains there. The company reflects the changes in corporate America over the course of the twentieth century.

Further Reading

O'Boyle, Thomas F. *At Any Cost: Jack Welch, General Electric, and the Pursuit of Profit.* New York: Vintage, 1999.

Schatz, Ronald W. *Electrical Workers: A History of Labor at General Electric and Westinghouse, 1923–60.* Urbana: University of Illinois Press, 1983.

GENERAL MOTORS (GM)

General Motors or GM was founded in 1908 as a conglomeration of numerous U.S. automotive companies. At the time, Ford was the dominant company in the industry because of its cheap and reliable Model T. Customers had to pay cash and had their choice of color, as long as their choice was black. By contrast, GM developed a wide range of cars for every taste and purse. It also loaned buyers the money to purchase its cars. As a result, it was the world's largest automaker from 1931 until 2007, before Toyota displaced it (although GM regained the top spot again in 2011). Until the 1980s, GM was the largest private employer in the United States, when Wal-Mart claimed that honor.

Given its history, GM always had a large variety of different brands, or companies, within it. It was able to market Chevrolets to the middle class and Cadillacs to the more affluent. Like other successful U.S. corporations, the company was top-heavy with management, and broadly unionized. Started in the United States, GM soon became an international company, manufacturing vehicles in 31 different countries. The company fell behind Japanese automakers in quality and the technology of auto making, although it remained profitable by concentrating on large vehicles and trucks. In 2008, the U.S. government assumed control over the company, although it sought quickly to move past its role as "Government Motors." Throughout its travails, the company remained a popular automaker in Europe and especially China.

Further Reading

Keller, Maryann. *Rude Awakening: The Rise, Fall, and Struggle for Recovery of General Motors.* New York: Morrow, 1989.

GERMAN GENERAL WORKINGMEN'S ASSOCIATION

Formed in 1863, under the leadership of the socialist Ferdinand Lassalle, this group was instrumental in launching the German labor movement. Lassalle believed that workers must first acquire the vote and then use it to transform private enterprise and wage labor into a fully cooperative system that would treat workers fairly. A number of German cooperative societies and artisans were attracted by this notion, which appealed to older ideas of guild structure while meeting modern industrial and political conditions. The new association did well for a time but suffered from poor leadership after Lassalle's death in a duel in 1864. It was increasingly outstripped by the more strictly political Marxist Social Democratic Party, and it merged with the party in 1875. The united group made a bow to the idea of producers' associations (a compromise that infuriated the purist Marx), but in fact, its program was Marxist. Nevertheless, the Lassallean movement had helped launch the most important trade unions in Germany.

See also Franchise; Utopian Socialists

Further Reading

Geary, Dick. *European Labour Protest, 1848–1939.* New York: St. Martin's Press, 1981.

GERMANY

German industrialization began a bit late by West European standards. Most parts of Germany retained the guild system into the 1840s; this helps explain the absence of German inventions in the early period. Separate states retarded commerce until the formation of an internal customs union (the Zollverein) in the 1830s. States even introduced different rail gauges, hampering transportation. German textiles suffered badly from British competition.

But German coal mining and metallurgy expanded rapidly in the 1830s. Iron production grew at the rate of 14 percent per year in the 1840s to supply the new rail network. German iron and coal resources were excellent and benefited further by the acquisition of Lorraine in 1871 after the Franco-Prussian War. National unification in the 1860s removed local impediments to trade, and a booming population provided labor and markets.

German industrialization had several special features. Once launched, growth was very rapid. The special concentration on heavy industry focused the economy and linked it to military goals. Government involvement was extensive. Germany was also a center of business combination; mergers and trade associations allowed businessmen to intensify their political and economic power. Capital-intensive heavy industry, the role of big investment banks, and government backing furthered the growth of cartels. Two or three firms predominated in industries like chemicals and electrical equipment. By the late nineteenth century, there were 300 cartels in Germany, with extensive market control and political influence. Steel and coal cartels set production limits for each member, to keep prices up.

The speed of German growth antagonized many traditional social elements, like artisans and small shopkeepers. Conflicts with labor and socialism—the German Socialist Party was the largest in the world by 1914—pushed big business to back repressive measures. These traits have been seen as part of Germany's "special path" (Sonderweg) in modern history and suggest how such a modern society could also generate Nazism amid the dislocations following World War I and the Great Depression. Historians have also noted, however, how many aspects of Germany's industrial history resemble those of other societies; the comparative judgment is complicated.

Germany's special economic zeal resumed after World War II, with the rapid growth of the Federal Republic of Germany, as the nation regained a decisive share of world economic leadership. Germany suffered in the immediate postwar period. Most of its cities and factories had been extensively bombed. Millions of soldiers and civilians had died; the country had to absorb more than 10 million refugees. Four different powers occupied it. Yet West Germany roared back, thanks in part to the generosity of the U.S.-led Marshall plan, the reconfiguration of institutions by the occupied powers, and German desire to move ahead. By 1960, economic production was almost three times that of 1950. Living standards rose. Germany was a free-market country but gave strong rights to workers, who elected members to the boards of directors of major companies.

East Germany suffered from its occupation by the Soviet Union. The Soviet Union had been ravaged by the Nazis and shipped entire factories to the east. Stalin stripped much of Prussia and gave it to Poland. Shortages of food were common until 1960. Before the war, Eastern Germany, especially Berlin, had supported Socialist and Communist parties. Communists imposed a police state. When workers struck in 1953, the government responded with tanks and soldiers. Hundreds died. The German communist writer Bertolt Brecht observed that a leading trade unionist complained that the riots resulted in the people losing the confidence of the government. Brecht caustically observed that it would be easier for the government to "dissolve the people, and elect another." Instead, East Germany became one of the most repressive societies on earth, with a massive government bureaucracy that spied upon its citizenry.

By 1990, East Germany collapsed, and the two Germanys reunified. That prospect was not without its critics, especially from European countries deeply worried by the military implications. The process was far more expensive than estimated. Many of the East Germany industries were shut down as inefficient. The new government raised living standards throughout the former East Germany. The country relocated its capital to Berlin, and rebuilt much of the city which had remained isolated in the postwar regime. Ironically, some East Germans expressed nostalgia for the communist regime, which provided employment and a clear set of rules for what to do. The German economy rebounded sharply in the 1990s, exporting cars, appliances, engineering, and machinery to the world.

See also European Union (EU); Krupp; Siemens

Further Reading

Detwiler, Donald S. *Germany: A Short History*. Carbondale: Southern Illinois University Press, 1999.

Henderson, W. O. *The State and the Industrial Revolution in Prussia, 1740–1870*. Liverpool, UK: Liverpool University Press, 1958.

Landes, David. *The Unbound Prometheus: Technical Change and Industrial Development in Western Europe*. Cambridge: Cambridge University Press, 1969.

Lidtke, Vernon. *The Alternative Culture: Socialist Labor in Imperial Germany*. New York: Oxford University Press, 1985.

GILCHRIST-THOMAS

This process allowed fuller use of the important iron ore deposits in Lorraine (held mostly by Germany in the 1870s) and Sweden, which were excessively high in phosphorous. A variety of engineers worked on this chemical problem, but the answer was found by two British amateurs, Sidney Gilchrist Thomas, a police court clerk, and his cousin Percy Carlyle Gilchrist, a chemist in a Welsh iron works. By mixing limestone with molten iron and relining blast furnaces, they were able to draw the phosphorous out. Major steel companies like Wendel and the Rheinische Stahlwerke paid small sums to lease the patent rights on the process and began a huge expansion of production in 1879. (Unlike many inventors, they carefully patented their invention.) The process was fundamental to the spectacular rise of German heavy industry. Gilchrist and Thomas were the last examples of the great early industrial tradition of artisan-tinkerers as sources of invention; from this point

English metallurgist and inventor Sidney Gilchrist Thomas (1850–85). (Getty Images)

almost all major gains came from research divisions in big companies. Sidney Gilchrist Thomas left all of his fortune to philanthropy to benefit steel workers.

See also Inventions; Iron and Steel Industry; Open Hearth; Research and Development (R&D)

Further Reading

Thomas, Sidney Gilchrist. *Memoir and Letters of Sidney Gilchrist Thomas.* Edited by Robert William Burnie. London: John Murray, 1891.

GLASSMAKING

The art of glassmaking extends back to ancient times—about 3000 BCE. Until late in the Industrial Revolution, it was a highly skilled operation, with glass containers individually blown and window and mirror glass hand pressed. Volume was limited, and considerable artistry was involved. Demand for glass rose in the nineteenth century, and window glass was particularly sought after. With discoveries in electricity, lightbulbs had to be blown; the first bulb was produced in 1879 in the Corning Glass Works. By the 1880s, glass companies in Europe and the United States expanded the processing of glass, using larger melting pots to stir the substance as it was made from sand and soda. A semiautomatic machine for making bottles was also introduced in France in 1859. Less skilled workers were used, and several labor conflicts suggested that skilled workers were beginning to feel threatened. Still, major technological developments lagged simply because the product was so fragile. In 1897, a continuous process for annealing plate glass was developed by a Pennsylvania company, cutting three days from the production time required for a sheet of plate glass. In 1902 a Belgian, Emile Fourcault, invented a machine to draw a continuous sheet of glass. The following year a machine to make bottles automatically was introduced in Ohio, while a French inventor devised laminated glass. Developments in glass composition and manufacturing were fairly steady thereafter, with a window-glass drawing machine introduced after 1908 and an automatic machine to blow electric lightbulbs invented in 1926.

Glassmaking became a major factory industry, and the skill component involved was dramatically reduced.

Like many aspects of industrialization, glass has been revolutionized by science and electronics. Smart phones use new forms of smart glass that allow users to interact with their handheld computer while protecting fragile components. Smart glass that can adjust its level of opacity or adjust how much heat is allowed through it is available. Advances in material sciences make it theoretically possible to generate solar power from windows.

Further Reading

Flannery, James L. *The Glass House Boys of Pittsburgh: Law, Technology, and Child Labor.* Pittsburgh, PA: University of Pittsburgh Press, 2009.

Scott, Joan. *The Glassworkers of Carmaux.* Cambridge, MA: Harvard University Press, 1974.

Skrabec, Quentin R. *Glass in Northwest Ohio.* Charleston, SC: Arcadia, 2007.

GLOBAL WARMING

Fossil fuels powered the Industrial Revolution, at first coal, then oil, and then natural gas. One by-product of burning fossil fuels, as well as other economic activities, has been to rapidly increase amounts of carbon dioxide in the atmosphere by about 360 billion tons since 1850. By 2010, there was 45 percent more carbon in the atmosphere than in 1750, when the Industrial Revolution began. This is the highest level of carbon over the last 800,000 years, leading most scientists to conclude that human activity caused carbon levels to rise.

Scientists have concluded that carbon dioxide, as well as other gases, such as methane, are strongly correlated to human activities such as industry, cattle farming, and burning forests to create farmlands. The net result of these gases is to trap heat from the sun, thus warming the planet and changing the climate. A vast number of factors affect climate, which has varied wildly over the last million years. But carbon is relatively stable, long lasting, and strongly correlated to human activity, so it is often discussed in terms of global warming.

The human activities that contribute to global warming reveal the impact of the Industrial Revolution on the world. Three-quarters of the carbon released into the atmosphere came from burning fossil fuels. Roughly a third of fuel was burned to run industries or generate electricity. Another third of the fuel was used to power trucks and cars, and another third to heat or cool homes. The Industrial Revolution has allowed humans to remake their built environment, allowing it to be heated, lighted, and filled with things that provide humans with ease and pleasure. Much of the remaining carbon was released as people cut down forests to provide fuel or natural materials for urban areas, or turned forests into pastures and farmland.

The countries that contributed the most greenhouse gases in the mid-2000s were, not surprisingly, the countries where the Industrial Revolution had the most impact: the United States, Europe, and China. Other important contributors were developing countries such as Brazil and India; countries that contributed enormous amounts of minerals and agricultural goods (such as Australia or South Africa); and countries that contributed agricultural products, oil, and gas (such as Russia and some African countries). Although Western Europe contributes to global warming, its contribution is proportionately less than others, in part because it burns less gasoline per capita (compared to the United States) and uses less coal to generate electricity (as compared to China).

The fact that fossil fuels have been the path to greater wealth, and that there are so many countries and industries that produce greenhouse gases, is suggestive of the problems in coordinating an effective response to this issue.

Regulating energy usage raises the problem known as the "prisoner's dilemma." If everyone could cooperate, then an optimal outcome could be achieved. However, if one person (or country) defects, everyone else pays the price for cooperation, allowing the free rider to enjoy the benefits of both a cleaner environment and using cheaper but dirtier fuels. Thus coordination must occur among numerous countries simultaneously. However, for some, the temptation to become a free rider is almost irresistible. Industrializing countries, such as China and India, point out that they did not become wealthy during the first 200 years of the Industrial Revolution, so why should they limit burning coal now that they are on the verge of becoming wealthy? After all, the pattern of Western countries is to remediate environmental problems after they become affluent. The Kyoto Protocol, negotiated in the 1990s, allowed poorer countries to use more coal than wealthier ones. As a result, in the 2000s the United States dropped out of the Kyoto Protocol.

Environmental regulation is thorny enough within one country. Cleaner air generates economic benefits, such as fewer deaths and illnesses due to respiratory problems. Those benefits are often more than enough to offset the higher prices for fuel. If the benefits of clean air are diffuse, limiting pollution imposes costs on "dirty" companies, such as coal companies that supply electric utilities. Dirty industries have deep pockets, and they have resisted environmental regulations. It might be smarter for a society to factor in all the costs of fossil fuels, but those that will be most affected tend to resist.

One form of resistance has been to call into question the science behind global warming. Starting in the 1980s, energy companies funded research and groups that questioned whether the earth was warming, whether human activity was behind it, and what, if anything, should be done to counter it. The tactic proved successful in turning a scientific debate into a political one. In the United States, "climate skepticism" has become an article of faith for Republicans. Strategies that Republicans once endorsed and worked for, such as reducing "acid rain" emissions in the 1980s, became, as of 2009, extreme socialist ideas. Certainly, there have been dramatic and rapid climate changes in the relatively recent past. Volcanic activity has triggered mini-ice ages as recently as the Middle Ages. As noted above, climate is extremely complex, and many factors will take place. However, it seems likely that as the planet warms at a historically unprecedented pace, changes will occur that will affect the industrialized world.

As the planet becomes hotter, more water will evaporate, and the planet as a whole will become wetter. So, it is likely that winters will produce more snow; some will become wetter (such as the northeastern United States). The weather systems will become more extreme, with stronger storms and heat waves. Some regions will become drier, such as much of sub-Saharan Africa, Western Australia, and the southwestern United States. Richer countries or cities may well be able to build desalination plants or recycle enough water to continue much as they are. Poorer countries will not have that luxury. As of 2011, Yemen is the first country to have effectively run out of water. Its aquifers are dry; drought and the resulting hardships have taken an economic toll, and the result is decreased social and political stability.

The weather will become less predictable, which will have important consequences for agriculture. Today there are more people, with higher expectations, and less potential farmland than ever before. Richer people eat more dairy and meat, which takes up to 16 times more crop land than raising grains or legumes. In the 2000s, more and more crop land was devoted to raising biofuels. Several hundred years ago, there were severe droughts in Iowa and surrounding states that lasted decades. New technologies may well offer solutions. But many cards from the Industrial Revolution (tractors, fertilizers, hybrid crops) have already been played. Countries such as Saudi Arabia once raised crops, relying on water extracted from aquifers. Now that that water is gone, they have turned to buying cropland in Africa.

Should global warming melt the ice in Greenland or Antarctica, another major effect will be on coastal cities and regions that will have to confront greater risks of flooding. Hundreds of millions will be affected.

The effects on natural habitats and biodiversity could well be severe. Humans are generalists, but many species of plants, birds, insects, and mammals, etc., are not. For instance, species adapted to alpine climates have nowhere to go if mountaintops get too warm. This trend has already been observed. Many species will be stressed and therefore more susceptible to disease or pests. One credible scientific estimate suggests that by 2100, climate change and habitat loss combined could cull one-third of all species from the planet. The loss of bees from a province in China, the result of what has been called colony collapse disorder, meant that fruit trees had to be pollinated by hand. It is possible but costly and cumbersome. Bees help pollinate around one-third of the value of all crops worldwide.

Numerous scientists have called for countries to place a tax on carbon. Consumers would have the financial incentives to insulate their homes or shift to smaller cars. A carbon tax would likely encourage new industries to emerge, such as solar, wind, or bioengineered ethanol, that at present cannot compete with fossil fuels. Already there are enormous sums being invested by companies in the hopes of becoming the company that develops a clean source of fuel. It is also likely that the number of people will decline in the future as richer individuals generally have smaller families. Ironically enough, the threat of global warming was caused by the Industrial Revolution; humanity's best hope lies in the next revolutionary change.

Further Reading

Weart, Spencer R. *The Discovery of Global Warming*. Cambridge, MA: Harvard University Press, 2008.

GLOBALIZATION AND THE INDUSTRIAL REVOLUTION

Globalization and the Industrial Revolution have been intertwined since the middle of the nineteenth century. Globalization would have been impossible without the technology and increased output provided by the Industrial Revolution. In turn, globalization has facilitated the spread of industrialization and has encouraged a variety of policies to promote, but also to regulate, the process internationally. The relationship remains close in the early twenty-first century, even as globalization expands.

Globalization centers on a rebalancing between local and global forces in shaping various aspects of human behavior. Global influences accelerate: they involve increased contacts among different societies literally around the world, and also the introduction or intensification of global processes and institutions, such as multinational corporations or international agencies. The range of interactions expands at the same time. Migration and disease transmission date far back in the human experience in generating external impacts on individual regions. With globalization, enhanced trade, cultural connections, political processes, and even environmental changes now add to the list.

Historians did not devise the concept of globalization. The Japanese introduced a relevant term as early as the 1960s, but English-language reference began in the 1990s, in economics and other social sciences. The assumption of most globalization theories was that something dramatically new had opened up fairly recently, thanks to new technologies like the Internet (effectively launched around 1990) and international economic policies and institutions such as the World Bank and International Monetary Fund (effectively established in the late 1940s). Indeed, a group of historians—terming their field the "new global history"—continue to insist that the processes they study establish a massive and growing gap between the human experience from the late twentieth century onward and all that has gone before.

This framework, in turn, helps explain initial European industrialization: the Industrial Revolution built on global trade contacts and capital amassed in the centuries before 1800, and it also built on European efforts to gain new competitive advantages over Asian, and particularly Indian, manufacturing.

But these early phases of globalization were preliminaries, not the full system. Modern globalization really began to take shape after 1850, and historians' main contribution to defining the whole phenomenon rests heavily on the identification of clearly modern global processes a century and a half ago.

Late nineteenth-century globalization rested on a number of factors, but the elaboration of industrial technology was crucial. As larger groups of historians have begun to analyze globalization, however, the picture has expanded somewhat. Several studies argue for a multistage development of globalization, with important steps taken as early as a thousand years ago. (One historian even advances the idea of "archaic" globalization, to denote the initial phases, making outright globalization a more recent, but partially successor, phenomenon.) The trade routes and expansion of trade and sailing technology, introduced primarily by the Arabs, suggest a first stage of globalization as early as 1000 CE. Then in the fifteenth century, armed with knowledge about trade possibilities derived from the Mongol era, European explorers set out to find more direct routes to Asia, and in the process, of course, introduced the Americas and Pacific Oceania to global contacts for the first time.

Technology was critical to the process of globalization; the introduction of steam shipping began to revolutionize global transportation after about 1840 (before that point, early steamships required such frequent refueling that they had limited impact). Soon, added to this were transcontinental rail lines and the Suez, and later the Panama, canals. More goods and people could be carried over long distances and faster than ever before. Interiors previously closed to global contacts—as in parts of Africa—were opened by river steamers and rails. Communication accelerated as well, with the introduction of the telegraph and, soon, transoceanic lines. Organizationally, growing business corporations developed international operations through trade subsidiaries, branch factories, and vertical linkages to obtain raw materials and to promote sales of the growing array of industrial products. The first international nongovernmental organizations emerged initially to combat slavery, but by the 1880s, they extended into other areas such as women's rights. Governments themselves began to arrange certain matters on a global basis. New conventions set up transnational postal service for the first time, or provided standards for the treatment of prisoners of war.

During these same initial decades, just as globalization had resulted from the Industrial Revolution, it began to spill back into industrialization in turn. Many of the most sought-after new international arrangements focused on facilitating contacts relevant to trade and other economic activities. Thus the postal agreement helped manufacturers send correspondence to far-flung countries, whereas before communications had to be hand-carried. In 1883, a Paris Patent Convention set up arrangements whereby inventors in signatory nations could apply for international patent protection within 12 months of invention, so that this vital service no longer depended on citizenship—a reflection and further cause of a now-global economy. Other arrangements involved global shipping patterns. All of this developed slowly, as various nations signed on gradually over time, but the principle of using global political contacts to facilitate international business and industry was clearly established.

Globalization, at this point, also spurred developments in products and technology. International expositions flourished, beginning with the great Crystal Hall exhibit in London in 1851. Here were places where people from various countries could observe machines and goods from around the world. Imitation accelerated, thanks to new global contacts. Many countries, like Russia in the 1850s and Japan in the 1890s, began to set up department stores in imitation of this Western innovation, and the stores in turn initially featured Western craft and factory goods.

This initial round of modern globalization was clearly Western dominated, part of the brief but crucial Western monopoly of industrial power. Not surprisingly, as many regions gained new political and economic capacity, there was pushback against this version of internationalism. The Russian Revolution in 1917, and particularly the later rise of Stalin and his vision of "socialism in one country," pulled the Soviet Union away from many aspects of globalization, though technically communism had its own vision of what global action might involve. Japan sought its own separate economic and political empire from the 1930s through World War II, and Nazi Germany in its own way sought alternatives to globalization. The second quarter of the twentieth century saw globalization in partial retreat. Many countries looked for ways to protect themselves from outside industrial competition, hoping to develop industrial sectors independently.

But globalization continued to operate even in these decades. The range of many international businesses expanded, and the global scope of the Great Depression indicated how closely tied together many economies were. A new element arose as well: the formation of the International Labor Office (in 1919), associated with the new League of Nations, saw various efforts to win international agreements to curb some abuses of labor associated in part with industrialization. From 1923 onward, for example, a variety of conventions sought to reduce the use of children in factories and other sectors. Over time, global discussions and standards did encourage the growing reduction in child labor in almost every part of the world, and the rise of school requirement in its stead.

Globalization returned more obviously to center stage, in many ways beginning in the late 1940s. New technology was again crucial. It was at this point that jet travel began to go global, with lines for example to Australia and South Africa (the concept of jet lag was introduced in 1963). International telephone and radio linkages steadily improved, and satellite communication soon after greatly accelerated both communication and cultural transmissions. Along with technology, new international agreements, though initially complicated by the Cold War, provided a framework for greater financial and economic coordination. Countries that had previously pulled away from globalization, like Japan, Germany, and the United States, became eager global players. In 1978, the Chinese government made its historic decision to open unprecedentedly to global contacts, and in 1985, under Mikhail Gorbachev, Russia began to do the same. Both countries assumed that their further industrial advance depended on global participation. Only a few small countries, such as North Korea, now held out against the global tide. There were still hosts of impediments to global contacts (such as passport and security controls, made worse by the rise of global terrorism), and many concerns and resistances, including continued nationalism, but there was no question that global contacts reached new levels, becoming arguably the most powerful force for change in contemporary world history.

Globalization thus offers a roughly 150-year history, with important earlier precedents. Its advance has been uneven, at times actively and effectively opposed. Its early iterations were marked by Western dominance, but more recently the economic rise of China, India, Brazil and other players makes globalization at least somewhat more multifaceted. The historical framework for globalization must not be equated with assumptions of progress. Many observers have seen real gains from globalization, but one can also mark a host of drawbacks and disputes—as is obvious in the field of exploitation of labor. Polls in the early twenty-first century suggested that more people feared aspects of globalization (beginning with concerns over loss of cultural identity, but including anxieties about economic displacement) than welcomed them, though this undercurrent hardly seemed to hold the process back.

Much debate also focused on whether different regions now suffered or benefited from the global economy, and here too the evidence varied. Perhaps ironically, people in some of the poorer regions, like Africa, tended to see growing global participation as good for their economies, whereas workers in established industrial countries, like the United States or France, were less certain.

By the early twenty-first century, globalization involved a range of international organizations and agreements designed to facilitate industrial growth. Efforts to stabilize financial markets, encourage lower tariffs, or provide international loans to spur local industry were examples on the policy side. Multinational corporations emerged in this new stage of globalization, with production facilities in a host of different regions to take advantage of favorable cost factors. But globalization now also involved new efforts to provide some global controls. A host of international conferences sought to win global agreement on limitation on pollutants. Various international nongovernmental organizations, or NGOs, called attention to local labor or environmental abuses. Globalization also involved the emergence of a range of shared consumer tastes—for certain kinds of popular toys, for example—that depended on global sales from the growing range of production centers. The interrelationships between globalization and ongoing industrialization were intricate.

Further Reading

Hopkins, A. G., ed. *Globalization in World History*. New York: Norton, 2002.
Mazlish, Bruce. *The New Global History*. New York: Routledge, 2006.
Robertson, Robbie. *The Three Waves of Globalization*. New York: Zed Books, 2003.
Stearns, Peter N. *Globalization in World History*. New York: Routledge, 2010.

GOLD STANDARD

The gold standard, by which the value of money is pegged to the supply of gold, was an integral part of the international banking system under which national currencies were converted upon demand into gold. It arose in the late eighteenth century with the rise of British economic power and lasted until the 1930s when Britain could no longer enforce it. Allowing merchants to trust the currencies of foreign merchants through the gold standard helped to facilitate international trade. The gold standard broke down, however, during periods of political turmoil and war, such as in the late eighteenth and early nineteenth centuries during the French Revolution and Napoleonic Wars, and during World War I.

The gold standard was a central feature of laissez-faire economic policy, and it was an important mechanism in regulating the international economy throughout the nineteenth century. Countries had strong incentives to keep trade surpluses to maintain gold reserves (and hence the strength of their currency). Although from the 1790s to the 1890s the United States was a net importer of capital, consistently running a trade deficit, it remained on the gold standard and retained the confidence of bankers. When a country experienced a depression, people often converted their money into gold, and the government (or central bank) defended the value of the currency by buying gold from other banks, thus attracting capital to the country. Other central banks (particularly the Bank of England) cooperated by lending the affected government capital to maintain the gold standard.

Although new discoveries of gold in nineteenth-century South Africa and the United States expanded the de facto money supply, the gold standard also placed a check upon inflation because the amount of gold was relatively inflexible. With the financial demands of the American Civil War on the federal government, the gold standard was partially abandoned (from 1862 until 1879) in favor of nonredeemable paper currency or "Greenbacks." The issuance of paper money resulted in substantial inflation that favored debtors, such as farmers, who could repay loans with "cheaper" money. Bankers successfully argued that the government should return to the gold standard, which as a result contracted the money supply throughout the 1880s and 1890s. Prices of agricultural and manufactured goods fell relative to the price of gold, and farmers and other debtors had to repay their loans with more expensive money. Farmers in particular complained that they were being "crucified upon a cross of gold."

By World War I, the gold standard had begun to break down as an international system. The decline of the British economy prevented the Bank of England from maintaining the system's inviolability by intervening to aid troubled currencies and economies. The unwillingness of the United States or other creditor countries to assume Britain's role in maintaining the standard was a contributing factor to the breakdown of international trade in the 1920s and 1930s, and countries went off the gold standard and devalued their currencies to cheapen their exports. By 1936, all the major industrialized countries had abandoned the gold standard. The Bretton Woods Agreement of 1944 established new mechanisms (under the guidance of the United States) to regulate international trade and banking. The dollar (backed by gold reserves) became the standard international currency, although by 1971 the failing economy of the United States had forced its government to abandon the convertibility of dollars into gold.

The history of gold reveals the complex relationship between national currencies, industrialization, and the global economy. The volatility of currency after the 1970s suggested to some the need to return to a gold standard. The Austrian school of economics, which mistrusted fiat currency, became popular in conservative circles. Others read that history differently, seeing a national currency as a critical part of why some countries such as China and Japan were able to manage their trade by making exports more affordable.

See also Banking System; Finance Capital; Populism

Further Reading

Eichengreen, Barry. *Golden Fetters: The Gold Standard and the Great Depression, 1919–1939.* New York: Oxford University Press, 1992.

GOMPERS, SAMUEL (1850–1924)

Samuel Gompers was an English-born cigar worker who became the first head of the American Federation of Labor. With the exception of one year, he led the organization from its formation in 1886 until his death in 1924. Cigar workers were a skilled, literate, and radical group of workers who frequently hired a person to read to them newspapers, books, and articles on labor issues and socialism while they worked. Thus early in his life, Gompers was influenced by socialism, although he is best known for laying the conservative foundations upon which the U.S. house of labor was built. Gompers believed that workers would not benefit from "utopian" goals of cooperatives, independent political parties, or unions of unskilled workers who could not easily force employers to recognize their

President of the American Federation of Labor for nearly 40 years, Samuel Gompers helped shape the American labor movement by eschewing political and revolutionary aims. (Library of Congress)

unions. Gompers instead advocated "pure and simple unionism," eschewing political affiliations, radical tactics, or socialist goals in favor of wages, benefits, and moderate political reforms.

See also Congress of Industrial Organizations (CIO); Industrial Unions; Industrial Workers of the World (IWW)

Further Reading

Greene, Julie. *Pure and Simple Politics: The American Federation of Labor and Political Activism, 1881–1917*. New York: Cambridge University Press, 1999.

Kaufman, Stuart Brace. *Samuel Gompers and the Origins of the American Federation of Labor, 1848–1896*. Westport, CT: Greenwood, 1973.

GOODYEAR, CHARLES (1800–1860)

Charles Goodyear invented the vulcanization of rubber, which allowed crude rubber to retain its elastic and waterproof qualities at high and low temperatures. He was investigating how rubber was affected by mixing it with sulfur when he spilled or left some of the mixture on a hot stove—the result set him on the road to uncovering the process. However, Goodyear was unable to retain patent rights in Europe or effective control of the process in the United States. He died penniless in 1860; the company that bears his name was formed in 1898 by Benjamin Franklin Goodrich.

See also Inventions

Further Reading

Barker, Preston Wallace. *Charles Goodyear: Connecticut Yankee and Rubber Pioneer*. Boston: Godfrey L. Cabot, 1940.

Slack, Charles. *Noble Obsession: Charles Goodyear, Thomas Hancock, and the Race to Unlock the Greatest Industrial Secret of the Nineteenth Century*. New York: Hyperion, 1999.

GOULD, JAY (1836–92)

Jay Gould was a speculator and railroad tycoon who built a great fortune during the building of a national network of railroads in the nineteenth century. After making a small fortune on Wall Street, Gould entered the railroad business in 1867 by joining the board of directors of the Erie Railroad. In the 1860s and 1870s, railroads were rapidly expanding, and great fortunes were made and lost by issuing stock, frequently in a watered-down form, and manipulating the setting of freight rates in a rough-and-tumble struggle for access to capital and control of markets. The Erie eventually went bankrupt, but not before Gould bested Cornelius Vanderbilt, who remarked after his experience with Gould that "it never pays to kick a skunk." In 1885, Gould was forced by the Knights of Labor to sign a union contract on one of his western railroads; within a short time, however, Gould had crushed the union.

See also Great Strike of 1877; Railroads

Jay Gould rose from poverty to become a railroad tycoon. He was alleged to have said that he could hire half the working class to kill the other half. (Library of Congress)

Further Reading

Klein, Maury. *The Life and Legend of Jay Gould*. Baltimore: Johns Hopkins University Press, 1986.

GREAT DEPRESSION (1930s)

The Great Depression was a lengthy, severe global economic crisis that had far-reaching social and political consequences. The Depression affected every country in the world economy, which meant the only major exception to the Depression was the Soviet Union. The crisis was severe not only in industrialized countries such as Britain, Germany, and the United States but also in countries or colonies that primarily exported agricultural goods or raw materials, such as Argentina, Ceylon (Sri Lanka), and South Africa.

The root causes of the crisis were not only the tendency of the capitalist system to overproduce goods but also the political and economic resolution of World War I. That war required Germany in particular to pay large reparations to France, England, and other allies; Germany's ability to export goods and services to foreign markets was limited because of high tariffs. The economies of the major European allies, England, France, and Italy, were weakened by the economic costs of the war. Even in the United States, the Roaring Twenties had many "sick" or troubled industries, including steel, coal, and textiles. The U.S. government's demands that their World War I allies repay their war loans, regardless of their ability to pay, spurred demands by the European allies that a devastated Germany honor its reparations. The result was a severe inflationary spiral in Germany that undermined the faith of many of its citizens in parliamentary democratic government. The financial crisis soon extended to world trade as many countries raised their tariffs in an attempt to protect domestic industries and raise the revenue for financial obligations. At the same time, overproduction in agricultural and raw materials in areas such as Latin America caused lower earnings and reduced the markets for industrial exports from Europe and the United States. Between 1929 and 1933 world trade diminished by about 70 percent.

Although there were important differences among the ways that industrialized countries attempted to resolve the crisis, varying from the New Deal in the United States to fascism in Germany and Italy, there were some common themes. Even among many businessmen, faith in the market's ability to resolve the crisis was severely eroded. The gold standard, which had been currency's previous mark of stability, was abandoned. Beginning with fascist Italy, many countries adopted some form of corporatism, which meant that the government attempted to mediate the interests of different social groups or classes. Governments everywhere took a larger role in the economy: the United States preferred to subsidize and coordinate private industry, while the Italian government had a larger direct involvement in its own economy than any other country except the Soviet Union.

The failure of industrial countries to resolve the Depression was a major contributing factor not only to the rise of fascism in Japan, Spain, Italy, and Germany but also to World War II. In the wake of that war, there was a widespread effort on the part of industrial countries to coordinate tariffs, stabilize currencies, and attempt to resolve diplomatic and trade disputes peaceably. Many observers see the financial crisis that began in 2007–8 as having parallels with the Great Depression. Many have termed it the "Great Recession."

See also Bretton Woods Agreement

Further Reading

Garside, W. R., ed. *Capitalism in Crisis: International Responses to the Great Depression*. New York: St. Martin's Press, 1993.

Nash, Gerald D. *The Great Depression and World War II: Organizing America, 1933–1945*. New York: St. Martin's Press, 1979.

GREAT LEAP FORWARD

The Great Leap Forward began in 1958 and was an attempt, led by Mao Zedong, to catapult China into the industrial era by harnessing the Chinese people's revolutionary zeal. In the first (and only) five-year plan, China borrowed heavily from the Stalinist model of development and emphasized heavy industry. Mao felt that the Soviet model of development left agriculture relatively underdeveloped; Mao sought to utilize the reservoir of potential labor and energy in the countryside so that China could "walk on two legs." The status of technicians and economic planners declined in favor of rural communes that sought not only to increase output of grains but to help the Chinese steel industry grow by 15 percent a year by building small pig-iron furnaces. Mao's plan failed and resulted in widespread economic and political chaos. The Great Leap Forward also helped to precipitate the split with the Soviet Union in 1960.

Further Reading

Lippit, Victor D. *The Economic Development of China*. Armonk, NY: M.E. Sharpe, 1987.

GREAT MIGRATION

The Great Migration is the term for the mass movement of black workers from the southern United States to urban industrial centers in the North, West, and South in the early twentieth century. Until World War I, industrialists blocked black Americans from factory employment, arguing that they were inherently unfit for industrial labor. When the war caused industrial production to explode and interrupted established patterns of trans-Atlantic immigration, industrialists responded by actively recruiting southern blacks. Although hundreds of thousands of black men, women, and children became industrial workers and urban dwellers in the South, the northern dimension of the Great Migration was most influential in transforming the culture, politics, and economics of the black community.

Although blacks were denied equal access to jobs, housing, and public facilities, northern blacks earned more money and had greater freedom to form their own organizations and institutions than their counterparts in the South. Furthermore, northern blacks were able to vote, a fact that eventually undermined the political support for segregation within the Democratic Party. Blacks' experiences with unions were particularly problematic. During World War I, unions affiliated with the American Federation of Labor attempted to organize the mass-production industries of meatpacking and steel. Most unionists found it difficult to accept blacks as full-fledged union members; consequently, most black industrial workers

Typesetters work at their keyboards in 1941 at *The Chicago Defender*, an African American newspaper. (Library of Congress)

remained skeptical of "the white man's union." Strikes to establish unions failed, and many blacks crossed picket lines; the competition for jobs helped to contribute to the violent race riots that shook many northern cities in 1919. Most blacks had realized that the North was no paradise, though the mass migration back to the South, which many southern whites had predicted, failed to materialize.

Although urban dwellers (both black and white) frequently viewed migrants as fresh from the fields, most black migrants had had some experience with industrial employment. Traveling to Chicago, New York, or Los Angeles was frequently the culmination of a process in which southern blacks took jobs in local sawmills, regional industrial centers, and southern cities. Even after black men and women found urban jobs, they retained social ties with friends and family by periodically returning to the South, often to work for a period before returning to industrial employment. Interrupted by the Great Depression, the Great Migration began again in the 1940s and continued until the 1970s, when deindustrialization decimated the urban black community.

See also Dual Labor Markets; Urbanization

Further Reading

Trotter, Joe William, ed. *The Great Migration in Historical Perspective: New Dimensions of Race, Class, and Gender.* Bloomington: University of Indiana Press, 1991.

GREAT STRIKE OF 1877

By 1877, railroads were the largest single employer of U.S. workers. In the midst of a severe economic depression, railroad owners repeatedly slashed wages, and eventually workers responded by refusing to operate equipment in what became known as the Great Strike of 1877. Attempts by companies to run the trains with managers or strikebreakers led to bloody confrontations among militia, workers, and sympathizers from working-class neighborhoods. After militia members killed several demonstrators in Pittsburgh, workers destroyed a great deal of railroad equipment and temporarily drove the militia out of the city. Although the strike eventually failed, it raised the specter of working-class insurrection established by the Paris Commune of 1871. The strike's failure and the subsequent blacklisting of militants convinced many union leaders that only conservative tactics could preserve workers' organizations. Among the most lasting results of the strike were the professionalization of the National Guard and the establishment of armories in working-class neighborhoods to prevent similar riots.

See also Knights of Labor

Further Reading

Foner, Philip S. *The Great Labor Uprising of 1877.* New York: Monad Press, 1977.

GREEN REVOLUTION

The "Green revolution" (1960s) involved new agricultural technology, chemical fertilizers, and more productive seeds, developed mainly by U.S. agricultural experts, to increase output in many Third World countries. The Green revolution had particularly great impact on India and Southeast Asia. Indian food production had not kept pace with population growth, forcing food imports in the 1960s and threatening famine; the results severely reduced industrial growth. The Green revolution restored India's self-sufficiency in food, allowing resumption of overall economic growth in the 1970s. The revolution also benefited those farmers with enough money to invest in new materials, widening rural divisions and leaving the rural majority still desperately poor; it did not assure a general improvement in economic conditions, though it may have prevented deterioration.

Further Reading

Perkins, John H. *Geopolitics and the Green Revolution: Wheat, Genes, and the Cold War.* New York: Oxford University Press, 1997.

GREEN TECHNOLOGY

Green technology is the application of science to protect the environment. Examples include water filtration and treatment, environmental remediation, solid-waste management, energy conservation, and renewable energy.

Water treatment systems date back to the late nineteenth century. The science behind them was outdated; it owed more to the ancient idea that cities were, like humans, governed by humors. Removing wastes and introducing clean water was seen as necessary to keep the body politic healthy. Nonetheless, the new systems did much to reduce the spread of infectious water-borne disease and to reduce mortality.

Industrial cities that lacked rivers, such as Los Angeles, were able to tap dammed reservoirs hundreds of miles away. A vast system of canals and dams developed to support the creation of a megacity in the Southern California desert. Rain might fall only intermittently, but the suburban residents retained the assumptions of a wetter, Eastern climate and so irrigated the land to keep alive their grassy lawns and golf courses. Water-intensive industry and agriculture also developed. That model spread through the southwestern United States and also in countries in the Persian Gulf. After the 1970s, Saudi Arabia tapped underground aquifers and desalination plants to grow hay to feed dairy herds. One Persian Gulf city-state built a massive indoor ski slope.

But such development was not sustainable; underground aquifers ran dry, and river systems were overtaxed. By the early twenty-first century, water treatment systems were working to develop a new model of water treatment, recycling water from sewage plants for reuse for irrigation.

Architects have developed new ways to incorporate green technologies so that buildings are less energy intensive. Buildings consume about one-third of all energy, so that is as important as developing energy-efficient transportation. Insulation and

In this photo taken September 2009, farmers along with their sheep stand near the construction site of a wind-powered farm in Shangyi, Hebei, China. (AP/Wide World Photo)

more-energy-efficient appliances or lighting is one means to "go green." Buildings can also incorporate solar panels on the roof, and even in the windows, so that buildings produce energy as well as consume it. Buildings contribute to the heat-island effect that keeps cities several degrees warmer than their surrounding regions. A relatively simple way to reduce heat-island effect is to use lighter-colored tiles on the exteriors. A more comprehensive, and expensive, fix is to build living roofs, with grasses, etc.

Green technology will become increasingly important in the future, as humans either reduce their impact on the environment or use technology to do what nature used to do for free.

See also Global Warming; Renewable Energy

Further Reading

Madrigal, Alexis. *Powering the Dream: The History and Promise of Green Technology.* Cambridge, MA: Da Capo Press, 2011.

GROUP OF EIGHT (G8)

The Group of Eight, or G8, began as a Group of Six. The forum was established by France in 1975, for the world's leading industrial countries to help discuss mutual economic and political problems, providing some additional leadership to the world's economy. Initial members were France, Italy, Germany, the United Kingdom, Japan, and the United States. Canada was added in 1976, creating a long-standing Group of Seven. Then after the end of the Cold War, the group added Russia. The group's leaders met annually, and key ministers, including finance ministers, met more frequently throughout the year. The initial impetus for the group was the 1973 oil crisis. Over time, topics for annual discussion included labor issues, health, economic development (including policies toward developing nations), the environment, trade barriers, and several political issues. By the early twenty-first century, environmental issues gained further ground, with discussions of innovations in energy efficiency and other matters.

The Group of Eight, and its predecessors, encountered criticism for high-handed decisions based on sheer industrial and military power. Trade policies were attacked for providing insufficient space for the poorest countries. By the early twenty-first century, annual meetings were usually greeted by large protests and groups' concerns about global poverty, consumerism, and other issues; security measures for the meetings increased space. While the Group increasingly reached out to other, new industrial powers, its representativeness became questionable, and in 2008 it was replaced by the Group of Twenty.

See also Group of Twenty (G20)

Further Reading

Bayne, Nicholas, and Robert Putnam. *Hanging in There: The G7 and G8 Summit in Maturity and Renewal.* Brookfield, VT: Ashgate, 2000.

Kokotsis, Eleanor. *Keeping International Commitments: Compliance, Credibility and the G7, 1988–1995.* New York: Garland, 1999.

GROUP OF TWENTY (G20)

The Group of Twenty (G20) had two origins. First, beginning early in the twenty-first century, a group of nations with growing economies, such as Brazil and India, organized to gain a greater voice in world economic affairs. They were concerned about the narrow views of the Group of Eight (the dominant industrial powers plus Russia), particularly in trade policies that might discriminate against rising economies by protecting certain inefficient sectors. An initial group of 20 of these countries first organized in 2003; the membership fluctuated thereafter. The dominant Group of Eight increasingly reached out to some of these same countries to join in discussions of agricultural policy and other matters. Indeed, as early as 1999, an initial group of 20 had met in Germany.

It was, however, the severe financial and economic crisis of 2008 that prompted leading industrial countries, including the United States, to call officially for a new, larger group to replace the Group of Eight in recurrent discussions of global economic coordination. The formation of this new group, including numerous Asian,

Latin American, and other members, in addition to the original eight, really symbolized the global expansion of economic and industrial power. China's strength, for example, as an industrial exporter and creditor nation could not be ignored in dealing with the severe dislocation of financial markets in 2008–9. Provision of better global financial regulation headed the list of topics in initial meetings. The Group also discussed the challenging problem of the imbalance between nations with unusually high consumption and debt levels, headed by the United States, compared to high-product and -export countries, like China and Germany. Predictably, smaller industrial powers, like Norway and Singapore, protested their exclusion from the group.

See also BRIC (Brazil, Russia, India, China); China; Group of Eight (G8)

Further Reading

Lopez-Claros, Augusto, Richard Samans, and Marc Uzan. *The International Monetary System and the IMF and the G-20*. Basingstoke, UK: Palgrave Macmillan, 2007.

HAMMER, ARMAND (1898–1990)

Armand Hammer was a U.S. businessman (and art collector) best known for his role as a trader and entrepreneur in the Soviet Union. Hammer grew up in poverty, the child of Russian immigrants. His father became a doctor and was also a fervent communist activist. Armand Hammer took over his father's failing drug business and made a fortune selling tincture of ginger (a concoction that contained alcohol) during the early phases of Prohibition. In the early 1920s, Hammer traveled to the Soviet Union and used his father's reputation as a good communist to establish business deals. Hammer prospered during the New Economic Policy period by importing grain and Ford tractors and exporting furs, leather, and lumber for a 5 percent commission on each end of the deal. He also established a pencil factory, which enabled the fledgling regime to forgo imports from Germany; when his production costs dropped, Hammer exported the product. His real money was made by being a front for the Soviets to sell art in the West. After he lost favor with the Soviet regime in the 1930s, he concentrated on building a fortune in the United States, largely in the oil industry. After 1961, Hammer again helped arrange deals between the Soviet Union and the United States. Hammer reveals how even communist governments needed entrepreneurs and how businessmen could survive within such systems only based on personal contacts.

Armand Hammer was an international industrialist and oil tycoon, a peace advocate and philanthropist, and a secret communist agent who built factories in the Soviet Union. (Library of Congress)

Further Reading

Epstein, Edward Jay. *Dossier: The Secret Life of Armand Hammer.* Upland, PA: Diane, 2001.

HARGREAVES, JAMES (D. 1778)

Hargreaves, a weaver by trade, was the inventor of the spinning jenny (c. 1764, patented in 1770). He utilized earlier British inventions that had tried unsuccessfully to automate part of the manufacturing of thread and yarn. Growing demand for the product had prompted the Society for the Encouragement of Arts, Manufactures, and Commerce to offer a prize for a spinning machine, which Hargreaves won. His jenny used a wheel to rotate the spindles that wound fiber into thread, but the drawing out and twisting of the fiber were mechanized, whereas on the traditional spinning wheel these processes were performed by hand. Early jennies contained only eight spindles, but the number was rapidly increased. Although it was operated by hand power and was used in the home, the principles of mechanizing the twisting process could later be applied to powered equipment. The jenny thus advanced proto-industrial manufacturing while paving the way, technically, for outright industrialization in cotton spinning.

See also Arkwright, Richard

Further Reading

Hills, Richard L. *Power in the Industrial Revolution.* Manchester, UK: Manchester University Press, 1970.

HEAVY INDUSTRY. *See* Iron and Steel Industry

HOLDING COMPANY

A holding company seeks to control other companies by holding strategic amounts of their stock. This allows the holding company to amass technical expertise, patents, and capital and to exert a monopolistic influence on a market. In many cases, a holding company (such as American Telephone and Telegraph or U.S. Steel) holds the stock to own or manage its subsidiaries. In Japan, holding companies such as Mitsubishi were called zaibatsus (or financial cliques) and exercised enormous influence after the Meiji era. The Japanese government provided zaibatsus with informal subsidies; in the case of Mitsubishi, the subsidies supported the company's shipping monopoly. The zaibatsu controlled a network of other companies through an internal bank, intermarriage, and appeals to loyalty. Although formally disbanded during the U.S. occupation of Japan, zaibatsus still function in all but name.

See also Cartels; Corporations; Finance Capital

Prince Alwaleed Bin Talal of Saudi Arabia, chairman of Kingdom Holding Company (right), hands New York City mayor Rudolph Giuliani a check for $10 million for relief efforts on October 11, 2001. (AP/Wide World Photos)

Further Reading

Josephson, Matthew. *The Robber Barons: The Great American Capitalists, 1861–1901.* New York: Harcourt, Brace, 1934.

Prechel, Harland N. *Big Business and the State: Historical Transitions and Corporate Transformation, 1880s–1990s.* Albany: State University of New York Press, 2000.

HOLY MONDAY

The idea of taking Monday off was an old custom among European artisans in many countries. Many craftsmen argued that if Sunday must be devoted to the family, they also needed the next day free from work in which they could pursue their own leisure interests—often including a good bit of drinking. This day became known as Holy Monday. Some factory workers, when their wages were high enough to permit the indulgence, maintained the Holy Monday tradition as well. Employers, including craft employers eager to regularize their workers' habits as their share in the industrialization process, fought Holy Monday vigorously, fining workers for absences and threatening dismissal. Here was a quiet battleground between older customs of more leisurely work and the new demands for regular timing and pace brought by the Industrial Revolution. Gradually, the Holy Monday tradition declined, though lower worker productivity on Mondays (thanks to recuperation from the weekend) leaves a trace of the tradition even in advanced industrial societies today.

See also Discipline; Work

Further Reading

Stearns, Peter N. *Paths to Authority*. Urbana: University of Illinois Press, 1978.

HOMESTEAD LOCKOUT (1892)

A lockout is essentially a strike by the owner, and in the case of the Homestead Lockout, the owners were Andrew Carnegie and his partner Henry Clay Frick, who refused to allow their employees into the steel mill until workers repudiated their union. The showdown was widely covered in the press of the time. It was seen as a contest between the growing economic power of monopolists and workers who saw "trusts" as incompatible with the political ideals of the United States. The local government was sympathetic to the workers, and the entire community rushed to repulse armed Pinkerton guards whom owners had hired to suppress the strike. Several workers and Pinkertons were killed. Workers won the battle but lost the war. At the urging of Frick, Pennsylvania's governor called in the state militia, who helped to crush the union. The lockout revealed the limitations of craft unionism and workers' political rights in the face of the growing power of large industrialists.

Further Reading

Krause, Paul. *The Battle for Homestead, 1880–1892: Politics, Culture, and Steel*. Pittsburgh, PA: University of Pittsburgh Press, 1992.

HONDA MOTOR COMPANY

This company was founded in 1948 to produce motorcycles. It did not produce automobiles until 1962, but by the mid-1980s, Honda was the third-largest car company in Japan. By the 1980s, Honda produced 60 percent of the world's motorcycles by producing high-quality, fuel-efficient engines and aggressively appealing to the middle class, claiming that "you meet the nicest people on a Honda." A relative maverick within the Japanese system, Honda is not part of a zaibatsu or "group." In 1974, the Japanese government encouraged its carmakers to curb their exports to the United States, but Honda refused. That year, Honda introduced its innovative CVCC engine, which drastically reduced auto emissions without the use of a catalytic converter. In 1979, Honda built a factory in Marysville, Ohio, and by 1985, it was the fourth-largest carmaker in the United States.

See also Japan; Toyota; Zaibatsus

Further Reading

Sakiya, Tetsuo, and Timothy Porter. *Honda Motor: The Men, the Management, the Machines*. New York: Kodansha USA, 1982.

Soichiro Honda inspects plans for a Honda plant in Marysville, Ohio, in 1977. (Honda)

HOURS OF WORK

Industrialization lengthened the working day and required more disciplined forms of labor. Struggles between workers and industrialists over the length of the working day became an enduring tension of industrial society. In the early nineteenth century, most industrial workers labored 6 days a week, 12 or more hours a day. Trade unionists struggled for a shorter workday, often arguing that this would protect women and children. Employers resisted shortening the workday, arguing that it would make their factories unprofitable and allow workers more time for drinking. Working-class advocates of the shorter workday maintained that increased leisure would not only alleviate unemployment but allow workers sufficient time for rest, a decent family life, and opportunities to improve their minds. Although many strikes fought for shorter working hours, the most significant gains came as a result of political agitation, for example, that of the Chartists in England. Hours for children and women were often regulated by law before those of adult men.

As a result of strikes and political agitation, the working day for most U.S. and Western European workers had fallen to 10 hours a day, 6 days a week, by 1900. The trend was far from universal, however. Although the 8- or 10-hour day had been common in the United States' iron and steel industry of the 1880s, the destruction of unions in the 1890s allowed industries to institute a 12-hour day and a 7-day week. Workers knew furnaces needed to be run continuously or else they became damaged, but they maintained that employers could afford to hire more workers and shorten the workweek. Until the 1920s, when workers' protests and the muckraking accounts of journalists resulted in an 8-hour day, steelworkers had to endure the "long turn" every other Sunday when they would work two back-to-back turns. One steelworker recalled that by three in the morning of the long turn, you could die and not even notice.

Until the 1920s, workers' calls for a shorter working day had often been linked to their demands for greater control over the workplace. Employers refused to cede their control of the workplace but did reduce their workday, so that by the 1940s a 40-hour week had become the norm. Despite periodic demands for a 30-hour week, most unions dropped the quest for shorter hours. By the 1970s, the working day of most workers in the United States began to lengthen as people worked longer (or took additional jobs) to compensate for falling wages. By the late 1980s, the average U.S. worker was working the equivalent of an extra month a year, and the trend is accelerating as real wages continue to fall. Due to their strong unions, workers in Western Europe came to enjoy far more leisure; though daily hours of work might slightly exceed U.S. workloads, most European workers enjoy at least six weeks of vacation a year. In South Korea, Japan, and other Pacific Rim industrial countries, unions are weaker, and a six-day workweek is common for factory workers. Among white-collar employees in Japan, mandatory (and unpaid) overtime is compulsory and karoshi (death from overwork) remains a serious problem.

See also Dual Labor Market; State, Role of the; Workers' Control

Further Reading

Cross, Gary. *Time and Money: The Making of Consumer Culture*. London: Routledge, 1993.

Roediger, David R., and Philip S. Foner. *Our Own Time: A History of American Labor and the Working Day*. New York: Verso, 1989.

Schor, Juliet B. *The Overworked American: The Unexpected Decline of Leisure*. New York: Basic Books, 1992.

HOUSEWORK

Industrialization has radically transformed the nature of housework. In the nineteenth century, the growing separation of the family from economic production meant that the unpaid labor necessary for social reproduction and preparing workers for the labor market (that is, housework) increasingly fell on women alone. Prior to industrialization (and for much of the nineteenth century), before a woman could cook, clean, or wash, she had to spend an hour or two hauling water into the house and then manipulating the stove to heat it. Chopping and hauling wood to heat the home and water also required a substantial amount of time and effort. Although entrepreneurs created numerous labor-saving devices, most were of limited utility, and the favorite "labor-saving device" for those who could afford it was a maid or servant. Most servants in the United States were Irish, German, or Slavic women immigrants and, increasingly in the twentieth century, black women. Advances in technology did ultimately influence housework, however, and by the mid-nineteenth century, most women in cities used coal instead of wood, which burned hotter and required less work. Feeding the stove or furnace (and periodically cleaning the stove and house of soot) was still a burden nonetheless. Sewing machines made making clothing at home easier, though it could still be a time-consuming chore.

The most significant advances came later in the nineteenth century, with indoor water, gas, and then electric lights (which did not leave soot); still, many working-class families in the United States did not receive these amenities until well into the twentieth century. Also in the twentieth century, electrically powered machines such as mechanized washing machines or electric vacuum cleaners began to ease the burden of middle- and then working-class women's housework. Most scholars of housework have observed that industrialization did not free women from housework, because standards of cleanliness rose in tandem with the advances of new technology. Furthermore, many jobs once done by men (such as delivering produce) were shifted onto women. These observations notwithstanding, the demands of housework had declined sufficiently in the twentieth century to allow middle-class women to dispense with their servants and begin a career, as well as to take on the demands of housework—or the "second shift." It is worth noting that many white working-class women and most black women had always worked.

In most of Europe and the United States, the demands of housework have been addressed by new technologies adopted by individual families. Nineteenth-century socialists advocated that many of the demands of housework be solved by using new technology to collectivize the tasks. The Soviet Union attempted to free women from housework by establishing state-run (and subsidized) daycare centers, laundries, and restaurants. This experiment was successfully implemented by many Eastern European societies after World War II but has been abandoned with the return to market-driven policies. Housework continues to be a significant burden for women in all societies.

The financial crisis that began in 2007–8 has shifted things somewhat. Previously, both parents were employed in working-class families. Unemployment, especially among men, has caused more to take greater responsibility for home and family. Scholars will be interested to see if that pattern continues.

See also Women Industrial Workers

Further Reading

Cowan, Ruth Schwarz. *More Work for Mother: The Ironies of Household Technology from the Open Hearth to the Microwave*. New York: Basic Books, 1983.

HYDROELECTRIC POWER

As demand for electricity went up in the 1870s, with the invention of the electric motor, street lighting, and other developments, the need to expand generation became obvious. One quick recourse involved use of hydroelectric power—water power—to generate electricity. By the 1880s, hydroelectric lighting systems were being installed in mountainous sections of central Europe and Scandinavia. Tramways were powered by hydroelectric generation. Large factories, already using water power, found it more convenient to produce electricity and apply it to motors for the machines in the plant.

Hydroelectric power did not require any new inventions outside the electrical field. The hydraulic turbine had been invented in 1832, and by the 1880s it was possible to design a turbine to meet the requirements of any power site, from a small mountain stream to Niagara Falls. The first electric plant at Niagara, opened in 1881, had two turbines. A new powerhouse was begun in 1891, with 10 turbines connected with generators rated at 5,000 horsepower each. Europeans tended to emphasize smaller installation but in large numbers. Switzerland had 561 plants with less than 100 horsepower by 1914, but only 6 plants with 10,000 horsepower or more. Like all electrical power generation, hydroelectric power focused increasing attention on long-distance transmission. Research on this subject began in the

Edward D. Adams Station Power Plant in Niagara Falls, New York, built in the 1890s. (Library of Congress)

1880s, with experiments steadily improving efficiency from initial levels of 39 percent energy loss. Work in Italy on alternating current, begun in 1886 by Circhi and then carried on by others, including Nikola Tesla in the United States, allowed transmission over more than 100 miles with less than 10 percent loss by the early 1900s.

Further Reading

Rouse, Hunter, and Simon Ice. *A History of Hydraulics*. New York: Dover Publications, 1963.
White, Richard. *The Organic Machine: The Remaking of the Columbia River*. New York: Hill and Wang, 1996.

HYUNDAI

Created by entrepreneur Chung Ju Yung, this company was one of the mainstays of South Korean industrialization after World War II. Chung Ju Yung was a villager who walked 150 miles to Seoul to take a job as a day laborer in the 1940s. He soon opened a modest business of his own, which expanded steadily as the South Korean economy began to take off after the Korean War. By the 1980s, Hyundai had 135,000 employees and offices in 42 countries around the world. Visually, it governed Korea's southeast coast, building ships and automobiles. The highly paternalistic company built thousands of housing units for its low-wage labor force and sponsored technical schools to supply technicians. It used traditional rituals to tie workers to each other and to the company, building an arena for tae kwon do, the Korean martial art, and beginning workdays with group exercises. Hyundai workers seemed to respond favorably, putting in six-day weeks with three vacation days per year and participating in reverential ceremonies when a fleet of cars was shipped abroad or a new tanker launched.

See also Japan; Korea

Further Reading

Kirk, Donald. *Korean Dynasty: Hyundai and Chung Ju Yung*. Armonk, NY: M.E. Sharpe, 1994.

IMMIGRATION AND MIGRATION

Migration occurs when people move (either permanently or temporarily) from one country or region to another—generally from farms to cities or rural industrial centers (such as coal mining camps). Immigration is the movement of migrants to a new country; emigration occurs when people leave a place. Although famines, wars, and ethnic or religious conflict have affected migration flows, the most common reason for the mass movement of people is economic. The common image that preindustrial life was a settled and stable one is simply wrong. Even before the Industrial Revolution, many poor peasants migrated to other regions to find seasonal work and artisans in the journeyman stage traveled to find work and build up their skills.

Industrialization built upon these earlier migration patterns and transformed them. By creating new centers of employment (often in cities), industrialization facilitated the permanent shift of millions of people from "field to factory." Many migrants were initially "sojourners," that is, temporary migrants who frequently traveled short distances, but most became urban workers. Industrialization also made migration easier through improvements in transportation technology (canals, railroads, and steamships). The ongoing process of industrialization, migration, and immigration resulted in transforming the composition of most countries involved in the world economy.

In the sixteenth and seventeenth centuries, the dramatic decline of indigenous population of the Americas (over 80% died after contact) and the rise of silver mines and plantations for sugar, rice, and tobacco created an enormous demand for labor that colonial powers generally filled through the enslavement of several million Africans as well as with free European laborers. This pattern continued in the nineteenth and twentieth centuries because the rapid industrialization of the United States created a large demand for workers. Apart from African slaves, most immigrants prior to the 1830s came from Britain and Germany. During the early phases of industrialization, the Irish were slotted into the unskilled labor market. Many of the servants in industrial cities were Irish women. Many, though not all, migrants from England, Wales, Scotland, and Germany became artisans and skilled workers. In addition to their labor, many of these workers contributed to the development of the trade union and socialist movements.

In the past, historians assumed that migrants were "the uprooted"— overwhelmed by the difficulties of finding work and creating identities for

Most immigrants to the United States were first received in Ellis Island's Examination Hall, photographed here in 1904. (Library of Congress)

themselves in a new country. Although historians still document the frequently harsh experiences of migrants, most historians today view migrants as "transplanted" and emphasize migrants' creative/adaptive strategies. Moreover, migrants introduced new foods, terms, and cultural practices to their host society. Curry and tandoori are firmly part of English cuisine, just as bagels, spaghetti, and tacos are in the United States. Migrants used their family or personal contacts to find out information about local working or housing conditions; after they migrated, these contacts were helpful in finding jobs (chain migration). To the enduring frustration of trade union organizers, many migrants judged their difficult working and living conditions abroad against even worse conditions at home—a factor that inhibited protest. However, once workers believed they had been wronged, their immigrant cultures were often a formidable base for solidarity. For instance, one of the largest (and generally unacknowledged) strikes in the United States was conducted in 1867 by Chinese immigrants working on railroads in California.

During the "second" Industrial Revolution (late nineteenth to early twentieth centuries), Eastern and Southern Europe became the United States' primary source for industrial laborers. There were important differences between migrants: the vast majority of (largely impoverished) Slovak villagers ended up as laborers in Pennsylvania's coal mines and steel mills, while better-off Czech migrants settled in the Midwest as artisans or farmers. Many Italians were "birds of passage" and frequently returned to Europe (or migrated again to Argentina). In the Western part of the country, Asian and Mexican migrants built railroads and worked in the mines or on the plantations. By 1924, nativist sentiment and the demands of the American Federation of Labor succeeded in passing laws that drastically reduced immigration. Changes in the law meant that during the Great Depression of the 1930s, immigrant radicals (or simply unemployed immigrants) were deported.

Migrants were also an important factor in colonial regimes. In the nineteenth and twentieth centuries, plantations in Asian and African colonies created large-scale movement of workers. During the nineteenth century, the British Imperial government encouraged the settlement of several million Indian laborers to work the rubber, tea, coffee, and coconut plantations of South and East Africa, Sri Lanka, and Malaysia. By 1948, there were more than a million Tamil laborers in Sri Lanka (then Ceylon). The newly independent Ceylonese government sought to repatriate several hundred thousand of the now unwanted workers. The Indian government refused to accept the return of these laborers, fearing that it would set a precedent that might result in the influx of several million impoverished workers. While a substantial number of these "Indian Tamils" (many of whose families had lived two or three generations in Ceylon) were expatriated, many others were rendered stateless—a status that many still hold nearly 50 years later.

After World War II, most immigrants to the United States came from Latin America or Asia. Many Mexican, Haitian, and Puerto Rican migrants came because their economies were faltering or collapsing; many Cubans, Salvadorans, Vietnamese, and Filipinos came because their countries were experiencing substantial political upheaval or revolutions. Many of these immigrants did not find factory jobs but obtained work in the service sector as cooks, waitresses, and janitors. The political concerns of the Cold War were an important factor in influencing immigrants' experiences. In the 1980s, Nicaraguans were assumed by the U.S. government to be political refugees from Nicaragua's leftist Sandinista government (and because they could find work legally, they faced less abuse from employers), while Salvadorans, whose right-wing government was supported by the United States, were assumed to be "economic refugees" and had difficulty obtaining legal work.

Even before World War II, other industrial areas besides the United States were magnets for immigrants seeking factory jobs from poorer, agricultural societies pressed by population growth. British industry in the nineteenth century used many Irish workers. Poles in the early twentieth century migrated to the industrial regions of Britain, Germany, and France. After World War II, immigration to industrial Europe came from Africa, Turkey, the Indian subcontinent, and the Caribbean. As in the United States, many immigrants found work in the unskilled sector, with better factory jobs reserved for the native born. Though less dependent on immigrant labor (having a substantial pool of underemployed people in its own hinterland), postwar Japan also imported workers from Korea and Southeast Asia, another example of how the labor needs of industrialization, together with global population growth, continued to create dramatic patterns of population movement.

Europe became a major center for immigrant workers since the 1970s. Germany and Sweden attracted numerous Turkish workers. In some cases, the pattern of migration built off of colonial relationships: North Africans migrated to France; Indians and those from the West Indies found work in Britain.

After the oil price hikes of 1973 and 1979, the Middle East became a major source of work for migrants throughout Asia. Millions of Indian and Pakistanis found jobs building the booming cities or maintaining the oil fields. In some instances, such as in Dubai, more than 80 percent of the workforce was made of up immigrants. Immigrants fill jobs from the lowest levels (nannies, domestics, restaurant workers) to the top (university professors, engineers, bankers).

Workers' remittances to their families are a major source of income for developing countries. Mexico receives more money from workers living abroad than it does from the sale of petroleum. In many countries, like the Philippines, migration is a way of life. Good providers find jobs as nurses in the United States, or domestic workers in the Persian Gulf. Migrant workers build relatively large homes for their children, who are, ironically enough, often raised by Filipino nannies as well as family members. More than half of all Puerto Ricans have migrated from that island, almost all to the United States. Worldwide, at least 200 million workers have crossed borders to find work. That does not include those who migrate long distances within their country, which is common in countries as diverse as China and South Africa.

See also Argentina; Dual Labor Market; Great Migration; Urbanization; World Systems Theory

Further Reading

Bodnar, John. *The Transplanted: A History of Immigrants in Urban America*. Bloomington: Indiana University Press, 1985.

Moch, Leslie. *Moving Europeans: Migration in Western Europe since 1650*. Bloomington: Indiana University Press, 1992.

IMPERIALISM

Although empires have existed for thousands of years, the Industrial Revolution was influenced by, even as it significantly changed, the meaning of imperialism. As one historian has pointed out, "Empires and emperors were old, but imperialism was new" to the late nineteenth century—the term "imperialism" came into popular usage only in the 1880s. It referred to the rapid spread of European conquests in Africa, Asia, and the Pacific. Beginning in the seventeenth century, global commercial empires provided Britain and France with surplus capital to finance their industrialization efforts—in Portugal and Spain, however, colonial possessions did not significantly aid industrialization. Throughout much of the nineteenth century, Britain's colonies (notably India, South Africa, and some Caribbean islands) provided it with a reliable supply of raw materials and a captive market for industrial goods. Particularly in the late nineteenth century, many industrial or industrializing countries sought relief from a prolonged depression (caused in part by overproduction) in imperialism. Between 1875 and 1914 countries as diverse as Britain, Germany, Japan, and the United States quickly conquered and colonized Africa and most of Asia—a total of one-quarter of the world's surface.

Imperialism provided "metropolitan" countries not only with cheap raw materials and captive markets but with an opportunity to build common political ground for capitalists, the middle class, and workers. Although relatively few Europeans,

Americans, or Japanese actually migrated to a colonized country as workers, supervisors, or administrators, all members of the metropolitan country were made aware (through the mass media) of their nation's superiority over technologically (and allegedly morally) inferior peoples. As such, imperialism provided much-needed social and political stability to metropolitan countries experiencing tremendous class polarization.

Besides outright conquest, industrialization offered technologically and economically advanced countries new ways to control other regions. Throughout the nineteenth century, England's superior industrial production provided it with de facto economic control over nominally independent nations in Latin America. Countries like Argentina were dependent upon Britain to buy its exports of raw materials (in this case meat, hides, and grain). When Britain suffered a depression or when world war closed shipping lanes, Argentina's economy was hit hard, and it could not afford to purchase manufactured products. The attempt by Latin American nations to modernize their economies drew them further into Britain's economic orbit as they sought technical expertise and capital. Until 1914, Britain was the world's foremost lender, and this position gave its bankers a powerful amount of control in structuring the economies of Latin American nations.

In the twentieth century, the attempts of other industrialized countries—notably Japan, Germany, and Italy—to replicate Britain's economic success through outright imperialism resulted in the devastation of World War II. Global conflict so weakened the metropolitan centers that most of the countries colonized during the previous four centuries were able to gain their independence. The present ability of industrialized countries to use loans and other means to control the terms of trade (and, by extension, the economies) of decolonized nations has caused many to term the new relationship neocolonialism. Imperialism is a charge often hurled at Western countries for military interventions. Controlling access to valuable raw materials is often seen as the motivation.

See also Decolonization; Finance Capital; Neocolonialism; World Bank; World Systems Theory

Further Reading
Hobsbawm, Eric. *The Age of Empire: 1875–1914.* New York: Vintage, 1987.

IMPORT SUBSTITUTION

Import substitution is the practice whereby governments encourage domestic production of goods previously imported. In the 1930s the weakening demand in Europe for meat and hides from Argentina meant that the country could not afford to import manufactured goods; in response, the government supported the rise of domestic industries. Iran adopted similar policies in the 1920s and 1930s to reduce its economic dependence on Europe. In South Korea and Taiwan in the 1950s, textiles were among the first industries encouraged by their government. Import substitution is typically (or hopefully) a prelude to an economic "takeoff" that will lead to the production of goods that can be exported. In the case of Taiwan, an export-oriented garment industry developed in the wake of the successful industrialization of the textile industry. Even when a full industrial revolution does not develop, import substitution spreads mechanization and forces the world's industrial leaders to concentrate on more advanced production sectors.

See also Foreign Trade

Further Reading

Green, Duncan. *Silent Revolution: The Rise and Crisis of Market Economics in Latin America.* New York: Monthly Review Press, 2003.

INDIA

By the middle of the twentieth century, India was one of the 10 largest participants in world trade, yet Indian society as a whole was only partially industrialized. By the time of its independence in 1947, industrial production was concentrated near Bombay, along the country's western coast, and in the east, in the region surrounding Calcutta. However, the level of mechanization in India was low, and its output of manufactured goods per person was increasing at a slower rate than industrializing countries such as Mexico. Even today, though India has a large industrial sector, its rural population engaged in agriculture is even larger and growing fast.

Hewlett-Packard employees work at the company's Business Process Outsourcing call center in Bangalore, India, August 7, 2007. (AP Photo/Aijaz Rahi)

The successes and limitations of industrialization in India were strongly influenced by its economic development as a British colony from the mid-eighteenth century until 1947.

British imperial policy favored British-manufactured goods and displaced Indian textile makers, who were forced to produce for the lower ends of local markets where low profit margins retarded investment in industrial production. From the early nineteenth century until the 1940s, India was an important market for Lancashire's textiles, and as British manufacturers lost other markets, they sought to adjust the tariff to protect the Indian market. Nevertheless, industrial textile production did begin to develop in India in the 1850s, although it did not really blossom until the 1870s. By 1914, India was the world's foremost supplier of jute (twine and bagging for cotton) and its textile mills were significant on the world market. After the 1920s, Indian entrepreneurs began to displace expatriate British managers of industrial facilities, a process aided by a strong Indian entrepreneurial tradition and the ideological demands of the growing nationalist movement. However, large industrial companies, such as that of Jamshed Tata (by the 1940s, the world's twelfth-largest steel company) were rare.

Although commodity production of tea, cotton, and jute transformed much of the Indian countryside into plantations that produced raw materials for the world market, most Indians remained peasants, and land holdings remained small. Unlike Argentina, where the entire population became dependent upon the cash economy, India was still dominated by more or less self-sufficient peasants. Literacy rates under the British remained low until the twentieth century, when they slowly began to rise. The poverty and relatively low productivity of the countryside acted as a drag on the expansion of the industrial sector. For instance, although the Indian railroad system is one of the world's largest, it is chronically short of rolling stock to transport its passengers, and the situation is exacerbated by the many Indians who cannot afford to pay but manage to ride anyway.

After independence, the Indian government sought to accelerate industrialization by providing credits to crucial sectors such as steel and electrical power and by expanding the country's school system. Major urban centers grew rapidly, often beyond the ability of the government to provide basic services. The parliamentary form of government, frequently jettisoned by newly independent revolutionary or nationalist governments elsewhere, proved remarkably resilient in India, although preindustrial loyalties of caste and religion provided the basis for divisive conflicts. The country also has a vibrant newspaper industry, which often exposes corruption in government. Industrial production has continued to expand, helping to produce sizable working and middle classes, but most Indians are hard-pressed peasants. By the 1990s the country was able to produce sophisticated military equipment, such as nuclear weapons, but much of its population remained mired in poverty.

Since the 1990s, Indian industrialization has greatly expanded. South India became a center for software writing and call centers. Mumbai (Bombay) has become a major center for finance. Yet older problems remain: the country's infrastructure and creaky bureaucratic government hampers development, and the country lacks the capacity to produce or transmit enough electricity. In the 1990s, the government signed a deal for a natural gas power plant in Mumbai that enriched the Enron corporation. Later, an Indian entrepreneur found that it was cheaper and easier to ship coal from Indonesia to India to generate electricity because the national railroads were too unreliable.

See also Back Office; Outsourcing

Further Reading

Tomlinson, B. R. *The Economy of Modern India, 1860–1970.* New York: Cambridge University Press, 1993.

INDUSTRIAL REVOLUTION. *See* Causes of the Industrial Revolution

INDUSTRIAL UNIONS

Industrial unions are organizations that represent all the workers at a particular firm or in an entire industry. Rather than consisting only of skilled workers, industrial unions also include the unskilled and the semiskilled machine operators. After a work process has been sufficiently subdivided or automated, employers can easily replace workers, thus making solidarity between skilled and unskilled workers during strikes an absolute necessity if unions are to survive or succeed. Because of the long history of racism, sexism, and nativism in the craft unions of the United States, industrial unions in that country often developed a philosophy of representing all workers regardless of race, gender, religion, or national origin. In Europe as well industrial unions had a social agenda because they frequently developed in tandem with labor or Social Democratic parties. Revolutionary anarcho-syndicalist unions were also influential in France, Spain, and Latin America.

The significance of industrial unions becomes clear only in the context of the history of their predecessors, craft unions. In the early phases of industrialization, unions were generally made up of highly skilled craft workers. Unskilled workers were frequently not able to join the unions, sometimes because skilled workers felt that the unskilled did not have the requisite technical skills, social status, or personal self-control to regulate the organization of their workplace. In the nineteenth century, a few British trade unions opposed extending the franchise to all workers. Furthermore, there was often a fair amount of day-to-day tension between the skilled and the unskilled. One of the legacies of the artisanal mode of production was that skilled workers often continued to direct unskilled workers on the job site.

By the late nineteenth century, employees, particularly in mass-production industries, were increasingly organized on a national basis, through either industrial firms or cartels, which allowed them to bypass the local and regional organizations of most craft unions. Many workers saw the need for industrial and national organization, but the actual dynamics of union organizing made industrial unionism an elusive goal. In 1880, for instance, unskilled dockworkers in London established a union, but the organization was destroyed by an employer counteroffensive in 1893. In the United States, a massive influx of immigrants from eastern and southern Europe accompanied the cartelization of mass-production industries. Many native-born residents or more recent immigrants from northern Europe viewed the new immigrants as undesirable, and furthermore as a cause of the decline of workers' organizations and standards of living. In the 1870s and 1880s, the Knights of Labor attempted to organize all workers regardless of skill, race, or gender. After some stunning initial successes, the union unraveled, in part because many workers refused to accept black members, although the primary reason was that unskilled workers had little leverage on their employers. The national federation of craft unions, the American Federation of Labor, largely retreated from social and political concerns, as did the mass-production industries, choosing largely to concentrate on the economic or "bread-and-butter" concerns of its skilled members. By the turn of the century, however, national confederations of unions were established in Germany, England, and France, and they all had at least 1 million members. Industrial unions that united workers across skill levels gained ground, particularly in heavy industry, in the chemical industry, and among dockworkers.

Industrial unions were not well established in the United States until the formation of the CIO in 1935. Led by the United Mine Workers, the CIO organized important mass-production industries such as steel, auto, electrical equipment, rubber, and aircraft. In many unions, radicals and socialists were organizers and often gained local office; several CIO unions had close ties with the Communist Party. Blacks, women, and immigrants gained a wider, though far from full, voice in the workplace and in the unions. Many workers used the CIO as a political vehicle, although not a revolutionary one; the CIO helped to make industrial workers a crucial component of the Democratic Party and Franklin Roosevelt's New Deal. The power of the CIO was perhaps strongest between 1946, when several million workers struck to regain or improve their standard of living, and 1948, when the CIO helped reelect Democratic president Harry Truman in a stunning political upset.

At the height of its power, the CIO was undermined by changes in government policies. In 1947 Truman confronted a Republican Congress, which overturned his veto to pass the Taft-Hartley Act, a law that greatly restricted the actions of the CIO. Unions were prohibited from making political contributions, the closed shop (in which new workers were automatically enrolled in the union) was banned, and all union officials had to guarantee that they were not communists. To abide by the last provision, the CIO drove 11 unions with communist ties out of their federation, and most were destroyed by both the government and other unions "raiding" their members. Although former CIO unions continued to grow in numbers and influence until the 1960s, the growing conservatism of labor law has made it more difficult to organize new workers, and today most industrial unions are declining with their industries.

In Europe, industrial unions had a different history. The fascist regimes in both Germany and Italy restricted the independence of unions, although in the postwar period industrial unions affiliated with Social Democratic parties regained much of their previous strength. In many cases, unions won not only better wages and social benefits but a direct role in shaping industrial policy. Often, union leaders are also members of corporate boards of directors.

Although Soviet workers were also organized in industrial unions, in practice these were almost completely dominated by the communist governments. In the early 1980s, however, Solidarity, an independent industrial federation of Polish workers, emerged and forced the government to make important political and economic concessions before it was temporarily suppressed. Unions also played an important role in the transformation of the Soviet Union in the 1980s and 1990s. Chinese unions are essentially Stalinist; independent unions are illegal. Chinese workers have led thousands of strikes, and sometimes the government allows them to elect representatives to the Communist unions or to form independent welfare committees. For instance, in 2010, striking workers at a Honda plant called for an independent union.

The concentration of workers in industry has given them common experiences and employers and has made it possible for workers to organize to overcome common problems. Throughout the history of industrial unions, their formation and health have frequently been influenced by political as well as economic trends. Repressive regimes often suppress trade unions and even murder trade unionists. There are also cases of industrial unions weakening or toppling repressive governments, as in Poland and South Africa in the 1980s, or the actions of Nigerian oil workers in the 1990s. The most serious challenge to industrial unionism probably lies in the increasing power of multinational corporations to shift production from one country to another. Although there are instances of industrial unions cooperating across national borders, that chapter of history largely remains to be written.

See also Confédération Générale du Travail (CGT); Division of Labor; Socialism

Further Reading

Lichtenstein, Nelson, and John Harris Howell. *Industrial Democracy in America: The Ambiguous Promise*. New York: Cambridge University Press, 1993.

INDUSTRIAL WORKERS

Industrial workers have often been at the forefront of work organization and labor discipline. In the late eighteenth century, merchants organized decentralized "putting out" systems of production that employed rural workers working in their homes. In the nineteenth century, work was centralized in factories, and industrial workers experienced tighter supervision, longer hours of work, and a faster work pace—a regime that quickly extended to other workers. Thus industrial workers differed from craft workers, who had different traditions and work sites. By the end of the nineteenth century, industrial workers were increasingly concentrated in large factories where industrialists could achieve greater levels of efficiency from new forms of work organization, such as the moving assembly line. In the 1920s, there were over 60,000 workers in Henry Ford's River Rouge automobile factory—an extreme case but one that exemplified the tendency toward the rapid growth and centralization of industrial workers.

Many Marxists in the nineteenth century believed that the expansion of the Industrial Revolution and of industrial workers would create a unified, disciplined, and politically conscious class that would fight for socialism. Industrial workers were certainly at the forefront of most Social Democratic parties and movements, but the substantial differences between workers' skills, wage levels, and political expectations (often influenced by race, gender, or ethnicity) made class solidarity problematic. Industrial workers were not the whole working class, though they were the most rapidly growing segment. Early in the twentieth century, Lenin observed that whereas many people called industrial workers "proletarians," this was a political identity, not a demographic one. More workers aspired to be the foreman in the factory, or a small business owner, than the militant who wanted to overthrow capitalism.

Because of the importance of industrial firms to the economy, organizations of industrial workers have often wielded great political and economic strength. Russian factory workers were essential in toppling the czar in the communist revolution of 1917. However, most industrial workers eschewed revolution for reform. In the United States, the formation of the Congress of Industrial Organization in the 1930s created durable unions of industrial workers and strengthened the New Deal. Although "globalization" of industrial production had always been a reality, this trend began to accelerate in the 1960s and 1970s, undermining the importance of industrial workers in industrialized countries. Industrial workers began to decline numerically in the most advanced industrial economies. As late as the 1970s, strikes by British coal miners toppled national governments; in the mid-1980s, the crushing of a coal miners' strike by Margaret Thatcher's government had enormous political symbolism.

See also Black Workers; Dual Labor Markets; Industrial Unions; Postindustrial Economies; Proto-industrialization; Welfare State; Women Industrial Workers

Further Reading

Montgomery, David. *The Fall of the House of Labor: The Workplace, the State, and American Labor Activism, 1865–1925*. Cambridge: Cambridge University Press, 1987.

INDUSTRIAL WORKERS OF THE WORLD (IWW)

The Industrial Workers of the World (IWW) were formed in 1905 as a revolutionary syndicalist union. The founding convention in Chicago brought together socialists, anarchists, and veteran hard-rock miners (copper, lead, etc.),

Industrial Workers of the World (IWW) demonstrate in New York City, April 1914. (Library of Congress)

radicalized by bitter struggles with mining companies in the western United States. The goals of the fledgling union were high; one participant called the formation of the union the "constitutional convention of the working class." The IWW bitterly criticized the conservatism of the American Federation of Labor (AFL) and sought to organize all workers, regardless of skill, race, or nationality, into unions. They believed industrial unions would allow workers to "bring to birth the new world from the ashes of the old." The IWW led numerous militant strikes, and about 3 million people passed through the organization until it was destroyed by the U.S. federal government after World War I. Although the IWW still exists, its influence radically declined in the 1920s and most militant Wobblies (as IWW activists were called) joined the Communist Party. Here and there, a few anarchists organized effective local unions, such as one of steelworkers in Cleveland in the 1940s.

Unlike most unions that grew out of the social solidarity of skilled workers in relatively stable neighborhoods, the Wobblies built a union movement among transient workers, particularly in the Great Plains and in the West. In the early 1900s, farming was partially mechanized, but farmers still relied on large numbers of migrant laborers to harvest their crops. Living conditions for workers were crude, and workers put in long hours. However, if the crops were not harvested in a timely fashion they would spoil, and Wobblies frequently exploited this situation by urging workers to strike, or more commonly to simply work slower or to sabotage equipment. The union was represented by traveling delegates who collected dues from workers in the fields. The most common form of traveling for these hobo-workers was by hopping freight trains, and Wobblies would sometimes enforce solidarity by allowing only union men to ride in "their" boxcars. A similar tradition arose among timber workers, particularly along the West Coast, but also in the pine woods of the South. The IWW organized white and black workers into the union, an act that cost numerous union men their lives. Violence at the hands of vigilantes was a common form of retaliation on the IWW, and part of the reason that Wobblies advocated "striking on the job"—their term for sabotage—was that traditional strike methods were not only futile, but could even be fatal. Union activists did try to defend their civil liberties, and when small-town police prevented Wobblies from speaking, the union frequently flooded the town with union men until the city fathers tired of paying to put up union men in their jail. The IWW opposed World War I, and Wobblies' advocacy of sabotaging the war effort brought them into conflict with the newly formed FBI. Fear of the Bolshevik revolution led the United States into a full-blown "red scare" after the war ended, and many Wobblies were lynched or murdered and their organization destroyed.

See also Workers' Control

Further Reading

Dubinsky, Melvyn. *We Shall Be All: A History of the Industrial Workers of the World.* Chicago: Quadrangle, 1969.

INFLATION AND DEFLATION

Inflation describes a condition of systematically rising prices. Prices can increase because the supply of money expands (when the stock of precious metals grows or governments print more money), driving up the price of goods, or inflation can occur when demand exceeds the amount of goods available. Deflation is the reverse: either because supply exceeds demand or because the amount of money in circulation diminishes, prices fall. Economic historians debate the relative importance of money supply versus supply and demand for goods. When money supply drops in relation to business activity, the value of the unit of money goes up; in inflation the reverse prevails. But efficiency (tending to cut costs and prices) or growing consumer demand (tending to raise them) plays a role as well.

During the early industrial period in most Western countries, an inflationary situation did not prevail. Prices went up during the Napoleonic Wars, when military demand and supply shortages created bottlenecks; this encouraged further industrialization in Britain. But during much of the nineteenth century, prices were stationary or falling; money supply declined in relation to the growth of economic activity, while increased output kept pace with or outstripped demand. Temporary inflation occurred when harvests were bad, driving food prices up, but there was no systematic trend. Deflation was the more normal pattern as industrial production increased the amount of goods in circulation, driving down prices. Limits on money supply based on gold, tending to reduce prices, helped motivate businessmen to seek ways to cut costs to continue making profits. New gold supply from California, in the early 1850s, created some inflation, but this ended in 1857 and deflation resumed.

Inflation began to loom as a greater problem around 1900, when consumer demand sometimes exceeded supply. New discoveries of gold in Australia (1851), South Africa (1887), and the Klondike (1896) began to increase the money supply, helping to relax the deflationary pressures. Several protests against rising prices occurred after 1900. Rampant inflation occurred during and after World War I, when governments spent massive amounts of money without raising taxes, thus increasing overall demand. French prices stood at an index of 356 in 1919 (1913 = 100), 509 in 1920. Austrian inflation reached a multiplier of 14,000, and German and Russian levels were far worse. These inflationary conditions could temporarily spur industry, because businessmen were eager to borrow for expansion knowing that, as prices continued to go up, their debt would be less costly when it came time to repay simply because the unit of money would be worth less. But post–World War I inflation was ultimately destabilizing, hurting people on fixed incomes, encouraging speculation rather than solid investment, and reducing overall confidence. Thus inflation was a major factor in Europe's interwar economic woes. Britain, running against the tide, deflated its prices by returning to the gold standard in the 1920s, but this made British exports more expensive and hurt the economy. The British abandoned this policy during the Great Depression of the 1930s, when prices fell everywhere.

Inflationary tendencies continued, though at a lower rate, in the industrial world after World War II, and governments tried hard to keep the problem in check. Rapid inflation in many developing countries, like Brazil and South Africa, was a major economic problem after World War II; demand, including government expenditures, went up rapidly, raising prices and reducing the value of money. This trend could discourage foreign investment and certainly depressed living standards for most wage earners, though industrial growth often continued. Cases of deflation, while rarer, also existed, such as Japan for decades after 1987.

The history of inflation during the period of industrialization suggests that rampant price increases are socially and economically damaging. The relationship between milder inflations and economic growth is less clear; at some points, by making credit cheaper, it stimulates borrowing, which can in turn increase industrial capacity. At the same time many late twentieth-century governments, stung by the post–World War I experience, sedulously attempt to keep price increases at moderate levels even at the expense of short-term economic growth.

See also Business Cycles

Further Reading

Feldman, Gerald D. *The Great Disorder: Politics, Economics, and Society in the German Inflation*. New York: Oxford University Press, 1993.

INFRASTRUCTURE

Successful industrialization efforts have relied not only on new technology or entrepreneurialism but on the creation of a physical and social infrastructure in which economic change could take place. Infrastructure refers to facilities like roads, sewers, or schools that are essential to economic life but not directly productive.

Physical infrastructure projects have generally been the responsibility of the state. European governments helped support industrialization by building canals and railroads. The Japanese government also sponsored expansion of port facilities and shipyards, a vital part of industrialization in a country dependent upon ocean trade. Chinese industrialization after 1978 still retains an important role for government, for instance, in building a system of high-speed trains. In the United States, federal, state, and even local government helped to finance the building of nineteenth-century transportation networks such as roads, canals, and railroads and, in the twentieth century, highways and airports. The Erie Canal greatly expanded exports of grain and manufactured products from New York, and several other states attempted to duplicate New York's success. The federal government offered lucrative land grants to railroads in the West; the economic costs to a city or region that

A sewer system is constructed in Nebraska in 1889; water systems were just one example of how industrialization transformed daily life. (Library of Congress)

were bypassed by a railroad were severe, and therefore localities frequently under-wrote bond issues so that they could be linked to a main line. The decline of the U.S. railroad system in the twentieth century was caused in large part by the shift of federal subsidies to the automobile.

Although automobiles rapidly became the center of the U.S. economy, carmakers relied on the government to provide the street and highway network required for "mass automobility." Partly through a tax on gasoline, federal and state governments spent billions on highway construction—even more in the 1930s than in the more prosperous 1920s. The location of highways proved crucial to suburban land developers. Ironically, the government could build roads that made land more valuable, but it was prohibited (unlike many European governments) from purchasing land that would accrue in value after the construction of roads. European governments generally used gasoline taxes to subsidize public transportation, while most streetcar systems in U.S. cities were dismantled by a consortium of automobile and automobile-related companies. After World War II, the federal government launched a massive program to build "superhighways." Ostensibly a defense measure (an imitation of fascist Germany's Autobahn), the superhighway program, along with subsidies for suburban home ownership, helped to solidify the development of auto, home, and highway construction industries.

Industrialization has also relied on systems of mass education and universities. An educated workforce has provided the technical skills, flexibility, and discipline for latecomer industrializers to develop a modern system of manufacturing. The university system in the United States rapidly expanded after the 1862 "land grant" system to schools that offered technical and agricultural education. Engineering and scientific researchers quickly developed strong links with corporations and have provided much of their research and development. During the Cold War, government-sponsored military-related research provided an additional subsidy, both to the university system and to defense companies. The Japanese state built on the already strong pre-Meiji education system by emphasizing technical skills and nationalism. After their independence from Japan in 1945, South Korea and Taiwan expanded their education systems, particularly technical instruction, and their highly skilled workforce was a major contributing factor to the success of their industrialization drive. From the nineteenth century onward, public health facilities such as sewer and water systems have been vital features of industrial infrastructure, making industrialized cities more livable for workers and helping to improve their productivity.

Since the mid-1970s, most industrialized countries encountered a serious financial crisis. As a result, support for education has been limited or cut. In Europe, university students must pay an increasing amount of tuition, whereas the state once paid the entire amount; stipends to students have been reduced or fail to keep up with inflation. In the United States, direct and indirect subsidies to universities and education in general have been cut. Tuition rates for universities and colleges have risen at twice or more the rate of inflation. Technically, trained workers are still readily available, but an increasing number of skilled workers are underemployed or even unemployed. Particularly after the 1990s, Chinese leaders sought to expand the number of scientists and engineers. Government tried to create a group that could not just apply science to industry but also shift the center of innovation from the United States to China. Yet many university graduates are unable to find meaningful work. It is not easy for any country to arrive at the best balance between affordable education and an educated workforce that encourages technological innovation.

Faced with large deficits, governments often choose to delay maintenance of physical infrastructure. In the Soviet Union, where everything was owned by the state, roads, oil pipelines, and even nuclear power plants were allowed to deteriorate to the point of collapse. Stalin's five-year plans neglected infrastructure in favor of production, and the road and rail system suffered. Ultimately, this policy created production bottlenecks and environmental damage, contributing to the Soviet Union's industrial decline in the 1980s. The nuclear accident in Chernobyl resulted from these policies.

In the United States, the infrastructure of roads, bridges, and waterways, particularly in urban areas, has reached a critical stage. In the late 1980s, delays in repairing an underground tunnel (which would have cost several hundred dollars) eventually flooded much of downtown Chicago, resulting in businesses losing several hundred million dollars' worth of business. In the 2000s, a widespread concern emerged about the aging American electrical grid. Companies sought to shift to computerized systems, ones that can handle new forms of electricity, such as wind or solar, but the system suffers from years of neglect. The computer systems that handle airline traffic are so out of date that they contribute significantly to delays in airline traffic. Still, the political support for infrastructure spending is notoriously weak.

The financial crisis for industrialized states is undeniably critical, but among industrializing or nonindustrialized countries it is far more acute. In Africa, the university system is failing, and many development agencies refuse to provide aid, arguing that Africans will need only low-level skills anyway. In much of the continent, university professors earn more money working at development agencies than teaching students. Some have turned to driving taxis to make ends meet. Hundreds of Africans die each day because hospitals lack such necessities as rubber gloves. The global nature of the infrastructure crisis has led some scholars to wonder whether the industrial system has begun a process of "modernization in reverse."

The major exception to this process lies in East Asia, particularly in China. Airports through South East Asia were modernized following the financial crisis of the late 1990s. The Chinese government has greatly expanded its roadways, as well as creating more high-speed rail than the rest of the world combined.

See also Postindustrial Economies; Professionalization; "Second" Industrial Revolution; State, Role of the; World Bank

Further Reading

Hossein-Zadeh, Ismael. *The Political Economy of U.S. Militarism.* New York: Palgrave Macmillan, 2006.

Noble, David F. *America by Design: Science, Technology and the Rise of Corporate Capitalism.* New York: Knopf, 1977.

INSTRUMENTALISM

This term is used to describe a fundamental new attitude toward work that partially replaced the older belief that jobs should provide identity or be defined in terms of unchanging effort (what British unskilled workers called the lump o' labor). Instrumentalist workers accepted the idea that work could change and even intensify, if it was viewed as an instrument to a better life (higher earnings, shorter hours) off the job. Instrumentalist workers thus could bargain for gains in exchange for some loss of skills, diminished control, or interest on the job. Instrumentalist goals began to surface in the mid-nineteenth century among British skilled workers. They later spread even more widely among semiskilled factory workers in most Western industrial countries, and they influenced the goals of many labor movements.

See also Discipline; Standard of Living; Work

Further Reading

Stearns, Peter N. *Paths to Authority.* Urbana: University of Illinois Press, 1978.

INTERCHANGEABLE PARTS

As complex machines became more important in manufacturing, issues in their own manufacture loomed larger. Before the eighteenth century, most machinery and weaponry was assembled by hand, with metal pieces individually cut out for each item. The one exception was in boring cylinders for cannon, where some equipment beyond hand tools was used. Industrial parts manufacture was expensive. It was clear that production of parts separately, in large quantities, would be more efficient as soon as enough accuracy could be achieved that they were interchangeable in assembling the whole item.

As early as 1700, the Swedish engineer Christopher Polhem tried to manufacture accurate separate parts. He applied water power to all possible stages of production, assembling the individual parts later on. But the equipment available was too crude to have much effect. In 1785 a French manufacturer, Honoré Le Blanc, began to produce muskets with interchangeable parts, using standardized jigs to guide workmen cutting out the different segments. The results of his work were limited because hand crafting was essential, but they were being publicized by 1791.

A further breakthrough toward interchangeable parts was accomplished by Eli Whitney and Simeon North in making firearms under contract with the U.S. government, though Whitney claimed more uniformity than he really achieved. North's work, between 1798 and 1816, was more vital because he worked on uniform parts and the specialized machinery to make them in what became known as the "American System." By the early nineteenth century, guns could be produced in quantity by assembling standardized, accurately molded parts chosen at random in each necessary category. British manufacturers, some of whom worked for a time in the United States, began to produce pulleys and other equipment for the navy on the basis of interchangeable parts. Again, the security of a military contract was essential for the innovation required: Marc Brunel and Samuel Bentham designed 44 separate machines capable of producing most of the parts needed for a finished pulley block. The machines variously cut pieces, bored and shaped them, turned and riveted them, and polished the most exacting parts. Although some work still had to be accomplished by hand, machines enabled 10 semiskilled workers to do work otherwise requiring 110 skilled operatives. The principles of interchangeable parts were progressively carried into the manufacture of all sorts of machinery and equipment, including engines. Fully automatic machine building was not completed until the late nineteenth century, but interchangeable parts provided an essential basis for the mass production of crucial technology in growing volume and with decreasing costs.

See also Boring Machines; Machine Building; Springfield Armory

Further Reading

Pursell, Carroll W., Jr. *Technology in America: A History of Individuals and Ideas.* Cambridge, MA: MIT Press, 1981.

INTERNAL COMBUSTION ENGINE

This engine operates by means of a channeled explosion: as gases expand in a confined space, such as a cylinder, a piston is driven in the direction desired. The possibility of such a device, driven by regularly repeated explosions, was discussed as early as 1678 by Abbé Hautefeuille. The first practical version was developed only in 1859, however, when Etienne Lenoir brought forth a motor fired by a mixture of gas and air. The motor consumed too much gas to be practical, but the principle was established, and from then on, a variety of tinkerers and engineers worked on further development. N. A. Otto produced and patented the first practical gas engine in 1876, and within a few years, more than 35,000 of them were at work all over the world. This engine had many advantages over steam: it was more efficient, particularly in small industry, cleaner, and the feed could be automated, saving the labor of shoveling coal. Early motors were fixed in location, using gases emitted as byproducts from metallurgical factories. When liquid petroleum fuels were developed, the motor could also be mobile.

The greatest uses of the gasoline-powered internal combustion turned out to be in transportation, in engines for ships, and, ultimately, in automobiles. The motor's invention stimulated the search for new sources of petroleum, which was initially very expensive. Oil engines were in use in Russia in the 1870s, based on the great

Karl Benz, right, as he makes first test runs on the Ringstrasse in Mannheim, Germany, October 1885, with the world's first car powered by a gas combustion engine, a three-wheeler named "Velociped." (Associated Press)

Baku oil fields. Western-owned fields first emerged in Southeast Asia (1898) and Texas (1901); at this point, European navies began to convert to petroleum. By the 1920s, this fuel was rapidly displacing coal for many uses, creating a major rebalancing in labor forces and older industrial economies alike. Many coal-producing regions began to decline, and the scramble for control over oil fields became one of the major themes of the twentieth century.

Further Reading

Pursell, Carroll W., Jr. *Technology in America: A History of Individuals and Ideas.* Cambridge, MA: MIT Press, 1981.

INTERNATIONAL BUSINESS MACHINES (IBM)

International Business Machines (IBM) is a U.S.-based technology and computer company founded in 1911 as a merger of several other businesses. IBM brought together companies that had already made the punch-clock, scales, and an early mechanical sorter and computer (the Hollerith machine). IBM represents the long-standing ability of computers and high technology to revolutionize the industrial workplace, as well as the travails of a large U.S.-based corporation.

The Hollerith machines enabled IBM to complete large, complex sorting procedures such as the U.S. Census, sending out checks for Social Security, ascertaining who was Jewish under Nazi laws, and prioritizing shipments for the U.S. and Nazi militaries. IBM led the way in creating electronic computers, developing early mainframes, and computing languages such as Fortran.

The company's informal motto was "Think," although it encouraged conservative dress for its engineers. For years, it was a model employer, paying relatively high wages, with good benefits.

The company faltered as computing turned to personal computers. It lost out in terms of manufacturing either the hardware or the software for them. By the 1980s, Big Blue, as the company was known, had a bad case of the blues. Thousands were laid off. It relocated from its headquarters in Binghamton, New York, and the city did not recover. IBM then rebuilt itself, becoming an industry leader in building supercomputers. It developed key artificial intelligence (AI) programs, such as the Watson system that was the first AI program to beat a human chess master.

See also Artificial Intelligence (AI); Computers

Further Reading

Garr, Doug. *IBM Redux: Lou Gerstner and the Business Turnaround of the Decade*. New York: HarperBusiness, 1999.

INTERNATIONAL MONETARY FUND (IMF)

The International Monetary Fund (IMF) was established shortly after World War II as an international organization designed to oversee the global financial system. The purpose was to avoid the lack of regulation and impulse toward narrow national response that had helped establish the context for the Depression of the 1930s. In turn, the decision to launch the IMF was a crucial element of the policy shifts that helped propel economic globalization.

The International Monetary Fund was planned in 1944 and came into existence the following year, initially with 45 members. The goals at the beginning involved monitoring the economic policies of member states to stabilize exchange rates and maintain stable currencies, while also assisting in reconstructing the international financial system. Member countries contributed to an investment pool from which loans could be provided temporarily to help countries with a payments imbalance.

The influence of the IMF expanded fairly steadily, though during the Cold War communist nations systematically avoided the institution. Over time, the IMF has intervened to assist a number of countries hit by financial fluctuations, from Southeast Asia to Argentina. Typically, the IMF requires a borrower nation to undertake significant economic reforms, including increases in taxes, reduction of government budgets, and (often) a reduction of the state's economic role in favor

Participants of the Bretton Woods conference in 1944, where the framework for the postwar global economy was planned. (Library of Congress)

of greater free enterprise. This has won the IMF a great deal of criticism for being unduly influenced by Western, particularly American, principles and for limiting economic development opportunities for certain regions. Indeed, IMF governing structure gives disproportionate voting power to leading European countries and particularly the United States. And the organization has definitely not managed to prevent some severe cases of financial collapse. Finally, critics argue that IMF terms occasionally push countries to exploit resources heedlessly, in the effort to earn profits that will allow repayment of loans, even at the expense of longer-term environmental quality. On the other hand, the IMF gets credit for protecting the international financial system even when particular regions encounter difficulty. The role of the IMF was actually enhanced as a key international response to the banking and economic crisis of 2008–9, providing stabilization loans to a number of debtor economies particularly in southern and Eastern Europe.

The membership of the International Monetary Fund, initially disproportionately Western, has expanded steadily, and by 2010, 187 states were participating. Only a few countries, including North Korea, deliberately refrain from participation.

The collapse of the communist bloc around 1990 led to many new applications, and even earlier, most countries that freed themselves from colonial control quickly signed up for the IMF. Attractions included not only considerable protection of financial stability but also, for some of the poorer countries, additional development loans. The IMF proclaims its commitment to facilitating international trade and promoting high employment and sustainable economic growth. Efforts to broaden the governing base of the fund have not been fully resolved.

Further Reading

Moschella, Manuela. *Governing Risk: The IMF and Global Financial Crises.* London: Palgrave Macmillan, 2010.

INTERNATIONALS

The internationals were organizations that attempted to articulate and coordinate the interests and movements of the growing working class throughout the industrializing world. The fate of the three successive internationals has reflected larger transformations of socialist ideology and organization. The First International (1864–76) was formed by a collection of radicals, utopian socialists, anarchists, and unionists. The organization helped to spread radical ideas but fell victim to the conflict between the communist Karl Marx, who argued that workers' organizations needed to carefully study social and economic conditions before formulating their goals and actions, and the anarchist Mikhail Bakunin, a believer in spontaneous revolt. The Second International (1899–1920) was dominated by the socialist parties of Germany, France, and Austria, among others. Despite a long tradition of advocating the solidarity of the working classes, and therefore noncooperation with wars between industrial countries, all major socialist parties endorsed World War I.

The Third, or Communist, International (1919–43) arose out of the failures of the socialist parties and the dramatic success of the Russian Bolshevik Party. Although the Communist International initially asserted that workers' revolutions in countries such as Germany, Italy, or France would take precedence over conditions in Russia, the failure of revolutions in these countries led the Third International to demand allegiance to the Russian Revolution. Until Stalin dissolved this international in 1943 (out of solidarity with his allies in the fight against fascism), loyalty to the Bolshevik Party was ruthlessly and often brutally enforced. Although a failure in Western Europe, the Third International did promote revolutions in China and Eastern Europe.

See also Russian Revolution (1917)

Further Reading

Haupt, Georges. *Aspects of International Socialism, 1871–1914: Essays.* New York: Columbia University Press, 1986.

INTERNET

To say that the Internet has revolutionized daily life is an understatement. It would be an exaggeration, however, to say that the Internet has changed human existence as much as the agricultural or industrial revolutions. The changes wrought by the Internet are akin to how telephones, electricity, and railroads changed society. Each technology spurred new technologies and businesses and changed the ways people lived, thought about themselves, and the world around them.

The Internet has its origins in the Cold War. After the Soviet Union launched Sputnik, the United States set up ARPA (Advanced Research Projects Agency, later DARPA). ARPA was given the task of funding research to ensure that the United States kept ahead of the Soviet Union in terms of technology. The U.S. military wanted to ensure its command centers could communicate in the event of a nuclear blast that disabled telephone systems. By 1968, ARPA had worked with several universities, mostly in Southern California, and laid wiring that allowed communication between their computer systems. Numerous software-engineering problems were identified and solved. ARPAnet was born; and within a few years, 15 universities had joined, a harbinger of future popularity.

The system went through several incarnations before 1991 when the general public took notice of it as "the World Wide Web." The World Wide Web was a European initiative. The first commercial applications were allowed in the mid-1980s, but the business of the Internet really took off in the mid-1990s.

Like the telephone, the internetwork connects users, although unlike the telephone, it connects multiple users simultaneously. As with telephony, the Internet

Amazon.com distribution center in Seattle, 1997. (Associated Press)

has helped to radically and rapidly break down time and space; the difference is that the Internet has engendered a faster rate of change. Within 25 years, the revolutionary communication device of one generation (e-mail) has been largely abandoned by younger users for social networking sites such as Facebook. It is either comforting or maddening to know how quickly the cutting edge becomes passé as still newer generations of users rely on novel forms of interaction (Twitter or texting). In each case, however, the Internet's model of an interactive network of users is updated and refined.

The Internet has the power to flatten traditional relationships. In the 1990s, Airlines learned they could sell tickets directly to customers. Internet-based middlemen saw an opportunity to sell unused seats. Traditional travel agents almost completely disappeared. The Internet made it easier to outsource back-office functions, such as telephone help desks, to overseas. Later, more skilled work followed; for instance, X-rays can be taken in one country and read in another. The music industry has been transformed by networks of users sharing electronic music (often in violation of copyright laws). The result has been a decline in the profits of record companies, although not their elimination. Many bands have found it fun and profitable to supply recorded music "directly" to their fans over the Internet.

In certain senses, there is nothing new in a new form of technology making it harder for established businesses or professions to maintain their viability. Railroads could bypass towns that had been important hubs when trade went via canal or river. Long-distance trucking and the highway system made it possible to set up businesses far from a railroad line. When people traveled internationally by steamship, towns like Cairo and Cape Town were well known because ships stopped there on the way to somewhere else. Jet planes bypassed these cities.

Like the railroads a century before, companies in the Internet era quickly realized that huge profits could be made as more and more business was conducted over the web. But like earlier generations of businessmen, they were not quite sure how. In the late 1990s, vast sums were invested in the "dot-com," or technology, bubble. For a few months, Priceline, a company that sold airline tickets via the Internet, was worth considerably more than any number of major airlines who owned real assets and had a history of making money. Priceline made money in only one quarter of its existence, and its price fell by about 99 percent from its highs; however, it did stay in business. Other dot-com companies, such as Amazon, helped put brick-and-mortar bookstores out of business, and then began to sell virtually everything else.

Businesses that operated over the web avoided a major cost of brick-and-mortar businesses: a network of stores that needed to be "branded" and maintained to attract customers. Companies like Netflix transformed the movie rental markets by allowing customers to build a list of movies they wished to watch on the web, using software to recommend choices. Unlike chains of video rental stores, Netflix sent the DVD through the mail; eventually brick-and-mortar chains went out of business. When Netflix decided to stream movies and television into the home, cable companies saw the threat. Cable, unlike Netflix, has to pay for and develop a physical infrastructure to deliver their product to consumers. In 2010, one-third of all Internet traffic in the evening was movies streamed into homes.

To borrow a phrase from author Thomas Friedman, the Internet is "flattening" the world. India was able to use the Internet to accelerate its pace of modernization. But the accelerating pace of change makes it harder for those countries, regions, or classes to close the gap. Most of sub-Saharan Africa has extremely limited Internet connections (as well as roads, water systems, etc.). Even within developed countries, Internet access can vary widely between urban and rural areas. Within most societies, Internet access is generally a function of class, as the richest portion of society has the best access to it. While the unemployed do not have to stand in long lines to file a claim or apply for jobs, jobless workers generally have the most limited access to the Internet.

See also Back Office; Computerization

Further Reading

Ryan, Johnny. *The History of the Internet and the Digital Future.* London: Reaktion Books, 2010.

INTERSTATE COMMERCE COMMISSION (ICC)

The Interstate Commerce Commission (ICC) was established by an act of Congress in 1887 to regulate railroad rates after great political pressure from farmers who depended on railroads to get their goods to market. The enormous power railroads exercised over interstate commerce and the frequent use of rebates to favored customers (subsidized by higher rates paid by other consumers) helped to legitimize the creation of the ICC, which was authorized to prevent "unjust or unreasonable" charges. What "unreasonable" meant in practice was unclear, and because railroad companies exercised great influence on the regulatory board, the ICC's interpretation of that term frequently favored cartels. Railroad companies themselves had requested government regulation because fierce competition between companies was resulting in the ruin of many railroad lines.

The ICC is an example of the important role government frequently plays in regulating markets, often by limiting competition among firms. In the early years, however, informal rate agreements came undone as firms undercut their competition. The regulatory power of the ICC has extended to all surface transportation: rails, trucks, water traffic, pipelines. Many regulators today leave the ICC for careers with rail or trucking firms.

See also Populism; State, Role of the

Further Reading

Kolko, Gabriel. *Railroads and Regulation, 1877–1916.* Princeton, NJ: Princeton University Press, 1965.

INTERVENTIONIST GOVERNMENT

Interventionist governments adopt explicit policies to affect economic and social patterns. Pinpointing the role of government—the degree and impact of government intervention—in the Industrial Revolution is difficult. All industrial revolutions have involved government action. All have also required government to stop enforcing certain traditional policies—like supporting guild restrictions on technological innovation. Government roles have varied, however, and they have been debated; liberal economists have attacked government in the name of open competition, a particularly important theme in the industrialization of Europe and the United States.

Some of the common policies governments have adopted to encourage industrialization include promoting technological knowledge by sponsoring commercial fairs and technical schools; expanding educational systems; using government funds and rights of eminent domain to sponsor big improvements in infrastructure, such as railway development or the modernization of ports; and using police and laws to help limit worker protest, particularly during early industrialization. Even within this category variety exists. Most governments backed educational growth (in the United States, this was initially up to state governments), but Britain lagged a bit, in part because of uncertainty that this was an appropriate government activity. Although all governments helped railroad construction, the British government did relatively little, whereas the United States gave huge public lands to private companies; the French government planned and built the tracks but let private companies run the lines under state license; and the German government built and operated most lines directly.

In general, later industrializers relied on governments for more intervention to spur economic growth than had been the case in Western Europe and the United States. Governments could help a society like Russia catch up technologically and also compensate for lack of capital and entrepreneurial tradition. The Japanese government, with its powerful Ministry of Industry, was even more active than its Russian counterpart, building most of Japan's initial heavy industry directly. Pacific Rim industrializations in the 1950s and 1960s involved extensive government planning, for example, in encouraging exports; thus the Taiwanese government during the 1960s installed elaborate planning mechanisms designed to make the most of limited capital and resources, while rapidly expanding schools and technical learning. Many industrializing areas, including India and Latin America, also relied heavily on government intervention to further their process of change. Latin American governments, reacting to the 1930s depression, took a quite activist economic role. Brazil, for example, built a new steel industry and then launched a successful computer sector under government sponsorship. Only in the Soviet Union, Eastern Europe, and China, however, did a government try to run the industrialization process entirely, doing away with virtually all private initiative. The results were not impressive, particularly once computerization began to affect society.

Government intervention in the economy has been somewhat cyclical. In the early industrialization of the West, liberals focused strongly on getting government out of the business of protecting older methods; some also fought high tariffs, though with varying degrees of success. After 1850, government intervention tended to increase. Governments helped organize investment capital, as in the big banks sponsored by the Second Empire regime in France. Armaments expenditures rose, in part to provide markets for heavy industry. Governments began to intervene in labor conditions by regulating children's and women's labor, supervising safety, and, beginning in the 1880s, providing some social insurance programs. The general idea here was to use government inspection and some tax monies to limit the worst abuses of industrial operations. In most industrial countries of the twentieth century, this approach blossomed into the welfare state, in which governments offer a wide range of social programs to protect its citizens economically against the worst problems of aging, unemployment, and illness. Increasing concern with environmental regulation after World War II added yet another regulatory area.

In the 1970s, world opinion shifted again to oppose too much government regulation. A number of governments have sold off selected state enterprises—thus Mexico "privatized" over half of its government companies in the early 1990s. Free-market competition was encouraged in China after 1978 and then in Vietnam, both communist countries. In the 1990s, India also began to reduce government regulations and encourage foreign business. The idea was that too much government activity, even if helpful at first, proved stifling. The prosperity of the West and Japan, with extensive private sectors, and the failure of the Soviet command-economy system in Russia, helped spur this move. Government policies still vary—the United States is unusual in having no government planning office. Almost everywhere, however, intervention is much more extensive than it was in the nineteenth century, and the proper mix continues to be debated.

See also Child Labor; Laissez-faire; Ministry of International Trade and Industry (MITI); Social Insurance; State, Role of; Welfare State

Further Reading

Gordon, Linda, ed. *Women, the State, and Welfare.* Madison: University of Wisconsin Press, 1990.

Haggard, Stephan, and Chung-in Moon. *Pacific Dynamics: The International Politics of Industrial Change.* Boulder, CO: Westview, 1989.

Skowronek, Stephen. *Building a New American State: The Expansion of National Administrative Capacity, 1877–1920.* New York: Cambridge University Press, 1982.

Smith, Thomas. *Political Change and Industrial Development in Japan: Governmental Enterprise, 1868–1880.* Stanford, CA: Stanford University Press, 1955.

INVENTIONS

Inventions were crucial in setting off and sustaining the Industrial Revolution. Early inventions, occurring mainly in eighteenth-century Britain, were designed to improve productivity within the existing economic system; thus they focused on domestic manufacturing. With the steam engine, inventions began to apply directly to the need for factories and novel sources of power. Many countries contributed to the list of important industrial inventors. Britain headed the pack, but France and the United States contributed strongly; by the late nineteenth century, Germany and Sweden joined in, particularly in electronics and chemicals.

Inventions had occurred before, of course, though often anonymously. Until the fifteenth century, Asia, particularly China, had provided world technological leadership; for example, China had introduced printing, paper, and explosive powder. The focus shifted to Western Europe several centuries before the Industrial Revolution. During the eighteenth and nineteenth centuries, the pace of invention greatly surpassed all historical precedent. Several millennia previously, around 4000 BCE (that is, several millennia after the introduction of agriculture), a number of vital discoveries converged: the invention of writing, the wheel, the use of metals. These inventions spread over many centuries, however, and thereafter the rate of major invention actually was fairly slow. The rate and scope of inventions in the Industrial Revolution were thus unprecedented.

What caused the surge of invention around the onset of industrialization? Analyses must take account of individual genius, but this factor does not explain timing. New opportunity, in the form of growing markets for goods, was clearly involved. Most inventors were quite conscious of working to fill a need. Once the wave of inventions began, each one triggered the next. That is, new devices for weaving created greater need for thread, which provided a target for inventors to think about the spinning process. Early machines created needs for making machines more efficiently—hence another target: devising interchangeable parts that could be turned out more easily. Along with opportunity came new scientific discoveries that guided many inventors. New knowledge about the behavior of gases contributed directly to improvements in the steam engine; study of electricity led to the telegraph and the electric motor. Science also provided inventors with a belief that nature could and should be understood and controlled, and that technical progress was both possible and desirable.

Most early inventors came from artisanal backgrounds, though there was diversity. British artisans especially, with no strict guild tradition and with incentives provided by patent protection, seemed to have a genius for devising new methods. This early kind of inventor is often dubbed "artisan-tinkerer." Some early inventors, with or without an artisanal background, received scientific training and only a few had artistic experience clearly relevant to design. Some inventors proved to be very bad businessmen and ended in poverty, their devices exploited by other entrepreneurs. Others were quite successful, either by themselves or in partnership with men who could provide capital. Many inventors gained great prestige in a society that was coming to value economic growth.

The style of invention began to change by the 1830s, and the artisan-tinkerer tradition faded by the 1870s; Gilchrist and Thomas, in metallurgy, are sometimes called the last of the breed. Increasingly, trained engineers and scientists, often working in teams in university or industrial laboratories, produced the significant inventions. Big businesses and governments realized that invention was too important to be left to chance, and the need for more training and laboratory funding became essential. More formal research and development work underlay many nineteenth-century inventions in industrial chemistry and electronics.

See also Engineering; Interchangeable Parts; Patents; Technology

Further Reading

Habbakuk, H. J. *American and British Technology in the Nineteenth Century: The Search for Labour-Saving Inventions.* Cambridge: Cambridge University Press, 1962.
Hounshell, David A. *From the American System to Mass Production, 1800–1932: The Development of Manufacturing Technology in the United States.* Baltimore: Johns Hopkins University Press, 1985.
Kranzberg, M., and C. W. Pursell Jr., eds. *Technology in Western Civilization.* Vol. 2. New York: Oxford University Press, 1977.

INVISIBLE HAND. *See* Smith, Adam

IRAN

Iran in 1900, and even 1925, was a nonindustrial country, with less than 10 percent of its gross national product (GNP) coming from manufacturing. During the nineteenth century, reform-minded intellectuals, worried about the country's ability to maintain independence against Western pressure, urged an industrialization program. Finally, with a new government in 1925 under the nationalist leader Reza Shah Pahlevi, serious change began to arrive.

The government essentially sponsored and directed an early industrial revolution, such that by 1941 about 20 percent of the GNP resulted from industry. The government organized technology exhibits, so that Iranian businessmen could learn about developments abroad. It mounted high tariffs on industrial goods, to protect infant factory industries at home. It allowed selected foreign manufacturers—for example, a Czech sugar refinery—to set up operations. A key goal was import substitution, and Iran became one of the first countries to practice this policy systematically: trying to replace foreign manufactured products with the output of new, local factories. The policy was costly: considerable investments were required, and the goods were often more expensive, and/or of lower quality, than foreign exports would have been. The difference was paid by consumers and by taxpayers (mainly peasants), from whom the investment funds were drawn. But the result did move Iran into the ranks of developing industrial nations, a considerable achievement and the leading example, in the Middle East, of the effectiveness of state-run economic change.

During the 1950s, after considerable tension, Iran gained greater control over its oil reserves, which provided a major new source of foreign earnings. The result directly stimulated some industries, in the area of refineries and petrochemicals.

It also provided investment funds for further industrialization. In 1967, the government encouraged the formation of the Industrial Development and Renovation Organization of Iran, deliberately to promote diversification of industry to avoid undue dependence on oil. Over 40 years this huge conglomerate partnered with private industry, including some foreign firms, in a wide variety of holdings.

Iranian industrial development was set back in the aftermath of the revolution of 1979 and particularly the bitter war with Iraq in the 1980s, during which a number of industrial facilities were bombed. Recovery began in the 1990s, with new government programs to spur additional development. In 1991, Iran joined many other countries in attempting to rebalance between state and private sector activity, to allow a greater range to private enterprise. Almost 200 state firms were sold off to private investors, and the program continued after 2000. By this point, upward of 30 percent of the labor force was directly employed in the industrial sector, and during the 1990s, Iran's economic growth rate surpassed 5 percent per year. Overall, Iran by the early twenty-first century was a significant industrial player, although without the thorough transformation or resultant economic dynamism usually associated with a full industrial revolution.

Further Reading

Floor, Willem. "Industrialization in Iran, 1900–1941." Working Paper, University of Durham, Centre for Middle Eastern and Islamic Studies, 1984. http://www.dur.ac.uk/sgia.

Karshenas, Massoud. *Oil, State and Industrialization in Iran*. New York: Cambridge University Press, 1990.

IRON AND STEEL CORPORATION OF SOUTH AFRICA (ISCOR)

In the late nineteenth and early twentieth centuries, South Africa experienced dramatic economic growth, especially in gold mining, but the country had no industrial base. In 1928, the Republic of South Africa created the Iron and Steel Corporation of South Africa (Iscor) to manufacture steel, the basis for modern industry, as well as to create jobs for poor whites. By 1934, the company began production. Iscor required the government to give it capital and to negotiate with other countries and companies to give Iscor market share. But the company made vast quantities of steel and dramatically expanded during World War II when the country was isolated because of submarine warfare. The steel the company made allowed South Africa to industrialize. After World War II, its economy expanded faster than any country in the world, except for Japan.

Iscor was a microcosm of racial apartheid, or white minority rule. Some white politicians and workers sought to ban blacks from the company, but whites were too expensive for the company to rely on exclusively. About half the workforce was black, a much lower proportion than any other industry in the country. Whites controlled most of the skilled positions. Over time, the company created a

A miner watches as a 120-ton truck moves iron ore and rock to a crusher at the Thabazimbi open-pit mine owned by Iscor in 1996. (Charles O'Rear/Corbis)

mini-welfare state for whites, subsidizing housing and training. Wages were not terribly high, but pensions and benefits were generous. After 30 years, workers could retire at 100 percent of their pay; pensioners also received annual cost of living adjustments. Blacks were paid a sixth or less than white workers. As in all industries, African workers were packed into crowded dormitories; if they caused trouble, they were fired and sent back to the rural "homelands" to starve.

Apartheid relied upon state-controlled companies like Iscor to manufacture steel, to run the railroads, to build weapons, even to build housing. These companies ensured a measure of macroeconomic planning, and provided a means to employ, and ideally train, the country's large class of poor whites.

Apartheid and Iscor came under pressure in the 1980s. African youth protested in the black townships (the black quasi-urban areas outside cities). Workers formed unions. Political groups that the government had banned began to reform. The country slid toward civil war.

Iscor proved a test case of privatization. The company was sold in 1989, chiefly to white banks, insurance companies, and company executives. A democratically elected government came to power in 1994, but it made little difference to how the company was run. In a few years, the company shed the vast majority of its workforce and continued to make low-cost steel. The end of apartheid and international sanctions against South African companies allowed Iscor to legally export coal, iron ore, and steel. In the 2000s, Iscor continued to employ few blacks in skilled or managerial positions.

The old apartheid divisions continue to divide workers. Most whites belong to a union that grew out of the ultra-conservative political movement that sought to preserve apartheid; the largest black union is affiliated with the ruling African National Congress.

The company was acquired by Mittal steel, the world's largest producer. Ironically, the company is owned by an Indian-born entrepreneur. The company continues to be the largest steel maker in sub-Saharan Africa, with three of the world's lowest-cost steel mills.

Further Reading

Morris, Mike, and David Kaplan. "Labour Policy in a State Corporation." *South African Labour Bulletin* 2, no. 6 (January 1976): 21–33.

IRON AND STEEL INDUSTRY

The iron and steel industry was a crucial component of the industrialization process, particularly in the "second" Industrial Revolution. Cheap and abundant iron and steel eased the development of railroads, machine building, and armaments in Britain and undergirded the country's economic and military strength. Because iron and steel were necessary for the development of other manufacturing as well as for a modern military, many governments (German, Japanese, Russian, and Soviet) stimulated the rise of heavy industry for its military as well as economic importance. Jamshed Tata, a late nineteenth-century industrial leader in India, believed that the country's future strength (after it ceased being a colony of the British Empire) would require a strong iron and steel industry. In fact, until the 1980s, the overall economic and military strength of a country was generally measured by its steel production.

Iron had been produced by ancient Indians, Chinese, and Africans, and in the seventeenth century, the process began a slow but significant technical change in England and then throughout Europe. Beginning in 1619, English iron makers, confronting diminishing supplies of wood, began to replace charcoal with coal as the fuel for the smelting process (by which iron ore is heated and transformed into iron). Horse and, later, steam power was used to blow air over the baths of molten iron, and the air intensified the heat in the blast furnaces. In the seventeenth century, iron puddling was developed in England, which allowed higher-quality iron to be produced.

The demand for iron began to explode in the 1830s as the railroad industry demanded huge amounts of iron for its locomotives, rails, and rolling stock. The rapid expansion of railroad networks spurred the expansion and technological development of the iron and steel industry. The world's premier steel industrialist, Andrew Carnegie, named his first steel mill after the head of the Pennsylvania Railroad, J. Edgar Thomson. By using Bessemer converters, Carnegie was the first to produce steel rails, which were cheaper and far more durable than those made of iron. The Thomson Works was the first mill to rationally integrate all of the steps in making steel, and it achieved new economies of scale. Carnegie brought together the facilities to create iron (blast furnaces), convert iron into steel (Bessemer converters, later open-hearth furnaces), and rolling mills to give the metal the proper temper. (By the 1960s, the dramatic decline of the railroads nearly caused the Thomson Works to close.)

Steel mills required vast numbers of unskilled laborers, although about one-quarter of all steel workers were highly skilled; they operated furnaces, cranes, and railroads, or repaired machinery. Employers made distinctions between skilled and unskilled workers in terms of pay and status. In the United States, most skilled workers, until the 1930s, were native-born white Protestants. Conflict among workers hampered the creation of an industrial union in steel until the 1930s. The union enabled some Catholic workers, but almost no black workers, to rise into the ranks of the skilled. Work in steel mills was notoriously dangerous. Around the beginning of the twentieth century, in Pittsburgh, over a hundred men were killed in an average year. Even after the work had become much safer, employers blocked women from the mills, and steel workers developed a distinctive masculine ethos around their strength and ability to withstand the extremes of heat and danger of the furnaces.

The availability of increasingly cheap steel helped to revolutionize many aspects of daily life. Mass-produced nails allowed U.S. builders to eschew complicated joints in favor of frame houses. Steel wire enabled telegraph companies to connect national communication networks. In the late nineteenth century, steel wire permitted the construction of such engineering marvels as the Brooklyn Bridge and, by 1919, the paper clip. By the 1910s, steel beams made possible the construction of skyscrapers; steel plate had already transformed shipping and naval warfare. Steel pipe allowed oil companies to drill and transport oil along lengthy pipelines.

Steel was essential for industry and warfare. To build a modern navy and to industrialize, the Japanese government subsidized the construction of a steel industry in the late nineteenth century—even though the country had no iron ore and meager coal deposits. Stalin recognized the importance of steel and made it a top priority of his first five-year plan. In the 1920s and 1930s, illiterate peasants, revolutionary workers, and foreign technicians struggled in the Ural Mountains, under incredibly harsh weather conditions, to construct the blast furnaces and rolling mills required for an industrial economy.

From the 1890s until the 1940s, the United States was the world's largest and most advanced steel maker. After World War II, however, there was an explosion of iron and steel production throughout the world. German, British, Russian, and Japanese mills not only were rebuilt, but their capacity was greatly expanded. Many new producers emerged in countries as diverse as South Korea, Brazil, Poland, and China. The result was an enormous worldwide surplus of production. A good deal of it was exported to the United States as steel, automobiles, or appliances. Large U.S. companies failed to reinvest enough capital to remain competitive, and many of the country's mills had closed by the 1980s. Parts of U.S. mills were sold to firms in China, Brazil, and South Korea.

One major development in the industry in the 1990s was the development of truly international companies, with production plants in several different countries. U.S. Steel did this in a minor way; Mittal steel in a more ambitious fashion.

See also Accidents; Carnegie, Andrew; Deindustrialization; Iron and Steel Corporation of South Africa (Iscor); Mittal, Lakshmi; Tata, Jamshed; United States Steel

Further Reading

Brody, David. *Steelworkers in America: The Nonunion Era*. Cambridge, MA: Harvard University Press, 1960.

Carr, J. C., and W. Taplin. *History of the British Steel Industry*. Cambridge, MA: Harvard University Press, 1962.

Hinshaw, John H. *Steel and Steelworkers: Race and Class Struggle in Twentieth-Century Pittsburgh*. Albany: State University of New York Press, 2002.

Warren, Kenneth. *The American Steel Industry, 1850–1970: A Geographical Interpretation*. Pittsburgh, PA: Pittsburgh University Press, 1973.

ISLAM AND INDUSTRIALIZATION

Islamic societies long lagged behind the West and parts of East Asia in industrialization. Some analysts, as a result, have wondered if there are aspects of Islam that actively inhibit industrial development. Some claim that Islam has limited scientific inquiry and has generated hostility to new ideas as potentially heretical. One study found Islam negatively associated with economic growth, in contrast to most Christian religions. Other scholars point to more specific aspects of Islam and Islamic tradition. Islam prohibits charging interest on loans, which might limit investment (though many Islamic banks find alternative mechanisms); a long-standing emphasis on partnerships, which could be ended at will, may have complicated the formation of larger and more durable business units and encouraged reliance on personal ties rather than more modern business structures; and rules that required distribution of inheritance among surviving family members may also have

The mix of the modern and traditional: an Iranian man prays near butane storage tanks in the mid-1950s. (Getty Images)

constrained accumulation of large amount of capital. These various business features may have promoted overreliance on state bureaucracies that distrusted innovation.

Against this cultural approach, other scholars note how friendly Islam has been, historically, to merchant activity and business motives, if properly combined with religious duties. They argue that it is not Islam but rather particular historical experiences nearer to modern times, including some governments imposed by invaders that sought to exploit taxation rather than encourage economic growth. They note how Western economic and political interference undermined many efforts at innovation from the early nineteenth century onward. Finally, particularly in Arab Muslim countries, it is rapid population growth and resulting youth unemployment that seem to provide the greatest source of economic instability (though fertility rates are now falling).

It is also important to note the successful economic growth, particularly in recent decades, of many Islamic countries. Malaysia and Indonesia have both expanded rapidly, in terms of per capita product, since 1980. Turkey has become the world's fifteenth-largest economy with substantial industrialization. Several recent analysts suggest that these developments show that, while many Islamic countries do face development challenges, it is unlikely that religion is a fundamental factor or that the problems are somehow inherent in basic culture.

Further Reading

Kuran, Timur. *The Long Divergence: How Islamic Law Held Back the Middle East*. Princeton, NJ: Princeton University Press, 2011.

Lewis, Bernard. *What Went Wrong?: The Clash between Islam and Modernity in the Middle East*. New York: Oxford University Press, 2002.

Noland, Marcus, and Howard Pack. *The Arab Economies in a Changing World*. Washington, DC: Peterson Institute for International Economics, 2007.

ISRAEL

This new state, established in 1948, quickly built an industrial base. Earlier Jewish settlers had extended commercial agriculture by setting up new irrigation systems and producing goods like fruits and eggs that could be sold abroad. New Israeli settlers from Europe had many craft and commercial skills, and extensive foreign aid, particularly from the United States, supported the industrialization effort. Israeli industrialization focused on the production of consumer goods, including construction materials, for use within Israel and potential export. Development of an armaments industry was also a high priority. Israel gained extensive export sales in the West, Turkey, and parts of Africa. Imports were essential to provide necessary raw metals and advanced machinery. By the 1960s, a quarter of the population worked in manufacturing, and Israel was the clear industrial leader in the Middle East.

Israel has become one of the leading industrial states in the world, ranking 17th in the size of the national economy despite a small population and limited resource base. During formative years, periodic wars with Arab neighbors, and even in recent times, high levels of military expenditure, were other constraints on industry.

Fairly steadily however, and building particularly on a skilled labor force and high levels of education, the new nation also advanced its industrial base. Initial emphases included diamond cutting (a craft, however, not a factory industry), but also chemicals and armaments, with substantial exports in all of these fields. The nation also proved adaptable as other industrial opportunities opened up, and in contrast to many countries in the region, it invested heavily in industrial research. By the 1990s, Israel had expanded its industrial concentrations to include medical electronics, telecommunications, agro-technology, and computer hardware and software. Many foreign high-tech firms, including leaders in the United States, set up their initial foreign research branches in Israel. These various developments helped increase the nation's industrial output by 20 percent in the 1990s, when many advanced industrial economies showed slower growth rates.

Further Reading

Bregman, Ahron. *A History of Israel*. New York: Palgrave Macmillan, 2003.
Rosenzweig, Rafael. *The Economic Consequences of Zionism*. New York: Brill Academic, 1997.

ITALY

Italy's industrial revolution developed relatively late, certainly in comparison with most of its neighbors to the north. Until the 1860s, Italy was disunited politically, which constrained economic change and prevented any systematic policy. The country's lack of relevant natural resources, especially coal, was another clear limitation. Social conditions also played a role. In the south particularly, inefficient, large estate agriculture bottled up a great deal of labor in impoverished conditions, again complicating economic change. By the later nineteenth century, these various limitations, combined with rapid population growth, propelled large numbers of Italian peasants to emigrate to the Americas.

Following the lead of other European countries, a few pilot factories were established by the middle of the nineteenth century, particularly in the north Italian state of Piedmont, where political leadership encouraged economic development. Real breakthroughs, however, awaited the very end of the nineteenth century. By this point, the example of other countries became increasingly compelling. The government mounted high tariffs to help develop and protect national industry from 1887 onward. Furthermore, new technologies allowed the harnessing of water power for electricity generation, and in the mountainous north these sources of hydroelectric power helped compensate for the lack of coal. Between 1890 and 1914, hydroelectric capacity increased by 150 percent. Significant industrial companies sprang up in metallurgy, textiles, chemicals, and rubber. A new automobile industry also took off rapidly, principally around the new Fiat firm; this sector would ultimately become Italy's leader in exports. Rapid industrial growth in and around key northern cities exacerbated the economic gap between north and south

Italy, creating an unusually intense regional imbalance as industrialization progressed, and one that has not been entirely erased even today. While, overall, Italy was still largely agricultural by 1914, economic growth, based on industrialization, was substantial.

Under fascism following World War I, Italian industry continued to develop, though there were no striking advances. Mussolini tried to support some economic development in the south. Under his auspices, particularly in response to the Depression (which initially hit the nation hard), the government took over many industrial and transportation firms, mainly under the Institute for Industrial Reconstruction. Pressing workers to accept lower wages, this policy did shield Italy from some of the worst economic dislocations of the 1930s after the first shock of bank collapse. Under fascism, the state controlled around 40 percent of the economy.

Italy's real industrial surge occurred somewhat unexpectedly after World War II and the replacement of fascism by a democratic political system. Various sectors boomed in the 1950s, largely at the hands of private companies, but organized as well by careful economic planning from the central government. Production in heavy industry, automobiles, and other branches rose rapidly, and for the first time industry, rather than agriculture, became the principal source of national income. Most companies remained small; Fiat was the largest, and it was still family owned. Italian growth for a time outstripped that of most other European countries, propelling Italy clearly into the ranks of significant global economic powers. For many years, until the oil crisis of 1973, growth rates surpassed eight percent annually, and for a brief time, Italy became the fourth-largest economy in the world, in a pattern understandably known as the "Italian economic miracle." Even the south, with the help of government investment from the Fund for the South, began to participate to an extent, particularly in light industry, aided as well by the discovery of oil in Sicily (though, overall, Italy continued to depend heavily on energy imports). Thanks to population control but above all to new economic opportunities at home, Italian emigration decreased rapidly, and standards of living rose dramatically during the second half of the twentieth century. Italian growth stagnated somewhat in the 1990s, causing concern, but performance improved in the 2000s.

Further Reading

Di Matteo, Massimo, and Paolo Piacentini, *The Italian Economy at the Dawn of the 21st Century*. Burlington, VT: Ashgate, 2003.

Hildebrand, George. *Growth and Structure in the Economy of Modern Italy*. Cambridge, MA: Harvard University Press, 1965.

Hilowitz, Jane. *Economic Development and Social Change in Sicily*. Cambridge, MA: Schenkman, 1976.

Kindelberger, Charles. *Europe's Postwar Growth*. Cambridge, MA: Harvard University Press, 1973.

Smith, Dennis Mack. *Italy, a Political History*. Ann Arbor: University of Michigan Press, 1997.

J

JACQUARD, JOSEPH (1752–1834)

One of the leading French inventors of the early Industrial Revolution, Jacquard devised a machine for weaving nets. His main contribution, the Jacquard loom, wove complicated figured patterns, advancing the industrial manufacture of high-quality cloth by allowing the application of power machinery to designs that were not geometrically repetitious. It used punched holes to guide the machine in producing any particular pattern, facilitating alterations of a design; much later, this innovation was applied to early computers.

Further Reading

Derry, Kingston, and T. I. Williams. *A Short History of Technology*. Oxford: Oxford University Press, 1961.

JAPAN

Many of Japan's institutional arrangements that made its industrialization possible (a highly skilled, low-wage workforce and coordination between industrialists and the government) were established in the late nineteenth century as the country struggled to develop an economically viable empire. Japan isolated itself until the 1850s, but became a quick learner of industrialization, world trade, and power

Joseph Marie Jacquard's mechanical loom, showing swags of punched cards on which the pattern to be woven was encoded. (Heritage Images/Corbis)

politics. As other Asian countries became outright colonies of industrialized European powers or found their independence severely compromised, Japan quickly mastered industrial production and became a colonial power in its own right. In 1895, Japan won from the Chinese government commercial concessions in Korea and annexed Taiwan; in 1910, it formally annexed Korea. In 1905, Japan achieved great-power status when it decisively defeated the Russian navy. Not all foreign adventures were successful. Japan's intervention in the Soviet Union in the 1920s was financially costly and provided no lasting benefits. However, Japan's colonies provided Japanese companies with access to raw materials (coal in Korea, food in Taiwan) and markets for industrial goods. Its war with China in the 1930s was initially successful, but led it to war with the United States in 1941, which proved disastrous.

Beginning in the Meiji Restoration, the Japanese government subsidized certain zaibatsus or "financial cliques" and allowed them to monopolize key areas of the economy. In return, the zaibatsus helped the government to achieve its national economic goals. A key component of Japan industrial development strategy was to keep its wages low as a competitive advantage. This approach meant, however, that the domestic market was always underdeveloped and zaibatsus were forced to go abroad in a search for markets as well as to find natural resources. The Japanese government also encouraged the manual production of silk cloth by women (who had been sold into labor by their families). Here was a vital source of foreign currency to help support industrial purchases and supplies. By the 1930s, Japan's strategy was paying off with factory production expanding rapidly, and Japan made large inroads into the markets of other imperial powers. Japanese textiles had captured half of the Indian market (previously an exclusive preserve of British manufacturers). Japan was the second-largest exporter to Morocco (after France), and when tariffs were raised on colonial markets, it aggressively exported to Latin America. Other industrialized countries retaliated by raising tariff barriers—a major factor contributing to Japan's attempt to grab what it needed by force.

Japan's war for the annexation of Manchuria in 1931 and its subsequent attempt to militarily construct an "Asian Co-Prosperity Sphere" throughout the Pacific was a desperate gamble to gain access to raw materials and markets. Military production was also the rationale for creating an automobile market, since the Japanese government wanted to have an independent supply of trucks and jeeps. The result, World War II, did not go as planned, for at the war's end, Japanese industry was decimated; millions of demobilized soldiers and unemployed colonial officials and expatriates competed for what few jobs remained.

In 1945, the United States intended to limit Japan's industrialization, but by the late 1940s, confronted with a communist government in China (and then a war in Korea), the U.S. government favored the reindustrialization of Japan and limited punishment of its fascist leaders. Partly at the insistence of its allies, the United States required that Japan remain demilitarized, which shifted the focus of Japanese business and government to its domestic market. Japan expanded its domestic economy through Fordist strategies of raising the purchasing power of its working class (although weak unions meant that wages always fell well short of advances in productivity). The lack of military spending did not end the close cooperation between government and businesses and eventually turned into a strategic advantage as Japanese companies (unlike many of their U.S. counterparts) specialized in civilian products. Japan's export drive accelerated in the late 1960s and 1970s to offset the rising prices of raw materials, particularly oil.

By the 1980s, Japan was running a substantial trade surplus with many of its trading partners, particularly the United States. Throughout that decade, Japan spent heavily abroad, in both productive and highly speculative investments. Within Japan, a major real estate and stock market bubble developed. When it burst in the late 1980s, the Japanese economy struggled to recover, leading to what many economists term a "lost decade" of sluggish growth.

See also Imperialism

Further Reading

Itoh, Makoto. *The World Economic Crisis and Japanese Capitalism*. New York: St. Martin's Press, 1990.
Sumiya, Mikio, and Koji Taira. *An Outline of Japanese Economic History, 1603–1940: Major Works and Research Findings*. Tokyo: University of Tokyo Press, 1979.

JAPANESE SYSTEM OF EMPLOYMENT

In the Japanese system of employment, large companies offer their permanent employees a lifetime of job security in return for extreme loyalty. Under this system, workers are paid on the basis of their seniority, not on the job being performed. The earnings of an employee typically start out low and peak after about 20 years with the firm; real wages decline rapidly thereafter. The lure of eventually earning higher pay is an important factor in preventing workers from leaving their jobs or protesting such practices as mandatory overtime or relocation to a new part of the country. Not every employee is eligible for the system; large auto factories, for instance, rely on large numbers of temporary workers who are laid off during slack periods or when the factory is being retooled. Women are far more likely to be temporary workers who work on a piece-rate basis. The system began to take shape in the 1920s, when advancing industry began to require more skilled workers. As the system spread, it promoted company loyalty and weakened independent unions. As a result, Japan has one of the lowest levels of economic inequality among industrial economies, despite having some of the most limited social welfare mechanisms. The system of lifetime employment began to weaken in the 1990s.

Further Reading

Gordon, Andrew. *Labor and Imperial Democracy in Prewar Japan*. Berkeley: University of California Press, 1991.

Japanese corporations typically provided long-term security in exchange for long hours; here "salary men" commute to work on a train. (Tokyo Space Club/Corbis)

JOINT STOCK COMPANIES

These capitalist enterprises, which combine funds from several investors, originated in the investment needs of long-distance trading firms in Britain. Partnerships were formed for each voyage, but during the seventeenth century, the partnerships evolved into a durable investment in a company. The company would decide on particular ventures without needing to assemble a new partnership each time. Various joint stock companies developed, but the East India Company and its new charter of 1657 is taken as the first common use of this method of organization. Similar companies developed in the Netherlands at about the same time. Unlike partnerships, joint stock companies also issued stocks that could be transferred to other owners.

Although early joint stock companies applied mainly to trade, they were also available for industry. A number of metallurgical and mining ventures, in France and Germany as well as Britain, required so much capital that the joint stock form was essential. Most early railroad companies were also joint stock ventures. Joint stock arrangements were much more novel outside Western Europe; the first ones appeared in Russia only in 1864, for commercial banking. The principle of the joint stock company also underlay the later development of the corporation, though the latter required additional legislation to limit the liability of each investor. Under traditional joint stock arrangements, any one investor could be held liable for the entire debts of the enterprise, which obviously discouraged use of the form, particularly by smaller capitalists.

Further Reading

Josephson, Matthew. *The Robber Barons: The Great American Capitalists, 1861–1901.* New York: Harcourt, Brace, 1934.

Micklethwait, John, and Adrian Wooldridge. *The Company: A Short History of a Revolutionary Idea.* New York: Modern Library, 2003.

JOURNEYMEN. *See* Artisans

KAIPING MINES

These mines played an important role in early Chinese industrialization and highlight the difficulties the process encountered in the late nineteenth century. The mines, north of Tianjin, were opened in 1878 to provide coal for steamships plying Chinese rivers and canals. The first permanent railroad in China was built in 1881 to carry Kaiping coal to the Chinese-owned steamer fleet. (An earlier rail line had been built by Europeans but was torn up by the Chinese government in protest against imperialist interference.) The mines ran up large debts, and the steamship line—the China Merchants' Company—was badly administered and lost ground to British companies working the Chinese rivers. The mines were taken over in 1900 by a foreign consortium headed by the American Herbert Hoover. The early venture was an exception to China's general policy of neglect, as industrialization was mainly brought in by foreigners in their newly-acquired treaty ports, and its rocky start both reflected and furthered the nation's indecisiveness about modern industry at this point in its history.

See also Imperialism; Latecomer Industrialization; State, Role of the

Further Reading

Carlson, Ellesworth C. *The Kaiping Mines: 1877–1912.* Cambridge, MA: Harvard University Press, 1971.

KAISER, HENRY (1880–1967)

In the 1930s and 1940s, Henry Kaiser helped to develop the U.S. West and built an industrial empire by employing mass-production techniques in construction and shipbuilding. Another crucial factor in Kaiser's success was to take

Industrialist Henry J. Kaiser. (Library of Congress)

advantage of contacts within the New Deal government, which loaned Kaiser capital and purchased many of his products. In the 1930s, Kaiser helped to coordinate construction of key infrastructure projects, including the Hoover and Grand Coulee dams, which provided the West Coast with enough power to rapidly expand its industrial production of aircraft and ships during World War II. During the war, Kaiser adapted the assembly-line techniques of the automobile industry to shipbuilding. Practically from scratch, Kaiser trained and housed a massive workforce, and by the end of the war Kaiser's shipyards had built one-third of the U.S. merchant fleet.

Further Reading

Foster, Mark. *Henry J. Kaiser: Builder in the American West.* Austin: University of Texas Press, 1989.

KAWASAKI SHIPYARD

The Kawasaki shipyard was set up by the Japanese government when it realized that building steamships was a vital national response to Western industrialization. The shipyard also played a crucial role in moving Japan away from wider dependence on imports of European machinery. In 1907, the yard produced the first locomotives and coaches in Japanese history, thus replacing several decades' reliance on Western supply for the nation's burgeoning rail network and foreshadowing the boom in heavy industry after World War I, as Japan moved into its second stage of industrialization.

Further Reading

Sumiya, Mikio, and Koji Taira. *An Outline of Japanese Economic History, 1603–1940: Major Works and Research Findings.* Tokyo: University of Tokyo Press, 1979.

KAY, JOHN. *See* Flying Shuttle

KEYNESIANISM

Keynesianism refers to the economic theories and policies of John Maynard Keynes (1883–1946). Keynes was a British economist who rejected the laissez-faire verities of the nineteenth and early twentieth centuries. In 1923, he wrote *A Tract on Monetary Reform*, which attacked the gold standard, previously considered the only way to ensure the stability and strength of national currencies. But Keynes is best known as the "author" of "interventionist" government, arguing in the midst of the Great Depression of the 1930s that governments could play a positive role in managing their national economies, particularly by using deficit spending to stimulate buying power ("priming the pump") and ending the downward economic cycle.

Keynes's theories were adopted by the New Deal state in the United States and were an important theoretical underpinning of the welfare state in Europe. In practice, Keynesianism viewed the state as the manager of industrial capitalism, controlling and directing public and private investment during booms and stimulating demand by aiding the unemployed during its "busts." Although Keynesianism has become viewed as inherently inflationary, Keynes urged the British government to finance wartime expenditures through compulsory savings (saving bonds) to avoid inflation during World War II. The British government, however, preferred more traditional methods of financing, and serious inflation did ensue. Keynesian theories (although not those of Keynes himself) were applied to the postwar institutions of international banking, trade, and development through the establishment of the World Bank/IMF. More active government planning and spending helped protect postwar industrial economies from severe depression.

Political conservatives were uncomfortable with the increasing role of government in the economy and society, fearing that, instead of managing capitalism, it was opening the door to "creeping socialism." In practice, however, conservative politicians (along with their Liberal, Labour, and Social Democratic counterparts) accepted Keynesianism in Britain and the United States. By 1971, archconservative Richard Nixon publicly confessed, "I am a Keynesian." However, the economic crisis of the mid-1970s proved immune to Keynesian economic measures; the attempts to stimulate a recovery from the depression that began in 1973 resulted in both sluggish growth and inflation: stagflation. Although Ronald Reagan formally rejected Keynesianism in favor of supply-side economics, the massive deficits that he ran up in the 1980s (and the resulting economic expansion) suggested that Reagan owed more to Keynes than he wished to acknowledge.

The largest challenge to Keynesianism arose in Europe and the United States following the economic crisis of the early 2000s. A variety of governments eschewed Keynesian approaches to the problems of unemployment, following austerity programs that various conservative political parties argued would result in faster growth and balanced budgets. In a few instances, notably the Baltic republics, austerity worked, or was least painful. In many cases, such as Greece, Ireland, Spain, and after 2010, the United States, the results were slower or even resulted in negative economic growth and prolonged and painful mass unemployment. In Southern Europe, youth unemployment is over 50 percent, higher than at any period since the Great Depression.

See also Bretton Woods Agreement; Fordism; Long Waves of Capitalism; Military-Industrial Complex; Socialism

Further Reading

Collins, Robert M. *The Business Response to Keynes, 1929–1964.* New York: Columbia University Press, 1981.

Heilbroner, Robert L. *The Worldly Philosophers: The Lives, Times, and Ideas of the Great Economic Thinkers.* New York: Simon and Schuster, 1986.

KNIGHTS OF LABOR

The Noble and Holy Order of the Knights of Labor was formed in 1869 as a secret association of Philadelphia tailors, but by the early 1880s, it had around 100,000 members of all trades throughout the United States. The Knights were an industrial union, which meant they were open to workers regardless of their craft (or lack of one). The idea that all employees of one company should belong to one union instead of separate craft unions made sense to many workers who were aware of the growing national organization and power of industrialists. Unlike the American Federation of Labor, the Knights did not define its membership simply by occupation; it allowed almost anyone to join (except bankers, lawyers, gamblers, and liquor dealers) who wanted to improve the status of laboring people. Farmers, small businessmen, and wage workers were members. Unlike most unions, women were allowed to join, and after 1883, black workers could join segregated locals; however, Asians were rigorously excluded.

In 1884, railroad workers went on strike (against the advice of the Knights' leadership) against an operation owned by Jay Gould. The intercraft solidarity of the strikers was successful, and by 1886, 700,000 people had flooded into the Knights, making it the largest union in the country. In 1886, however, Gould provoked the Knights into another strike in which he decisively defeated the union.

Leaders of the Knights of Labor in 1886, honoring founder Uriah Stephens (shown in portrait) who died in 1882. (Library of Congress)

In the public mind (or at least that of the mass media), the events of 1886 linked the moderate Knights with radical and socialist union advocates. In 1886, Chicago was wracked by a number of strikes seeking to establish the eight-hour day; Chicago Knights participated in a solidarity rally with socialists and anarchists in Haymarket Square. The rally ended in disaster; someone (most historians believe it was an agent provocateur) threw a bomb that killed several policemen; the police opened fire, killing several demonstrators. Haymarket became a rallying cry among radicals, particularly after several immigrant anarchists were executed on the basis of very flimsy evidence; Haymarket was also the basis of the first red scare in the United States. Most Knights were not socialists, but the association damaged the respectability of Knights in the eyes of many middle-class sympathizers. More damaging, managerial counteroffensives similar to that of Gould decimated the strength of the Knights throughout their former strongholds. By the early 1890s, the Knights were in irreversible decline.

In practice, the Knights combined elements of trade unionism with the political ideals and specific reforms of a social movement. The Knights also set up producer cooperatives. Throughout the 1880s, the Knights established themselves in many industrial areas as a force in local government, but they failed to establish themselves as a permanent Labor Party. By defining "labor" broadly, the Knights allowed many people to identify with their movement but also enabled other parties to borrow their rhetoric to win back voters. Particularly in the South, the Knights' real and imagined emphasis on racial equality led many whites to eschew the Knights.

See also American Federation of Labor (AFL); Racism

Further Reading

Fink, Leon. *Workingmen's Democracy: The Knights of Labor and American Politics*. Urbana: University of Illinois Press, 1983.

Rachleff, Peter. *Black Labor in the South: Richmond, Virginia, 1865–1890*. Philadelphia: Temple University Press, 1984.

KRUPP

The Krupp family pioneered modern heavy industry in Germany, in the coal-rich Ruhr region, and went on to enter the ranks of the German upper class by the later nineteenth century. Alfred Krupp was born in 1812 into a merchant family in Essen. His father had not done well, twice being swindled by partners when he tried to establish steel factories. Alfred set about to repair the family fortunes. He was sent to work in a factory at the age of 13 and the next year launched his own operation on the basis of a meager inheritance. Adept at using advanced technologies developed by others, he single-mindedly pursued a policy of expansion, branching from the manufacture of scissors and hand tools into metallurgy and mining.

The Krupp firm, further developed by Alfred's descendants, became one of the great integrated companies in Germany, creating a vast investment market from raw materials such as coal to finished products such as armaments. Later Krupp leaders played a significant role in national policy, encouraging military expenditure and producing much of the artillery used on the German side in the world wars. The Krupp conglomerate was modified by the victorious allies after World War II but continued under managers outside the family.

See also Corporations; Iron and Steel Industry; Latecomer Industrialization; Military-Industrial Complex

Further Reading

Landes, David. *The Unbound Prometheus: Technical Change and Industrial Development in Western Europe*. Cambridge: Cambridge University Press, 1969.

KULAKS

Although kulaks were wealthy Russian peasants who spearheaded commercial agriculture in the villages after 1905, this was primarily a political, not an economic, category developed by the Bolsheviks in the years following the 1917 revolution. Although the Bolsheviks had distributed land to the peasants, their support was weakest in the countryside, and kulaks were often blamed for withholding grain—which allowed the Bolsheviks to escape responsibility for the state's contribution to shortages because of poor planning. During the Stalinist period of the collectivization of agriculture, kulaks' cattle, horses, and grain were especially subject to seizure.

Kulaks themselves could be deported to forced labor camps or prison. Stalin's methods were particularly brutal; in many cases, peasants' seed grain was seized, and the state allowed millions in the countryside to starve. Although wealthy peasants were most vulnerable to deportation, it was quite easy for a vengeful official or a spiteful neighbor to label anyone a kulak. The "dekulakization" of the countryside convinced many peasants to emigrate to industrial centers to escape the harsh punishment the Stalinist regime meted out to opponents, real and imagined, of its rural policies.

See also Lenin, Vladimir Il'ich; New Economic Policy (NEP)

Further Reading

Fitzpatrick, Sheila. *Stalin's Peasants: Resistance and Survival in the Russian Village after Collectivization*. New York: Oxford University Press, 1994.

KYOTO PROTOCOL

The Kyoto Protocol is the most famous and important of several international agreements aimed at curbing global warming. It forms part of the United Nations

Delegates from 150 countries at the formulation of the Kyoto Protocol in 1997; it sought to lower the emission of greenhouse gases. (AP Photo/Katsumi Kasahara)

Framework Convention on Climate Change and was formulated in Kyoto, Japan, in 1997. As of 2011, 191 nations have ratified the Protocol.

The goal of the agreement was to get nations to commit to a reduction of greenhouse gases (such as carbon, sulfur, methane) and other combined gases held to be responsible for global warming. Signatories pledged to reduce greenhouse emissions by 5.2 percent from the 1990 level.

Concerns about global warming, based on industrial and other chemical emissions, had been growing for years, and several international conferences had already discussed the issue (notably the Earth Summit in Rio de Janeiro in 1992). The Kyoto accords meant to advance the agenda through a legally binding international agreement. Signatories could either reduce emissions directly or arrange other compensations to the same effect. Several subsequent meetings occurred during the early twenty-first century to monitor progress.

Many critics argued that the Protocol asked too much of established industrial nations without controlling developing areas where emissions were also rising rapidly. The United States refused to ratify for this reason among others. In the decade after the Kyoto conference, many signatory countries did not in fact make much progress in emissions control, though a 2009 study argued that the industrialized countries probably would meet their target, reducing emissions by 11 percent. The whole subject, including the fate of the Protocol, continues to occasion much debate.

Further Reading

Depledge, Joanna. "Tracing the Origins of the Kyoto Protocol." United Nations Framework Convention on Climate Control, August 2000. http://unfccc.int/resource/docs/tp/tp0200.pdf.

Manne, Alan S., and Richard G. Richels. "The Kyoto Protocol: A Cost-Effective Strategy for Meeting Environmental Objectives?" http://www.oecd.org/dataoecd/38/53/1923159.pdf (accessed January 2011).

L

LABOR TURNOVER

This term refers to the frequency with which workers leave any given firm or industry—the greater the frequency, the higher the turnover. High labor turnover is normally undesirable for a firm because it requires recruiting and training a series of new workers, rather than relying on increasing experience and loyalty.

High labor turnover was endemic in the early Industrial Revolution in most regions. Changing jobs gave workers a sense of control over their lives and some hope for a slightly better future. Some workers, of course, could not leave a firm because they were too poor or insecure, and some were sufficiently skilled that they did not wish to leave. Early New England factories, for example, had a very stable skilled worker core. Many workers, however, even risked considerable poverty for the sake of changing jobs and getting some break from the normal routine. Some (such as black migrants from the U.S. South) returned to the countryside periodically, particularly during harvest periods when rural labor was in demand. Others wandered to different cities, simply hoping for a better break. Geographical mobility was extensive in the nineteenth century, often complicating family life. Artisanal tradition had involved a good bit of wandering for young workers as part of training; this tradition carried over to industry in some cases. Even unskilled workers, like Slavic immigrants to the United States, shifted jobs frequently. Frequent economic recessions encouraged turnover, because workers, who were often fired during slumps, developed no loyalty to particular firms. In boom times, different firms deliberately tried to woo workers away from their rivals to build their own labor force with more experienced operatives.

High labor turnover translated into striking statistics. The average Japanese worker in 1900 stayed with a firm less than two years. Turnover was often particularly high among women, who as supplementary earners were likely to quit work upon marriage and tended to move around a lot. Turnover in the Ford automobile factory around 1908, with a large staff of immigrant workers, was as much as 1,000 percent per year.

Employers made major efforts to reduce turnover, particularly among the harder-to-replace skilled workers. They instituted paternalist programs, like company housing or mutual aid, so that workers would lose more than a job if they left the company. Early industrial firms often offered bonuses for workers who completed a multiyear contract. In 1915, Ford instituted a $5 day for unskilled workers who showed steady work habits and a respectable home life. Japan's massive program of employment security, launched in the 1920s, was aimed at the turnover problem.

Not all these measures worked; particularly in Europe and the United States, workers' desire for flexibility and their resentment of industrial conditions generated a long-standing turnover problem. Turnover did tend to decrease with time, however, for older workers with family responsibilities had less flexibility than their younger counterparts. Likewise, workers who bought into consumerist goals, wanting to maximize their earnings, might take fewer risks in changing jobs. The history of turnover in the industrial economy provides important insight into patterns of work and employer-worker relations.

See also Immigration and Migration; Scientific Management; Work

Further Reading

Meyer, Stephen. *The Five Dollar Day: Labor, Management, and Social Control in the Ford Motor Company, 1900–1921.* Albany: State University of New York Press, 1981.

Stearns, Peter N. *Lives of Labor: Working in a Maturing Industrial Society.* New York: Holmes and Meier, 1975.

LABOUR PARTY (BRITISH)

British working-class politics have been distinctive. Many British workers long backed either the Liberal or the Conservative Party, both of which, after workers got the vote in 1867, paid some attention to working-class demands. Despite, or perhaps because of, a strong union movement, Marxism did not catch on, though some efforts were put forward by Marxist leaders. The Labour Party took shape in the 1890s. Formed in 1900 as a merger of labor groups, the Labour Representation Committee grew slowly, but a House of Lords decision that unions could be sued (Taff Vale case) gave it new support by 1906. As it gained, the party was heavily influenced by unions and also by the intellectual Fabian Society, an articulate socialist group advocating deep-seated reform rather than revolution.

By 1919, the party replaced the Liberals as one of the two top British political forces. Its rule during 1945–51 installed the British welfare state with an extensive national health plan, government-built housing, and nationalization of key industries like coal mining as a means of reducing the power of capitalists over workers. The Labour Party abandoned its socialist positions in the 1980s, but it has remained the largest left party in Britain.

Further Reading

Eley, Geoff. *Forging Democracy: The History of the Left in Europe, 1850–2000.* New York: Oxford University Press, 2002.

LAISSEZ-FAIRE

The economic doctrine of laissez-faire, or "let do," emphasizes the importance of allowing individuals to pursue their economic self-interest free from government interference. Acquisitive individualism provides the best motives for people to work hard and innovate, and free competition among individuals is most conducive to economic progress and prosperity.

Laissez-faire doctrines developed in the eighteenth century and served as the basis for the economic writings of Adam Smith, whose *Wealth of Nations* was the most influential treatise during the early Industrial Revolution. The doctrines were opposed to the principles of mercantilism, which had called for extensive state intervention. Most economists continued to support laissez-faire ideas through the middle of the nineteenth century. The philosopher and economist John Stuart Mill, for example, wrote in 1848

Scottish philosopher and political economist Adam Smith. (Library of Congress)

that "every restriction of competition is an evil, and every extension of it, even if for the time injuriously affecting some class of laborers, is always an ultimate good." Laissez-faire advocates opposed old restrictions on innovation like the guilds; they attacked tariffs; and they often argued against combinations of working people that might restrict wage competition. Government, in the laissez-faire view, should be nothing more than a policeman, making sure that competitors play fair and do not conspire to limit individualism.

Laissez-faire ideas were very influential in early industrialization in Western Europe and the United States. Old regulations were abolished, allowing freer introduction of new technology and freer expansion of business. British policy, particularly, was affected by laissez-faire, and the size of British government actually shrank somewhat in the mid-nineteenth century. Many businessmen embraced laissez-faire ideas, though they often used them selectively. It was not uncommon for an American industrialist to advocate laissez-faire against some incipient trade union or labor law, while asking for tariff protection or a government land grant to a new railway company.

The importance of laissez-faire ideas continued into the twentieth century, although in practice they seem less important in increasingly interventionist states. The ideas became more complicated as the size of business units grew; should giant corporations be allowed to develop or should the government limit them in the name of really free individual competition? Many laissez-faire advocates also expanded their notion of essential government services, as in arguing that publicly supported school systems were needed. In addition, laissez-faire ideas were attacked as leading to excessive capitalist profits and inadequate attention to the needs of the working class and the poor. Socialist theorists developed alternatives to the laissez-faire vision, and their ideas increasingly affected actual policies. Finally, most societies that industrialized later, like Russia and Japan, made no pretense of embracing literal laissez-faire, for they used government policies openly and actively. On the whole, then, the impact of this doctrine declined after the early industrial period in the West, but its imagery remained powerful, particularly in the United States.

See also Liberalism; Social Darwinism; State, Role of the; Subsidies

Further Reading

Heilbroner, Robert L. *The Worldly Philosophers: The Lives, Times, and Ideas of the Great Economic Thinkers.* New York: Simon and Schuster, 1986.

LATECOMER INDUSTRIALIZATION

Societies that industrialize well after the initial industrial revolutions of Western Europe and the United States have some special advantages and disadvantages. These "latecomers," including Japan, Russia, and more recently the Pacific Rim, have been able to imitate advanced technology and business forms; they did not have to start back at early British industrial levels. They can also copy ingredients of the process that developed more haphazardly in the West—as in setting up formal education systems early on. On the downside, however, late industrializers always face intense competition from established factory centers; it takes decades to rise to the top level, and some industrializers, like Russia, have not yet managed to do so. Interference from more advanced industrial competition is always a problem. Latecomers typically lack the capital or the culture that induced industrialization in the West; they have to change more structures to clear the decks for industrialization. Thus Japan's civil strife in the 1860s altered political forms, and then the Meiji reforms began to alter Confucian culture in the interests of introducing more scientific training. Russia tried to industrialize with less prior change and paid the price in revolutions in 1905 and 1917, when structures and cultures altered with a vengeance.

Latecomer industrializers always have to encourage, but also manage, imitation of foreigners as well as outright foreign investment. Japan was cautious in this regard; Russia was less so until the 1917 revolution, when foreign contacts were limited. Latecomers usually employ the state to help organize capital and form many industrial companies outright; this stratagem compensates for some other deficiencies. They must also must find goods to export to earn foreign exchange to pay for pilot equipment. Japan emphasized silk production, Russia foods, and raw materials. Sometimes latecomer industries, pressed to catch up, may be even more careless about environmental problems than other industrial societies; this was certainly the case in Soviet Russia, Eastern Europe, and China. Latecomer industrializers, in other words, face some specific issues that differ from those of other societies, even as they engage in what is broadly speaking a common process.

Further Reading

Gerschenkron, Alexander. *Economic Backwardness in Historical Perspective*. Cambridge, MA: Harvard University Press, 1962.

Stearns, Peter N. *The Industrial Revolution in World History*. 3rd ed. Boulder, CO: Westview, 2007.

LATIN AMERICA

Most Latin American countries gained their political independence in the 1820s and 1830s, but as exporters of raw materials, they remained economically dependent upon industrialized countries throughout the nineteenth and much of the twentieth centuries. Deindustrialization of traditional manufacturing workers occurred under the pressure of British industrial goods. Despite the new nations' economic and social reforms in the mid- and late nineteenth century, most of Latin America's population remained peasants, although an urbanized working and middle class emerged in Argentina, Brazil, and Mexico. In the 1940s, under Juan Perón,

Juan Perón, shown here with his wife, Eva, dominated Argentine politics from 1946 until his death in 1974, claiming to speak on behalf of the poor. (AFP/Getty Images)

Argentina began a policy of import substitution that succeeded in building an industrial economy. By the 1970s, Argentina's inability to export manufactured products began to undermine its industrial economy.

After World War II, the Mexican and Brazilian governments sought to build the infrastructure for successful industrialization (roads, rails, electrical, and educational systems). In the 1980s, both countries began to attract export-oriented factories from Europe, Japan, and the United States. The results were underwhelming in Mexico, where living standards plummeted in the 1990s. The Brazilian case was far more successful. By the 2010s, Brazil was investing in other Latin American countries, leading to both a sense of regional pride and concern that Brazil would occupy the dominant role historically played by the United States.

See also Maquiladoras; World Bank; World Systems Theory

Further Reading

Keen, Benjamin, and Mark Wasserman. *A Short History of Latin America*. Boston: Houghton Mifflin, 1984.

LAWRENCE, ABBOTT (1792–1855)

One of the early New England industrialists, Abbott Lawrence headed a group of Boston financiers who built a textile center at a site on the Merrimack River—now Lawrence, Massachusetts—in 1845. One of his partners, his brother William, had already set up the first corporation to manufacture woolen goods. The partners built a stone dam to harness water power and erected rows of workers' houses to attract a labor force and economize on wages. That drew large numbers of immigrant workers to what was one of the classic one-industry communities in the United States. The new company was a second-generation textile operation, far larger than its predecessors and with greater capital resources.

Lawrence and his fellow investors also had unusual political influence, which allowed the company to regulate waterways in the Connecticut basin, to the detriment of many local farmers and artisans. The city of Lawrence also gained fame much later, in 1912, as the center of a huge and bitter strike involving over 20,000 workers that led to some improvements in worker conditions in the textile industry. In the 1920s, many Lawrence mills failed or moved south in search of cheaper labor.

Further Reading

Pursell, Carroll W., Jr. *Technology in America: A History of Individuals and Ideas*. Cambridge, MA: MIT Press, 1981.

LE CHAPELIER LAW (1791)

Enacted in 1791, during the liberal phase of the French Revolution, this law abolished guilds and forbade other worker associations. It was designed to promote free competition and innovation by holding down labor protest. The law signaled the basically middle-class character of this phase of the French Revolution, and it was similar to antilabor rules in most early industrial societies. The law was fully repealed only in the 1880s. Up to that point, the French government retained the right to intervene against labor organizations and arrest leaders.

Further Reading

Friedland, Paul. *Political Actors: Representative Bodies and Theatricality in the Age of the French Revolution*. Ithaca, NY: Cornell University Press, 2002.
Lefebvre, Georges. *The French Revolution*. New York: Columbia University Press, 1964.

LEE KUAN YEW (1923–)

Lee Kuan Yew was the first prime minister of Singapore when it became self-governing. Lee at first attempted to maintain a commonwealth with Malaysia, but by 1965, he had led the ethnically diverse city-state to full independence. Under British rule, Singapore had always been an important commercial port; Lee sought to supplement that activity with industrialization. Exports were vital, as internal markets were far too small to absorb industrial production, and Lee eventually encouraged a shift from production of labor-intensive goods to more

The first prime minister of Singapore, Lee Kuan Yew. Under his rule, the city-state became fully independent. (Associated Press)

capital-intensive ones. Singapore's strategic location, its skilled workforce, its pro-trade policies, and its efficient government allowed it to make good use of foreign capital. Lee used the government to promote economic policies that fostered industrial growth, full employment, and a rising standard of living; elections and civil liberties, however, were suppressed under one-party role. Lee's experiment succeeded in creating a wealthy, export-oriented industrial society with a well-educated population and remarkably efficient government.

See also Pacific Rim

Further Reading

Turnbull, C. M. *A History of Singapore, 1819–1988*. 2nd ed. New York: Oxford University Press, 1988.

LENIN, VLADIMIR IL'ICH (1870–1924)

Lenin was a founder of the Russian Social Democratic Workers' Party (Bolsheviks) and the leader of the 1917 Russian Revolution. A fervent Marxist who argued that international capitalism created the conditions for proletarian revolution even in Russia, Lenin believed that his party would be the vanguard of workers' struggles, guiding workers away from reformist goals and toward socialism. The Bolsheviks' highly disciplined cadres helped the fledgling revolution survive the myriad problems it confronted, including counterrevolution and invasion by England, Japan, and the United States. However, in the face of war, the Bolsheviks refused to allow workers' organizations to function independently, and workers' soviets and newspapers were suppressed or strictly controlled; gradually, economic, political, and military planning were taken over by the Bolsheviks.

Although fiercely anticapitalist, Lenin proved remarkably flexible in adjusting to the economic and political chaos provoked by world war, revolution, counterrevolution, and civil war. During the civil war, industrial facilities were nationalized, that is, taken over by the state, and most goods were no longer sold in the market but were instead produced by quota and distributed through rations. After the civil war, production was a fraction of what it had been in 1913, and Lenin launched the controversial New Economic Policy, which reintroduced markets for many products, particularly agricultural goods.

Lenin believed that industrialization would spread the conditions for socialism throughout the country. Before he died, Lenin warned the Bolshevik Party to beware of the growing power of Joseph Stalin, but it was too late. Lenin's life, party, and revolution provided a blueprint for many revolutionaries, particularly in underdeveloped countries, who sought to industrialize and build socialism at the same time.

See also Kulaks; Stakhanovites; World War I (1914–18)

Further Reading

Fisher, Louis. *The Life of Lenin*. New York: Harper and Row, 1966.

LIBERALISM

This political movement originated in Western Europe during the eighteenth-century Enlightenment under the influence of the political theories of philosopher John Locke. Many liberals supported industrialization, and many industrialists in Europe, the United States, and Latin America were liberals, at least in orientation. Liberalism gained ground in Europe beginning in the 1820s, the same time the Industrial Revolution was taking shape. Revolutions of 1830 in France and Belgium thus were liberal, at least initially.

Liberal political movements believed in constitutional government and personal rights such as freedom of religion and the press. They backed the spread of education and were hostile to traditional restrictions on economic freedom, such as guild regulations. Some liberals believed in laissez-faire. In general, however, liberals did not seek systematically to exclude government from economic activity. Many businessmen, though politically liberal, supported tariffs; this was true, for instance, in the United States. Liberal leaders often urged government involvement in measures to promote economic growth, such as railroads. Some liberals, as they learned more about working-class misery, came to back certain reforms, like child-labor legislation. As the nineteenth century wore on, groups like the British Liberal Party supported increasing government intervention in the area of welfare. A Liberal government in Britain enacted the National Insurance measure of 1911, which first provided unemployment insurance. Similarly, liberals in the United States backed increasing government intervention during the New Deal.

Liberalism, in sum, was rarely entirely identical with the narrow interests of industrialists, though they were often linked to liberal groups in the nineteenth century. Always eager for individual freedoms, liberals often urged government-backed reforms. Therefore liberalism necessarily varied greatly from place to place and tended to change over time; as liberals became more interventionist, they usually lost most business support, as in Western Europe and the United States by the early twentieth century.

Liberalism never widely caught on in Russia and Japan, and industrial revolutions in these countries had little to do with liberal policies. In Latin America, liberalism was an active movement in the nineteenth century. Liberals usually backed government encouragement for industry. Their eagerness for economic growth could lead them to impose harsh measures on groups—for instance, indigenous groups through the world—linked to more traditional economic practices. As in the United States, liberals often tried to press Indians to support private property and other "modern" concepts and were quite willing to coerce in the name of progress.

Except in the United States and to an extent Britain, nineteenth-century liberalism failed to catch on with working-class groups. This could result in growing identification of liberalism with the cause of business—as in Germany after 1871—and in a growing loss of liberal power thanks to the rise of socialism. Still, liberal beliefs and policies, though variable, related to the growth of industry in the West during crucial decades of the nineteenth century. In the late twentieth century, liberal beliefs in relatively free markets and low tariffs revived almost worldwide as a means of encouraging global industrial development.

See also Classical Economics; Protectionism

Further Reading

di Ruggiero, Guido. *A History of European Liberalism*. London: Oxford University Press, 1927.

Love, Joseph, and N. Jacobsen, eds. *Guiding the Invisible Hand. Economic Liberalism and the State in Latin American History*. New York: Praeger, 1988.

LIGHT INDUSTRY

This term refers to consumer goods industries, like textiles, leather, processed foods, tools, and (more recently) small appliances. Different industrial revolutions placed different emphases on light as opposed to heavy industry. Russian (and Soviet) industrialization was notorious for underplaying light industry, to the detriment of consumer standards. Communist China paid closer attention to light industry. German industrialization also stressed heavy industry, in part because British factory imports weakened German textiles during the period of 1820–30. By contrast, France and Italy, with poor iron and coal resources, emphasized light industry strongly, developing small, mechanized factories and shops. Within any industrialization process, light industries typically employ more women than heavy industry does and offers lower wages in part because of more intense price competition among relatively small firms.

See also Electronics; Women Industrial Workers

Further Reading

Landes, David. *The Unbound Prometheus: Technical Change and Industrial Development in Western Europe*. Cambridge: Cambridge University Press, 1969.

MacFarquhat, Roderick, and John K. Fairbank, eds. *Cambridge History of China*. Vol. 15. New York: Cambridge University Press, 1991.

Stearns, Peter. *The Industrial Revolution in World History*. 3rd ed. Boulder, CO: Westview, 2007.

LINEN

Linen was one of the most commonly used fibers in preindustrial Europe. It was made from flax, a plant that could be widely grown throughout most of Europe. Linen production was hard to mechanize, however, because the fiber broke easily. Factory production began, haltingly, only in the 1840s. Linen products thus declined in the face of factory cottons and wools, and linen goods became a low-paying, largely female craft specialty. Traditional linen-producing areas, like rural

This 1783 painting of flax production shows how much early industrial production was done in the home. (Library of Congress)

Brittany, parts of Belgium, and Ireland, suffered growing unemployment. Ironically, commercial linen production increased on the eve of industrialization, serving the need for military uniforms during the Napoleonic Wars; in Northern Ireland, linen weaving was as essential as the potato for the survival of rural Protestant families. This earlier demand made subsequent deindustrialization all the more severe.

See also Textiles

Further Reading

Landes, David. *The Unbound Prometheus: Technical Change and Industrial Development in Western Europe.* Cambridge: Cambridge University Press, 1969.

LITERACY. *See* Education and Literacy

LONG WAVES OF CAPITALISM

Most people are aware of the "boom-bust" cycles of capitalist economies from personal experience or from reading the newspapers. Over the last 80 years, economists have increased their knowledge of the causes of business cycles, and their recommendations have influenced the policies of government, greatly reducing the length and severity of depressions (now termed recessions). However, social scientists have begun to investigate the causes and consequences of much longer economic cycles that take decades to resolve. These "long waves" of capitalist development include short-term business cycles within them but are spread throughout the entire world system of trade. Unlike business cycles, the resolution of long-wave cycles involves the transformation of a wide variety of business, social, and political institutions and relationships.

The generally accepted periodizations of cycles of economic expansion are late eighteenth century to 1815, 1850–73, 1897–1914, and 1945–73. Periods of global depression are 1815–50, 1873–97, 1920–45, and 1973 to around 2007. Although economic growth occurs within depressionary cycles (such as the one since 1973), living standards of workers remain stagnant or decline, unemployment grows, and many industries and firms (such as steel in most industrialized countries) become unprofitable. Such periods of depression or crisis destroy the social, political, and business institutions that developed in the previous expansionist cycle and had enabled capitalism to expand and grow. When new institutional arrangements are constructed, capitalism begins to expand.

During the 1890s, for instance, the rise of monopoly capitalism not only centralized financial and productive power in the hands of cartels and corporations (in contrast to the relatively competitive period that had preceded it), but labor relations were also transformed. In the United States, craft unions in the iron and steel industry were crushed in the Homestead Lockout, and railroad unions were tamed through a number of bloody confrontations. The weakness of workers relative to industrialists facilitated a faster pace of work, the creation of more intense forms of workplace discipline such as Taylorism, and, eventually, the moving assembly line. The rapid expansion of production required that industrialists develop new relationships with consumers, encouraging a consumer culture through aggressive advertising and credit. This complex of institutional arrangements proved highly successful through the 1920s, but the Great Depression of the 1930s revealed corporations' inability to manage the entire economy. In the 1930s and 1940s, a new set of institutional relationships developed that gave the state a far larger role in managing the industrial economy.

See also Capitalism; Fordism; Keynesianism; Mass Marketing; New Deal; Welfare State

Further Reading

Gordon, David M., Richard Edwards, and Michael Reich. *Segmented Work, Divided Workers: The Historical Transformation of Labor in the United States.* New York: Cambridge University Press, 1982.

Mandel, Ernest. *Long Waves in the History of Capitalism: The Marxist Interpretation.* Cambridge: Cambridge University Press, 1978.

LUDDITES

In the late eighteenth and early nineteenth centuries, laws and customs that had protected the wages and working conditions of British workers were gradually overturned, ignored, or abandoned. In 1809, regulations governing the woolen industry were repealed; in 1813, the apprentice system was suspended, and the next year, the minimum wage. In addition, as steam-powered looms and shuttles were introduced to the textile industry, previously skilled workers' wages fell and working conditions deteriorated. Luddites were bands of disaffected British workers and artisans who resisted the new order and wrecked machinery during the late eighteenth and early nineteenth century. The rioters came to be called Luddites because factory owners were warned ahead of time

This illustration from 1812 is titled "The Leader of the Luddites"; note the leader is wearing a woman's bonnet and directing a well-armed mob. (Associated Press)

of retribution by "Ned Ludd" or "General Ludd" (a probably mythical leader) if they did not agree to changes in wages and working conditions. Luddites raised bread-and-butter issues but also resented and resisted the degradation of political rights and social status of artisans and workers in the early phases of the Industrial Revolution. Workers turned to Luddism after trade union actions had been banned by the government and workers could find no relief in the courts or Parliament. After the Combination Acts, unions continued to operate in secret and ostracized, beat, or sabotaged "blackleg," or nonunion, workers and artisans. Luddism was an extension of this activity, and like many preindustrial "riots," Luddites relied not only on the social solidarity of a group of protestors but on a wider community as well. The riots sometimes occurred in daylight, and the secrecy of the actions could have been betrayed by other workers who witnessed the riots. One police informer reported that "most every creature of the lower order both in town and country are on their side." Some magistrates also sympathized with workers' hostility to machines.

Luddites sometimes accomplished their immediate aims of a rise in wages, although riots also led to severe repression by the government. By 1812 (in the midst of a war with Napoleon), armed Luddites clashed with both mill owners and the army, and over 10,000 troops were in the field against General Ludd. The protests threatened to become a national movement aimed at changing the government that had ignored their plight and denied them their traditional rights. Repression won the day, however, and enough workers were hung to break the movement. The fact that industrialization at this point was a largely rural phenomenon hampered workers' ability to communicate with each other and coordinate activities. Many Luddites became members of the Chartist movement, although there was not another mass insurrection of workers that threatened the government. The sabotage of new machinery and ostracism of strikebreakers remained fixtures among English workers, but the slow legalization of trade unionism and the gradual extension of the right to vote to male propertied workers throughout the nineteenth century made the insurrectionary activity of Luddites appear bizarre to later historians and workers. Attacks on machines were nevertheless common in many early industrial periods, such as France in the 1820s. By the twentieth century, the term Luddite referred to anyone who futilely and irrationally seeks to oppose new technology.

See also Arkwright, Richard; Moral Economy

Further Reading

Sale, Kirkpatrick. *Rebels against the Future: The Luddites and Their War on the Industrial Revolution.* Cambridge, MA: Perseus, 1996.
Thompson, E. P. *The Making of the English Working Class.* New York: Pantheon, 1963.

MACHINE BUILDING

This industry was both a result of industrialization and vital to its expansion. New inventions in textiles and the steam engine obviously had to be manufactured. At first, prototypes were made by industrialists like James Watt, and traditional metal shops were used to provide materials; but ultimately, the industry had to emerge on its own. The Boulton-Watt collaboration involved a machine tools shop in which numerous steam engines could be constructed. Real progress in developing procedures for the production of standardized machine parts awaited the very end of the eighteenth century and beyond. Increased knowledge in the manufacture of clocks and other precision instruments played a crucial role. New equipment included accurate lathes, on which machine parts could be cut; various types were available by the late eighteenth century. All-metal lathes, pioneered by Henry Maudslay in England and David Wilkinson in the United States, constituted a significant advance, for they provided minutely accurate screws for machines. New boring engines allowed more accurate construction of metal cylinders for use in engines. Lathes and boring engines set the basis for the development of interchangeable parts, which a Swedish engineer, Christopher Polhem, had worked on as early as 1700. By 1785, a Frenchman named Le Blanc was making muskets on the basis of interchangeable parts, presumably by cutting patterns for each part to guide the workmen. The most influential achievements stemmed from the firearms manufacture organized by Eli Whitney and Simeon North in the United States, as well as from the manufacture of naval pulleys in England. Different machines cut and bored each part identically, so that machines could be assembled by putting them together.

Early machine-building operations depended on skilled workmen. Most shops were small, and, although the skills were new, an essentially artisanal atmosphere prevailed. Much labor was recruited from the ranks of trained metalworkers. Skilled unions, like the Amalgamated Society of Engineers in Britain, brought these workers into the ranks of craft organization. Later in the nineteenth century, a new generation of inventions permitted more automatic machine construction. Automatic riveting and boring machines, attached to electrical or gasoline engines, allowed semiskilled workers to build equipment like ships' engines and locomotives. These developments greatly expanded output—for example, in World War I, when women workers were widely used. They also produced important labor conflict over the boundaries between skilled and factory operatives.

See also Wilkinson, John

Further Reading

Derry, Kingston, and T. I. Williams. *A Short History of Technology*. Oxford: Oxford University Press, 1961.
McNeil, Ian. *An Encyclopaedia of the History of Technology*. New York: Routledge, 2002.

MALTHUS, REVEREND THOMAS ROBERT (1766–1834)

Thomas Robert Malthus was a British middle-class economist. He is most famous for his argument that whereas population can expand geometrically (1, 2, 4, 8), food production can expand only arithmetically (1, 2, 3, 4). Malthus's insight influenced Charles Darwin, who saw that competition within and between species was inevitable.

Malthus observed that throughout human history, wars, plagues, and famines placed checks on population. People who were influenced by Malthus's ideas on population defended the refusal of the British government to intervene massively in the Irish famine, since the deaths of Irish peasants were "inevitable." It was after reading Malthus that Thomas Carlyle declared economics to be the "dismal science." Malthus was the first economist to try to figure out the causes and consequences of what he called "gluts," which later economists would term depressions. Malthus's followers (Malthusians) tended to oppose welfare for the poor, which they thought would increase their birthrate. Some Malthusians worked hard to encourage birth control in the nineteenth and early twentieth centuries within middle-class reform organizations but also in some labor movements.

See also Population Growth

Further Reading

Heilbroner, Robert L. *The Worldly Philosophers: The Lives, Times, and Ideas of the Great Economic Thinkers*. New York: Simon and Schuster, 1986.

MANAGERS

A manager is someone who directs a business or professional operation without owning it. Whereas people like managers existed before the Industrial Revolution, the term and the importance of managerial activity result from advancing industrialization. In the early Industrial Revolution in Western Europe and the United States, most factories were managed by their owners, or at least by one member of an owning partnership. Maintaining older values, many factory owners placed great emphasis on the importance of their personal direction of most basic activities. They tried to run the factory, oversee supplies and sales, and keep up with the latest technology. If they needed additional staff help, they often turned to family members.

Fairly quickly, however, it became clear that expanding factories could not operate as a one-man band. Some activities had to be released to managers, who would take basic directions from owners but would have considerable latitude in running day-to-day operations. The expansion of corporations, where ownership was diffuse, also required increasing recruitment of managers. By the late nineteenth century, most industrial operations (and also many department stores, public utilities, and other activities) depended on direction from managers. Most managers were recruited from middle-class ranks. Some regretted the fact that they could not own outright; a number of British managers in the later nineteenth century believed that they had been downwardly mobile. But talented individuals could rise into management as well.

Managers on average had somewhat different interests from owners, and the tone of the industrial economy may have changed as operation was separated from ownership. Many managers were more highly educated than owners and in a better position to apply new technology and to organize systematic industrial research. During the twentieth century, the professional levels of management expanded; in Europe, for example, a "new breed" of manager took over many large enterprises after World War II, with backgrounds in engineering, economics, or law. Managers sometimes applied a longer-term perspective to their operations than owners did, less concerned about short-term profits. They may also have been more willing than owners to share some decision-making power with trade unions, less concerned with defending every conventional owner prerogative and more eager for labor peace. These distinctions cannot be applied in every case, but it is possible that the rise of management over more traditional owner direction contributed to other shifts in industrial operations from the late nineteenth century onward.

See also Bureaucracy; Scientific Management

Further Reading

Chandler, Alfred. *The Visible Hand: The Managerial Revolution in American Business.* Cambridge, MA: Belknap Press, 1977.

Nelson, Daniel. *Managers and Workers: Origins of the New Factory System in the United States, 1880–1920.* Madison: University of Wisconsin Press, 1975.

MAO ZEDONG (1893–1976)

Mao Zedong led the Chinese Revolution (1949), which brought the Chinese Communist Party to power. Mao was the first communist to emphasize the peasantry, rather than the urban working class, as a revolutionary force. As the leader of China, Mao sought to develop industry, but he also focused a great deal of attention on transforming the countryside. Collectivization of agriculture occurred more slowly and with less brutality than in the Soviet Union. The first five-year plan was carried out from 1953 to 1957. It was somewhat successful but was followed by the overly ambitious Great Leap Forward. Mao's ideology stressed not only the necessary role of the revolutionary party but also egalitarian principles. Egalitarianism was emphasized during the Cultural Revolution (1966–69); for example, piece rates

Mao Zedong, a leader of the Chinese Communist Party until his death in 1976. (The Illustrated London News Picture Library)

for industrial workers were abolished and were reinstalled only in 1978 under Deng Xiaoping. Mao's policies, while sometimes inhibiting industrialization, helped to develop China's human and physical capital.

See also China; Chinese Communist Party

Further Reading

Spence, Jonathan. *Mao Zedong.* New York: Penguin Books, 2006.

MAQUILADORAS

Maquiladoras are foreign-owned, export-oriented manufacturing plants located in Mexico. After 1945, Mexican workers could legally migrate to the United States through the bracero program, until it was terminated in 1964 by the United States. In 1965, Mexico and the United States began the Border Industrialization Program to create jobs in northern Mexico, thereby stemming illegal immigration. Under the maquiladora program, Mexican laws that limited foreign investment and U.S. import tariffs were relaxed. By the late 1980s, over 300,000 Mexicans worked in over 1,500 factories throughout Mexico.

In the 1960s and 1970s, most maquiladora factories were in low-wage, labor-intensive industries such as garment making and electronics, and the majority of the employees were women. Although wages were relatively high for Mexico, working conditions were harsh (job-related diseases and injuries were common) and labor turnover was high. Since the 1980s, more capital-intensive industries such as automobiles have entered Mexico, and maquiladoras employ more skilled workers and professionals, an increasing number of them men. Some technologically advanced firms have developed in Mexico to provide services to foreign-owned factories.

Downward pressure on wages is intense. The North American Free Trade Agreement created widespread unemployment as American agricultural products flooded the market. Furthermore, because more people migrate to maquiladora areas than can find jobs, unemployment remains high in industrializing regions.

(Millions more migrated to the United States.) The Mexican government has discouraged workers from forming independent unions. Critics of the program also point out the burden that unrestrained industrialization and urbanization has placed on the delicate desert environment. The benefits of the system to the process of Mexican development are widely disputed.

Initially, the maquiladora program worked to the advantage of corporations in the United States that sought to take advantage of relatively cheap labor to win shares of foreign markets. The program became a more important source of foreign revenue to Mexico, however, after the collapse of oil prices in the early 1980s. In the wake of the devaluation of the Mexican peso, labor prices became even cheaper than before, and investment from Japan, Europe, or Canada accounted for half of all new investment in Mexico. Because of their Mexican factories, Japanese and European corporations can circumvent tariffs or quotas set by the United States. Since the approval of the North American Free Trade Agreement in 1994, the maquiladora program, with its problems and potential, continues to expand. Scholars predict that more small and medium-size companies will also take advantage of the opportunities for investment in Mexico.

See also Deindustrialization; Division of Labor; Foreign Trade; Import Substitution; Postindustrial Economies

Further Reading

Fatemi, Khosrow, ed. The Maquiladora Industry: Economic Solution or Problem? New York: Praeger, 1990.
Fernandez-Kelly, Maria Patricia. For We Are Sold, I and My People: Women and Industry in Mexico's Frontier. Albany: State University of New York Press, 1984.

MARCONI, GUGLIELMO (1874–1937)

Marconi, an Italian engineer, developed what was first called wireless telegraphy, or radio. He was born into a wealthy Irish-Italian family and was early drawn to the study of electromagnetic waves. On his father's estate, he first set up an apparatus to receive and send signals by electrical waves, reaching longer distances than any had ever done before. The Italian government was uninterested, so Marconi sought funding in England, taking out a patent in 1896.

He formed the first wireless company the following year, installing wireless sets in British lighthouses. He sent the first wireless message across the Channel, a distance of 85 miles, in 1899. Radios were soon used on ships and proved vital in signaling emergencies. Marconi built a station to send signals across the Atlantic in 1901, managing to send a very faint "S" sound. Marconi continued to add to the distance radio messages could be sent, later experimenting with short waves. He commanded an Italian radio division in World War I.

Marconi's radio method involves the beam system, to and from aerials. A cathode-ray tube system was developed at almost the same time by Ferdinand

Marconi helped revolutionize communication; here operators learn their trade at a Marconi wireless school in New York, ca. 1912. (Library of Congress)

Braun. The two men shared the Nobel Prize for physics in 1909. Radios soon became vital not only for faster and more flexible communication but also to transmit entertainment, thereby adding to the growing stock of consumer items.

Further Reading

Nobel Foundation. *Nobel Lectures: Physics 1901–1921*. Amsterdam: Elsevier, 1967.

MARKETS

People have traded commodities in markets for millenia, but the market as a system whereby land, goods, and labor (or services) can all be treated as commodities only arose in Europe in the last 500 years. In addition to the social and economic changes engendered by the rise of capitalism, the expansion of the market system helped to create an entirely new scholarly discipline: economics.

Adam Smith was one of the first economists to investigate the operation of the market system. Smith argued that competition among producers in a free or unregulated market becomes self-regulating—producers that attempt to overcharge customers are displaced by manufacturers with more modestly priced or better quality wares. The self-regulating nature of the free market, or what Smith termed the "invisible hand," became an important fixture of laissez-faire economic theory, which opposed governmental regulation of businesses or intervention to aid the poor. Smith castigated the assumptions of mercantilist governments that assumed that international trade was a zero-sum game; instead, Smith argued, free trade would allow different countries to specialize in products or services in which they developed a comparative advantage. However, Smith acknowledged that the government was not the only limit on free markets and noted that producers frequently attempted to circumvent the market by fixing prices or establishing cartels.

Despite the importance of laissez faire as an ideology, even in the nineteenth century virtually no markets were free; they were regulated by national or imperial governments. Although the Industrial Revolution had made it possible for manufacturers to produce vastly increased amounts of goods, the question of who would buy these goods was more problematic, and access to markets, whether domestic, colonial, or foreign, was of crucial importance to industrialists. The success of latecomer industrializers all depended upon government's direct subsidies (notably the railroads) or indirect subsidies via tariffs. The quest for markets for individual goods was a contributing factor to the rise of imperialism.

Labor markets reflected the impact of growing numbers of workers selling their labor. Employers often tried to undercut pressures that might have raised wages by encouraging an increase in the labor supply. For example, industrialists often attracted immigrant workers to industrializing countries or used growing numbers of women or children.

By the late nineteenth century, the rise of large-scale corporations and cartels changed the dynamics of the market system. By acquiring their own sources of raw materials and transportation via vertical integration, corporations created "internal markets" for goods, services, and labor. For instance, U.S. Steel had its own "captive" iron and coal mines whose products were transported to steel mills on the corporation's own system of ships and trains. The steel was sold to affiliated companies that produced ships, railroads, and skyscrapers. Competitors faced high costs to enter industries with technically advanced corporations that could also manipulate the market by dumping products at a loss, launching crippling lawsuits, or pressuring other corporations to boycott the newcomers' goods. Thus, although the invisible hand of the market does eliminate inefficient producers in the long run (often by competing corporations or cartels), in the short and medium run, the "visible hand" of the corporation plays a decisive role. Since the early 1980s, many corporations have turned to more flexible arrangements with their work forces and suppliers.

See also Back Office; Capitalism; Mass Marketing; Outsourcing; Postindustrial Economies; Profit; Protectionism

Further Reading

Chandler, Alfred D., Jr. *The Visible Hand: The Managerial Revolution in American Business.* Cambridge, MA: Belknap Press, 1977.

Heilbroner, Robert L. *The Worldly Philosophers: The Lives, Times, and Ideas of the Great Economic Thinkers.* New York: Simon and Schuster, 1986.

MARSHALL PLAN

In 1947, Secretary of State of the United States George C. Marshall (1880–1959) proposed a plan to rebuild the countries devastated by World War II. In the wake of the war, Marshall feared that Europe's economy would continue to decay and eventually fall under the influence of local communists and the Soviet Union. In the words of its namesake, the policy was directed "not against any country or doctrine but against hunger, poverty, desperation, and chaos. Its purpose should be the revival of a working economy in the world so as to permit the emergence of political and social conditions in which free institutions can exist." At a point when capitalism was politically vulnerable, the Marshall Plan subsidized the expansion of the system of private enterprise.

The Marshall Plan offered a sharp contrast to the debilitating burdens placed on the defeated powers after World War I. Between 1945 and 1952, the United States offered approximately $20 billion in grants (and several billion more in loans) to former allies and enemies in Europe and Asia. The Marshall Plan prevented economic bottlenecks from developing and encouraged the reindustrialization of Europe to expand world trade (and, coincidentally, to provide an immediate market for U.S. capital goods). The Marshall Plan allocated its grants only to countries that structured their economies along procapitalist lines; furthermore, countries were required to coordinate their economic planning to stimulate an international division of labor (this ultimately resulted in the Organization of European Economic Cooperation). The Soviet Union refused to accept the conditions of the Marshall Plan and prevented Eastern Europe from accepting grants or loans from the United States.

George C. Marshall developed the U.S. plan to rebuild the economies of Europe after World War II. (Library of Congress)

In both economic and political terms, the Marshall Plan was a remarkable success. Between 1950 and the late 1960s, Western Europe underwent a period of rapid economic growth. By 1963, the European economy was 250 percent larger than it had been in 1940. Furthermore, Western Europe enjoyed a period of social cohesion that allowed the liberal parliamentary system to take hold in Germany, Italy, and other industrial countries. The Marshall Plan undermined the appeal of the communist strategy of industrial development that yielded relatively lower standards of living for the majority of its citizens. The Marshall Plan established one crucial aspect of foreign aid in the post–World War II era: capital loaned to recipient nations has to be spent in contracts with firms from the lending nation. However, nearly all subsequent aid through the World Bank or the U.S. Agency for International Development was in the form of loans, not grants.

Further Reading

Wexler, Imanuel. *The Marshall Plan Revisited: The European Recovery Program in Economic Perspective*. Westport, CT: Greenwood, 1983.

MARX, KARL (1818–83)

Karl Marx was a German philosopher whose all-embracing analysis of capitalism has endured as a basis for studying economics, society, and politics. Marx had an important influence on the nineteenth-century socialist movement through his numerous polemical and analytical writings on economics and contemporary political events. Marx often collaborated with Friedrich Engels, and their work has had a profound influence upon many activists, workers, and scholars.

Marx was born to a middle-class Jewish family that sent him through the German university system. Marx earned a PhD, but the anti-Semitic policies of the Prussian government prevented him from obtaining a faculty position, and Marx plunged into a career as a liberal journalist working as editor for the *Rheinische Zeitung* in Cologne. Marx's polemics caused the government to suppress the paper. By 1843, Marx had embarked on a journey through France, Belgium, and England. Partly in response to his contact with socialistic workers, Marx began to work out a critique of capitalism, which in his view inherently alienated workers; Marx also elaborated a humanistic vision of communism in which people's physical, social, and psychic needs would be realized.

By the late 1840s, Marx had started to work out his theory that the driving forces of history have been changes in forms of production. Marx viewed capitalism as a revolutionary force that not only dramatically increased the productive capacity of humanity through the Industrial Revolution but transformed all social and political relationships as well as cultural and intellectual forms. In Marx's view, the revolutionary forces unleashed by capitalist and industrial production would periodically cause crises (more profound than depressions) that could enable the working class to someday come to power. Marx and Engels were commissioned by a group of revolutionary workers to write the *Communist Manifesto*, which appeared in print during the revolutions of 1848. Repression, however, not workers' republics, was the immediate result of these revolutions, and Marx spent the rest of his life in self-imposed exile in England.

Despite the failure of the 1848 revolutions, Marx continued his work in exile, throwing himself into organizing the first workers' International, writing for newspapers, commenting on political events of the day (such as the Paris Commune of 1871), and producing his monumental study of capitalism. Marx received some money from his writings, but his chief support came from Engels, whose family owned textile factories—still, Marx and his family lived in poverty. Many of his writings were published posthumously by Engels. Marxism became the leading intellectual support of socialism and communism, though it was subsequently adjusted and modified. Marx's insights about social classes and power inform much research on the Industrial Revolution to this day.

See also Lenin, Vladimir Il'ich; Long Waves of Capitalism; Primitive Accumulation; Surplus Value; Utopian Socialists

Further Reading

Marx, Karl. *Capital: A Critique of Political Economy*. New York: International, 1967.
McLellan, David. *Karl Marx: His Life and Thought*. New York: Harper and Row, 1974.

MARXISM

Marxism is the intellectual tradition that applies the theories and methods of Karl Marx (1818–83) to history, economics, and society. Although Marx is generally known as an economic theorist, his work attempted to depict the dynamic historical relationships among economics, society, politics, and culture. The social and intellectual history of Marxism has been influenced by the development and reorganization of industrial capitalism and the working class itself.

Marx argued that the economic development of societies and the struggle between social classes have been the forces behind fundamental historical change. Marx saw history as a constant struggle between classes over the means of production. In his day, the crucial struggle pitted workers against capitalists, and Marx foresaw that workers would triumph and that an egalitarian society of abundance with no government would eventually follow. Consequently, Marx himself and many Marxists were involved in what Marx termed the "workers' movement" (trade unions, Internationals, and socialist parties). However, Marxism was not so much a theory of insurrection as a way to guide workers toward socialism through a better understanding of the workings of capitalism. When Marx began his analysis of capitalism, the Industrial Revolution was still a recent phenomenon and the working class still relatively small. Ironically, it would be the consolidation of industrial capitalism through what Marxists termed monopoly capitalism and imperialism that would throw Marxism and the socialist movement into turmoil. As a few large companies took over most production—monopoly capitalism—and Europe expanded its colonies, working-class conditions became more complex, which generated various disputes about Marxist predictions and prescriptions.

Marxism provided a grand revolutionary theory of history and a scathing critique of capitalism, and it impressed many workers and political leaders. But Marxism was a fractured and argumentative intellectual tradition, claimed and contested by those who believed that a classless society could be won only via revolution (such as communists) and those who favored more gradual reforms (such as Social Democrats). These divisions became more pronounced during World War I, when many reformists supported the war—in violation of their pledges to international solidarity among workers—while revolutionaries opposed the war. After the war, the split between reformists and revolutionaries deepened. Revolutionaries helped create the first "workers' state" in relatively backward Russia, but failed to in the more advanced industrial countries with stronger social democratic parties such as Germany, Austria, or Hungary. From 1919–20, insurgent workers in Germany and Austria attempted their own revolutions and were repressed by social democratic parties.

Since the 1920s, Marxism has been strongly influenced by the Leninist tradition, which gave the crucial role of leading the workers' movement to the highly disciplined workers' party, rather than to the trade unions. Because communists were the only major group who resisted fascism in France and Italy, Marxists enjoyed an important political and intellectual role after World War II. Furthermore, Marxism-Leninism became an important ideology for revolutionaries in Latin America and in decolonization struggles in Asia and Africa. Marxist-Leninists began to argue that although industrialization was necessary for a socialist society, revolution itself was more likely in countries on the periphery of the world system.

In Europe, communist and social democratic parties helped to improve the standards of living of workers via the welfare state; ironically, most communist parties became nearly as reformist as social democratic parties. And though communist parties in Eastern Europe, Asia, or Latin America improved living standards for the mass of its citizenry, none were able to either create a classless society of abundance or govern with any semblance of democracy. In fact, many dissident Marxists began to argue that the Soviet Union's Communist Party had itself become a new ruling class. The loyalty to the Soviet Union demanded by Communist parties stifled the creativity of Marxist intellectuals, whose work was generally of a lower quality than before the 1920s. In fact, after the 1940s, an increasing number of Western Marxists refused to affiliate with Communist parties, and the center of Marxist thought decisively shifted to the university system. In the postwar world, investigations into philosophy, art, history, and literature—rather than economics, organizing, or politics—became the norm for Marxists in Western countries.

The growing crisis and subsequent collapse of socialism in the Soviet Union, Eastern Europe, and the rest of the world has caused many Marxists to renounce the possibility, and even desirability, of a socialist society. Within radical circles, Marxism nonetheless retains some intellectual vitality.

See also Communism; Russian Revolution (1917); Stalinism

Further Reading

Anderson, Perry. *Considerations on Western Marxism*. London: Verso, 1976.

MASCULINITY

The Industrial Revolution undermined traditional masculinity but permitted important new expressions of masculine power and competence. Industrial workers had little access to property, but because preindustrial masculine maturity had been based on ownership, workers continued to insist on trying to control their wives and children. Industrial work forced men to labor under the supervision of others and reduced the demand for many traditional masculine skills, such as weaving. Even sheer strength could be challenged by machines, as the nineteenth-century U.S. folk song "John Henry" demonstrated. For the growing middle class, industrialization meant office work, where, again, masculine physical prowess could be hard to demonstrate.

Men in both the middle and the working classes reacted to these challenges by vaunting masculinity in new ways from the late eighteenth century onward. Many European and American men sought sexual domination over women: taunts and even violent sexual attacks against women workers increased during the period of early industrialization. Middle-class men in Western Europe and the United States in the mid-nineteenth century promoted the ideology that men were the stronger sex, alone capable of work and political action, whereas women, gentle and moral, were essential to care for the home. Workers and reform-minded businessmen alike supported laws that limited women's hours of work, thus promoting the domestic sphere as proper for women while also making them less competitive in the workplace. Workers often excluded women from trade unions and limited their role in protests, while developing a strongly masculine leisure culture that emphasized drinking, fighting, and sports. This working-class machismo lasted well into the twentieth century. Crucial to all urban classes was the nineteenth-century emphasis on the man as principal breadwinner, whose arduous work and earnings were vital for his family's survival. Men who proved incapable of supporting their families were considered abject failures.

Some of the initial assertions of masculinity were modified as women demanded new rights. Nevertheless, the industrial definition of masculinity, the product of major changes and stresses, continues to exercise some influence.

See also Dual Labor Markets; Feminism; Franchise

Further Reading

Carnes, Mark, and Clyde Griffen, eds. *Meanings for Manhood*. Chicago: University of Chicago Press, 1990.
Stearns, Peter N. *Be a Man: Males in Modern Society*. Rev. ed. New York: Holmes and Meier, 1990.

MASS MARKETING

Mass-marketing systems, designed to sell products to a large number of buyers, arose in the late nineteenth century as corporations sought to capture or create large-scale demand for a rapidly increasing volume of products. Before the 1850s, merchants advertised the availability and prices of their wares in local newspapers; by the 1860s, companies had begun to aggressively advertise their products using pictures, stories, and photographs in newspapers and national magazines. Companies sought to differentiate their products from those of their competitors and were able to take advantage of improvements in packaging technologies (canning, paper wrappers, and so on) to build a distinctive "name brand" for household products such as soap, canned foods, and kerosene as well as more expensive items such as sewing machines and farm implements.

The sewing machine was the first major "consumer durable." By the 1870s, its manufacturers had developed many of the production, advertising, and distribution techniques that would later be applied to most products. In the 1830s and 1840s, sewing machines were unwieldy, relatively expensive items, and disagreements among companies over who held patents to crucial technologies discouraged improvements. In the late 1850s, companies established a "patent pool"; as a result,

Advertisement for sewing machines in 1875. (Courtesy of Kathryn Ledbetter)

the quality of machines improved and prices eventually dropped. In the 1860s, for example, the members of the patent pool sold less than 80,000 units a year, but by the mid-1870s, sales had risen to over 350,000 a year—with many of the machines exported to England and other foreign markets. Singer emerged as the dominant company, in part because customers could place an order with a traveling sales agent or purchase a sewing machine directly from the company rather than depending on large retail outlets.

After the 1870s, mail-order commerce increased as department stores took advantage of the lower postal rates that resulted from the completion of a national railroad network. In 1872, the Montgomery Ward company published its first catalog, and by the 1890s, many other companies, notably Sears, Roebuck and Co., had also published massive catalogs. Mail-order catalogs, important in their own right for increasing the sales of certain products, offered residents of isolated rural communities a wider range of products. The catalogs also helped spread the culture of consumerism beyond the middle-class patrons of urban department stores. Mail-order catalogs became such a fixture of U.S. culture that many observers lamented the decision of Sears, Roebuck and Co. to cease publication of its annual catalog in the late 1980s.

By the end of the nineteenth century, industrialists had created national and international markets for a wide variety of products. Large corporations or cartels, such as Westinghouse and General Electric, had the resources to take advantage of the emerging advertising industry and were in the best position to exploit national markets. Early on, corporations sold not only their products but their corporate image. In 1908, for instance, AT&T advertised the virtues of a "regulated private monopoly" in the telephone industry. By the 1910s and 1920s, advertising increased in importance for corporations and solidified as an industry in its own right. In the heady days of the 1920s, advertisers claimed that by stimulating demand, they could even end the phenomenon of business cycles, in which production and employment fluctuated radically.

One of the most important pioneers of mass marketing was Henry Ford, who mass produced the Model T, a durable, cheap "car for the great multitude." Ford's business became the world's largest industrial company, but by the late 1920s, General Motors had begun to produce Chevrolets that offered consumers more options than Ford's Model T. Although a few industrialists, notably Ford, believed advertising was a waste of money, even he found it necessary to advertise to compete with General Motors. By the late 1920s, carmakers were attempting to lure customers by subtly changing each annual model. Critics charged that companies refused to use all of their new technology in each new model and, in fact, engineered a short product life—what was called "planned obsolescence."

Certain mass-produced and mass-marketed products have come to symbolize the appeal of industrialized countries' consumerism. Companies such as McDonald's, Coca-Cola, and Levi's have developed world markets by offering consumers a strictly standardized product produced in conditions closely resembling an assembly line. According to these companies' considerable advertising, consumers are purchasing not only food, drink, or clothing but flexibility, freedom, and fun.

See also Cartels; Multinational Corporations (MNCs); Sloan, Alfred P.

Further Reading

Marchand, Roland. *Advertising the U.S. Dream: Making Way for Modernity, 1920–1940.* Berkeley: University of California Press, 1985.

Tedlow, Richard S. *New and Improved: The Story of Mass Marketing in America.* New York: Basic, 1990.

MASS MEDIA

Mass media, communications outlets designed for mass consumption, emerged first in the form of large-circulation daily newspapers. Middle-class papers like the *New York Tribune* began bidding for larger audiences after the mid-nineteenth century, but the true mass press, selling to 1 to 2 million readers, arrived in the 1890s with offerings like the *London Daily Mail* or the *Berlin Lokal-Anzeiger.* Industrial technology was essential to the mass media. Improvements in printing, which can be dated to the 1830s, included faster, steam-driven presses and methods of translating photographs to the printing press. Cheaper manufacturing of paper came in the 1850s from using wood pulp instead of rag. In the 1890s, automatic composing machines allowed semiskilled typesetting from keyboards to replace highly skilled manual setting. Advances in photography facilitated illustration.

Industrialization also created large urban audiences—literate, but eager for entertaining, even sensationalized, fare. Bold headlines, simple writing, and features such as sports, women's columns, and comics offered readers escape from the daily routine. Advertisers reached these consumers with eye-catching pitches for cosmetics, clothes, bicycles, and diet products. Advertising revenues helped keep prices low; mass-circulation papers sold for just pennies in 1900.

The principles of mass newspapers—advanced technology, simple and dramatic messages, and abundant advertisements—extended to later mass media, from radio to television. Those same principles were applied to the Internet and, ultimately, to new social media such as Facebook.

Mass media has been dramatically remade since the 1980s. Newspaper and magazines suffered large declines in readership. Television was remade by cable, satellite, and Internet streaming. The technological revolutions have created new levels of competition with vast opportunities for wealth and enormous risks for not adjusting to the new realities.

See also Advertising; Telecommunications

Further Reading

Briggs, Asa, and Peter Burke. *A Social History of Media: From Gutenberg to the Internet.* Malden, MA: Polity Press, 2009.

Mills, C. Wright. *The Power Elite.* New York: Oxford University Press, 1956.

McCORMICK, CYRUS (1809–84)

Cyrus McCormick helped to mechanize farm production by inventing and mass producing farm equipment, such as the mechanical reaper he perfected in the 1830s. His invention allowed horse power to be substituted for human power, a significant advantage for large-scale grain farmers on the enormous prairies of the United States. McCormick ensured high-quality products by building his own factory and adopting mass-production techniques. He guarded against competitors by carefully patenting his subsequent inventions. McCormick's acumen as a businessman, utilizing advertising and advancing credit to customers, gave him a near monopoly on agricultural implements for much of the mid-nineteenth century.

See also Mass Marketing

Further Reading

Pursell, Carroll W., Jr. *Technology in America: A History of Individuals and Ideas.* Cambridge, MA: MIT Press, 1981.

MEATPACKING

Beginning in the seventeenth century, preparation of meat was controlled by small-scale commercial butchers. In the late nineteenth century, large corporations with centralized production facilities (packing houses) displaced local butchers, effectively industrializing this branch of food processing. The new companies relied on a detailed division of labor along "disassembly lines" to produce meat that was canned or shipped fresh via refrigerated railroad cars through national (or, in the case of Argentina or Australia, international) distribution networks. In the United States, corporate meatpacking followed the development of large-scale commercial cattle raising and helped to spur the creation of factory-like feedlots in which hundreds of thousands of animals were prepared for slaughter. In *The Jungle*, Upton Sinclair savagely described the brutal working conditions of immigrant workers in the Chicago meatpacking industry in the early twentieth century. Middle-class readers focused on the images of rotten and spoiled meat and pressed for government inspection—leaving workers to struggle alone to improve working conditions, for durable industrial unions were not established until the 1930s.

In the mid-twentieth century, industrialists took advantage of trucking technology by locating smaller packing houses in rural areas, near a ready supply of animals and frequently nonunion labor. The result has been a return to conditions akin to *The Jungle*. The faster line speeds cause serious health problems for workers and for consumers; for instance, fecal matter routinely gets dripped onto the meat. However, regulation can be effective. The same factories that produce for the European Union have considerably lower rates of disease as the disassembly line runs considerably slower.

See also Armour, Philip Danforth; Industrial Unions

Further Reading

Barrett, James R. *Work and Community in the Jungle: Chicago's Packinghouse Workers, 1894–1922*. Urbana: University of Illinois Press, 1987.

Schlosser, Eric. *Fast Food Nation: The Dark Side of the All-American Meal*. New York: Houghton Mifflin, 2001.

Sinclair, Upton. *The Jungle*. Memphis, TN: St. Lukes, 1988.

MECHANIZATION

Mechanization refers to the replacement of human skill or power by machines. Powerful forces encouraged mechanization: the Industrial Revolution involved a shift from human, wind, and animal power to steam, electricity, and oil as the logic of capitalism forced employers to attempt to replace workers with machines whenever possible. The basic principle of mechanization relied on power-driven machinery to produce more than workers could manage with hand tools. Mechanization began first in the eighteenth century in manufacturing processes (such as textiles or shoemaking), but by the early nineteenth century, mechanization had proven to exercise a pervasive and powerful influence over the lives of ordinary people.

This Currier & Ives print, ca. 1876, pays homage to some major inventions of the nineteenth century, including the steam press, telegraph, locomotive, and steamboat. (Library of Congress)

Even when people did not come into direct contact with machines, mechanized products replaced previously homemade goods such as textiles or candles, encouraging a greater dependence upon the market.

By the late nineteenth century, mechanization had completely transformed the homes of ordinary people with domestic production equipment, such as sewing machines, and manufactured consumer items, such as kerosene lamps and factory-produced rugs and wallpaper. By the 1920s, the spread of electric power, combined with central heating and indoor plumbing, allowed new levels of comfort for middle-class families—changes that were accompanied by new standards of cleanliness. The spread of air conditioners later in the century allowed many people to control indoor temperature throughout the year. The spread of air conditioning to urban workers and the southern United States has had the effect of slowly undermining older forms of summertime sociability that centered on the front porch. As people have gained greater control over their environment, distinctive regional forms of architecture have declined and have been replaced by standardized tract housing.

Mechanized transportation and communication has transformed people's sense of time and space. Railroads and steamships lowered the costs of the postal system, allowing increased business and personal communication. Telegraph networks accelerated this process and enabled newspapers to cover national and international news with greater speed. Prior to the electric streetcar, most people lived within walking distance of their workplace, but by the late nineteenth century, the middle and upper classes in the United States could commute from semirural suburbs. By the 1910s, the automobile accelerated the process of suburbanization, and the decentralization of business was influenced by "automobility" and telephone networks that facilitated communication between branches of a corporation. The Internet, cell phones, and other handheld electronics continue to accelerate the effects of mechanization on daily life.

See also Automation

Further Reading

Giedion, Siegfried. *Mechanization Takes Command: A Contribution to Anonymous History*. New York: Norton, 1969.

MEIJI RESTORATION

Japan was the first non-European country to successfully industrialize. In the mid-nineteenth century, Japan was a feudal society, closed to contact with the world and dominated by a class of warriors, or samurai; today it is the world's most advanced producer of automobiles, steel, and electronics. Japan's rapid transformation began in the 1850s, when Russia, the United States, and Britain forced the Tokugawa government to open Japan's ports to commerce. The response of the Japanese government to this external challenge to its authority laid the groundwork for Japan's industrialization. The Meiji restoration was the period between 1868, when the Japanese emperor called Meiji, or "enlightenment," was "restored" to power, and 1912, when the emperor died.

The opening of Japan to foreign traders created a political crisis for the nation's ruling class of samurai warriors. The crisis was eventually resolved by restoring (at least symbolically) the emperor as the nation's leader. The Meiji restoration was less a return to monarchy, however, than a complete transformation of the social and economic basis of the nation from feudalism to capitalism. A small group of bureaucrats (acting in the name of the emperor) enacted far-reaching land reform. Samurai were quickly stripped of their feudal privileges in exchange for cash stipends; many samurai became bureaucrats in government and industry. Although Japanese farmers had extensive experience with commerce, they could no longer pay their taxes in kind (for instance, with rice) but had to use cash. Common lands previously used by poorer peasants to gather wood or graze cattle were sold to individuals. The economic surplus gathered by the state provided the basis for industrialization schemes.

The Meiji government also transformed education, stressing nationalism, loyalty to the emperor, and technical fields of study over Confucian ethics. Japan had had high rates of literacy before 1868, and the Meiji regime improved upon this tradition. Universities were established to train the new bureaucratic, business, and technical elites. The Meiji government actively supported industrialization by establishing facilities and then selling them off to favored companies, which generally received monopolies. In the 1870s, the Mitsubishi zaibatsu (business combination) was given a government loan to buy a shipping company previously owned by a European company. Other zaibatsu were also extended remarkably favorable terms to purchase factories, although the government itself ran the railroads, telegraphs, and armories. The government favored policies that kept wages low to maintain a competitive advantage in world markets.

Although the government's policies caused widespread hardship for the majority of the population and centralized economic power in a few hands, Japan did avoid becoming reliant upon foreign producers or banks. For instance, the Japanese government relied on foreign technicians to set up a centralized mint and banking system, but unlike the governments of China and India, the Japanese government expelled the foreigners within 10 years. In fact, the government's concern with developing itself as a major military power was a dominant theme in its pursuit of industrial development. As one historian observed, "By 1910 Japan had completed the largest battleship in the world, the *Satsuma*, but had built no textile machinery at all."

See also Enclosure Movement; Imperialism

Further Reading

Akamatsu, Paul. *Meiji 1868: Revolution and Counter-Revolution in Japan*. New York: Harper and Row, 1972.

MELLON, ANDREW (1855–1937)

Andrew Mellon was the son of a prominent Pittsburgh banker, Thomas "Judge" Mellon. Andrew Mellon joined his father's bank in 1874 and assumed control of it in 1882. Mellon built his fortune by supplying capital to emerging industries and gaining substantial holdings in such industries such as oil (Gulf Oil), aluminum (Aluminum Company of America or Alcoa), and coke making (Koppers). Always alert for business opportunities, Mellon helped to establish a construction firm that made locks for the Panama Canal. In 1921, President Warren G. Harding named Mellon secretary of the treasury, a post he held until 1932. Mellon favored lowering taxes on the wealthy and paying off government debt, policies that became the subject of much derision during the Great Depression. An indication of his wealth (and taste) can be gauged by the fact that Mellon's personal donation of art and capital constituted the initial collection of the National Gallery of Art.

See also Finance Capital

Further Reading

Cannadine, David. *Mellon: An American Life*. New York: Knopf, 2006.
O'Connor, Harvey. *Mellon's Millions, The Biography of a Fortune: The Life and Times of Andrew W. Mellon*. New York: John Day, 1933.

MERCANTILISM

This set of economic beliefs dominated European thinking during the seventeenth and much of the eighteenth centuries. It fit well with the growing military and diplomatic competition among national monarchies. Mercantilists sought economic systems that would maximize national wealth; above all, they wanted to increase the supply of precious metals and the tax base of the national government. Believing that the total wealth of the world was a fixed quantity, mercantilist theories advocated measures that would help one's own nation get a larger slice of the pie, automatically diminishing other nations in the process.

Characteristic mercantilist devices included high tariffs to promote internal manufacturing; promotion of exports; abolition of barriers to internal trade and improved roads; acquisition of colonies to assure cheap imports of raw materials that would not diminish the national supply of gold; and detailed regulations to encourage consumption of goods produced at home, to promote national industries, and so on. France, under Louis XIV and his finance minister Colbert, became a mercantilist center in the late seventeenth century. A version of mercantilism called cameralism spread in central Europe, helping monarchs like Frederick the Great of Prussia to promote the cultivation of potatoes to increase population (another mercantilist goal), to encourage foreign merchants to settle in Prussia, and to sponsor expositions to promote new technology.

Mercantilism helped prepare the way for industrialization in some respects. Promotion of shipbuilding or tariff protection of new industry could have positive results. For instance, mercantilist encouragement to exports spurred some industry and trade. Detailed regulations of methods of work attempted by Colbert, however, probably dampened innovation. By the middle of the eighteenth century, economists were attacking mercantilist ideas, arguing that wealth was not a fixed entity but could be increased, and claiming that unfettered competition, not protection and regulation, would best serve prosperity. Adam Smith was the liberal economist who most decisively unseated mercantilist beliefs. However, elements of mercantilism unquestionably survived, particularly in the temptation to use tariff policy as an element in national competitions, even though the theory itself disappeared.

See also Laissez-faire; Protectionism; World Systems Theory

Further Reading

Hecksher, Eli. *Mercantilism.* London: Allen and Unwin, 1935.

Ormrod, David. *The Rise of Commercial Empires: England and the Netherlands in the Age of Mercantilism, 1650–1770.* New York: Cambridge University Press, 2003.

Wallerstein, Immanuel M. *The Modern World System.* Vol. 2, *Mercantilism and the Consolidation of the European World Economy, 1600–1750.* Berkeley: University of California Press, 2011.

MERCHANT CAPITAL

Merchants helped to break down feudalism in Western Europe and supplied nascent industrialists with capital, raw materials, and markets; in short, merchants played an important role in the Industrial Revolution. Merchants actually profited, however, from circulation of commodities, not from production. Therefore merchants could work with a variety of social forms other than wage labor, such as slavery and sharecropping. "Merchant capital" is how some historians have described the double role that merchants have played not only in the circulation of commodities but in the creation of social systems within the world system. According to the Marxist view, merchant capital is opportunistic and strengthens social systems that rely on unfree labor—even as it helps draw those societies deeper within the nexus of production for the market. Merchants have also sometimes distrusted industrialization and looked down on industrialists as newcomers and exploiters.

See also Profit

Further Reading

Fox-Genovese, Elizabeth, and Eugene D. Genovese. *Fruits of Merchant Capital: Slavery and Bourgeois Property in the Rise and Expansion of Capitalism.* New York: Oxford University Press, 1983.

Miller, Joseph C. *Way of Death: Merchant Capitalism and the Angolan Slave Trade, 1730–1830.* Madison: University of Wisconsin Press, 1988.

Southern sharecroppers helped enrich many plantation owners and merchants through the debt-lien system; this photograph is from 1939. (Library of Congress)

MERCHANTS

Merchants are people who trade goods, and their social and economic role long predates industrialization. All urban societies have merchants, and some traditions, such as that of Islam, give merchants a vital social status.

Merchants have been essential to industrialization in many ways, even as industrialization has forced important changes and even hostility among merchant groups. European merchants had been expanding their activities well before the Industrial Revolution, indeed since the Middle Ages. Trade overseas, from the fifteenth century onward, helped establish new markets for manufactured goods while bringing new capital to European shores. By the eighteenth century, various merchants were stimulating a domestic market to express new tastes for products such as textiles and pottery. Merchants also helped organize the expanding domestic manufacturing system to supply goods for their trade. Urban merchants bought quantities of raw material that were distributed to workers in their homes, and then returned as finished products to the merchants for wider sale. In all these ways—by stimulating markets, acquiring capital, and promoting manufacturing—merchants helped set the stage for industrialization in Europe and the United States.

Nonetheless, many established merchants suffered from industrialization. They disliked the change. They found factories dirty and despised the upstart industrialists who, however, might well soon be earning more money than their conservative colleagues. Many old merchant firms failed; such failures were a common pattern in Meiji Japan. Other enterprises survived but stagnated, their families sometimes producing intellectuals, like the Brahmins of Boston, critical of industrial life in the name of higher cultural values. Still other established merchants partnered with new entrepreneurs, supplying capital but staying out of the factory itself.

Industrialization quickly generated new needs for merchant activity. Merchants willing to innovate and devise new methods of disposing of vast quantities of goods participated directly in the ongoing Industrial Revolution. Pioneers of department stores—in the United States, mail-order operations—helped fuel industrial sales. Many innovations utilized some of the same principles of standardization, division of labor, and intensive direction of workers that had proved successful in factories. At this level, the Industrial Revolution stimulated a great change in merchant life, including new opportunities and access to new wealth.

Industrial cities also generated growing numbers of smaller merchants, who also sold a multiplying array of goods to rising urban and village populations. Some shopkeepers expanded, becoming full-blown merchants. Others, however, preserved a family business—the famous mom-and-pop store—and hovered uncertainly on the edges of the industrial world. Many shopkeepers disliked aspects of industrialization, including the expansion of big corporations. Many, drawing their clientele from workers, sympathized with labor protest. By the late nineteenth century, some had turned to rightist movements like the anti-Semitic parties in France and Germany to express their insecurity in a world increasingly dominated by big business. This shift underlaid anti-industrial protest through the fascist decades of the twentieth century and again demonstrated the complexities of the relationship between merchants and the industrial economy.

See also Causes of the Industrial Revolution; Department Stores; Domestic Manufacturing; Entrepreneurial Spirit; Merchant Capital

Further Reading

Braudel, Fernand. *The Wheels of Commerce.* New York: Harper and Row, 1979.
Cipolla, Carlo, ed. *The Fontana Economic History of Europe.* 5 vols. London: Fontana, 1970.

MERGERS

Mergers, the joining of two or more companies together, occurred at all stages of the Industrial Revolution. They were part of the reason for the growth of average firm size, as bigger firms offered efficiencies and economies of scale over their smaller counterparts. Many early industrial firms merged smaller operations as partnerships. In the late nineteenth century, mergers played a vital role in vertical integration, in which companies developed operations at all stages of the production process, from new materials to finished goods. Steel companies like Carnegie merged with coal mines, creating a chain of reliable supply, from raw materials up to the finished product. Shipping companies like Japan's Mitsubishi merged with shipbuilding operations. Mergers also began to allow companies to gain new international subsidiaries, a pattern that accelerated in the twentieth century. Mergers might be friendly junctures, like the partnerships in the early textiles or pottery industries, or unpleasant takeovers of weaker rivals. In capitalist countries in the twentieth century, some mergers had nothing to do with productivity advantages but with stock manipulations and tax breaks, raising questions about the impact of certain mergers on the overall economy.

See also Corporations; Multinational Corporations (MNCs)

Further Reading

Buder, Stanley. *Capitalizing on Change: A Social History of American Business.* Chapel Hill: University of North Carolina Press, 2009.

Josephson, Matthew. *The Robber Barons: The Great American Capitalists, 1861–1901.* New York: Harcourt, Brace, 1934.

METHODISM. *See* Religion

MEXICO

The present Mexican government was born in a long and bloody revolution (1911–20), in which peasants and workers sought to gain access to land and decent jobs. The struggle was inconclusive; workers and peasants gained many legal rights, but they were enforced sporadically. Mexico's chief assets in this period were mineral—by 1920, Mexico was the world's second-largest oil producer, and the industry was nationalized in 1938. Some industrial development had occurred before the revolution—in brewing, for example—but the revolution itself devastated the economy. The government encouraged industrial growth after World War II with a strong emphasis on steel, petrochemicals, and infrastructure projects such as improving roads and electrical systems. Over a quarter of the labor force entered the manufacturing sector and began to acquire some consumer goods. Although the economy grew rapidly, it failed to provide decent jobs to many workers and peasants, many of whom migrated to the United States for seasonal or permanent employment.

The large role of the state (which accounted for one-fifth of all jobs) was reversed in the early 1980s, when falling oil revenues and a mounting debt crisis pushed Mexico's elite to deregulate large parts of the economy. Many foreign companies have set up factories in Mexico, but living standards remain low. Migration to the United States accelerated in the wake of the North American Free Trade Agreement in 1993. In the 2000s, wages from workers abroad earned Mexico more income than petroleum.

See also Maquiladoras

Further Reading

Hamnett, Brian R. *A Concise History of Mexico*. New York: Cambridge University Press, 2006.

MIDDLE CLASS

The middle class is not easy to define. As it emerged in the nineteenth century in Western Europe, it fell beneath the aristocracy; its members did not have titles, and although they did not possess as much wealth as the great magnates, they did rise above the working classes. Middle-class people did not work with their hands; instead, they normally owned property or had a professional skill. On average, their educational levels were higher than those of the working classes.

Many members of the middle class had developed a common culture. They believed in science and in the importance of business and economic growth; they expounded their faith in progress and liberal values. Members of the middle class wanted political rights and constitutional government; they adhered, at least in principle, to an ethic of hard work. Many of these values informed the willing participation of the middle class in the Industrial Revolution, in which they served as factory owners and merchants or as lawyers or doctors assisting other segments of the middle class.

An early advertisement for Ford indicates that travel via car had quickly become central to middle-class sensibilities. (Library of Congress)

At the same time, however, certain segments of the middle class, even while embracing seemingly common values, responded to the Industrial Revolution quite differently. An older segment of the middle class, sometimes called the bourgeoisie, was accustomed to preindustrial urban life. They thought in terms of security, not change, and did not willingly invest in new industry. Some of these people opposed industrialization outright, sympathizing, for example, with working-class protest against factory conditions. Some merchants thus backed strikers in factory towns, such as Paterson, New Jersey, or supported Luddism in England.

Professional people often resented the wealth of factory owners. During the Industrial Revolution, many professionals updated their credentials, claiming access to important new knowledge (like advances in medical science) and imposing new tests and licensing procedures. These new professional standards helped doctors and lawyers participate in industrial society, but tension still arose. Individual professionals sometimes supported labor movements or other activities directed against industrialists. Thus a professor of philosophy, Jean Jaurès, spearheaded French socialism around 1900.

The most successful factory owners pulled away from the middle class into a new upper middle class with special ties to the aristocracy. Even in the United States, where no aristocracy existed, a plutocracy emerged after the Civil War that had little contact with ordinary middle-class folk, though they might advocate some common values.

In the late nineteenth century, a lower middle class developed, composed of people with no property but engaged in nonmanual occupations such as school teaching or clerical work. Again, this group could share middle-class values—it was much less likely to unionize, for example, than blue-collar workers—but its employment conditions resembled those of other workers.

Analyzing the middle class during the Industrial Revolution means, then, understanding the tension between shared conditions and values and very different specific reactions, including attitudes to industrialization itself. The middle class did, however, define standards of polite behavior, support generally liberal politics, and foster business and technological change that on balance provided a favorable context for industrial growth. It tended to criticize real or imagined working-class habits, like heavy drinking, in the name of respectability. Societies that began to industrialize later, like Russia by the 1890s, also developed a middle class in the process, though the group was smaller and spoke with a weaker political voice. Middle classes, defined in terms of mid-level wealth, business, or professional commitment, and some shared values, have also been identified in societies with growing industrial sectors in the twentieth century, such as Latin America and India.

In industrial societies themselves, middle-class definitions have become still more complicated during the twentieth century. In the United States, growing affluence and the dominance of some middle-class values led a vast majority of the population to claim it was middle class by the 1950s. Blue-collar workers joined the class, in their own estimation, simply because of a shared standard of living. As more members of the middle class became employed as technicians, managers, and professionals rather than as independent owners, several criteria of the nineteenth-century middle class clearly changed. Middle-class culture also evolved. The kind of respectability defined in the nineteenth century obviously shifted when the middle class embraced consumer values more fully, tolerated more expressive sexuality, and fostered new roles for women. Some core values, however, including faith in science and technical progress, survived. As nonmanual labor expanded, the middle class naturally grew quite rapidly, making it a still vital ingredient of industrial society.

See also Ruling Class; White-Collar Workers

Further Reading

Ghosh, Suniti. *The Big Indian Bourgeoisie: Its Genesis, Growth and Character.* Calcutta: Subarnarekha, 1985.

Pilbeam, Pamela. *The Middle Classes in Europe, 1789–1914*: France, Germany, Italy and Russia. Chicago: Lyceum, 1990.

Stearns, Peter N., and Herrick Chapman. *European Society in Upheaval: Social History since 1750.* 3rd ed. New York: Macmillan, 1992.

MIDDLE EAST

This historic region between the Mediterranean and the Indian Ocean now consists of many nations and varied economies. As a whole, the Middle East was slow to respond to Western industrialization. The dominant Ottoman Empire was not an innovator in economic policy, and Muslim tradition discouraged imitation of Christian Europe. The region lagged behind technologically in the seventeenth and eighteenth centuries. The growth of European military power led to takeovers of key areas (particularly in North Africa) by the mid-nineteenth century and to increased political and commercial pressure on the Ottoman Empire itself. Several reformers, notably Muhammed Ali in Egypt, attempted to spur industrial growth, without major success. The Ottoman Empire did begin to encourage mining and infrastructure; a postal system was established in 1834, a telegraph system in 1855, and railway construction began in 1866 onward. In the meantime, European commercial influence grew. Oil was discovered in the Middle East early in the twentieth century, and for decades it was exploited mainly by Western companies. In 1912, a European conglomerate formed the Turkish Petroleum Company to exploit reserves in Iraq; Saudi Arabia was dominated by the U.S. Standard Oil Company beginning in the 1930s.

Successful industrial efforts began to take shape, though slowly, after World War I. A new regime in Iran practiced the policy of import substitution; that is, it set up enough factories to supply most national needs and reduce dependence on imports. Iran also managed to retain some control over its oil reserves. Turkey meanwhile developed its own industrial base. In 1961, after individual oil-producing nations gained more control over oil profits by nationalizing or heavily regulating the Western companies, the leading oil producers formed the Organization of Petroleum Exporting Countries (OPEC). This strategy increased oil profits immensely by providing investment funds, and petroleum-based industries, technical training, and some wider industrialization all increased. To be sure, no full industrial revolution occurred; climate, population growth, and heavy military expenditures all hindered rapid development. Nonetheless, substantial industrial sectors existed in most Middle Eastern countries by the late twentieth century.

Further Reading

Goldschmidt, Arthur, Jr., and Lawrence Davidson. *A Concise History of the Middle East.* Boulder, CO: Westview, 2009.

MILITARY-INDUSTRIAL COMPLEX

When Dwight Eisenhower left the office of the U.S. presidency in 1961, he warned the country of the growing power of a "military-industrial complex." Eisenhower was referring to the increasingly symbiotic relationship between the military and the corporations that had become dependent upon military contracts during the Cold War. In fact, the relationship between the military and manufacturing has been important for 500 years.

The rising European economic dominance over the world system of trade in the sixteenth century was due in large part to Europeans' use of superior cannons and ships. Military competition among emerging European nation-states for control over shipping lanes and sugar plantations in the seventeenth and eighteenth centuries fostered the rise of the industrial system. England encouraged its manufacturers, particularly of cannons, guns, and ships, to compensate for the relatively few sailors and soldiers that it could muster.

Throughout the nineteenth century, the perceived military requirements of governments had an enormous impact on industrialization in many countries. Many of the new technologies and organizational innovations used in the development of the U.S. factory system were begun in the Springfield Armory, a weapons center in western Massachusetts. The global arms race among European powers throughout the nineteenth century expanded the industrial base of many countries as each government sought a domestic supply of armaments. Indeed, the Krupp family built an industrial empire by supplying the German government with military equipment. Russian industrialization resulted in no small part from the desire of the czars for military equipment. By the early twentieth century, the Meiji government of Japan had built its first battleship, though it had yet to build its own textile machinery. Although the British navy retained its dominance in the naval arms race prior to World War I, the British steel industry and shipyards did not keep up, and gradually these manufacturers became reliant upon the government to purchase its goods.

Although military spending stimulated the development of many industries, the human cost of this form of development has been staggering. The nineteenth-century arms race of the European "great powers" culminated in the deaths of millions of soldiers and civilians in World War I. The inability of industrialized countries to pay the financial and social costs of the World War I contributed to revolution in Russia, the decline of British military and economic power, economic chaos in Germany, and the rise of fascism in Italy and Germany. Many governments sought to escape from the Great Depression of the 1930s via what some have termed military Keynesianism. Backed by its powerful industrial cartels, Germany's fascist regime stressed military production. Many unemployed white-collar and middle-class professionals found new jobs and status in the military. The only resolution to the threats of fascism and depression was another world war whose social costs were also enormous.

Preparing for World War II allowed the New Deal government of Franklin Roosevelt to reinvigorate the economy of the United States. In industries as diverse as steel and aircraft manufacturing, the government financed the building of new factories, paid to train new personnel, allowed large corporations to manage the facilities, and then purchased the output. In contrast to World War I, profits were limited, although in World War II the contractors were much more likely to be large corporations or cartels than small businesses. After the war, the new factories were sold at a substantial discount to their corporate managers. Although many industries reconverted to civilian uses, the Cold War required that the economy remain on a permanent war footing. Resources were directed into the universities and the aerospace and computer industries. With the end of the Cold War in 1989, reconverting these industries to peacetime use became a challenge.

The military-industrial complex has proven difficult to dismantle. The "peace dividend" of the 1990s proved elusive. American military spending fell in that decade but remained higher in real terms than in the 1970s. In the 2000s, spending jumped to historically high levels following 9/11. The two ground wars proved costly, as did new types of industries, such as contractors who supplied intelligence or services to the government. One emblematic company was Blackwater, who provided thousands of highly paid security personnel in Iraq and elsewhere. Emblematic of the new era, there were more private contractors, including Blackwater, in Iraq than direct employees of the U.S. military. Private contractors did much of the reconstruction work in Iraq, which was more costly than the Marshall Plan, with far less to show for it.

See also Finance Capital; Imperialism; Iron and Steel Industry

Further Reading

Markusen, Ann R., and Joel Yudken. *Dismantling the Cold War Economy*. New York: Basic Books, 1992.
Schaeffer, Robert K. *War in the World System*. Westport, CT: Greenwood, 1989.

MINERS' FEDERATION. *See* Miners' National Union.

MINERS' NATIONAL UNION

This union, formed in 1863, was one of the first durable industrial unions in Britain. The strong community cohesion of miners' villages, plus the rigorous conditions of work, provided an excellent basis for unionism, and British miners played a major role in the national labor movement well into the twentieth century. At the same time, varying conditions in different mining areas made national coordination difficult; regional unions often predominated. The miners' union largely supported the Liberal Party, but in 1888 a radical segment split off and formed the Miners' Federation. This division launched a major growth period of industrial unionism more generally. A flurry of bitter strikes erupted as employers tried to increase miners' output. The federation played a significant role in the emerging Labour Party and in some of the great strike movements of British history, including the strikes of 1912–13 and the General Strike of 1926. At the same time, miners' notorious independence and spontaneity often caused them to race ahead of organized union structure, creating significant tensions between direct action and official federation policies.

See also Coal Miners; United Mine Workers (UMW)

Further Reading

Church, Roy A., and Quentin Outram. *Strikes and Solidarity: Coalfield Conflict in Britain, 1889–1966.* Cambridge: Cambridge University Press, 2002.

National Union of Mineworkers president Arthur Scargill opposing the plans of Prime Minister Margaret Thatcher to close numerous mines; the strike failed. (Associated Press)

MINIMATA DISEASE

This disease involved methyl mercury poisoning of residents of Minimata village and other communities who ate fish contaminated by the discharge from a chemical plant. The symptoms were classic mercury poisoning: death or a comatose state, loss of speech, or sensory-motor disturbances. By February 1972, 282 Minimata cases were reported, with 60 deaths. Wide publicity of this and several other chemical-poisoning cases in Japan ultimately provoked great concern. A small group of Japanese scientists worked for public awareness in the 1960s, leading to a strong environmental movement and more stringent regulations. The ruling party, concerned about a divisive political issue, adopted environmentalism as its own cause after this episode. Major lawsuits were directed against polluting companies, and heavy damages were assessed.

Further Reading

Jun, Ui, ed. *Industrial Pollution in Japan*. Tokyo: United Nations University Press, 1992.

MINISTRY OF INTERNATIONAL TRADE AND INDUSTRY (MITI)

The Ministry of International Trade and Industry (MITI) is the post–World War II name of a crucial bureaucracy that has shaped Japan's industrial policies from the 1920s through the present. MITI's roots originate in the Meiji era, with its direct predecessor, the Ministry of Commerce and Industry, which was founded in 1925. The ministry first changed its name in 1943 to the Ministry of Munitions, then to MITI in 1949. During the Meiji era, the government itself owned many factories, but MITI functions by establishing national economic policies and encouraging companies to meet its goals through low-interest loans, tax incentives, access to new technology, and foreign currency. MITI's experiences during wartime have shaped its postwar view that Japan is engaged in an economic struggle for survival whose success requires the resources of the entire country. Although critics of MITI fault its elitism and the favoritism it shows to large companies, MITI has engineered impressive economic growth: in 1975, the Japanese economy was more than 12 times larger than it had been in 1950, and it continues to grow.

MITI symbolizes the unique prestige and power of Japanese national bureaucracies, which before World War II had reported directly to the emperor, making bureaucrats relatively autonomous from elected officials. These prewar bureaucrats believed they represented national rather than narrow political interests, although this view became discredited as many Japanese came to blame the bureaucracies for launching World War II, a war whose results were disastrous for Japan. After the war, the U.S. occupation stripped the power of zaibatsus (financial cliques similar to holding companies) and military bureaucracies but allowed MITI to retain broad controls over the economy. As soon as possible—certainly by the 1960s—MITI restored the zaibatsu system in all but name, using its control over capital for investment and its access to foreign currency to rebuild heavy industry.

Although some Western observers argue that the Japanese "national character" accounts for MITI's power over the national economy, MITI was in fact responding to Japan's weaknesses after the war. Capital and foreign currency were in extremely short supply, and MITI directed what capital was available to projects that it felt would also help rebuild Japan's industrial power. The government's underwriting of loans allowed companies to expand well beyond what more fiscally orthodox bankers would have allowed. The result has been a system of highly concentrated industrial companies directed by cadres of market-oriented bureaucrats. Some observers argue that the system incorporates the flexibility of capitalism while disciplining it through rigorous national industrial policies lacking in the U.S. model.

See also South Korea

Further Reading

Johnson, Chalmers. *MITI and the Japanese Miracle: The Growth of Industrial Policy, 1925–1975*. Stanford, CA: Stanford University Press, 1982.

MITSUBISHI

The Mitsubishi Company has been one of the mainstays of Japanese industrialization from the mid-nineteenth century on. The company was formed by a feudal samurai, Iwasaki Yataro (1834–85), who had managed armaments procurements

By 1925, when this photograph was taken of a Mitsubishi plant, the company had become a dominant zaibatsu in Japan. (Library of Congress)

for a feudal lord, buying foreign weapons and ships. Iwasaki proved efficient in reorganizing older businesses for arms purchases. Under the Meiji regime, he set up an independent company while still assisting former feudal nobility and providing jobs for samurai. Iwasaki converted the company into his personal property in 1873, naming it Mitsubishi. He relied heavily on the loyalty of his staff of former samurai. Mitsubishi competed directly with the government shipping line for coastal trade, soon forcing it out of business by using more modern ships with a less cumbersome bureaucracy. In 1875, the government bought 11 new iron steamers, loaning and ultimately giving all of them to the new company with massive subsidies. The goal was to have Mitsubishi compete directly with U.S. and British companies in the trade between Japan and China—and by 1877, Iwasaki had bested the foreigners.

Mitsubishi began then to expand beyond shipping, thanks to its massive capital. It bought a maritime insurance company and moved into banking. Despite the widespread dislike of Iwasaki for his huge profits and overbearing personality, Mitsubishi withstood competition from a new shipping company, ultimately taking it over with government help. The conglomerate first borrowed and then bought a big shipyard from the government and also operated some coal mines. Expansion continued in the twentieth century, as Mitsubishi moved into metallurgy, armaments, and automobiles. Even before World War II, the company had proved adept in making collaborative arrangements with foreign firms like the U.S. company Westinghouse, which helped to update Mitsubishi's technology. By the 1960s, Mitsubishi had emerged as one of the great multinationals, with production facilities and export opportunities around the globe.

See also Military-Industrial Complex; Multinational Corporations (MNCs); State, Role of the

Further Reading

Patrick, Hugh, ed. *Japanese Industrialization and Its Social Consequences*. Berkeley: University of California Press, 1976.

MITTAL, LAKSHMI (1950–)

Lakshmi Mittal is one of the richest men in the world, and as of 2010 owns 40 percent of the world's largest steel company. He was born in 1950, in India. His father ran a steel company, and he worked for him, before forming his own company in 1976. He saw the economic possibilities in run-down steel firms, buying his first in Indonesia. Starting in 1989, he bought several state-owned companies, the first in the Caribbean, then Mexico, Kazakhstan, Poland, the Czech Republic, South Africa, and elsewhere. His strategy was to purchase only those companies that he could turn around and make a profit on within two years. State-owned firms maximized employment, a situation that Mittal rectified. The technology does not necessary need to be modernized if wages can remain low.

Mittal specialized in privatization, which has led to charges of political corruption. Steel making had largely been based in national economies; Mittal built one of the first truly international steel firms. In 2004, he merged with Arcelor the other largest international steel company. By the mid-2000s, the merged firm produced 10 percent of the world's steel and employed almost 200,000 workers.

Mittal is akin to Andrew Carnegie, who also drove labor costs lower and was able to reshape the market dynamics of the entire industry. He also represents the integration of the world's industrial economy.

Further Reading

Ruetter, Mark. "Who Is the Man Who Bought Sparrow's Point?" *MakingSteel.com*. Last modified September, 2005. http://www.makingsteel.com/whoishe.html.

MODERNIZATION THEORY

This theory was developed by U.S. sociologists during the 1950s and 1960s, although it built on earlier work by the great German sociologist Max Weber. The theory holds that a number of processes were intertwined in the development of modern industrial society. Therefore one could look at Western history as a model for a whole host of processes that other societies would have to go through to industrialize. One could develop various kinds of measurements to determine how "modern" a non-Western society was; perhaps, one could even set off a

Modernization theory suggested that mass education helps to usher in a novel way of thinking that contributes to rapid economic growth. (Morgan Lane Photography/Shutterstock)

modernization process by introducing some of the factors that had been involved in the process elsewhere.

Industrialization and accompanying technological change were unquestionably part of the modernization process, but the theory focused more attention on other features that could help prepare for industrialization or that would be wrapped up in industrialization itself. Political modernization consisted of developing new functions for the state and more efficient bureaucracy, plus attracting greater popular loyalty. In some renditions of the theory, political modernization should also consist of establishing democracy. Education was clearly part of modernization, and a modernizing state would necessarily develop an educational system. Population control was another widely accepted ingredient of modernization. So, too, new attention to children (including education) and, possibly, more intense affection factored into the process. Modernization for women meant a reduction in patriarchal controls, new legal rights, and greater education. Greater belief in science was a key element of cultural modernization. Some observers also talked of a modernized personality—open to change, eager for progress, individualized. On the basis of these criteria, modernization theorists defined some societies as modernizing and other societies as lagging in modernization.

Modernization theory has become less popular in the final decades of the twentieth century than it was in the 1950s and 1960s. Many historians have criticized its ethnocentrism: at its simplest, modernization theory argues that all societies should be measured on the basis of their resemblance to the West. Even in the case of Western history, modernization has been attacked for lumping too many separate developments together and implying that history moves in a single direction. Critics point out that industrialization did not always bring the same political forms (was Nazi Germany more or less modernized than democratic Britain?). It did not produce the same conditions and outlooks for workers as it did for the middle class, or for women as for men. (Again, at their simplest, modernized personalities sound very much like the standards developed for Western, middle-class males.) The industrial success of Japan further qualified modernization theory, for Japan became a leading industrial power without becoming Western; the idea that individualized personalities were essential to modernization was clearly silly, given the group-oriented style of modernized Japan.

Modernization is, nevertheless, a term in current usage. Its survival partly reflects unexamined assumptions; many U.S. citizens, for example, still judge other societies by their own and use the term modernization to cover this evaluation. The term has also come to have a narrower application. The word "modernization" is often applied to economic change to mean, essentially, industrialization or more intense industrialization; thus a reference to the "modernization" of the Brazilian economy usually means that manufacturing is increasing and more advanced technology is being used—that the economy is, in short, industrializing.

Though modernization is a contested term employed variously and vaguely, it may still be useful. Most societies in the twentieth century have undertaken some common kinds of change, partly in imitation of what the West did earlier: they have expanded education, improved public health, introduced more scientific training, granted new legal rights to women (including voting), adopted new technologies, and tried to improve the training of bureaucrats. Many countries have introduced these changes in hopes that they would foster greater industrialization. These similarities do not mean, however, that all societies have homogenized or that all are about to reach the same industrial level. Modernization clearly does not describe all major social patterns; in some "modernizing" societies, for example, crime goes up, while in others it goes down; in some "modernizing" societies, women lose economic functions, while in others they gain new ones. Used carefully to describe some limited but important changes that have been associated with industrialization, modernization may still be a valid historical term. Certainly many policy makers, from the leaders of postindependence India, to Witte, Lenin, or Gorbachev in Russia, have believed that certain kinds of changes might induce greater industrialization, and they have agreed on what a fair number of these changes are.

Modernization theory is an ambitious attempt to explain patterns associated with industrialization by looking at history. The theory can be rejected. If used, it must be defined carefully in the knowledge that it can be rendered poorly and that it definitely does not describe the whole of modern history.

Further Reading

Black, Cyril E., et al. *The Modernization of Japan and Russia.* New York: Free Press, 1975.
Levy, Marion J., Jr. *Modernization and the Structure of Societies.* Princeton, NJ: Princeton University Press, 1966.
Rozman, Gilbert, ed. *The Modernization of China.* New York: Free Press, 1980.

MONEY

Money has played a crucial role in the rise of capitalism, the modern world system of trade, and the Industrial Revolution. In early industrialization, many people had to adjust to a money-based economy rather than subsistence production and barter. The idea of working for money was distasteful to some, but monetary operations became increasingly accepted. Establishing a common currency was frequently a difficult task for national governments, but once accomplished, it greatly facilitated domestic and international trade. By the fifteenth century, gold and silver coins were used as currency. They were gradually replaced by promissory notes (redeemable in specie) that were issued by individuals, banks, or governments. By the late eighteenth century, the gold standard had emerged as a de facto international monetary standard, and most national currencies could be converted into gold. By the 1920s, money increasingly meant paper currencies that were not redeemable for gold but were backed by the credibility of national governments and the strength of national economies. After World War II, an increasing amount of money changed hands in the forms of checks and credit cards, continuing the trend away from the gold standard.

Further Reading

Ferguson, Niall. *The Ascent of Money: A Financial History of the World*. New York: Penguin Press, 2008.

Josephson, Matthew. *The Robber Barons: The Great American Capitalists, 1861–1901*. New York: Harcourt, Brace, 1934.

MONOPOLY CAPITALISM

Monopoly capitalism was the term developed by Marxist economists who sought to understand the transition from a competitive economic system in the eighteenth and early nineteenth centuries to one dominated by a relatively small number of cartels and corporations, a process that began at the end of the nineteenth century. Spearheaded by financiers, large-scale corporations and cartels began to dominate the increasingly complex industrial production processes in key sectors of the economy, such as steel, oil, and chemicals. The monopoly positions of these companies generally enabled them to maintain their technological superiority, thereby limiting the ability of newcomers to enter the market. At the same time, profits rose and controls over labor increased as a result of limits on competition.

The state played an important role in the formation of monopolistic firms. In Europe and Japan, governments actively encouraged the establishment of cartels that could take advantage of economies of scale. In fact, the developing modern states in Germany and Japan were themselves shaped by the industrialization process led by monopolistic companies. The decline of laissez-faire economic practice caused widespread unease among workers and especially the middle classes in the United States. Although in the early 1900s "trust busters" such as Theodore Roosevelt became a staple of reformist politics, the government did little to prevent the formation of monopolies in the auto, steel, chemical, and electrical equipment industries. Since the 1940s, in fact, all industrialized governments have actively subsidized monopoly firms, particularly those in the military sector.

Monopolistic companies were the first to use scientific management in their workplaces. Companies established dense layers of white-collar bureaucracies to supervise employees and to keep track of the goods and services passing through the corporations' own "internal markets." Some Marxists argued that the concept of monopoly capitalism also applied to Eastern Europe and the Soviet Union, whose governments likewise relied on policies of scientific management, vast bureaucracies, and military spending. New firms have emerged in capitalist societies to compete with established monopolistic companies, but until the 1970s, the trend toward centralization appeared to be a global phenomenon. The fall of Stalinist regimes throughout the world and the dramatic decline in the numbers of people employed by powerful corporations such as U.S. Steel and IBM have led some economists to argue that the world has entered a new historical stage—that of the postindustrial economy.

See also Finance Capital; Imperialism; Sherman Antitrust Act

Further Reading

Baran, P. A., and P. M. Sweezy. *Monopoly Capital: An Essay on the U.S. Economic and Social Order*. New York: Monthly Review, 1966.

Braverman, Harry. *Labor and Monopoly Capital: The Degradation of Work in the Twentieth Century*. New York: Monthly Review, 1974.

MORAL ECONOMY

E. P. Thompson used the term "moral economy" to make sense of how and why poor people resisted the extension of capitalism in the eighteenth century. In the preceding centuries, bread and grain were sold for set prices, and the moral economy of the poor (who perceived "fair" prices to be just) contrasted sharply with the emerging values of market economics. During periods of economic hardship, the poor rioted, sometimes merely seizing grain or bread but other times selling it at "fair" prices. These riots were not always disorderly: in many cases, rioters turned over to the miller or baker not only the money the rioters had collected but also the empty sacks! In the workplace, the moral economy tended toward a stable production process with few changes in the pace of work and informal controls and favors between employers and employees.

Rioting was an important part of the preindustrial political culture of European cities. For centuries, elites had used "the mob" to mobilize popular support for their policies, and poor people had rioted when their conditions deteriorated—for instance, when the price of bread increased or other forms of hardship arose. Appealing to the moral economy of paternalistic elites via riots proved to be a relatively effective way for the poor to protest the encroachment of laissez-faire capitalism. By the early nineteenth century, however, the ruling class had become firmly wedded to the emergent values of the market, and without the tolerance of elites, bread riots and similar protests became far less effective.

The preindustrial moral economy of the poor influenced later movements such as Luddism, cooperatives, and socialist utopianism. Building on Thompson's work, historians have examined the alternative values of the poor as they have been expressed in churches, trade unions, and everyday life.

See also Corn Laws; Women

Further Reading

Thompson, E. P. "The Moral Economy of the English Crowd." *Past and Present* 50 (1971): 76–136.

MORGAN, JOHN PIERPONT, SR. (1837–1913)

J. P. Morgan created an enormous financial empire, the "House of Morgan," that dominated U.S. economic life in the late nineteenth and early twentieth centuries. Morgan was the son of a wealthy banker, Junius P. Morgan, and through their connections to English banks, the Morgans became a conduit for capital to U.S. firms and the U.S. and Latin American governments. In 1877, the Morgans loaned the U.S. government enough money to pay the salary of its army until Congress could reconvene and appropriate the money. In 1893, J. P. Morgan helped to stop a panic among railroad companies and as a result acquired a controlling interest in many of the companies. Morgan also helped to create several enormous industrial firms, such as General Electric, International Harvester, and the first billion-dollar corporation—U.S. Steel. Morgan controlled his holdings through a system of interlocking directorates, whereby members of the firms' boards of directors sat on other companies' boards and represented the interests of the Morgan family.

Financier John Pierpont Morgan in a photograph taken in 1902. (Corbis)

See also Finance Capital

Further Reading

Carosso, Vince P. *The Morgans: Private International Bankers, 1854–1913*. Cambridge, MA: Harvard University Press, 1987.

MORSE, SAMUEL F. B. (1791–1872)

Morse invented the first successful electric telegraph and the Morse code. Like several other U.S. inventors, including Robert Fulton, Morse was an artist as well as a scientist, with scientific training at Yale and artistic work in England. (After a difficult apprenticeship, he became a well-known portrait painter.) He learned from a shipboard conversation in 1832 that electricity could be sent across wire, and he immediately thought of the telegraph. Making his idea a reality required amassing savings from his art, however, and he was not able to demonstrate a prototype until 1837. A partnership improved the financial picture, though Morse was able to interest neither the U.S. Congress nor foreign backers. A widely publicized display in 1842 failed, but Morse did win some congressional funding in 1843 and strung a telegraph wire from Washington, DC, to Baltimore. The first message, in 1844, was "What hath God wrought?" Telegraph systems spread widely thereafter, becoming vital to business and military communication. Morse won great fame at home and abroad and amassed considerable wealth.

Further Reading

Pursell, Carroll W., Jr. *Technology in America: A History of Individuals and Ideas.* Cambridge, MA: MIT Press, 1981.

MULTINATIONAL CORPORATIONS (MNCs)

Multinational corporations (MNCs) are companies that operate simultaneously in several different countries. For instance, Ford Motor Company is one of the largest automakers in the United States, the largest in Europe, and has major facilities in South Africa, Brazil, India, and Japan. Ford's "globalization" started early: in the 1920s Ford had factories in 19 countries. If Ford were a country, its GNP would be larger than those of Hungary and Israel combined—and oil companies such as Exxon are still larger.

One aspect of multinational corporations is takeovers of each other; here the head of Kraft announces that Philip Morris, its parent company, was taking over Nabisco in 2000. (Rick Maiman/Sygma/Corbis)

MNCs frequently have diversified portfolios. Philip Morris was originally a maker of tobacco products, but by the 1980s, it had become the world's second-largest food producer and the seventh-largest industrial firm in the United States. Beginning in the 1940s, Ford extended credit to its customers so they could buy its cars, but in the 1980s it followed the lead of Japanese carmakers and diversified into all forms of banking. By the early 1990s, Ford was the United States' second-largest lender, with $115 billion in loans.

Although MNCs are headquartered in one country, the fact that they operate in numerous countries makes it in their interest to act as good "corporate citizens." MNCs typically staff their overseas branches with foreign nationals and make contributions to local charities and politicians. Before World War II, Henry Ford both personally received a medal from Adolf Hitler and became one of the top three suppliers of military goods to the United States. Ford's German operations also supplied the Nazi army.

The "home" country of an MNC generally receives the profit from overseas operations. For instance, General Motors' European and Asian companies subsidized the U.S. division throughout the tough times of the 1980s. However, an MNC's first loyalty is to itself and self-interest transcends national allegiances. One U.S.-based watchmaker built a factory in American Samoa that enters the United States tariff-free. The president of the company explained that "we were able to beat the foreign competition because we are the foreign competition." In the 1980s, Ford cut its payroll by over 100,000 workers, mostly in the United States, and built its most efficient, modern plant in Mexico. Although Ford's close financial connection to Mazda (dating from the 1970s when Ford bought one-quarter of its Japanese rival) allowed Ford to reopen a Michigan factory, much of the design work for the car assembled in Michigan was done by the Japanese, and the engines were produced in Mexico. Ford has been working to produce a "world car" of one design that can avoid tariffs and be manufactured within the national boundaries of any of the several different countries in which Ford operates plants.

Some economists argue that, since the mid-1970s, the global industrial economy has become more flexible. Large companies such as IBM, General Motors, or U.S. Steel had by this period become "dinosaurs," precipitating a shift of the center of economic activity and entrepreneurialism from huge enterprises to small and medium-size companies. In many cases, however, MNCs have simply chosen to subcontract manufacturing or design work to smaller companies. In Germany and the United States, large companies generally experience the fastest growth—and have the smallest chance of going out of business. Japanese multinationals such as Mitsubishi continue to diversify product lines and establish operations in every inhabited continent. MNCs retain enormous advantages: for instance, to stay competitive in the computer or superconductor industry, companies must be able to invest $1 billion into a new product line—well beyond the capacities of most entrepreneurs.

Most MNCs are based in industrialized countries, and the vast majority of global investment and trade by these corporate giants occurs in Europe, North America, and East Asia. About 20 percent of MNC investment occurs in industrializing countries and only 2 percent in Africa. While the "lean and mean" MNCs survive in the "postindustrial" global economy, their former workers and the communities that once housed factories or offices do not fare particularly well. Whereas unemployment and poverty are highest in nonindustrialized countries, even in the United States more than 15 percent of the population lives below the official poverty line, and industrial jobs—the traditional avenue of upward mobility—have been disappearing.

Since the 1970s, the power of MNCs has grown, in relative terms, vis-à-vis the power of nation-states. As noted above, many MNCs are larger than small or medium-size countries. Even large, powerful countries such as the United States attempt to regulate MNCs only loosely. Approximately 60 percent of foreign-owned companies operating in the United States do not pay tax to the federal government. Foreign-owned MNCs often "lose" money in their U.S. subsidiaries by overcharging for parts or services, thereby avoiding taxes. Ultimately, however, governments regulate international trade, and even the largest MNCs have responded, albeit reluctantly, to the policies of industrialized countries.

See also Cartels; Deindustrialization; Entrepreneurial Spirit; Foreign Trade; Monopoly Capitalism; Postindustrial Economies

Further Reading

Barnet, Richard J., and John Cavanaugh. *Global Dreams: Imperial Corporations and the New World Order*. New York: Simon and Schuster, 1994.

Harrison, Bennett. *Lean and Mean: The Changing Landscape of Corporate Power in the Era of Flexibility*. New York: Basic Books, 1994.

NANOTECHNOLOGY

Nanotechnology involves the study and manipulation of matter at an atomic or molecular level. (A nanometer is a billionth of a meter.) The theoretical basis for nanotech goes back to 1959, and practical work began a decade later. By the early 1980s, scientists began to be able to take images of surfaces at the atomic level. By the early 1990s, nanotech-engineered catalytic materials were developed. They are used in the refining of oil and water treatment. Nanotech fibers or polymers can reduce the buildup of bacteria in facilities, thereby reducing waterborne illnesses. Nanotechnology was added to clothing so that it resisted stains, to sunscreen so that it was more effective at filtering out the sun, and to creams to enhance medicines' antimicrobial properties.

Boosters see enormous potential in the approach, from manipulating DNA to developing vastly improved polymers and drugs. Nanotech had potential applications to more efficient batteries for cars and cell phones as well as computer design. Critics point to the long history of new technologies with unanticipated consequences, like DDT. The new technology could result in new forms of pollution or create an invasive species that cannot be controlled.

As of 2011, about three to four new nanotech applications are coming out a week; there are already several hundred applications in the marketplace. The applications enhance traditional materials by making them lighter, stronger, and more energy efficient. They also can use less material since it is possible to lay down layers of film one atom thick.

This leads a few scientists to be concerned that "nanotechnology" is traditional materials science in a new marketing label. The motivation behind the relabeling is that the nanotech "brand" leads to more funding for research or higher prices for a product. In effect, a nanotech bubble could have developed that will actually impede real nanotech research.

Nanotechnology represents the continued interactions of university-based scientists, corporate research labs, and national governments to develop new technologies that continue to change the world around us.

Further Reading

National Nanotechnology Initiative website. http://www.nano.gov (accessed May 16, 2012).

This 1966 photo shows a NASA lander on the moon; this major technological achievement was part of the wider effort by the United States to beat the Soviet Union in the Cold War. (NASA)

NATIONAL AERONAUTICS AND SPACE ADMINISTRATION (NASA)

The National Aeronautics and Space Administration (NASA) was created in 1958 by the U.S. government. When the Soviet Union launched the first satellite in space in 1957, many believed the Russians' scientific and technical expertise had triumphed; the U.S. government desperately sought to counter this notion by succeeding in the space race. By 1968, NASA had landed a man on the moon. The space program helped to develop the system of satellite communications and weather prediction as well as military capabilities such as spying and attack warnings. By the 1970s, satellite communications were commercially viable, and in the 1990s, the amount of data transmitted via space continued to expand rapidly. Although many technologies spun off from NASA have proved commercially viable, military applications provided much of the political impetus for programs such as the Space Shuttle, which helped the United States develop and maintain its lead in space-based intelligence-gathering systems in the 1980s and 1990s.

See also Military-Industrial Complex

Further Reading

McCurdy, Howard E. *Inside NASA: High Technology and Organizational Change in the U.S. Space Program*. Baltimore: Johns Hopkins University Press, 1993.

NATIONAL MINERS UNION

Formed in 1856, the National Miners Union (NMU), led by Alexander MacDonald, attempted to build a national organization of coal miners in Britain. Because a previous national federation, the National Union of Miners, had been destroyed by a disastrous 1847 strike, the NMU opted for a less confrontational style. It attempted to improve workers' lives through parliamentary action rather than through strikes, and it achieved some success in the 1860s. Miners' wages had largely been stagnant since the 1840s; and in the 1870s, in part due to new levels of unionism and a boom in heavy industry, wages of miners finally improved. In the 1880s, employers counterattacked and once again succeeded in lowering wages; the NMU disappeared in that decade, supplanted by the more militant Miners Federation of Great Britain.

See also Miners' National Union; United Mine Workers (UMW)

Further Reading

Church, Roy A., and Quentin Outram. *Strikes and Solidarity: Coalfield Conflict in Britain, 1889–1966*. Cambridge: Cambridge University Press, 2002.

NATIONALISM

Nationalism and nation-states often appear to be permanent and natural, if problematic, features of world society. Yet nationalism is a relatively recent phenomenon that has been fundamentally shaped by the development of international capitalism and industrialization over the last 250 years.

Some historians argue that a sense of nationalism—an intense emotional bond shared among citizens of a country—is best understood as an "imagined community." Because the vast majority of the members of this national community will never meet each other, the bond between them (even if heartfelt) must remain for the most part abstract and "imagined." Moreover, before people can be French, Brazilian, or Japanese, the national identity must be conceptualized and articulated (or imagined) by nationalist movements, intellectuals, or the state.

By the sixteenth century, most European states were becoming more powerful, a process aided by the emerging world system. The quest for colonies and new markets placed new military and administrative demands on governments, but new sources of taxes and profits allowed central governments to build more powerful armies and bureaucracies—which strengthened their hand vis-à-vis the aristocracy. The emerging form of government could not rely on the old forms of deference and the authority of feudalism. Nationalism became an important way for these new states to legitimize themselves to their populations.

Since the sixteenth century, the rapid spread of printing presses facilitated the diffusion of ideas through books, pamphlets, and newspapers—publications that arguably reshaped the mentality of literate and even illiterate people by subtly imposing national identities and boundaries on their mental landscapes. Pamphleteers played an important role in spreading nationalist and democratic ideas during the English revolution of the mid-seventeenth century and during the American and French revolutions of the late eighteenth century. It might be more appropriate, however, to speak of a plurality of nationalisms developing in a country than of the development of a single national identity; different movements and social classes often vigorously contested the national image promoted by the government. For instance, radical revolutionaries attempted unsuccessfully to address economic inequality as well as questions of political rights and representation in the midst of the English, American, and French revolutions. The process of defining what the nation would mean and who would be a citizen required decades to resolve. Throughout the nineteenth century in Europe, Latin America, and the United States, property-less workers struggled to obtain the vote. Although poor white workers in the United States obtained the franchise in the 1830s, the question of the rights of blacks contributed to the American Civil War and was not resolved until the 1960s. Some scholars argue that racialized slavery and imperialism have shaped the boundaries of specific national identities and nationalism more generally.

Nationalism contributed to industrialization. Nation-states such as Britain or France that had had "bourgeois revolutions" led the way in creating the legal and physical infrastructure that supported the process of industrialization. At the same time, new urban workers, torn from traditional local loyalties, were often open to the solidarity of nationalism. Even states without strong parliamentary systems found nationalism to be an important aid in the industrialization process. Since the Meiji era, the Japanese government has sought to instill a nationalist sensibility that accepts the necessity of sacrifice of ordinary people to industrialize. The government was notably successful in using the education system to promote reverence for the emperor in particular, and respect for authority in general. Right-wing movements created an acutely nationalist sensibility that helped propel Japan to war with the United States. Certainly, "mass" state institutions such as the military or public schools have enabled governments to shape the national identities of its citizens.

These institutions, as well as the new forms of propaganda found in radio, film, and television, have been important features of the new nation-states that emerged in Africa and Asia as a result of decolonization in the twentieth century. African countries developed the weakest national institutions, such as schools, and the weakest identities. A weak state cannot aid industrial development, and a country without industries often lacks the wealth to support national institutions: a vicious cycle. Many African states, like the Democratic Republic of the Congo or Zimbabwe, possess a much smaller industrial base, or lower living standards, than they did at independence. Most of the world's "failed states" are in sub-Saharan Africa.

Ironically, until the 1980s, many scholars believed that in places with "stable" nation-states, such as Europe, nationalism was declining in importance. The bloody conflicts that have shaken the former Soviet Union and much of Eastern Europe have demonstrated that nationalism is still a potent force. Some of the new states, especially those farther from Western Europe, experienced declining standards of living, although all were formed on the premise that shared national identities would result in stability, democracy, and prosperity.

Since the mid-1970s, the increase of global economic insecurity has contributed to a sharp rise in nationalism even within established nation states. For instance,

British nationalism has not simply continued "naturally" from older nationalist traditions but has undergone a transformation, in part economic and in part political. The relative decline of British industry had been a trend since the late nineteenth century, but in the 1970s, deindustrialization began to result in the wholesale loss of jobs in coal mining, steel, and other manufacturing districts—causing cuts in the social services formerly provided by the welfare state. At about the same time, the press began to emphasize a "crime wave" that implicitly blamed disorder on South Asian and particularly Afro-Caribbean immigrants. The Conservative Party, led by Margaret Thatcher, successfully articulated a new set of nationalist values that stressed self-reliance (as opposed to reliance on the welfare state), the need for cooperation in industrial relations (as opposed to workers' support for unions), and the return to "traditional" values (in contrast to new immigrants).

See also Chartism; Emancipation and Reconstruction (United States); Ethnicity; Imperialism; Racism; Revolutions of 1848; State, Role of the

Further Reading

Anderson, Benedict. *Imagined Communities: Reflections on the Origins and Spread of Nationalism*. London: Verso, 1983.
Balibar, Étienne, and Immanuel Wallerstein. *Race, Nation, Class: Ambiguous Identities*. London: Routledge, Chapman and Hall, 1991.

NATIONALIZATION

Nationalization occurs when a national government assumes ownership of an industry or a sector of the economy. Advocates of nationalization believe that government can provide services more cheaply than private companies, that only governments can treat workers fairly, or that only government can provide the capital necessary for an industry to survive. Whereas mail service in the United States has been a government monopoly since the 1790s, the main movement toward the nationalization of industry began in the late nineteenth century, when unions and socialist parties agitated for government control over monopolistic industries. In 1894, a resolution in the relatively conservative American Federation of Labor called for the nationalization of the rail and utility industries—radicals had wanted all industries nationalized. The most extreme case occurred in the Soviet Union when the state seized control of the entire economy after 1928. However, most scholars view nationalization as occurring within a market economy—resulting in what some have termed "state capitalism." Many European and Latin American Social Democratic parties called for the government to assume control of key industries as a prelude to socialism.

Nationalization has often been adopted by weaker industrializing countries. Under Italy's fascist government of the 1920s and 1930s, a latecomer to industrialization, around 40 percent of the economy was nationalized. Although the government used socialistic rhetoric to justify government intervention, in practice

In 2006, the Bolivian government sought to break a pattern of neocolonialism by nationalizing the country's oil and natural gas; the banner reads "Nationalized: Property of the Bolivians." (AFP/Getty Images)

the regime sought to socialize losses and privatize profits. Beginning in the 1920s, South Africa's government ran important industries, such as railroads and steel, because private firms were unable or unwilling to assume the risk. When the white-supremacist National Party came to power in 1948, it expanded the public sector to build a planned capitalist economy that provided decent jobs for whites. The question of compensation for existing companies was often controversial. Foreign companies in Mexico had underestimated the value of their holdings to avoid taxes and were paid a "fair" price. In Eastern Europe and Cuba, assets were often seized—a point that led to problems with foreign governments such as the United States. In the case of Mexico, a leftist nationalist leader seized control of the foreign-dominated oil industry in the 1930s and used the profits to expand the country's industrialization. Although many nationalized companies were sold during the 1980s, PEMEX, the national oil company, remains an important source of revenue, jobs, and national pride for Mexicans.

The best-known case of nationalization occurred in Britain after World War II. In 1945, the British Labour government launched a major wave of nationalization that brought the coal, steel, transportation (rail, canals, and long-distance trucking), and utilities industries under government ownership. Even the Bank of England was nationalized. By 1951, the government owned 20 percent of the economy. Other European countries also turned to nationalization, often to combat the popular appeal of communist parties. For instance, France's conservative postwar government nationalized a higher proportion of the economy than did Britain.

In the postwar period, many governments assumed control of key industries and continued the process of "socializing losses and privatizing profits." In 1944, France's conservative government took over many coal companies, banks, utilities, the Renault Auto Company, and munitions. (Rail and communications had been nationalized before World War II.) These measures were taken to keep the left from nationalizing even more of the economy.

Britain's Labour Party had argued that nationalization would be the first step toward building socialism, yet many specific plans for nationalization had been formulated by the Conservative Party in the 1930s. Clause Four of the British Labour Party read "to secure for the workers by hand or by brain the full fruits of their industry and the most equitable distribution thereof that may be possible upon the basis of the common ownership of the means of production, distribution and exchange, and the best obtainable system of popular administration and control of each industry or service." Although the Conservatives raised ideological objections to nationalization, they simply continued to manage the nationalized industries when they regained power in the 1950s. Even under a Labour government, managers from private corporations directed nationalized industries, and government-owned corporations were run on the same principles as private companies. One miner complained that "the mine bosses are the same … The Coal Board in London is made up of big bosses and ex-admirals … Nationalization hasn't changed anything." Although trade union leaders also helped to direct nationalized companies, most workers believed that "they had simply become bosses."

If nationalization did not result in socialism, nationalized industries did provide the basis for an expanded welfare state. Between 1945 and 1951, the nationalized British housing industry built over a million low-cost homes for workers. The nationalized telephone and communication industries provided good, low-cost services to consumers and decent wages for their workers. Because of free health care, pensions, and other forms of social spending, workers' standards of living rose—approaching those of the lower middle class.

These improvements notwithstanding, leftist critics of British nationalization pointed out that the industries that were nationalized had ceased to be profitable and that for every dollar of compensation, which was relatively generous, the government had to spend 80 cents to improve the industries. The only industry that was profitable at the time of its nationalization, steel, was privatized in the 1950s and then renationalized in the 1970s when it had become a liability to its owners. The resultant financial drain upon the state by national industries (combined with high military spending) plunged the British economy into periodic crises that culminated in the reduction of social welfare spending.

In the 1980s, the Conservative government of Margaret Thatcher argued that the English economy needed to be weaned from "socialism" and begin the process of privatization. In what was to be the model for many countries with nationalized industries, state-run companies were sold to private companies who generally slashed payrolls, raised prices, and reduced services. The trend toward privatization accelerated in the 1980s, in part because of market forces and in part because the World Bank and the International Monetary Fund often require that countries privatize companies to receive emergency loans. A symbol of the move away from nationalization came in 1995, when the British Labour Party abandoned Clause Four of its Constitution.

See also International Monetary Fund (IMF); Labour Party (British)

Further Reading

Cochran, Ben. *Welfare Capitalism—and After*. New York: Schocken, 1984.

NEHRU, JAWAHARLAL (1889–1964)

India's first prime minister after independence, Nehru differed from the great nationalist leader Mahatma Gandhi on the subject of industrialization. Gandhi's vision had embraced an India that returned to its heritage of traditional handicrafts. He viewed Western industrialization critically, and he did not want the class divisions and exploitation he saw in the West to mar modern India. Nehru disagreed, seeing poverty as India's most urgent problem. A socialist and intellectual, Nehru advocated centralized economic planning. Under his leadership, a system of five-year plans was initiated in 1951 that called for steady growth; heavy emphasis went to agriculture, however, simply because of the burdens of population growth. Funding for industry and mining went up in the second plan, 1956–61, and production in iron, coal, and power capacity began to rise rapidly (iron ore output almost tripled, while power capacity doubled). Although he emphasized the power of his Planning Commission, Nehru did not undermine private enterprise, which in fact became more profitable under his regime. Nonetheless, Indian industrialization struggled to produce enough jobs or goods to keep ahead of population growth.

Further Reading

Tharoor, Shashi. *Nehru: A Biography*. New York: Arcade Pub., 2003.

NEOCOLONIALISM

Neocolonialism is a term applied to countries that have achieved political independence but are still economically dependent upon "metropolitan" industrialized countries. For instance, many scholars have sought to understand why most of Latin America, which was freed of Spanish rule by the 1820s, remained an impoverished provider of raw materials to Britain, the United States, and other countries. Even Argentina, which by the early twentieth century had gained one of the highest standards of living in the world through its export of meat, hides, and grain, failed to fully industrialize, and for decades following the middle of the twentieth century, most Argentineans experienced a decline in their standard of living.

The history of colonialism is crucial for "underdeveloping" neocolonial countries. In Africa, European governments sought to develop their colonies into producers of raw materials such as copper, coffee, rubber, or food products. Infrastructure projects, such as railroads, connected ports with mines or plantations and were not designed to stimulate industrialization. If peasants were unwilling to work as wage laborers, taxation policies forced people to work to earn cash. The British government sometimes imported Indian laborers to work on the African plantations. Education was generally downplayed, because clerical or skilled positions were held by Europeans.

By the time these former colonies achieved independence, their position in the world system of trade had been established. Most postcolonial governments found it difficult to escape the colonial legacy. If they sought to industrialize, they needed to acquire technical skills, raw materials, and machinery from industrialized countries, which necessitated a greater dependence upon the exports of raw materials. During the 1960s and 1970s, newly decolonized countries in Africa and Asia as well as Latin America found ready sources of capital from private banks or development banks such as the World Bank. However, prices of raw materials plummeted before industrialization efforts could take off, and debtor nations found it difficult to make their loan payments. Short-term loans allowed countries to repay their earlier loans, but banks have increasingly forced governments to impose "structural adjustments" (cuts in the minimum wage, and food and education subsidies) to receive additional loans.

See also Decolonization; Development Theory; Finance Capital; Immigration and Migration; Imperialism; Perónism; World Systems Theory

Further Reading

Frank, André Gunder. *Latin America: Underdevelopment or Revolution*. New York: Monthly Review, 1970.
Rodney, Walter. *How Europe Underdeveloped Africa*. Washington, DC: Howard University Press, 1981.

NEOLIBERALISM, OR ECONOMIC LIBERALISM

Neoliberalism is the belief that lightly regulated markets generate high levels of growth and that government interventions in the market to advance social goals (a cleaner environment, higher wages, etc.) are generally expensive and counterproductive. Neoliberalism is a simplified version of the classic liberalism of the eighteenth and nineteenth centuries.

In the first century of the Industrial Revolution, liberals embraced the view that markets and individuals should be freed of government regulation, which tended to stifle freedom and efficiency. Economists like Adam Smith broke with the economic orthodoxy of mercantilism, which saw wealth in terms of how much hard currency a country could amass. Consequently, liberals believed England should

Milton Friedman did much to reinvigorate the advocates of free-market economics in the 1970s and 1980s from the University of Chicago. (University of Chicago News Office)

not try to protect local corn farmers but import cheaper grain. Consumers would benefit from lower prices and farmers would ultimately grow profitable crops that required no protection. Overall, the country would benefit from more efficient allocation of capital and labor. Free markets would allow countries to efficiently organize trade, which would have the result of raising the living standards and the power of the country.

Promoting individual freedom throughout society was also an important ideal. Contracts freely arrived at between individuals allowed each person to pursue his or her own self-interest. Consequently, liberals opposed slavery and aristocratic privilege. Liberals also opposed guilds, unions, and most forms of government regulation of workers' hours or wages, as these created new kinds of monopoly power. Liberals and liberal ideas were important in the American and French revolutions, as well as in their European and Latin American counterparts in the nineteenth century.

Liberal economic ideas gained dominance over the course of the nineteenth century, helping to erode the institutions of slavery and serfdom. Early in the century, the English navy helped suppress the international slave trade. England promoted the ideal of free trade, for instance, urging China to allow other countries access to its markets. Chinese products were high quality, and the only good the British could sell the Chinese was Indian-made opium. Cynics used this as an example of how the British "ruled the waves and waived the rules."

Liberal principles dominated polices in the United States. In the early nineteenth century, monopolies were discouraged because of the long history of colonial dissatisfaction with British companies such as the East India Tea Company. Until the advent of the railroad boom, laws helped keep companies relatively small, because of fears that large companies would exert undue influence on the political system. In the wake of the U.S. Civil War, the United States abolished slavery and adopted universal suffrage for men. With the United States as an example, European liberals and socialists agitated for widening the voting rights of poor men and won gains in the late nineteenth and early twentieth centuries. Expanding democratic rights proved infectious; voting rights for poor men opened the doors to women's rights over their own property and person, including the right to vote. Liberal democracy and free markets were spreading as ideals and practice spread throughout Western countries.

Liberalism also had an effect on Latin America. In the early nineteenth century, most of Hispanic Latin America rid themselves of rule by the Spanish. Many political elites sought to emulate countries like the United States and embraced liberal ideals such as popular sovereignty, open markets, and a rational worldview unencumbered by clerical influence. But traditional or quasi-feudal institutions (like slavery, debt peonage, communal land ownership, and the Catholic Church) were far stronger than in the United States. Peasants, most of indigenous background, generally opposed liberal reforms such as breaking up communal land holdings. The role of the Catholic Church was stronger than its counterparts in the United States, as much of the poor and elite, for different reasons, opposed anticlerical reforms. Politics split between Latin American liberals and conservatives, who battled it out for control of government, sometimes by force of arms.

In the United States, governments relaxed antimonopolist laws to allow capital-intensive industries, such as railroads, to emerge. But the reforms were limited, at first. Corporations enjoyed limited liability (investors' liability was limited to the amount of money they invested in the company), but corporations were able to go into only specific activities. A canal company could not own a bridge, bank, or shoe factory. By the Civil War, those limits were giving way, and after it, they collapsed entirely. Delaware relaxed its laws, allowing corporations to establish themselves quickly and with minimal oversight. By 1886, the U.S. Supreme Court ruled that corporations enjoyed the rights of "personhood" as defined by the Fourteenth Amendment to the Constitution. Corporations had the rights to property and free speech, including participation in the political process. The ability of states to regulate corporations was greatly curtailed.

Large corporations and banks began to operate as trusts, limiting competition, raising prices, and stifling technological innovation. Laws designed to limit corporate power often faltered. The 1887 law that created the Interstate Commerce Commission (ICC) was designed to regulate railroads, but the ICC was quickly "captured" by the industry it was meant to regulate. The Sherman Antitrust Act of 1890 was used initially against labor unions, although that began to change under President Theodore Roosevelt.

The rise of industrial corporations caused a shift in liberal thinking. Liberals began to use government as an instrument of reform. In the 1920s, English liberals created unemployment insurance ("the dole"), which addressed a long-standing problem that the market did not address. In part, liberals simply expanded the definition of "public goods." Adam Smith believed that government should play a role in building canals, schools, and bridges. In the face of a prolonged depression and ascendant totalitarian regimes in Germany and Russia, liberal democracies sought ways to put their citizens back to work without destroying free enterprise. For instance, the New Deal in the United States regulated banks but never seriously considered nationalizing them. New Deal regulations ensured that individual deposits were insured, and government insured banks against losses on loans to home owners as long as bankers followed government guidelines. The government limited the hours of work, abolishing child labor and establishing the norm of a 40-hour week, and established a minimum wage for industrial workers. So while the New Deal broke with laissez-faire orthodoxy, it operated on liberal assumptions that private enterprise remains the center of the economy.

In the postwar period, all of the liberal democracies with industrial economies operated on welfare-state principles. What was a public good expanded. Labour governments in the UK nationalized industries, such as coal, steel, and railroads. More conservative governments in France went further. European countries began or expanded public pensions or health insurance. The United States provided veterans with benefits that helped them to buy a house. The GI Bill also paid their tuition to university in addition to a stipend. Public universities expanded to absorb them. Home ownership and higher education had become public goods. During this period, living standards rose, and most accepted the role that government played.

There were discontents. Conservative thinkers and politicians warned that abandoning the ideals of limited government was akin to communism. In the 1930s, former president Herbert Hoover warned that the New Deal was unprecedented in the history of the republic and concentrated power into the hands of a few government bureaucrats rather than in the hands of millions of businessmen and consumers. Intellectuals such as Milton Friedman and Friedrich von Hayek developed critiques of the welfare state as simultaneously inefficient and coercive. Initially, such critiques made little headway as Keynesian economics and the welfare state were widely seen to have worked. For instance, even a relatively conservative president like Dwight Eisenhower raised the minimum wage.

By the 1960s, conservatives became better organized. Ronald Reagan emerged as a spokesman, first for General Electric, then for conservative causes. He attacked Medicare as socialized medicine. By the late 1960s, southern whites defected from the Democratic Party. Also critical to building political support for neoliberalism was the era of stagflation. As energy prices rose after 1973, inflation spiked, as did a prolonged recession. Keynesian remedies seemed to have little effect. If governments increased spending, then inflation rose, but the economy remained anemic. If the government cut spending and raised interest rates, inflation continued, and the economy worsened. Most European countries muddled through, but the Anglo-American world went a different way.

By 1981, Ronald Reagan was president and Margaret Thatcher the prime minister of the United Kingdom. Each politician moved his and her country in a more conservative direction, and each helped move neoliberal ideas into the mainstream.

The most important ideas were that government was inherently inefficient and controlled by elites. The free market was both efficient and democratic; it allowed individuals control over their lives, and could resolve social problems, such as racism, on its own. Consequently, governments should deregulate businesses and privatize what they owned. The entrepreneur was praised for innovation and risk taking, the consumers for their ability to choose for themselves how to spend their money.

In the United States, stagflation was beat by raising interest rates to punishingly high levels; many industries collapsed, taking their unions with them. Thatcher and Reagan engineered large tax cuts, arguing that they would pay for themselves. They did not, but the cuts proved politically popular. Reagan also increased military spending. In both Britain and the United States, the government helped undermine unions, which kept wages low. In the United States, the first two years of Reagan's presidency saw a deep recession; but when the economy began to recover, stimulated by enormous sums of borrowed money, it did so on a new basis. Heavy industry was in decline; finance and high technology (often with military applications) became the center of the new "service," or postindustrial, economy. Public debt increased, but the public did not seem to care, as the economies grew, and with it, jobs.

In 1981, Reagan observed that "government is not the solution, government is the problem." Even Democratic presidents, such as Bill Clinton, worked within this framework, declaring in 1996 that "the era of big government is over." Conservatives had long criticized the welfare state for borrowing money and for discouraging the poor from working. The new conservatives also relied on borrowed money, which financed tax cuts. In 2000, when George W. Bush ran for president, he argued that a new round of tax cuts would revive growth and be democratic; the result was an expansion of debt and anemic job growth.

The neoliberal template was exported to many countries after the 1980s through the International Monetary Fund and the World Bank. Milton Friedman trained numerous economists at the University of Chicago, and the "Chicago school" was taken around the world. Governments that needed loans, or conservative governments like the military dictatorships of Chile and Argentina, turned to the "boys from Chicago." Markets were deregulated. Public spending on education, health, and social welfare was reduced. Chile privatized its pension system. Laws supporting unions were rewritten or abolished.

The results were mixed. The process of "stabilization," or structural adjustment, was painful. Wages declined. Often, so did traditional industries, especially if they relied on public support or they supplied the domestic market. If government owned industries—banks, hospitals, etc.—they were privatized. Economic inequality rose, although, ultimately, so did export-oriented industries. Unions and the public often protested, although if it was a military government, it had little effect. In Chile, the financial sector grew, as companies offered everyone advice on how to invest pension money. The utopian promises of private investment proved just that, and after almost 30 years, the new system was reformed because too many individuals were left with nothing. In the case of Chile, the country has more export industries and did enjoy a long period of growth. In the case of Argentina, neoliberalism resulted in a boom that then collapsed in the late 1990s. Government spending was more sustainable, although frequently, payments to the IMF, the World Bank, or foreign banks became a major ongoing expense.

The neoliberal model was carried out in a wide variety of countries. In the case of the former Soviet Union, the "shock therapy" approach proved particularly disastrous. The old communist elite, or criminal gangs, were able to buy up public assets for a fraction of their real price. On the other hand, individuals could own their own apartments. In some cases, however, gangs killed elderly home owners to obtain their flats. Incomes fell. Life expectancy fell. Birthrates fell. Female employment fell, as men argued that they should be able to support their families. After a lengthy period of economic free fall, Russia began to recover. But it was a vastly different country than it had been before.

In China, communists engaged in some aspects of neoliberal reforms. Individuals were allowed to get rich; industries that could export goods were encouraged; public subsidies for many industries were decreased; the "iron rice bowl" (lifetime employment) was broken. Yet the Chinese did not reregulate or privatize. Government continues to provide macroeconomic guidance, sometimes identifying key industries that need to be built. The model of government involvement in the economy, to encourage the free market or specific companies or industries, is pervasive.

After 1996, the newly democratic South African government engaged in neoliberal policies, much to the surprise of its mostly white opponents, as well as the black unions and the Communist Party, both of which had supported the election of the African National Congress (ANC). The ANC feared that if it engaged in welfare state policies, it would end up like many newly independent black countries, which experienced real growth in education and health gains but were not able to sustain the spending because no new private industries emerged to absorb a more educated workforce. The ANC encouraged former state-owned companies, and there were many in South Africa, to shed workers. Private job growth proved anemic, although the government quickly put itself on a solid footing, paying off loans that the old apartheid government had taken to fight the ANC. The ANC did spend more money on social programs, extending electricity and water systems into impoverished black townships that never had the benefits of industrial society. Paying for water and electricity proved difficult, and savage battles erupted between blacks in townships and black public and private police over shutoffs. By the mid-2000s, roughly half the country survived on various low-level public payments such as pensions for the elderly, the poor, and for children. The government has stable economics, but the country is actually more unequal than it was under a minority, white-run government.

Further Reading

Harvey, David. *A Brief History of Neoliberalism*. New York: Oxford University Press, 2005.

NEURASTHENIA

This disease was defined and widely popularized in the United States by such doctors as S. Weir Mitchell in the 1880s and 1890s. Its symptoms ranged from fatigue to various psychosomatic complaints. Doctors attributed the causes of this disease, particularly in middle-class men, to the pace of industrial life: the ambitions and exertions of businessmen were unnatural, though socially useful. (Other groups might develop neurasthenia for other reasons: neurasthenic middle-class women, for example, were blamed for idleness; working-class male sufferers for debauchery.) Neurasthenia was an early term for the symptoms later known as nervous breakdown, stress, or "burnout." Whether fully real or partly imaginary, it was a disease closely connected to industrialization. Treatment consisted of healthy exercise and recreation, including vacations, and it provided a good formula to justify leisure for groups dominated by the industrial work ethic. Neurasthenia disappeared as a label by 1900, but the basic diagnostic category persisted in defining tensions stemming from industrial life.

See also Work Ethic

Further Reading

Gosling, F. *Before Freud: Neurasthenia and the American Medical Community*. Urbana: University of Illinois Press, 1988.

NEW DEAL

The New Deal is generally understood to be the period between 1933 and 1938, when President Franklin D. Roosevelt created the institutional foundations of the U.S. welfare state. Roosevelt was elected in the midst of the Great Depression of the 1930s, when millions were unemployed and both agriculture and industry faced crises of overproduction and underconsumption. Many historians agree that Roosevelt saved industrial capitalism from itself by alleviating the protracted social and economic crisis. To stimulate an economic recovery, Roosevelt involved the federal government in the economy (and in social concerns) to the largest extent since the Reconstruction after the Civil War. Although many of the particular programs were only partially successful, the New Deal signaled an end to the laissez-faire philosophy that had dominated federal peacetime policy.

During the first phase of the New Deal, Roosevelt undertook cautious economic reforms. The new president inherited an enormous crisis in the banking system. Public confidence in the banking system as a whole was falling because many banks could not allow depositors to withdraw their money due to ill-chosen speculative investments made by bankers during the 1920s. Rather than nationalize the banking system, as some observers demanded, Roosevelt called for a "bank holiday" and then passed a series of laws to put the private banking system on surer footing. New laws regulated banks' financial policies (requiring certain ratios of reserves to loans, for instance). Roosevelt also created the Federal Deposit Insurance Corporation (FDIC) to ensure that even if banks did fail, depositors would not lose their savings. The banking system recovered and confidence in the economy slowly grew.

Part of Roosevelt's National Industrial Recovery Act (NIRA) recognized workers' right to organize unions—marking an important change in the relationship between the federal government and the labor movement. Previous administrations had offered unions little support, and the dominant union federation (the American Federation of Labor) had come to oppose any alliance with government. Following NIRA, however, there was an upsurge in union organizing that ultimately resulted in the Congress of Industrial Organizations (CIO). The CIO unions actively lobbied the government to help poor people by intervening to strengthen labor laws, build low-cost housing, and create social security measures for the indigent, unemployed, and elderly.

The New Deal also offered subsidies to industry and agriculture. NIRA encouraged industries that raised wages to set higher prices to cause a mild inflationary cycle and stimulate the economy. Farmers were given price supports and paid to reduce acreage—a policy that drove many sharecroppers off the land. (Roosevelt did not want to alienate conservative southern Democrats by supporting black and white sharecroppers.) NIRA was eventually declared unconstitutional, but it formed the basis for subsequent programs. The New Deal stimulated new welfare measures to aid the elderly and unemployed; the Social Security system, initially intended to alleviate poverty among older Americans, ultimately encouraged mass retirements. In other areas, New Deal welfare measures were more limited than similar measures in European welfare states.

Although the New Deal helped stimulate the economy, the Depression truly ended only when the government began to prepare for World War II. The government not only placed military orders with business—in many cases, the government actually built the factories and allowed corporations to manage them. As the secretary of war remarked, "If you . . . go to war . . . in a capitalist country, you have to let business make money out of the process or business won't work." (The policy of "military Keynesianism" would continue to dominate economic planning during the Cold War.)

Because many of the government's subsequent social and economic policies originated in the New Deal or were inspired by it, historians generally argue that the New Deal actually extended into the 1970s. In the 1960s, for instance, government provided health insurance for all citizens over the age of 65. During the next decade, the political coalition of city dwellers, farmers, and white and black workers began to unravel, and the federal government's commitment to social programs, such as aid to cities or the poor, began to be sacrificed.

See also Industrial Unions; Social Insurance

Further Reading

Cohen, Lizabeth. *Making a New Deal: Industrial Workers in Chicago, 1919–1939*. New York: Cambridge University Press, 1990.

Hawley, Ellis W. *The New Deal and the Problem of Monopoly*. Princeton, NJ: Princeton University Press, 1966.

NEW ECONOMIC POLICY (NEP)

The Soviet Union was economically devastated by the political, social, and economic chaos created by World War I, the 1917 Russian Revolution, and the resulting civil war. In 1921, production of agricultural and industrial goods was a fraction of what it had been in 1913—depending on the industry, between 5 and 20 percent of 1913 levels. By contrast, industrial production across Europe was generally one-third to one-half its prewar levels.

During the civil war (1917–21), "war communism" was instituted and market controls abandoned; that is, industrial production was controlled by the government and agricultural goods were frequently requisitioned by Red Army units. Designed by Lenin to spur recovery, the New Economic Policy (NEP) allowed heavy industry, foreign trade, and banking to remain state monopolies, but private producers, particularly peasants, gained greater freedom to produce and sell agricultural and consumer goods. During the NEP period (1921–28), the Soviet Union also experienced social and cultural experimentation and a wide range of political debate among communists over how to build an industrialized socialist society.

Under the NEP, the state favored agricultural production and light industry—particularly those products directed toward agricultural use. As a result, peasants did produce and market more food, although severe drought in the Volga region caused famine, and international relief was allowed into the Soviet Union for the first and only time. By 1923, the price of agricultural goods had fallen by one-third against industrial goods, and planners as well as city dwellers worried that peasants would withhold grain in protest.

Many party officials were disturbed by the promarket attitudes of peasants, retailers, and small manufacturers—particularly the ostentatious wealth of the "nepmen" such as Armand Hammer. Although industrial production reached pre–World War I levels in 1926, unemployment among workers remained high, and some critics of the NEP argued that if industry was to be developed, the manufacturing sector would have to receive greater subsidies. Furthermore, many Bolsheviks remained skeptical of strengthening the peasantry, the social group with the weakest commitment to the revolution, and these Bolsheviks argued that if socialism was to be built, then workers, the chief supporters of the revolution, would have to see improvements in their standard of living. The NEP ended in 1928, when Stalin extended his dictatorial control over the Bolshevik party. That same year, Stalin instituted the first five-year plan, which ended the experiment with a "mixed economy" in favor of a state-run economy.

Further Reading

Fitzpatrick, Sheila, Alexander Rabinowitch, and Richard Stites, eds. *Russia in the Era of NEP*. Bloomington: University of Indiana Press, 1991.

NONGOVERNMENTAL ORGANIZATIONS (NGOs)

International nongovernmental organizations (NGOs) seek a variety of goals in various nations of the world, particularly seeking to define and enforce certain standards of behavior on governments and businesses. Many NGOs draw strength, memberships, and contributions throughout the world. Local groups coordinate with international NGOs to call attention to what they claim are abuses of various sorts.

The first international NGOs began to emerge in the nineteenth century, around campaigns to end slavery or protect women's rights. By the twentieth century, the numbers began to increase gradually, and key groups worked with formal international entities such as the League of Nations or the International Labor Office. By 1960, about 2000 international NGOs existed, but then the rate of formation accelerated greatly. There were nearly 4,000 by the 1980s, and even greater growth has occurred since that time.

Some of the most famous international NGOs, like Amnesty International, focus mainly on political issues, such as the treatment of prisoners or abuses of women. A number, however, deal with economic and labor issues. Environmental NGOs emerged in the late 1960s. An early organization, Friends of the Earth, boasted 700,000 members internationally by the 1990s and worked to advocate greater environmental regulation and call attention to violations of local or international standards. A more activist environmental group, Greenpeace, had offices in over 30 countries by the 1990s; it pressed multinational corporations or subsidiaries

NGOs help to shape world opinion; here members of Amnesty International protest U.S. treatment of prisoners at Guantanamo Bay. (Shutterstock)

operating in places like Indonesia, where government oversight was sometimes limited, to curb pollution and end other abuses. A number of other international NGOs focused on working conditions. The Dutch-based Clean Clothes Campaign, for example, set up branches in all major countries to fight against sweatshop practices by publicizing abuses and enlisting millions of signatories on petition campaigns to press prominent companies to address excessively low pay, forced overtime, and lack of safety. Many NGOs also struggled to defend trade unions and prevent retaliation against local labor leaders. Finally, a number of international NGOs worked on behalf of consumers by trying to assure product quality.

International NGOs did not revolutionize the industrial workplace by the later twentieth century. A number of governments kept them out, entirely or in part; this was the case, for example, in China. Small, local companies (sometimes working as agents for larger corporations) might be largely immune to pressure. But there were many successes as well. International NGOs were sometimes able to induce national governments to take action against flagrant environmental or labor abuse. A key tactic, particularly against well-known companies like Nike or Apple, was to combine wide publicity of dubious labor practices with encouragements to consumers in the affluent societies to boycott products of offenders. When stung, many corporations did pledge to improve working conditions in their branches in places like Vietnam, and while some promises were doubtless hollow, there were some real reforms. Sometimes the threat of international NGO attention alone could constrain questionable behavior. The same applied to environmental issues.

The rise of international NGOs was an important aspect of globalization in the world economy and served as at least a partial counterweight to the growing power of some of the rising multinational corporations.

Further Reading

Guha, Ramachandra. *Environmentalism: A Global History*. New York: Longman, 2000.

Hilton, Matthew. *Prosperity for All: Consumer Activism in an Era of Globalization*. Ithaca, NY: Cornell University Press, 2009.

Mazlish, Bruce. *The New Global History*. New York: Routledge, 2006.

Stearns, Peter N. *Global Outrage: The Origins and Impact of World Opinion from the 1780s to the 21st Century*. Oxford: Oneworld Publications, 2005.

O

OIL

Although petroleum was used in small quantities for lubrication, medicine, and lighting before the nineteenth century, industrialization helped to transform the quantity of oil available and the way it was used. The first commercial drilling for petroleum was done in 1859 in Pennsylvania. The industry relied heavily on science: even the initial refining of oil into kerosene in the 1860s relied on the research of university-trained chemists. The transportation of oil via pipelines clearly relied on the resources that other industrial fields had made possible. In the form of kerosene, oil quickly displaced other sources of artificial lighting, such as whale oil and coal gas. Cheap kerosene helped to lengthen the amount of time that ordinary people had for reading or working. Oil production quickly became a global phenomenon; the Russian oil fields of Baku quickly emerged by the 1890s as a source of oil for Europe, and the oil fields in East Asia and the Middle East were developed by the 1920s. By this point, oil was displacing coal as the staple fuel of industrial societies. Oil was vital to the Allied victory in World War I; one British general observed that they had "floated to victory on a wave of oil." In the twentieth century, oil became a fuel for automobiles and industry, and chemists helped to create many new products, such as plastics, and to transform old ones, such as textiles.

See also Energy; Rockefeller, John D.; Synthetic Fabrics

Further Reading

Yergin, Daniel. *The Prize: The Epic Conquest for Oil, Money and Power*. New York: Simon and Schuster, 1991.

OPEN HEARTH

The open hearth is a furnace that converts pig iron into steel. The iron is heated to extremely high temperatures, in large part by using special bricks that reflect heat back into the furnace. The open hearth produced steel more quickly and in larger batches than the Bessemer converter, although, like the Bessemer, the open hearth was also developed to circumvent the labor of puddlers, the highly paid workers who had stirred molten iron to remove impurities. Perfected by Charles and William Siemens in the 1860s and 1870s, the open hearth spread widely in the 1880s, when it was adapted to use cheaper grades of iron. Ironically, the open hearth created a new class of highly skilled workers, although because employers controlled the pace of technological change, open-hearth workers never developed the kind of workplace autonomy that puddlers had enjoyed. From 1900 until the 1950s, most steel in the world was produced in open hearths.

After World War II, new processes made steel faster and cheaper, although many U.S. firms operated their open hearths until the 1980s. The open hearth is an example of how industrialists accelerated technological change to expand production and to gain greater control over the workplace. The overreliance of American firms on the open hearth in recent decades suggests that eschewing technological innovation is dangerous in a global system of competitive capitalism.

See also Bessemer, Henry

Further Reading

Krause, Paul. *The Battle for Homestead, 1880–1892: Politics, Culture, and Steel*. Pittsburgh, PA: University of Pittsburgh Press, 1992.

OUTSOURCING

Outsourcing occurs when governments, companies, or other organizations hire contractors to provide a service that used to be done by workers employed by the organization. Cost, security, the need to obtain specialized equipment or expertise, or ideology can be reasons to outsource. Throughout the twentieth century, big factories had workers who repaired equipment, moved or rigged machinery, or did

Outsourcing shifted industrial production throughout the world; this photo shows the inside of a Chinese factory assembling electronics. (Hugo Maes)

electrical work. But there were jobs that were too big or too complex, and in those cases, work was done by outside contractors.

Contractors can reduce costs because those workers possess specialized knowledge, and/or are not eligible for pensions or benefits. They might also make employees question their job security, which some managers can find advantageous. In the South African steel industry, the majority of traditional employees have been laid off, although most have returned as contractors. Some former workers, especially whites, make more money; others, especially blacks, make a great deal less. But the net result has been to reduce labor costs for the industry.

Since the 1980s, many governments have outsourced work to save money, although in many instances, contractors charge more than government employees. An extreme example of this principle occurred in Iraq after 2003, when it was occupied by the United States and its allies. The U.S. military had contracted much of its supply and logistical support to private contractors, notably Halliburton, which had a long history in this area. Private security firms were also used extensively. Veterans of Special Forces could make 10 times the money they made for the government if they worked for private security firms such as Blackwater. Private contractors were also involved in interrogation of prisoners. In this instance, outsourcing substantially raised costs.

Further Reading
Klein, Naomi. *The Shock Doctrine: The Rise of Disaster Capitalism.* New York: Henry Holt, 2007.

OWEN, ROBERT (1771–1858)
Owen was a prominent cotton manufacturer who made a great deal of money in the early stages of the British factory system. A paternalist, he also sought to better his workers through factory schools and other measures. Troubled by growing class divisions and worker poverty, Owen turned, in the 1820s, to a variety of reform movements. He formulated an elaborate plan for social reorganization on a cooperative basis, whereby communities would organize work so that all people could benefit from "the increase of scientific productive power." His cooperative vision inspired a number of people, particularly artisans, to form utopian producer cooperatives. A number of these cooperatives were set up in the United States, such as the community in New Harmony, Indiana. In Britain, opposition to his vision led Owen to support direct working-class organization, and he helped form one of the first serious trade union movements during the 1820s.

Textile workers formed a Grand Central Union in 1829, and then a wider variety of union movements joined the Grand National Consolidated Trades Union of 1834, backed by Owen. It promoted Owen's cooperative goals but also talked of a general strike to win an eight-hour day. Owen believed that much shorter working time, given the power of modern industry, would easily suffice to "saturate the world with wealth." Employers resisted this new union with lockouts before any strike could be attempted, and it collapsed. Owen stands as a major representative of utopian socialism and early worker organization, but he is also a symbol of the troubled conscience that industrialization could induce in some of its beneficiaries.

See also Cooperatives

Further Reading

Crouzet, François. *The First Industrialists: The Problem of Origins.* New York: Cambridge University Press, 1985.

P

PACIFIC RIM

In the 1970s and 1980s, the rapid industrial growth of East Asian countries inspired some scholars to define the Pacific Rim, or countries that border the Pacific, as having replaced the Atlantic seaboard as the most important area of world trade. In the 1980s, the U.S. trade deficit with Japan increased from $14 billion to over $50 billion before declining by about one-fourth—a fact that affects the increasing amount of U.S. trade with Asia. Furthermore, cross-Pacific investment is an important aspect of corporate restructuring in both Japan and the United States and is particularly significant in Mexican and Latin American industrialization efforts.

Japan had long been an industrial nation, but the industrialization of the four "little dragons" (South Korea, Singapore, Taiwan, and Hong Kong) largely occurred after 1945. In part, the success of the little dragons was due to the Cold War policies of the United States, which extended generous financial and technological aid to these countries and eased tariffs for their exports. Military spending in the region was another boost to their economies; for instance, as late as 1960, about 10 percent of Japan's GNP came from military spending by the United States. These Asian countries all followed policies that encouraged the creation of low-wage, highly skilled workforces, and they used the state to direct resources toward companies that could export products onto the world market. Culturally, they all (like Japan) shared a Confucian heritage that encouraged cooperation and discipline. Until the late 1980s, Pacific Rim countries had authoritarian governments that limited workers' protest, and some maintain an authoritarian character to this day. Though the environmental costs have been high, and unions have been crushed, Pacific Rim countries have succeeded in building industrial economies that have dramatically raised the standard of living for most of their citizens.

The little dragons now face pressure from other Asian countries that seek to replicate their success by offering employers access to disciplined, low-wage workers. Beginning in 1978, China began to emphasize the role of the market in aiding its long-standing efforts to industrialize. The government dropped its barriers to foreign investment, and many employers from Europe, the United States, and particularly Japan and the little dragons have helped turn China, with over 100 million industrial workers, into the world's fastest-growing economy. Many of the abandoned steel mills in the United States have been shipped to China to supply its economy with metal. Chinese leaders are hoping that its industrialization effort will replicate the success of other Asian countries. Competition also increased from

Malaysia, Indonesia, and Thailand, which export to more industrialized parts of the Pacific Rim.

See also Deindustrialization; Maquiladoras

Further Reading

Aikman, David. *Pacific Rim: Area of Change, Area of Opportunity*. Boston: Little, Brown, 1986.
Thompson, Roger C. *The Pacific Basin since 1945*. London: Longman, 1994.

PANAMA CANAL

Construction of a canal to connect the Atlantic and Pacific oceans was begun by a French company in 1881, but the company soon went bankrupt. In 1903, President Theodore Roosevelt, who recognized the advantages of a Panamanian canal to international trade and to the U.S. Navy, helped to instigate a revolt in the then Colombian district of Panama. Roosevelt's administration quickly recognized the new regime, which in turn leased the United States a 10-mile wide strip of land for a canal that would be subject to U.S. sovereignty. Construction began in 1906 under the command of the U.S. military and was completed in 1914. The canal itself was a marvel of engineering. Entire mills in Pittsburgh were engaged in constructing components for its series of locks. Mechanized earth-moving equipment and modern medicines (to counteract malaria and yellow fever) were essential to completing the project. The canal symbolized the military and diplomatic power of industrialized nations over less industrialized countries and the increasing importance of oceanic trade; it also indicates the growing role that governments have played in developing crucial infrastructure projects.

See also Erie Canal; State, Role of the

Further Reading

McCullough, David. *The Path between the Seas: The Creation of the Panama Canal, 1870–1914*. New York: Simon and Schuster, 1977.

PARK CHUNG HEE (1917–79)

Park Chung Hee was the ruler of South Korea from 1961 until his assassination in 1979. Park came to power through a military revolt, and under his authoritarian rule, Korea became an industrial power. Park liked to think of his regime as a Korean version of the Meiji regime, whose reforms helped make Japan into an industrial giant. Under Park, companies that helped the government meet its five-year plans were subsidized. Unlike many military rulers, Park took pains to make sure that subsidized companies were economically efficient; companies were encouraged to invest and discouraged from expatriating profits abroad or into nonproductive assets. Park ignored parliamentary forms of government, such as

Park Chung Hee was president of South Korea, helping to usher in dramatic economic growth. (UPI/Bettmann/Corbis)

elections, but the U.S. government tolerated him because he was a committed anticommunist.

See also Rhee, Syngman

Further Reading

Amsden, Alice. *Asia's Next Giant: South Korea and Late Industrialization.* New York: Oxford University Press, 1989.

PATENTS

Patents are government-backed grants of exclusive use to inventors of new devices, designed to allow inventors a period of exploitation before others can legally use the devices. Patent owners can of course license to others. The idea is to provide a clear incentive to invent; if others could copy right away, the inventor would gain little advantage from his or her creative effort.

Modern patent law began in England in 1624, with the Statute of Monopolies. The law was passed at a time when royal power was under attack as part of a parliamentary effort to limit the king's right to sell special privileges to sell or manufacture. The law made an exception, however, for "the sole working" of "any manner of new manufactures" to the "first inventor and inventors of such manufactures."

Various court interpretations progressively refined this meaning of patent law. The patent system was criticized by manufacturers, who wanted the free use of inventions, but the system survived and became the model for patent law in many other countries, including the United States. France, for example, created new Patent Laws in 1791 as part of the revolution. Patent rights have a definite term of years, although they can be renewed; they are not designed to keep an invention from general use forever. Almost certainly, patent law helped spur the huge series of inventions in Britain in the eighteenth century, even though inventors did not always in fact profit from their work. Patent law also supported the capitalist system underlying most industrial revolutions.

Patents remain an important consideration for companies involved in manufacturing. Some high-tech companies have perfected the dark legal arts of invoking patent infringement, which makes technological innovation more expensive. Some companies, such as IBM, have profited enormously from their deep source of patents, even as their product lines have shrunken in size.

Further Reading

Adams, John N. "History of the Patent System." In *Patent Law and Theory: A Handbook of Contemporary Research*, edited by Thoshiko Takenaka, 101–31. Northampton, MA: Edward Elgar, 2008.

Derry, Kingston, and T. I. Williams. *A Short History of Technology*. Oxford: Oxford University Press, 1961.

PATERNALISM

Paternalism is an ideology that views employers and employees as members of the same "family," guided by the fatherly employers. Prior to the Industrial Revolution, much economic production did occur in the homes of artisans who assumed the role of both father and employer to their apprentices. However, many artisans abused and exploited their charges, and the abandonment of the artisanal guild system throughout the late eighteenth and early nineteenth centuries freed many journeymen from their onerous obligations, allowing them to find jobs earlier in life and thereby control more of their own work and home life. In the southern United States, slave owners espoused an ideology of paternalism, arguing that slaves were part of their family. Most freed slaves desired to reunite their own families and wanted little to do with their old "family," although some freedmen sought to use the ideology of paternalism to their advantage to obtain access to land or credit.

Paternalistic employers try to show that not all their decisions are based on market forces alone but that they care for the workers as individuals, take interest in their personal lives, and even provide housing and medical care. In the early nineteenth century, mill owners in Lowell, Massachusetts, found themselves obliged to adopt a paternalistic attitude to remain attractive to laborers in their new textile mills, many of whom were women from New England farms. The mills provided housing for the women and strictly regulated their time, requiring them to pray and attend educational courses because it was understood that, for them, wage labor was a temporary activity before becoming wives to farmers or artisans.

Textile mill owners sought to use paternalism to compensate for low wages—and to keep unions out of the mills. Workers who engaged in strikes could be evicted from company housing and denied access to the company store or doctor, which in rural areas were the only available facilities. Metallurgical companies in France and Germany used paternalistic devices such as company housing to benefit valuable workers, reduce wage levels, and expand employers' control over workers' private lives.

Paternalism has been a halfway house between preindustrial and industrial work relations, at the same time functioning as a coercive and "generous" way to manage a modern workforce. Steel companies in the United States engaged in "corporate welfare" in the 1910s and 1920s, offering skilled workers housing subsidies and opportunities to buy stock. Similar policies were followed by Tata, the Indian steel and auto firm. Union movements typically battled paternalism while trying to shift company spending to straightforward benefit programs such as pensions. Even after the U.S. steel industry was unionized, companies continued to hire the family members of "good" employees, offering a powerful incentive to work hard. In one case, eight members of one family worked at the same mill. Japanese companies have also used the ideology and practice of paternalism to encourage employees' loyalty to their corporations. Whereas some employees obtain lifetime employment, those who engage in strikes or refuse to transfer to a new factory can be summarily fired.

Further Reading

Dublin, Thomas. *Women at Work: The Transformation of Work and Community in Lowell, Massachusetts, 1826–1860*. New York: Columbia University Press, 1979.

PEASANTRY

Peasants are subsistence farmers whose relationship to the cash economy is limited either by choice or by lack of alternatives. The relationship of peasants to industrialization is important, if indirect. Despite a characteristic cautiousness, peasants often innovate, using new methods to increase food production for sale to urban markets or taking advantage of new opportunities such as education. Peasants are often a source of revenue for industrialization projects, which was certainly the case during the Meiji period in Japan, as well as in the Soviet Union. Governmental policies that demand taxes paid in cash (rather than in-kind payments or through labor) often force peasants to move off the land and become members of the working class. Peasant rebellions over inequitable land distribution have been a major factor in precipitating revolutions. In Russia and China, socialists unleashed a process of modernization that changed peasants' lives in unforeseen ways. For instance, the Soviet Union ultimately made land collectively owned, which the peasantry did not want. Industrialization and urbanization has reduced the total number of peasants, who are no longer the majority of the world's population.

See also Populism

Further Reading

Shanin, Teodor. *Peasants and Peasant Societies*. Oxford: Blackwell, 1987.

PERESTROIKA

Perestroika, literally meaning reconstruction or restructuring, was the economic policy adopted by Mikhail Gorbachev in the later 1980s to try to galvanize the economy of Soviet Russia. In a literal sense the policy failed, in that the Soviet Union continued to decline and ultimately split apart in 1989–91. However, elements of the policy have continued in post-Soviet Russia. *Perestroika* was an interesting attempt (somewhat like the economic reforms of China after 1978) to introduce elements of a market economy into a communist political structure.

The Soviet economy was lagging badly when Gorbachev came to power in 1985. It suffered from low worker morale, excessive bureaucratization, environmental degradation, and the burdens of high military spending. After decades of success in building a basic industrial economy, Soviet performance was now declining.

Gorbachev's attempts at economic reform encountered massive opposition from hard-line bureaucrats, but in 1987, he was able to loosen controls over state enterprises, giving them greater latitude to meet consumer demands. State companies

Perestroika allowed Western companies to expand into the Soviet Union; here musicians help celebrate the 15th anniversary of the world's busiest McDonald's. (AFP/Getty Images)

that could not support themselves were allowed to go under. In the following year, another reform allowed the creation of private companies for the first time since Lenin's New Economic Policy. Foreign trade was also liberalized, and foreigners were allowed to invest in joint ventures in the Soviet Union. Reforms under *Perestroika* were limited in many ways, with much state control remaining, and they did not produce much economic advance. They were also accompanied by various political reforms that allowed the emergence of new dissent, which, in turn, ultimately toppled the regime. However, Russian economic policy in the 1990s and 2000s maintained a mixture of state enterprise with private ventures, including foreign companies—a mixture different from the policies of most Western nations and also from policies in China. The result is debated: the Russian economy has advanced in recent years mainly on the basis of oil and raw materials exports, with fewer gains in the industrial sector per se.

Further Reading

Gorbachev, Mikhail. *Perestroika: New Thinking for Our Country and the World.* New York: Harper and Row, 1988.

Jha, Prem Shankar. *The Perilous Road to the Market: The Political Economy of Reform in Russia, India and China.* London: Pluto Press, 2002.

PERÓNISM

Perónism is the term for a populist form of corporatism practiced in Argentina by Juan Domingo Perón (1895–1974) and his followers. Under Perónism, the state intervened in the economy to benefit industry and workers. Perón was part of a June 1943 coup of young military officers; Perón rose to power by successfully appealing to the masses of urban poor, known as the "shirtless ones." Under his rule, trade unions gained impressive wage increases and the state provided generous social welfare benefits such as old-age pensions and unemployment relief. The political cost for this arrangement was that workers' organizations had to cede their independence to the state; Perón's wife, Evita, ran the unions until she died in 1952. Although Perónism favored workers and industrialization over rural landowners, the traditional political elites, Perón did not institute land reform and his overall strategy was not revolutionary. He used the state to control international trade and thereby use Argentina's agricultural surpluses to subsidize industry. The military ousted Perón in 1955. Though Perónistas and unions were periodically able to return to power, they have been unable to make the historic compromise of Perónism pay lasting economic or political dividends.

See also Corporatism; Fascism

Further Reading

Peralta-Ramos, Monica. *The Political Economy of Argentina: Power and Class since 1930.* Boulder, CO: Westview, 1992.

PERSONAL COMPUTER

Until the 1970s, the central processing units for computers were large mainframes. Those computers had become progressively smaller, more powerful, and cheaper, but they were not something the average person could afford or take home with them.

In the early 1970s, early personal computers (or microcomputers, as they were then termed) came into existence. They had small screens, displaying one line of text at a time. They required knowledge of programming languages and were not commercially successful. In the late 1970s, the first home computers were sold. IBM was an early industry leader, although Apple developed a sizeable niche (roughly 10–15% of the market). In 1977, about 48,000 PCs had been sold; by 1999, more than 100 million.

In the early 1980s, an IBM computer sold for roughly $3,000 (and cost 20% of that to make). Fifteen years later, vastly stronger and faster models were sold for $1,000 as "IBM clones" (as they were initially called) flooded the market.

Computers created an almost magical allure for businesses. Projects that had been time-consuming and cumbersome, such as typing long papers or doing

The Model T of personal computers: the IBM AT model, ca. 1984. (Bettmann/Corbis)

spreadsheets, became easier. Having managers develop their own charts and graphs enabled companies to lay off graphic artists. Similarly, the typing pool filled with secretaries went the way of the dodo. In the 1990s, computers supposedly heralded a "paperless office," although more paper was used than ever before. U.S. businesses did not realize enormous productivity gains, in large part because computers became a major distraction due to games, e-mail, and the Internet.

Computers became faster. In 1965 Intel's cofounder, Gordon E. Moore, correctly predicted that computers would double in power every two years. An extreme example is the average smart phone, which has vastly faster and more powerful software than was available to NASA in the 1960s. However, Wirth's law, commonly called "bloat," suggests that most of those gains will be absorbed by less efficient computer programs. One computer scientist showed that the 2007 version of Microsoft Office performed the same function in only half the time as its 2000 counterpart.

Personal computers have transformed the expectations of the middle classes. In the 1980s, parents bought PCs for college students so they could type papers. From the perspective of 1977, it was the stuff of science fiction that computers would replace "snail mail," or that they would provide a way to do video telephone calls, or download music and movies. Computers and the Internet reshaped commerce and have become a major environmental hazard. Computer games are a larger industry than movies. In the mid-2000s, there were tens of thousands of gamers "farming" computer games such as *World of Warcraft*. Commerce in this sector is greater than the GDP of Nepal.

Computers have shifted from a luxury item for the middle classes to a necessity; to something that is reshaping commerce, leisure, and even how our brains function.

See also Computerization; Electronic Waste or E-waste; Internet

Further Reading

Swedin, Eric G., and David L. Ferro. *Computers: The Life Story of a Technology.* Baltimore: Johns Hopkins University Press, 2007.

PETROBRAS

Petrobras is a Brazilian, partially publicly owned petroleum firm. It is the largest company in Latin America and has been ranked as one of the 10 largest companies in the world. Petrobras was set up in the 1950s as a government-owned monopoly. Brazil, like many developing countries, suffered from the quadrupling of oil prices in the 1970s and looked to domestic supplies to offset imports. By 2006, Brazil no longer imported oil. The company produces around 2 million barrels a day; Brazil has 8 billion barrels of reserves.

Most of Brazil's reserves of oil are offshore, where it is expensive and risky to extract it. Consequently, Petrobras has developed some of the world's largest deep-sea platforms. One giant well exploded in 2001. As oil prices climbed throughout that decade, Petrobras quickly returned to deep-sea drilling.

Petrobras has also been relatively successful in avoiding the "oil curse" whereby a few individuals siphon off the profits and leave the country with environmental problems. The company is far more transparent and accountable than its counterparts in Mexico, Venezuela, or Africa. However, the company also apparently gives out large numbers of no-bid contracts to politically connected firms.

Petrobras also invests in green energy, helping Brazil become a major producer of ethanol from sugar cane. The successes of Petrobras have helped Brazil's economy emerge as a major industrial power since the 1990s.

Further Reading

Rohter, Larry. *Brazil on the Rise: The Story of a Country Transformed.* New York: Palgrave Macmillan, 2010.

PETROLEUM. *See* Oil

PHARMACEUTICALS

The modern pharmaceutical industry arose in the late nineteenth and early twentieth century. There were drugs before then, but they were not developed on a scientific basis, and the ingredients and their quality could vary widely. Until government regulation developed, many drugs contained alcohol or opium. The modern industry was located in countries that had strong university systems and the ability to process drugs industrially: Germany, the United States, the United Kingdom, Switzerland, etc. Scientists discovered how to process powerful new drugs, such as penicillin, that defeated long-standing diseases. The public grew accustomed to "wonder drugs," such as antibiotics or the vaccine for polio, a view that scientists did little to discourage.

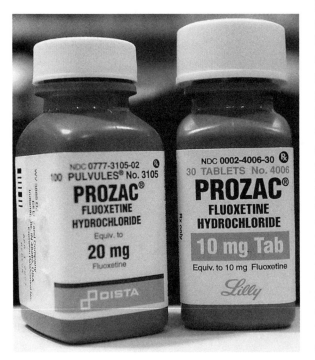

Prozac symbolized the diffusion of pharmaceuticals into daily life. (Stephen Chernin/Getty Images)

Over the postwar period, consumers enjoyed a steadily

increasing variety of drugs that transformed life. In the 1960s, "the pill" allowed women to engage in birth control by taking a mixture of estrogen and progestin. The drug atorvastatin was developed in 1985, which counteracted cholesterol. Levels of heart disease had been rising for decades as the result of an increasingly sedentary lifestyle and a richer diet; atorvastatin became one of the best-selling drugs of all time. Symptoms of mental illness also became treatable with psychotropic drugs. By the early 2000s, antidepressants had become so prevalent that an estimated 11 percent of U.S. women were taking some form of medication.

Even as drugs became more effective and widespread, drug companies became more vilified. Drug development was seen as political. The relatively slow development of drugs to counteract AIDS was viewed by many to be because the early sufferers of the disease were gay men. When a variety of drugs were developed, they greatly extended life but were not made available in Africa, except at prices that most there could not afford. The industry defended itself by pointing out drugs exist because of expensive research. However, much of this research is to ensure that drugs or processes are unique and can be patented. Most basic research is done with public money. Critics point out that the level of profit in the industry is high. In 2006, companies made a 20 percent profit rate on sales. For that reason, most countries closely regulate drug prices, with the United States as the largest exception.

Further Reading

Werth, Barry. *The Billion Dollar Molecule: One Company's Quest for the Perfect Drug.* New York: Simon and Schuster, 1995.

PIECE RATE

Piece rate refers to the practice of paying workers not by the hour or day but by the actual amount of work performed. The practice was a favored technique of so-called scientific management, which sought to increase productivity, generally by breaking up group tactics that aim at the restriction of labor. In the early twentieth-century steel industry in the United States, for example, many hourly wage workers could receive "tonnage" bonuses if they exceeded production quotas. Piece rates were often used in the automobile industry and the garment trade, which have a high degree of mechanization and labor that has been minutely subdivided. Many craft workers, in the building trades and elsewhere, used local unions to resist piece rates. Although the practice can operate to some workers' advantage, many workers and unionists criticize the practice as one in which workers are "sweated" for extra production.

See also Stakhanovites; Taylor, Frederick Winslow

Further Reading

Montgomery, David. *Workers' Control in America: Studies in the History of Work, Technology, and Labor Struggles.* New York: Cambridge University Press, 1979.

PINK-COLLAR WORKERS

The term "pink-collar workers" refers to white-collar occupations that have become thoroughly feminized, such as secretary, typist, and nurse, but in which "respectable" clothing is worn on the job. Pink-collar workers generally achieve less pay and status than their masculine counterparts. This inequity generally has more to do with the ways that work is geared to women than with the actual content of the work, although the two factors are frequently interdependent. In the late nineteenth century, telephone operators in the United States were usually men, and they received good pay and a large degree of latitude at work; when the job became feminized in the early twentieth century, women received lower wages and "required" closer supervision. In the mid-nineteenth century, secretarial work was a province of literate men who were well compensated for taking care of the correspondence (and keeping the secrets) of powerful men; female secretaries perform similar duties for fewer rewards.

See also Women; Women Industrial Workers

Further Reading

Norwood, Stephen H. *Labor's Flaming Youth: Telephone Operators and Worker Militancy.* Urbana: University of Illinois Press, 1990.

PINKERTONS

Pinkertons was a private detective and security firm founded by Allan Pinkerton (1819–84) in 1853. Although Pinkerton had himself been an advocate of

A group of armed Pinkerton guards travel in a wagon. (Securitas)

Chartism in England, in the United States his company earned its reputation by providing armed guards to companies during strikes. Pinkertons were often used to intimidate strikers and escort strikebreakers across picket lines; among unionists, the Pinkertons represented the power of corporations to transcend the power of elected governments by hiring their own private armies. In the Homestead Lockout of 1892, unionists succeeded in driving Pinkertons out of town—only to find themselves confronted by the Pennsylvania National Guard, which helped Andrew Carnegie run his mill with nonunion workers. The Pinkertons contributed to the fact that throughout the nineteenth and much of the twentieth century, strikes in the United States were violent affairs. As Jay Gould remarked, "I can hire one half of the working class to kill the other half."

Further Reading

Klein, Maury. *The Life and Legend of Jay Gould.* Baltimore: Johns Hopkins University Press, 1986.

Krause, Paul. *The Battle for Homestead, 1880–1892: Politics, Culture, and Steel.* Pittsburgh, PA: University of Pittsburgh Press, 1992.

PIPELINES

Pipelines efficiently transport large volumes of raw or processed petroleum, or natural gas, through steel tubes. Pipelines are an important part of the infrastructure or circulatory system of petroleum products that allow for a smooth-functioning industrial economy. As the price of energy rises, the flow of energy becomes ever-more critical.

The earliest pipelines go back to the 1860s in the United States. Pipelines allowed oil producers in the first oil boomtown to circumvent slower and more expensive teamsters who hauled barrels of crude along mud roads on horse-drawn wagons. Railroads still carried much of the volume in the late nineteenth century, although a major pipeline boom began in the 1920s, in part to circumvent the high prices established by railroad companies. Oil companies developed their own pipelines to link their refineries to major oil fields, or to link their refineries to urban markets. Another American pipeline boom began in the mid-2000s when natural gas companies began "fracking" gas from deep deposits of shale.

There are more than 1 million miles of pipelines in the world; there are 300,000 miles of pipe in the United States. Each year, at least 20,000 miles are added to this vast network.

Pipelines are typically invisible unless they spill, cause accidents, or their flow is interrupted. Nigeria's pipelines are notoriously leaky, in part due to construction, but also because criminals tap into the lines and siphon off product. Similar problems plagued the Iraqi industry after the U.S.-led invasion in 2003; a major source of revenue for the Iraqi insurgency was oil. One pipeline runs close to a vast Kenyan slum and attempts to siphon off oil lead to spills, which can catch on fire, resulting in numerous deaths.

The situation gets only more complex when pipelines cross international borders. The Russian energy producer Gazprom has shut off natural gas to countries, ostensibly over pricing; this is often seen as an attempt by the Russian government to exert its control over countries once part of the Soviet Union.

Further Reading

Smil, Vaclav. *Energy in World History*. Boulder, CO: Westview, 1994.

PLANTATIONS

Plantations were large farms that produced cash crops such as sugar, cotton, rubber, and tea. The owners (planters) of plantations or estates owned the land and frequently the labor force as well. The plantation system arose in the sixteenth century, particularly in the Americas, and produced many of the raw materials for the Industrial Revolution. Plantations have continued to shape the social and economic relationships of the countries that they dominated.

In the sixteenth century, sugar plantations established in the Caribbean and Brazil imposed harsh labor regimes on both African slaves and indentured servants from Europe. Planters gradually moved toward using African slaves as the main source of labor power—a decision that was based largely on economics—because planters could buy a slave for little more than it cost to hire an indentured servant for several years. The racialization of slavery also allowed planters to use poor whites as their political allies, for slave revolts were a constant fear in plantation societies. Slavery was abolished at different points during the nineteenth century throughout the world, but the plantation system survived and spread, relying on wage labor in some regions, bonded laborers, or peasants who worked part of the year for wages across much of Africa, Asia, and Latin America. Although workers were often paid in cash, working conditions remained harsh, and many peasants in the new colonies resisted becoming laborers for the plantations. British planters in Sri Lanka (Ceylon), Malaysia, and East Africa often used bonded laborers (bound to work for a period of several years) from India and China rather than, or in addition to, the domestic labor supply.

After decolonization, newly independent countries with developed plantation systems initially fared well in the international marketplace. Until the late 1960s, Sri Lanka was able to maintain its trade surpluses with industrialized countries in spite of its growing population. Sri Lanka's favorable balance of trade enabled it to create one of Asia's most developed welfare states, with an extensive university system and generous food, health, and transportation subsidies. The prices for Sri Lanka's main exports, tea and rubber, gradually fell, however. In the case of tea, other Asian and African countries (often at the urging of the World Bank) produced more tea—and the resulting oversupply caused prices to fall. Other countries also expanded their coconut plantations, and changing consumption patterns in Europe and the United States exacerbated the price fall. The price of rubber fell because the invention of synthetic rubber during World War II gave buyers an alternate supply. Sri Lanka's worsening balance of payments eventually caused its welfare state to collapse, and as people groped for a reason for the fall in their standards of living, tensions among ethnic groups degenerated into civil war. Like Sri Lanka, although not all countries with plantation systems have plunged into civil war, countries that entered the world system through the plantation system have often had a difficult time industrializing their economies. Plantation systems tend to depend on cheap labor and limited technology, poor workers depress the internal market for manufactured goods, and plantation employers can discourage the development of an industrial sector that would attract workers and raise wages elsewhere.

See also Development Theory; Neocolonialism; World Systems Theory

Further Reading

Wolf, Eric. *Europe and the People without History.* Berkeley: University of California Press, 1982.

PLASTICS

Plastic was first discovered by French chemists in 1828, but it is basically a twentieth-century industry. The term derives from the Greek word for "fit for molding." Plastics have various chemical compositions, derived from wood, cotton, and other materials, including ammonia and formaldehyde. Molding began in the United States about 1850 for novelty items such as combs and jewelry boxes, and plastics began to replace wood, ivory, and ceramics, at least for cheaper goods. Experiments continued in the United States; the greatest step occurred in 1907, when Leo Baekeland discovered phenol-formaldehyde resins, marketed under the trademark Bakelite. Cellulose acetate plastics were introduced in 1927, advancing the possibilities for heat molding. The plastics

The inventor of Bakelite cookware, Leo Hendrik Baekeland, had a profound effect on twentieth-century American life. (Union Carbide Plastics Company)

industry expanded rapidly as new materials and uses were discovered. A light industry, plastics spread widely in several early industrial revolutions of the twentieth century, such as that of Taiwan, providing opportunities in export sales in consumer goods. Workers in plastics are primarily involved with mixing the chemical materials, but there are also skilled jobs in shaping and in designing products.

Further Reading

Aftalion, Fred. *A History of the International Chemical Industry*. Philadelphia: Chemical Heritage Press, 2001.

POLAND

The industrialization of Poland began unevenly in the nineteenth century while the country was ruled by the Austrian, German, and Russian empires, though significant industrial centers arose in areas like Lodz. Many Polish workers emigrated to other European countries or to North America. A basic industrialization process was completed only after World War II. In 1945, Poland had great difficulties to overcome: one-fifth of the population had been killed, and the country's borders were redrawn—Stalin forcibly relocated millions of ethnic Poles from the Soviet Union into Poland, and large numbers of ethnic Germans were driven into East Germany. Stalin also denied Poland access to Western resources during the period of reconstruction, though Poland nevertheless managed to exploit its massive coal deposits and build an industrial economy.

Heavy industry was favored, though Polish communists allowed peasants greater control over the land than Soviet communists. Workers' discontent with harsh living conditions and lack of civil liberties periodically erupted in riots. In the 1970s, Poland borrowed heavily from the West to finance consumer goods for workers as well as new industrial projects such as shipbuilding, automobile factories, and food processing. Western Europe largely refused to open its markets to these goods, thus accelerating the crisis of the Polish state in the 1980s. After a period of hardship following the end of communism, Poland's economy benefited from its ability to trade with Western Europe.

See also East Central Europe

Further Reading

Dziewanowski, M. K. *Poland in the Twentieth Century*. New York: Columbia University Press, 1971.

POLICE REGULATION LAW

This law was introduced by Japan in 1900, after the first serious labor unrest broke out in the late 1890s. Several unions had emerged, and though they were moderate, they staged a strike in 1898 to protest the firing of "agitators" and to demand better treatment. The Police Regulation Law of 1900 made it virtually a crime to organize and lead workers out on strikes. Several labor groups, including a 1901 Social Democratic Party, were disbanded under this law. The law resembled provisions in other early industrial societies that had outlawed labor organizations, but it was enforced with particular severity. The Japanese union movement was stunted as a result, and workers turned increasingly to political action.

A Federation of Labor emerged in 1919, calling for revision of the Regulation Law. A major shipyards strike in 1921 against Kawasaki and Mitsubishi was broken up by army troops; 300 leaders were arrested, which made the remaining movement more radical. Finally, in 1925, the government became more flexible and revised the Regulation Law to eliminate restrictions on labor activities, though violence was still controlled and compulsory arbitration was required in some industries.

Further Reading

Mitchell, Richard H. *Thought Control in Prewar Japan.* Ithaca, NY: Cornell University Press, 1976.

POOR LAW (1601)

The Elizabethan Poor Law of 1601 responded to the growth of property-less workers as the English economy became more commercial. It authorized localities to provide aid (mainly in kind) to the poor and unemployed. This system seemed incompatible with the principles of an industrial economy, and it was reformed in 1834. Business leaders wanted more consistent policies that were not dependent on local whims, and they sought lower taxes; they were also convinced that many poor people abused the system, getting public aid when they should be working. The views of liberal economists, who were hostile to government assistance programs in the name of free competition, supported this change.

The Poor Law reform measure provided central controls over the system. Relief funds were cut and more rigorous tests were to be applied to applicants, so that able-bodied people were forced to work. Workhouses were established for those who did receive aid, and their conditions were deliberately made unpleasant and discouraging. Workers attacked this change—it was one of the causes of the Chartist movement—but the reformed system continued to be the basis for British relief of poverty until the twentieth century. While the Poor Law reform was intended to foster better administrative practices, it is rightly remembered for the punitive approach to poverty associated with many leaders of the Industrial Revolution.

See also Enclosure Movement; Underclass

Further Reading

Katz, Michael. *The Undeserving Poor: From the War on Poverty to the War on Welfare.* New York: Pantheon, 1989.

POPULATION GROWTH

Population levels are tied to industrialization in complex ways. Too much population, it has been argued, can prevent a full industrial revolution. Some demographic growth, however, is a vital economic stimulant. Many scholars argue that countries often benefit from immigration, as migrants often work harder than the native-born population. Finally, industrial revolutions cut population growth rates, with important consequences.

Most societies that industrialized had first experienced population growth. In Western Europe, massive population growth began about 1730. Levels doubled between 1750 and 1800 in Britain and Prussia; they increased 50 percent in France. The causes of this growth were the utilization of more efficient foodstuffs, notably the potato, and a coincidental reduction in epidemic disease; major plagues disappeared until a recurrence in the 1830s. Improvements in urban sanitation played a minor role. Better food and less disease meant that more children survived to adulthood, which increased the population and also augmented the number of available parents, increasing the population even more. This cycle continued for several generations. Population growth provided new markets for goods. It also made it more difficult to survive in agriculture; more and more rural children had to look for other work, for the land was insufficient to support them. Countries with lower population growth, like France, felt this pressure less and found it more difficult to recruit a factory labor force. Population growth generally forced workers to accept factory conditions, move to cities, or emigrate. In middle-class families, population growth could spur innovation. More children survived to adulthood and needed to be supported at a middle-class level; that fact could be a direct motivation for business expansion and investment in unfamiliar technology.

Too much growth, however, particularly in already crowded conditions, can drain some of the resources and capital needed for industrial investment. This argument has been used to explain why Latin America, India, and China have been slower to industrialize. However, Japan's population grew rapidly, thanks to new public health measures and improved agriculture, before and during the early industrial decades. Certainly, twentieth-century growth rates have been unprecedented in most nonindustrial countries, as China and India possessed a billion people each. Modern medicine and agriculture, fruits of international industrialization, spurred this growth. How great a problem population growth represents in terms of retarding industrialization is widely debated. South Korea is one of the most densely populated countries in the world, but it has managed to launch an industrial revolution. Many societies, like China since 1978, have actively sought to cut population growth to facilitate industrialization. Others, like India or sub-Saharan Africa, have experienced far slower declines in family size.

All successful industrial revolutions to date have led to rapid drops in birthrates, as families adjust to the fact that children can no longer earn money and devote more attention to improving their standards of living. Consequently, a cycle becomes started where many families have smaller numbers of children so they can afford them greater opportunities. This cycle is reinforced as women gain access to the kinds of birth control that industrialization created. Japan, Western Europe, Russia, and North America have all been affected by this demographic transition. It can be uneven, and some groups reduce their birthrates more rapidly than others; ironically, poorer groups often maintain higher rates (which was not the case before industrialization). The transition also increases the percentage of older people in the population. This new demographic structure presents novel problems to industrialized societies in the twenty-first century.

See also Demographic Transition

Further Reading

Bacci, Massimo Livi. *A Concise History of World Population*. Malden, MA: Blackwell, 2001.

POPULISM

Populism refers to farmers' protest movements. Since the fifteenth century, the rise of capitalism and industrialization has transformed the economic basis of farming throughout the world. Farmers (who are generally considered to be more market oriented than their relatively self-sufficient peasant counterparts) supplied burgeoning urban markets with agricultural goods but in the process became increasingly dependent on manufactured goods such as plows, bags, fertilizers, and tractors. Once farmers became enmeshed in the "cash nexus," they became vulnerable to variations in prices and demand for agricultural and manufactured goods. Farmers occasionally enjoyed relatively favorable "terms of trade," as for example during the period just before and during World War I. But in the late nineteenth century, farms began to become increasingly capital-intensive. Farmers needed money to purchase machinery, bringing them into contact with the banking system. In part because the late nineteenth century was a deflationary era, the result was the eviction of most small-scale farmers from the land. In response to the often negative changes that the industrialization process has wrought on their lives, farmers instituted a number of protest movements.

Beginning in the 1870s, farmers in the United States began to agitate against the fall of agricultural prices and the increasing cost of credit. What has become known as the Populist movement initially challenged railroad and manufacturing cartels, or "trusts," that charged high rates for transportation and necessary goods (such as bagging for cotton). Populists also targeted the federal government's gold standard policies that favored bankers over creditors by maintaining deflationary cycles. The Populists argued for a more flexible currency that, being based in part on agricultural production, would respond better to the needs of "producers" and not concentrate power in the hands of the banking system. At its height in the 1890s, the Populist movement's People's Party polled over 1 million votes even in the face of massive and brutal repression in the southern United States. It eventually "fused" with and disappeared into the Democratic Party. The Populists had an important

Mary Elizabeth Lease was a populist agitator, famously observing that farmers in Kansas needed to raise less corn and more hell. (Hayward Cirker and Blanche Cirker, eds., *Dictionary of American Portraits*, 1967)

influence on the course of political reforms, including railroad regulations, but they did not succeed in saving large numbers of small-scale farmers from economic ruin.

Not all farmers' movements have been failures, however. In twentieth-century France and Japan, farmers were able to pressure their governments for generous subsidies, allowing many small farmers to remain economically viable.

Populist movements face a variety of obstacles. The dispersed nature of settlement in the countryside complicates communication, and the often substantial class differences between richer and poorer (or landless) farmers make it difficult to articulate and maintain political unity. For instance, although Populists attempted to address the needs of both sharecroppers and farmers who owned their own land, the movement clearly favored wealthier farmers. Likewise, as a result of resistance by southern Democrats to the Populists' interracial politics, the movement maintained separate organizations for whites and blacks. In the twentieth-century United States, rich farmers were able to form powerful cooperatives (such as Sunkist) and influence federal policies, whereas sharecroppers had little luck influencing policies as their unions crumbled in the face of state and vigilante violence.

See also Agriculture; Kulaks; New Deal

Further Reading

Goodwyn, Lawrence. *The Populist Moment: A Short History of the Agrarian Revolt in America.* New York: Oxford University Press, 1978.

Shanin, Teodor. *Peasants and Peasant Societies.* Oxford: Blackwell, 1987.

POSTINDUSTRIAL ECONOMIES

Since the 1970s, employment in the manufacturing sectors of industrialized countries has been stagnant or in decline. In Europe, the United States, and Japan, jobs in "smokestack" industries such as steel, textiles, and automobiles have declined as companies have continued to institute automation or have shifted production to newly industrializing countries such as Mexico, South Korea, or China. The relocation of industrial production has been accompanied by advances in computer and communication technology that has allowed multinational corporations to coordinate the production and distribution of goods on a worldwide basis. Some observers believe that the result has been the emergence of a global "postindustrial" economy.

Many economists have heralded the emergence of a postindustrial economy that is based upon "high-tech" nonindustries such as computers, communications, and the service sector. For instance, from the 1950s onward, New York City has lost many of its blue-collar industries (printing, garments, metalworking) as policy makers have encouraged the rise of white-collar employment in media, finance, and real estate. Firms that continue to rely on rigid divisions between managers and workers fall victim to companies and nations that have more educated and flexible workforces. In the 1980s, many old industrial companies, such as IBM or General Motors, lost market share to newer, more nimble companies. Supporters of postindustrial theory point to the fall of the Soviet Union as a result of the failure of the country's communist planners to adapt to a more competitive global market, and many economists worry that firms in the United States may also lag in adapting to new realities.

Critics point out that postindustrialism is not so much a new era in economic development as an acceleration of industrialization on a worldwide scale, and note that the changes have neither empowered workers nor improved their standards of living. Whereas flexibility may be a virtue for companies in the global marketplace, "leaner" corporations have resulted in an increasing number of workers who are denied permanent employment. Since the 1980s, most of the jobs created in the United States, and increasingly in Europe and Japan, are low-wage, temporary positions. One historian has observed that "postindustrial" New York City has a wider gap between rich and poor than it did in the 1940s and that, after a brief boom in the 1980s, the number of high-wage jobs in finance and media was actually lower in the 1990s than it was in the 1970s. Particularly in the United States, workers' incomes since the 1970s (if adjusted for inflation) have actually fallen.

Postindustrial technologies may intensify industrial conditions of work. Though some people forecast big changes in work thanks to computer linkages—work may become more decentralized, more self-paced—it is also clear that computers can allow closer monitoring of the pace of work and afford supervisors new ways to keep track of what employees do on the job.

See also Dual Labor Markets

Further Reading

Harrison, Bennett. *Lean and Mean: The Changing Landscape of Corporate Power in the Era of Flexibility*. New York: Basic, 1994.

Harvey, David. *The Condition of Postmodernity: An Inquiry into the Origins of Cultural Change.* Oxford: Blackwell, 1990.

POTATO

The potato was a New World crop, originally domesticated in the Andes. Its use began to spread to Europe only at the end of the seventeenth century, when prejudices against new foods declined. The potato was an immensely efficient crop, allowing families to survive on smaller plots of land, which in turn fueled Europe's massive population increase in the eighteenth century—up to 100 percent in Britain and Prussia. Population increase stimulated markets for manufactured goods and also expanded the labor supply; both of these developments contributed directly to the Industrial Revolution. When diseases began to affect the crop, notably the potato blight of 1846–47, resultant famine generated new patterns of emigration. Large numbers of Irish immigrants swelled available industrial labor in the United States and elsewhere.

See also Agriculture; Population Growth

Further Reading

Crosby, Alfred W., Jr. *The Columbian Exchange: Biological and Cultural Consequences of 1492.* 3rd ed. Westport, CT: Greenwood, 1976.

PRIMITIVE ACCUMULATION

Primitive accumulation is a term developed by Karl Marx to explain the origins of wage labor, or how producers (future proletarians or members of the working class) lost economic alternatives to wage labor. He uses the term primitive not simply because force and robbery play a large role in this process but also because it is part of the prehistory of the capitalist era. He believed that the enclosure movement, by which the English aristocracy drove peasants from common grounds (fields and forests), was a classic example of primitive accumulation. Another example was when England forced Spain to allow English traders to supply African slaves to Spanish colonies. Marx wrote that "if money, according to Augier, 'comes into the world with a congenital blood-stain on one cheek,' capital comes dripping from head to foot, from every pore, with blood and dirt."

Marxists see primitive accumulation as an ongoing process, pointing to the privatization of public assets since the 1970s as an example from recent history.

See also Privatization; Slavery

Further Reading

Wolf, Eric. *Europe and the People without History.* Berkeley: University of California Press, 1982.

PRIVATE PROPERTY

Private property, a guiding principle of capitalist economies, emphasizes undisputed individual ownership of production goods, such as land, equipment, and business. Most societies that industrialized had fairly well-established laws about private property. Even inventions were protected as property by patent law. Russia, by abolishing serfdom in 1861 and then issuing more standardized legal codes, firmed up its property laws prior to industrialization. A few societies faced groups, such as Native Americans, wedded to more communal property concepts. The U.S. government and Latin American governments have pressed these groups either to isolate themselves or to accept private property arrangements as the basis for a more commercial economy, and significant tensions have resulted.

Though private property was not caused by industrialization, the industrial revolution exacerbated the division between property owners and nonowners. The people who controlled the factories and earned the main profits were owners. Workers were people who had no access to significant property; they were proletarians. Not surprisingly, many workers and many socialist theories attacked private property because it subjected certain people to the control of property owners at unequal rates of reward. Utopian socialists as well as Marxists argued for more communal arrangements, so that everyone would share in decisions and earnings. A few alternative communities were set up. Only the communist system, however, seriously attempted industrialization without significant private property. Under the Soviet system in Russia, and in later communist societies in Eastern Europe and China, the state owned factories in the name of the people. The system worked well for establishing basic industries, but it seemed to have broken down as a structure for keeping industrial growth going. Thus most communist systems between 1978 and 1985 began to tolerate more private property as an incentive for economic innovation.

Private property remains a legal bedrock for capitalist industrial societies. However, the growth of corporations from the 1870s onward progressively diffused ownership. Big industrial corporations are property, but they are not individual property as the early factories were. Industrialization in this sense also complicates property arrangements.

A country without clearly defined rights for private property can undermine industrialization efforts. Postcommunist Russia is notorious for having a weak "rule of law" regarding private property. Billionaires have found themselves in jail for annoying powerful politicians. Even successful cases, like China, struggle with how much autonomy from politicians should be granted to land or business owners.

Further Reading

Heilbroner, Robert L. *The Worldly Philosophers: The Lives, Times, and Ideas of the Great Economic Thinkers.* New York: Simon and Schuster, 1986.

PRIVATIZATION

Privatization is the sale of public assets to individual owners. In many capitalist countries, government nationalized critical industries such as railroads (the United Kingdom, France, India, South Africa, and Japan), electricity or gas companies

Demonstrators in the Bolivian water war in 2000, protesting the foreign-owned company that forced impoverished Bolivians to pay high rates for water. (AP Photo/Julie Plasencia)

(United Kingdom, France, South Africa), or declining ones, such as coal, steel making, shipyards, or automobiles. Nationalization promised to revitalize an important industry or run it in the public interest. The rise of neoliberal ideology in the 1980s, as well as the costs associated with public ownership, caused many governments to privatize industries. Unions in those industries typically resisted. In some cases, industries were renationalized, as most voters accepted that subsidies to those industries were too costly and that the country would benefit from free trade.

Numerous developing countries nationalized industries, or developed new ones. In many countries, the utilities and railroads, as well as oil companies, were publicly owned. When and if those countries needed International Monetary Fund (IMF) or World Bank loans, privatization was often the cost of obtaining credit. In Bolivia, the water system was privatized at the request of the IMF and the law made it illegal to collect rainwater. The new rates were high in a very poor country and weeks of protest followed, the so-called water war. The law was ultimately overturned.

In communist countries, all industries had been publicly owned. Capitalists as a group had been eliminated, often for decades, so identifying former owners, or potential owners, was problematic. As in many countries, there are charges of cronyism and corruption when new owners take over.

The definition of what is a public good varies widely from country to country, and between different political parties within one. Railroads and electric companies might be a public good. Most countries see health insurance as a public good. Germany, the Netherlands, and several other countries have heavily regulated private insurance; the United States has the least. Most countries see education as a public good, although some would say that governments should encourage privatization and a spirit of competition here as well.

Further Reading

Klein, Naomi. *The Shock Doctrine: The Rise of Disaster Capitalism*. New York: Henry Holt, 2007.

PRODUCTIVITY

Productivity describes the output generated by the average worker in a given factory, industry, or the whole economy, when calculated to include the costs of equipment and resources. The Industrial Revolution was intended to increase per-worker productivity by using new machines, greater labor specialization, and intensified supervision. Once an industrial revolution started, productivity tended to continue to expand, though in recurrent bursts rather than a steady progression, as new equipment and greater work discipline were introduced.

Early industrial revolutions could generate massive productivity gains in a given industry, but the simplest figures can be misleading. This is an area where the sophisticated quantitative methods of the "new economic history," or cliometrics, have provided important refinements over a conventional historical understanding. Mechanical spinning allowed a single operative to produce over 50 times as much thread as a hand worker could do, though some assistants were also involved on the machine. However, labor went into the machines, the fuel, and other costs, which makes actual productivity gains hard to calculate. Other equipment was less spectacular: early mechanical looms increased production by 50 to 100 percent per worker, which is why hand-loom weavers, if they concentrated on certain grades of cloth, long continued to compete. Again, overall productivity calculations are complex. When spinning and weaving of cotton (the most industrialized textile fiber) are considered together with the costs of machines and fuel, productivity gains in Britain have been estimated at about 3.4 percent per year by 1812 and at about 2 percent per annum until 1860. These gains seem relatively modest, but such sustained productivity gains were unheard of in world history until then.

Power-driven printing equipment, mechanical kneading machines for bread dough, larger metallurgical furnaces—these were other developments in the late nineteenth century that heightened productivity. The result was greatly increased output, with a labor force that did not grow correspondingly. In textiles, in fact, productivity gains allowed a smaller number of workers to generate rapidly rising output, and domestic workers were gradually cut back.

Early industrial revolutions did not, however, result in rapid overall productivity gains, which is one reason some historians dispute the term "revolution." The primary reason is that more productive methods were applied only to a small part of the economy, not to the whole. In Britain, by 1850 over 80 percent of cotton production was in mechanized factories, but only about 40 percent of wool production had been transformed. British woolens, as a result, had about 0.9 percent annual productivity improvement during the early industrial period—impressive over time, but not spectacular in the short run. Construction and other craft sectors, pressed to develop more efficient methods at least to some extent, had expanded, while agriculture remained extensive and operated with only limited new equipment (in Britain there was at most a 0.4 percent annual productivity gain). Furthermore, early industrialization required massive growth in coal mining where, except in transporting material from the mines, there was little technological innovation; as pits deepen, per-worker productivity might actually decline. Finally, the withdrawal of some workers from the formal labor force, such as most married women, was another constraint on overall productivity.

Productivity gains, then, varied greatly during early industrialization. High in cotton and also transportation, they were more modest in other textiles and in iron and sluggish in nonfactory sectors.

Later industrializations, applying new equipment and methods to more branches of the economy, often generated higher overall productivity improvements. This phenomenon formed the basis for national product growth rates of 9 to 10 percent in a number of twentieth-century cases: Japan in the 1950s and 1960s, Spain and Italy in the 1960s, and China in the 1980s.

Productivity improvements in individual industrial sectors, even in nineteenth-century industrial revolutions, remained fundamental, for increased productivity was the source of the greater output of goods that required new sales and export outlets and, ultimately, a new consumerist mentality. It was also the source of new tensions between employers and workers. Owners, to assure their own profits and pay for new equipment, had to arrange that most productivity gains not return to workers in the form of higher wages. Hence, they often tried to cut wages or, more commonly, to switch to hourly scales (rather than piece rates) so that more production would not result in higher earnings. Workers obviously recognized this strategy and sometimes felt cheated. Employers also began to press workers to augment their productivity even beyond what new machines assured when they realized how much productivity meant in terms of competitive costs and satisfactory profits. This realization informed the general efforts to speed the pace of work not only in factories but also in crafts and mines in the late nineteenth century. At the same time, however, higher productivity did ultimately allow higher living standards for many workers, plus shorter hours of actual work and fewer family members involved in work.

Industrialists, for their part, tended to press for higher productivity somewhat sporadically. When sales were good, there was little reason to change methods; more workers could be hired. One of the "purposes" of the economic cycle and recurrent slumps was to weed out less productive firms and prompt other industrialists to introduce a new round of technological innovation or other efficiencies so that prices could be dropped to induce more sales.

How productivity is shared is a major source of contention in industrial societies. In the nineteenth century, English and American workers benefited from rising productivity, as falling prices for goods meant that in real terms wages improved by roughly 1 percent per year. Certain industrialists or monopolies, such as the large railroads, accumulated fabulous fortunes. By the late nineteenth century, American workers, farmers, and small-business owners pushed for reforms, which were fought for decades and then enacted in the 1930s. During the post–World War II era, American productivity expanded and was widely shared. Incomes actually rose somewhat faster at the bottom of society than at the top. Since the mid-1970s, almost all of productivity increases went to the top 10 percent of society, the lion's share to the top 1 percent. By 2011, a protest movement emerged that charged the "1 percent" with rigging the economy and political system to favor itself over all others.

See also Business Cycles; Consumerism and Mass Consumption; Strikes; Technology

Further Reading

Mokyr, Joel, ed. *The Economics of the Industrial Revolution*. Lanham, MD: Rowman and Littlefield, 1985.

PROFESSIONALIZATION

Professionalization was the process by which university-derived knowledge came to be defined and regulated by the professional associations and the state. The Industrial Revolution created an unprecedented demand for specialized forms of information among engineers, accountants, and architects. The older professions of medicine and law increased their knowledge claims and public roles, carving out a strong position in industrial society. Professional associations limited entry into job markets, but, unlike trade unions, professionals, because they were assumed to operate in the public interest, were allowed a considerable degree of self-regulation.

Early on, engineering emerged as one of the most important professions in industrialization. Civil engineers proved crucial to the building of the Erie Canal and other infrastructure projects. Because most universities in the first half of the nineteenth century offered only classical training (languages, religion, and philosophy), scientists and entrepreneurs urged the formation of universities that could train engineers to apply scientific principles to manufacturing. France and Germany already had polytechnic schools for mining and civil engineers. Before 1850, several technical universities were established in the United States, and the passage of the Morrill Act in 1862 offered substantial federal support (land grants) for universities that offered technical or agricultural training. In 1870, approximately 100 engineers graduated from universities, and by 1914 over 4,000 graduates were joining the workforce each year.

Engineering associations were formed relatively early: in England in 1818 and in the United States in 1852. Professional associations distinguished between university-trained mechanical engineers and the large numbers of mechanical engineers who were skilled workers with extensive experience in machine-tool shops. The professional associations helped make university training a prerequisite for entering into the managerial ranks of industrial corporations, and most "mechanics" remained foremen. By the early twentieth century, a new discipline of industrial engineering had begun to emerge that applied technical expertise to making the workplace more profitable.

See also Research and Development (R&D); Science; Scientific Management; Taylor, Frederick Winslow; Technology; Work Ethic

Further Reading

Layton, Edwin, Jr. *Revolt of the Engineers: Social Responsibility and the American Engineering Profession*. Baltimore: Johns Hopkins University Press, 1986.

Noble, David F. *America by Design: Science, Technology and the Rise of Corporate Capitalism*. New York: Knopf, 1977.

PROFESSIONALS

Most preindustrial societies had a few groups that can be called professional, in that they were based on unusually extensive learning. In Europe doctors, lawyers, and priests or ministers formed the "learned professions." Industrialization combined with political and scientific change altered the nature of the professions during the nineteenth century. Most older professions developed more specialized training, so that they could better serve the needs of an industrial society and also so that they could maintain prestige in an age increasingly dominated by business success. Advancing industrialization required new kinds of legal knowledge, for example, and more rigorous scientific training in medicine also made sense in the industrial context. Doctors played a major role in public health regulations that improved conditions in industrial cities. In Europe during the late nineteenth century and by the 1870s in the United States, the older professions generally had upgraded their educational achievements, formed new professional associations, and advocated careful licensing procedures to certify appropriate attainment. Along with these changes, a number of new professions were spawned by industrialization. Engineering became a profession as formal training improved and examinations and licensing were introduced. Accounting became a profession in the early twentieth century; architecture, too, emerged as a new professional field. The overall expansion of professions related closely to growth and redefinition in universities, the source of most professional training. University academics themselves became another profession.

A number of important job categories took on characteristics of a profession, but incompletely. Librarians, for example, required training, but access to the training was relatively easy, and no rigorous licensing procedures applied; the same held true for schoolteachers. Occupations of this sort, dominated by women, did not achieve full professional status by the late nineteenth and early twentieth centuries. Meanwhile, the popularity of the term "professional," as a badge of special training and expertise, expanded into industrial societies. Many occupations, including professional sports, picked up the label. In general, the growth and definition of modern professions follows the needs for specialized knowledge generated by industrial economies.

Professional success has not, however, always accompanied industrial expansion. Because professionals base their claims for status on knowledge rather than money, they can take a somewhat distinctive view of industrial economies. Moreover, the popularity of professions often lures more people into their ranks than an economy can easily support. "Overproduction" of professionals occurred in Europe at the end of the nineteenth century (over a third of the trained doctors in France, for example, could not find relevant work), as well as in industrializing India in the 1990s and even to some degree in China in the 2000s. These factors can bring some professionals into opposition with industrial society, as they seek outlets in politics of protest or reform activities. Much of the socialist leadership around the world has come from the ranks of professionals. More recently, environmentalist causes gain greatly from professionals' support. Thus there remains a significant ambiguity in the relationship between modern professionals and ongoing industrialization.

See also Middle Class

Further Reading

Hatch, Nathan O., ed. *The Professions in American History*. Notre Dame, IN: University of Notre Dame Press, 1988.
Larson, Magali S. *The Rise of Professionalism: A Sociological Analysis*. Berkeley: University of California Press, 1977.

PROFIT

The desire to earn a profit—the money earned by a seller when prices exceed cost—is one of the strongest forces within capitalism and one that has profoundly shaped the development of the modern world economy and the Industrial Revolution. Yet industrial production is simply one way to earn a profit. Merchants, for example, circulate commodities (wool, cotton, or manufactured goods) to gain a profit, and although many merchants became (or financed) industrialists, merchants also relied on, or indeed helped to create, systems of slavery and other forms of coerced labor to supply raw materials for industrial production. Financiers played a crucial role in developing systems of factories in industrialized countries, but when markets for industrial goods become saturated (or industries become uncompetitive), bankers' desire for increased profits leads them to shift their investments into other forms of capital such as real estate or commodity speculation. The profit motive is a powerful and pitiless force that has been instrumental in building as well as destroying industry.

The profit motive resulted in exploitation and also the explosion of material goods, such as in this general store in 1898. (Library of Congress)

See also Deindustrialization; Finance Capital; Merchant Capital; Plantations; U.S. South

Further Reading

Heilbroner, Robert L. *The Worldly Philosophers: The Lives, Times, and Ideas of the Great Economic Thinkers*. New York: Simon and Schuster, 1986.

PROLETARIAT. *See* Industrial Workers

PROTECTIONISM

Protectionism stresses high tariffs to protect one nation's goods by taxing imports. Debates over tariff policy accompanied every industrial revolution. Most early industrial societies were protectionist—that is, they sought to protect infant industry, to foster it against often better developed foreign competition. More established industrial societies typically press for freer trade, hoping that they can sell their products in foreign markets where there is less technologically sophisticated competition. Many of these societies also want lower tariffs on foods and raw materials, so that there will be less pressure for higher wages. Tariff debates frequently pit industrialists against other interests. In Britain during the early nineteenth century, factory owners wanted low tariffs, particularly on food, while aristocratic estate owners pressed for protection. At almost the same time, in the 1820s and 1830s, U.S. factory owners in the North urged tariffs to protect their industries against the more advanced British competition, while southern planters urged free trade so that they would not face retaliatory barriers in trying to sell their agricultural products, headed by cotton, abroad.

Through most of the nineteenth century, Britain, with its industrial lead, advocated low tariffs. Ironically, British tariffs against Indian and other textile products in the eighteenth century had helped British factories get their start. British liberals supported free trade from ideological conviction, and some continental liberals agreed. Free-trade movements first began within Britain with attacks on high agricultural tariffs like the Corn Law. Free-trade advocates believed as a matter of principle that lower tariffs would cut prices for consumers and force producers to be maximally efficient. Some supporters of free trade simply wanted to improve their ability to export. Low tariffs in one's own country would help persuade other countries—potential markets—to cut their rates. After 1850, the British tried to negotiate freer trade with other countries, as in the Cobden-Chevalier treaty of 1860 with France.

As more countries began to industrialize in the late nineteenth century, tariffs tended to rise; most industrial nations, including the United States, raised their rates in the 1890s. The McKinley Tariff (1890), named after Senator (later President) William McKinley (1843–1901), aimed to protect industrialists, workers, and farmers from international competition. Typically, the Republican Party, of which McKinley was a member, advocated protective tariffs to shelter U.S. industries, whereas the Democratic Party supported tariffs only as a source of government revenue. McKinley's tariff was notable because it was far higher than most protective tariffs, and it was intended to be permanent and not just to support the rise of infant industries.

Rates in France hit 15 percent on most industrial goods, and the United States and Russia (a new industrializer) went even higher. Britain abandoned its advocacy of free trade after World War I when its industries faced growing competition. High tariffs almost certainly reduced international commerce and exacerbated the economic problems of the 1920s and 1930s, impeding trade, protecting inefficiency, and worsening conditions in the Great Depression of the 1930s.

This example encouraged more free-trade efforts after World War II, often led by the United States. Free traders continue to believe that extensive commerce allows everyone to benefit from lower prices and the most productive economic specializations, advantages that outweigh damage to a few less competitive sectors. A series of negotiations and agreements, plus regional tariff reduction pacts such as the European Economic Community and, later, the North American Free Trade Association (NAFTA), have dotted the economic history of the second half of the twentieth century. In 1994, the U.S. government approved a new General

Agreement on Tariffs and Trade (GATT) accord, designed to lower rates markedly around the world. At the same time, in the interest of protecting their factory sectors, many new industrializers, like South Korea, have hesitated to lower tariffs. Every industrial nation, including the United States, has certain products it seeks to protect either by outright tariffs or by other trade barriers. The debate continues, though the frankly protectionist climate of much early industrialization in the nineteenth century has definitely shifted.

See also Bretton Woods Agreement; Bülow Tariff (1902); Calico Act (1721); Laissez-faire; Smoot-Hawley Tariff (1930)

Further Reading

Bowden, Witt, Michael Karpovich, and A. P. Usher. *An Economic History of Europe since 1750*. New York: American Book, 1937.

PROTO-INDUSTRIALIZATION

This term was coined in 1972 by Franklin Mendels and has been elaborated by many socioeconomic historians, particularly in Germany. The term describes the rapid expansion of production between the sixteenth and eighteenth centuries in western and central Europe, where largely traditional methods were used in manufacturing but where market mechanisms increasingly came into play. Proto-industrialization is seen as a training ground for merchants and other directors in the process, who learned the kinds of business skills and capital accumulation later applied to industrialization per se. Workers loosened their ties to the land, becoming incipient proletariats. Proto-industrial workers learned to take direction from strangers and to work for a wage, and they acquired new habits, such as consumerism and greater sexuality, that would expand when the working class encountered the outright factory system.

Proto-industrialization is also seen as a factor in eighteenth-century population growth because people could earn at a relatively early age and not wait for inheritance of land. Thus sexual activity occurred earlier, with or without marriage. The proto-industrial concept has been applied to many other areas and periods as a description of the transition between traditional production and the novelty of industrialization. The theory has also been challenged, however, because it does not fit the facts for every region. In some cases, proto-industrialization actually delayed industrialization, and workers clung to home-based production instead of shifting to potentially more efficient factories. It is certainly clear that many proto-industrial regions lost ground to factory competition when workers and merchants proved unable to develop a factory system of their own, hence the deindustrialization of western France and of many women workers in the early nineteenth century. The concept of proto-industrialization seems to have won considerable but far from complete acceptance, even when carefully applied, as providing a framework for developments that led up to the industrial period.

See also Causes of the Industrial Revolution; Deindustrialization; Domestic Manufacturing

Further Reading

Gullickson, Gay. *Spinners and Weavers of Auffray.* New York: Cambridge University Press, 1986.

Kriedte, Peter, Hans Medick, and Jürgen Schlumbohm. *Industrialization before Industrialization.* New York: Cambridge University Press, 1981.

PRUSSIA. *See* Germany

PUDDLERS

Puddlers were highly skilled workers who refined iron after it came out of blast furnaces. Though a new category of workers in the nineteenth century, they were part of the aristocrats of labor whose relative privileges derived partly from their manual abilities to work iron but also from their ability to judge when the molten iron had sufficiently congealed. One puddler recalled that "none of us ever went to school and learned the chemistry of it [making iron] from books. We learned the trick by doing it, standing with our faces in the scorching heat while our hands puddled the metal in its glaring bath." Puddlers enjoyed a high degree of autonomy at work, which was codified in their union's elaborate work rules. Although industrialists frequently sought to circumvent puddlers' control over production, they were unsuccessful until the introduction of the Bessemer converter in the 1860s.

See also Workers' Control

Further Reading

Montgomery, David. *The Fall of the House of Labor: The*

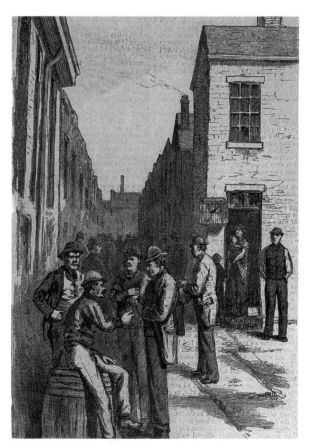

European Puddlers gather outside their headquarters in 1882. (Bettmann/Corbis)

Workplace, the State, and American Labor Activism, 1865–1925. Cambridge: Cambridge University Press, 1987.

PULLMAN, GEORGE M. (1831–97)

George Pullman established the Pullman Palace Car Company in 1867. Pullman sleeping cars were a common feature of train travel from the late nineteenth to the mid-twentieth century. Pullman wanted to provide his customers with a luxurious experience, and he employed only black workers as his porters to provide a sense of plantation-like service. Although the porter's costume was degrading, the position was, ironically, frequently the best job a black male could obtain; many porters were college graduates. The cars were manufactured (by native and immigrant whites) in the model community of Pullman, Illinois. One disgruntled worker reported that "we are born in a Pullman house, fed from the Pullman shop, taught in the Pullman school, catechized in the Pullman church, and when we die we shall be buried in the Pullman cemetery and go to the Pullman hell." A wage cut in 1893 pushed workers to revolt; in 1894, Pullman workers struck, and railroad workers boycotted Pullman cars. Pullman convinced the federal government to place mail bags in their cars so that the boycott interfered with the delivery of the U.S. mail. Confronted by company guards and federal troops, the strike quickly collapsed.

See also Paternalism; Railroads

Further Reading

Leyendecker, Liston E. *Palace Car Prince: A Biography of George Mortimer Pullman*. Niwot, CO: University of Colorado Press, 1992.